# Civil Disobedience and the German Courts

In the 1980s, the West German peace movement—fearing that the stationing of NATO nuclear missiles in Germany threatened an imminent nuclear war in Europe—engaged in massive protests, including sustained civil disobedience in the form of sit-down demonstrations. *Civil Disobedience and the German Courts* traces the historical and philosophical background of this movement and follows a group of demonstrators through their trials in the German criminal courts up to the German Constitutional Court—in which their fate was determined in two important constitutional cases. In this context, the volume also analyzes the German Constitutional Court, as a crucial institution of government, in comparative perspective. The book is the first full-length, English-language treatment of these events and these constitutional decisions, and it also places the decisions at an important turning point in German constitutional history.

**Peter E. Quint** is Jacob A. France Professor of Constitutional Law at the University of Maryland School of Law in Baltimore, U.S.A. His main research interests include American constitutional law and comparative constitutional law, particularly the constitutional law of the Federal Republic of Germany. He is the author of *The Imperfect Union: Constitutional Structures of German Unification* (Princeton University Press, 1997), as well as numerous articles on American and German constitutional law.

## The University of Texas at Austin Studies in Foreign and Transnational Law

General Editors: Sir Basil Markesinis and Dr Jörg Fedtke

The UT Studies in Foreign and Transnational Law series aims to publish books covering various aspects of foreign, private, criminal and public law, as well as transnational law. This broad ambition of the series underlines the editors' belief that, in a shrinking world, there is a growing need to expand our knowledge of other legal orders—national or supernational—and to publish books discussing comparative methodology and not merely describing foreign systems.

Titles in the Series

**The French Civil Code**
*J-L. Halpérin, trans. T. Weir*

**Judicial Recourse to Foreign Law**
*B. Markesinis and J. Fedtke*

**International Negotiation in the Twenty-first Century**
*A. Plantey, trans. F. Meadows*

**Civil Disobedience and the German Courts**
*P. Quint*

Forthcoming titles

**Human Rights in the Private Sphere**
*D. Oliver and J. Fedtke (2007)*

**Italian Private Law**
*G. Alpa and V. Zeno-Zencovich (2007)*

**The Protection of Human Rights in German and English Law**
*J. Fedtke and M. O'Cinneide (2008)*

# Civil Disobedience and the German Courts

## The Pershing missile protests in comparative perspective

Peter E. Quint

Routledge-Cavendish
Taylor & Francis Group
LONDON AND NEW YORK

First edition published 2008

Transferred to digital printing 2008
by Routledge-Cavendish
2 Park Square, Milton Park, Abingdon, Oxon, OX14 4RN

Simultaneously published in the USA and Canada
by Routledge-Cavendish
270 Madison Ave, New York, NY 10016

*Routledge-Cavendish is an imprint of the Taylor & Francis Group, an informa business*



Typeset in Times by
RefineCatch Limited, Bungay, Suffolk



*British Library Cataloguing in Publication Data*
A catalogue record for this book is available from the British Library

*Library of Congress Cataloging in Publication Data*
A catalog record for this book has been requested

ISBN10: 0–415–44285–0 (hbk)
ISBN10: 0–415–44353–9 (pbk)
eISBN10: 0–203–93300–1

ISBN13: 978–0–415–44285–5 (hbk)
ISBN13: 978–0–415–44353–1 (pbk)
eISBN13: 978–0–203–93300–8

This book is dedicated to the memory of
Friedrich K. Juenger (1930–2001)
and
Edward M. Wise (1938–2000),
friends, colleagues, and inspiring scholars of comparative law

# Contents

# Preface

In July 1986 I was invited to attend an oral argument at the German Constitutional Court in Karlsruhe. The case involved the convictions of several peace demonstrators for their exercise of civil disobedience as a protest against the stationing of NATO nuclear missiles in Germany. The arguments that I heard that day seemed to raise very complex and interesting problems concerning the relationship between criminal law and constitutional law in Germany in periods of political stress.

The case stuck in my mind, but some years passed before I was able to return to this subject and try to write something about it. By that time the decision of the case that I had heard on oral argument—which ultimately upheld the convictions by an equally divided vote—had been superseded by another decision in 1995, which in effect reversed many if not all of the protestors' convictions.

Trying to make sense of these cases involved a journey through many fascinating and complicated issues, including the philosophical basis of civil disobedience and the history of the German peace movement, with its background in the German student movement of the late 1960s. I have tried to assemble material from these various aspects of the problem in a way that will make an intelligible (and I hope compelling) narrative.

I am very grateful to the lawyers, judges and prosecutors, as well as former demonstrators, defendants and organizers of the peace movement, who were kind enough to discuss the varied aspects of these problems with me and, in many cases, to provide written materials from the period that would not otherwise have been available. I am very much indebted to these generous participants for their recollections—not only because they provided valuable information, but also because they helped re-create the less tangible "spirit" of this period of the German peace movement.

I also wish to express my gratitude for their invaluable support to successive deans of the University of Maryland School of Law, Donald G. Gifford and Karen L. Rothenberg, as well as to the fellows and staff of Clare Hall, Cambridge University, where the first draft of this book was written, and to Dame Gillian Beer, former president of Clare Hall, who presided over that admirable institution in the academic year 1999–2000 when I was a Visiting Fellow there. I am also greatly indebted to the directors, fellows and staff of the Max Planck Institute for Comparative Public Law and International Law in Heidelberg for their generous hospitality on a number of visits to the Institute and its marvelous library. Furthermore, I wish to thank the Federal Constitutional Court in Karlsruhe for kindly permitting me to consult the Court's archives on the sit-down demonstration cases.

For excellent research assistance, I am grateful to a succession of students at the University of Maryland School of Law: Mary K. Burgess, Sonia Cho, Carl Ehrhardt, Christina Herrmann, Gabriela Hurwitz, Leanne Lauenstein, Markus Rauschecker, and Zhen Zhang. Several friends and colleagues read part or all of the manuscript and provided perceptive and illuminating comments: Richard Boldt, Edward Eberle, Michael Greenberger, A. James McAdams, and Edward Tomlinson. The staff of the Law School's Marshall Law Library—and particularly Pamela Bluh and Maxine Grosshans—were unfailingly patient and resourceful in responding to even the most obscure requests. I am also grateful to Maureen Bakke, Angela Newman, and Marie Schwartz for excellent administrative and secretarial assistance.

Law in any system often involves the reciprocal interaction of rules of almost forbidding abstraction and generality with the concrete experiences of specific individuals often at moments of crisis in their lives. I have tried as well as I can to capture something of that reciprocity and interplay in the chapters that follow.

# Abbreviations

### Legal materials

| | |
|---|---|
| BGBl | Bundesgesetzblatt (Register of Statutes of the Federal Republic of Germany) |
| BGH | Bundesgerichtshof (Federal Supreme Court) |
| BGHSt | Entscheidungen des Bundesgerichtshofes in Strafsachen (Reports of the Federal Supreme Court in Criminal Matters) |
| BVerfGE | Entscheidungen des Bundesverfassungsgerichts (Reports of the Federal Constitutional Court) |
| BVerfGG | Bundesverfassungsgerichtsgesetz (Law Concerning the Federal Constitutional Court) |
| BVerwGE | Entscheidungen des Bundesverwaltungsgerichts (Reports of the Federal Administrative Court) |
| GG | Grundgesetz für die Bundesrepublik Deutschland (Basic Law of the Federal Republic of Germany) |
| I.C.J. | Reports of the International Court of Justice |
| LG | Landgericht (State Court) |
| OLG | Oberlandesgericht (State Appellate Court) |
| RGSt | Entscheidungen des Reichsgerichts in Strafsachen (Reports of the Imperial Court—Reichsgericht—in Criminal Matters) |
| StGB | Strafgesetzbuch (Criminal Code of the Federal Republic of Germany) |
| StPO | Strafprozeßordnung (Code of Criminal Procedure of the Federal Republic of Germany) |
| U.N.T.S. | United Nations Treaty Series |
| VersG | Versammlungsgesetz (Law Concerning Assemblies) |
| WRV | Weimarer Reichsverfassung: the Weimar Constitution |

## Periodicals

| | |
|---|---|
| AfP | Archiv für Presserecht |
| APuZ | Aus Politik und Zeitgeschichte |
| BayVBl | Bayerische Verwaltungsblätter |
| DRiZ | Deutsche Richterzeitung |
| FAZ | Frankfurter Allgemeine Zeitung |
| FR | Frankfurter Rundschau |
| JA | Juristische Arbeitsblätter |
| JR | Juristische Rundschau |
| JuS | Juristische Schulung |
| JZ | Juristenzeitung |
| KJ | Kritische Justiz |
| NJW | Neue Juristische Wochenschrift |
| NStZ | Neue Zeitschrift für Strafrecht |
| NVwZ | Neue Zeitschrift für Verwaltungsrecht |
| RJ | Rechtshistorisches Journal |
| StV | Strafverteidiger |
| SZ | Süddeutsche Zeitung |
| ThürVB1 | Thüringer Verwaltungsblätter |
| ZRP | Zeitschrift für Rechtspolitik |

# Introduction

In many countries of the world today, the principles and doctrines of constitutional law decide some of the greatest questions of politics and public life. Certainly, constitutional law often determines the scope and nature of governmental power and the relationship between the individual and the state.

Because constitutional principles are typically set forth in very general form, courts may be called upon to interpret these principles—and indeed to say, in some concrete form, what they actually mean. In many contemporary systems (but not all), the courts hand down these interpretations in the context of what the American Constitution calls a "case" or "controversy"—an actual dispute involving specific individuals and a specific event that gives rise to contrary positions advanced by the parties.

Cases and controversies of this sort are particularly likely to arise when the dispute involves the relationship between constitutional law and the "ordinary" doctrines of civil and criminal law. Generally speaking, this ordinary law is considerably older than the doctrines of constitutional law, and indeed it forms the background and furnishes many of the concepts for the development of constitutional law. Yet, conversely, constitutional law often influences, changes, or nullifies aspects—and sometimes very important aspects—of the ordinary law.

In the traditional "case" or "controversy", there is often a fundamental tension at the heart of a constitutional decision. Constitutional law may be viewed as a special branch of political theory and, as such, its spirit seems to push in the direction of broad statements of fundamental principles. Yet the role of a judicial opinion as the decision of an individual case may well push in the opposite direction—toward limited and specific statements of results.

But however this tension may be resolved in any specific instance, the historical and factual background of the individual case often has a significant effect on the development of the broader principles of constitutional doctrine. The way in which a particular case arises, its historical setting and the actions and personalities of its participants may be important in determining the constitutional principles that are ultimately formulated by the courts.

An excellent American example of this process is the famous case of *New York Times v. Sullivan.*[1] This important and influential decision arose against the background of the civil rights struggle in the southern United States—as well as the role of national newspapers in publicizing the hostile, and often brutal, reactions of southern officials to that movement. In response to this unwanted publicity, a police commissioner in Montgomery, Alabama—in a sense representing the political and social establishment of the region—filed a libel action against the *New York Times*, a northern newspaper, based on a civil rights advertisement that was critical of certain events in the south. The Alabama courts ordered the *Times* to pay huge damages—an amount that could have driven some newspapers into bankruptcy or, at the very least, seriously discouraged any vigorous coverage of the civil rights movement. But in a famous opinion, the United States Supreme Court rejected possible narrower grounds of decision and drastically reduced the ability of public officials to collect damages for defamation related to their official conduct.

The *New York Times* case has had broad repercussions that go far beyond the specific circumstances of the American civil rights movement: among other things, the "ordinary" law of defamation was profoundly altered by this decision and—in the view of many—the Court's entire view of freedom of expression was transformed. Some believe that the case marks the beginning of modern First Amendment doctrine.

When we examine these developments, the history of decisions like the *New York Times* case seems to fall into four general stages:

First, there are the specific factual circumstances of the case itself, as played out against the more general historical background. At this first stage in the *Times* case, we have the specific dispute that lay behind the defamation action of Commissioner Sullivan against the

[1] 376 U.S. 254 (1964).

*New York Times*, as well as the background of the case in the civil rights struggles of the 1950s and 1960s, including the role of the northern newspapers in that history. This first stage deals with what has happened in real life—before the case gets into the courts.

In the second stage, the specific facts of the case (as illuminated by its more general background) are filtered through the doctrines of the "ordinary" law—in this case, the defamation law of Alabama, as that law existed before the case reached the United States Supreme Court. At the time, the defamation law of Alabama resembled that of many other states in significantly favoring the complaining parties (plaintiffs) in these actions. For example, if a newspaper story could impair an individual's professional reputation, the paper might be liable for damages unless it could prove the truth of the statements "in all particulars". Moreover, the jury could assess "general" damages against the newspaper, even if the plaintiff could not show any specific economic loss. Accordingly, the Alabama courts upheld a $500,000 judgment against the *Times* because its advertisement contained minor inaccuracies concerning the conduct of the police.

In the third stage, the case moves from the problems of the ordinary law into the "higher" realm of constitutional law. In other words, a court applies constitutional principles to the result obtained under the "ordinary" law, and this process may alter, nullify, or transform the ordinary law. In the *New York Times* case, the United States Supreme Court found that—regardless of what the "ordinary" Alabama libel law said on the matter—the First Amendment required that a public official not be permitted to recover libel damages for statements made about his or her official conduct, unless the public official could show that the statements were made with "actual malice"—that is, "with knowing falsity or reckless disregard of the truth." This new constitutional rule required that Sullivan's libel action be dismissed.

Finally, in the fourth stage of this process, the constitutional doctrine that has been developed in this way detaches itself to some extent from the individual case and becomes part of the broader history and development of constitutional law. Indeed, if the decision is a particularly important one—like the *New York Times* case or, to take an even more famous American example, the epochal desegregation case of *Brown v. Board of Education*[2]—it may become part of the more general political and social history of its time. In

2 347 U.S. 483 (1954).

this fourth stage, the new constitutional doctrine may be subject to political accolades or attacks, and it may attract legislative support or attempted curtailment. Moreover, it may be subject to judicial expansion or contraction in its own continuing history and may have implications for many other areas of constitutional law.

In the *New York Times* case, for example, the Supreme Court's new test for defamation was soon expanded beyond the realm of actions by public officials to include defamation actions brought by so-called "public figures"—such as movie stars and other celebrities.[3] In addition, the *New York Times* case influenced the development of a new constitutional standard for defamation actions even when the plaintiff was not a "public figure."[4] Finally, it could well be argued that the *New York Times* case, and particularly the constitutional principles underlying the opinion, initiated the modern era of free speech doctrine in the United States—in which, as a practical matter, most forms of speech receive extensive constitutional protection through a set of relatively well-defined "categories" or specific constitutional rules.

Of course not all contemporary legal systems have the form of constitutional review that we see exemplified in cases such as *New York Times v. Sullivan*. Courts in the United Kingdom, for example, have no authority to invoke constitutional principles to invalidate statutes of Parliament—although in the past few years the courts have received expanded powers to apply European Union treaties, as well as the European Convention on Human Rights. The French Conseil Constitutionnel is authorized to invalidate newly adopted statutes before they are promulgated—but this process takes place in an abstract procedure without a specific factual situation or contending parties.

On the other hand, the Constitutional Court of the Federal Republic of Germany exercises a jurisdiction that is, in many respects, considerably closer to the American procedure of constitutional review. Of course, the Constitutional Court is sometimes authorized to decide constitutional questions in abstract proceedings that go well beyond anything that would be permitted under the American "case" or "controversy" doctrine.[5] Yet most issues in the Constitutional Court are decided in the context of a concrete case or controversy—

[3] *Curtis Publishing Co. v. Butts*; *Associated Press v. Walker*, 388 U.S. 130 (1967).

[4] *Gertz v. Robert Welch, Inc.*, 418 U.S. 323 (1974).

[5] See Art. 93(1)(1)–(2) GG.

although the method of reaching the Constitutional Court may be rather different from the avenue of approach to the Supreme Court in the United States.

In the German system, the distinction between constitutional law and the "ordinary" civil or criminal law is in a sense sharpened through the structure of the court system. One set of "ordinary" courts is responsible for the interpretation of the "ordinary" civil and criminal law, and the Constitutional Court is a special court—set apart from the ordinary court system—whose almost exclusive purpose is to decide constitutional questions.

In the Federal Republic of Germany—as in the *New York Times* case in the United States—the Constitutional Court is frequently called upon to decide cases with significant political overtones. Indeed, given the breadth of its jurisdiction, the political role of the Constitutional Court may well be greater than that of the American Supreme Court. As post-war constitutionalism in Germany was principally a reaction to the catastrophe of the Nazi period, many of these important political cases implicate issues suggested by the Nazi period and its aftermath. Among these cases are decisions dealing with the post-war role of the Nazi civil service, the tension between freedom of expression and right-wing political speech and organization, and the appropriate role of the German military in the post-war world.

Within the latter group, the German Constitutional Court, at various points in its history, has been called upon to decide issues raised by German rearmament and the inclusion of the Federal Republic of Germany in the military alliance of NATO. Although many of these cases involved significant principles of public law, the vigorous protests of thousands of citizens against certain military plans or programs have also involved prosecutions under the "ordinary" criminal law.

Prominent among these cases were the prosecutions of thousands of sit-down demonstrators who sought to block the entrances of American military bases—depots for NATO nuclear missiles—in the German peace demonstrations of the 1980s. This long series of protests—arising out of the ideological ferment of the student movement of the late 1960s and the ecological movement of the 1970s—introduced the phenomenon of civil disobedience into Germany. Accordingly, at the end of a long odyssey through the German court system, these protests evoked important discussions of civil disobedience by judges of the German Constitutional Court.

Indeed, the anti-missile sit-down cases may be readily analyzed in accordance with the four-stage scheme employed above in outlining the *New York Times* case. First, like the *New York Times* case, these cases arose out of a passionate and widespread political movement that called into question fundamental aspects of existing policy. Second—also like the *New York Times* case—these cases initially involved the application and interpretation of widely accepted, though sometimes challenged, principles of the "ordinary law." Third, like the *New York Times* case, the Constitutional Court eventually adopted a constitutional doctrine that substantially restricted the effect of the "ordinary" law—although this result came only in a second decision in 1995, after the Court had upheld the traditional interpretation of the criminal law (by an equally divided vote) in the 1980s. Finally, in the fourth stage, the Constitutional Court's decision of 1995 may be read together with other decisions of the same period to signal a new trend in German constitutional law—a trend that seems to involve a liberalization, or even "Americanization", of certain constitutional doctrines in Germany, including an increased skepticism of certain security claims of the state.

This book will undertake to analyze these complex and important German decisions in the four stages outlined above. But in addition to presenting a close examination of a particular set of constitutional issues, I hope that the analysis of these cases from beginning to end will result in illuminating certain important similarities and differences between the German and American constitutional systems in a more general way. Thus, at important points throughout the narrative, salient characteristics of German law and legal institutions will be compared and contrasted with counterparts in other systems—primarily in the United States but also to some extent in the United Kingdom and France. I hope, therefore, that American and English readers may be able to develop or deepen their understanding of the general structure and nature of the German constitutional system through this comparative examination of a specific constitutional problem.

In accordance with the structure outlined above, this book is divided into five chapters and an Epilogue. Chapter 1—which discusses the historical, philosophical and factual background of these cases—begins with a discussion of NATO's decision to deploy Pershing II nuclear missiles in West Germany, and the numerous demonstrations and sit-down blockades which that decision evoked, along with an analysis of the historical and philosophical background of the German peace movement and the forms of civil disobedience that it employed. The chapter concludes with an account of the blockades that led to the prosecutions in three separate sit-down cases, and we will follow the cases of these three sets of protestors throughout later chapters as well.

Chapter 2, which discusses the applicable issues of the "ordinary law," analyzes the criminal offense of "coercion" (*Nötigung*), under which thousands of protestors were convicted for their participation in the anti-missile sit-down demonstrations. This chapter also follows the specific cases of our three sets of protestors as they made their way through the German criminal court system.

Chapter 3 brings the cases of these sit-down protestors to the doors of the German Constitutional Court. This chapter describes the nature of the Constitutional Court in general and the arguments considered by the Court in the sit-down cases, as well as other important issues that arose at this point in the litigation.

Chapter 4 then shifts to the constitutional level of doctrine and analyzes the two great opinions of the Federal Constitutional Court dealing with the sit-down prosecutions of the peace movement. The first case, decided in 1986, generally upheld the convictions, but the second case, handed down in 1995, had the effect of reversing most or all of the thousands of convictions of the sit-down demonstrators.

Chapter 5 then seeks to place the Constitutional Court's decision of 1995 in the context of two other major constitutional cases decided by the Court in the same year—cases that were of equally great importance (or, some might say, notoriety). The chapter argues that these cases marked a high point in a new development in German constitutional doctrine and may represent a further step in what some theorists have seen as the "Americanization" of German political life.

The volume concludes with an Epilogue, which will bring the legal and constitutional story up to the present day. The Epilogue will also say some final words about the contemporary life of the litigants whose cases we have followed and whose lives were so greatly affected by the peace movement of the 1980s and by their prosecutions for participation in the sit-down demonstrations.

This book falls into a genre that is common and familiar in the United States but—as far as I have been able to determine—is very rare in Germany. There are numerous books in the United States that trace the progress of a constitutional case from its perhaps modest beginnings on the streets, through its journey in the lower courts, to its arrival in the halls of the Supreme Court, and even beyond. Notable examples of this genre may be found in many areas of American constitutional law.[6]

Such a focus on the history and development of a particularly important case is by no means surprising in the American legal culture, in which the individual case has arguably always been the most important legal event. In the continental systems in which the ideology of law tends to focus on codes, statutes, and academic

[6] For example, the classic account of *New York Times v. Sullivan* is Anthony Lewis, *Make No Law: The Sullivan Case and the First Amendment* (New York: Random House 1991). A second "*New York Times* case"—the famous litigation over the Pentagon Papers in 1971—is also the subject of a well-known analysis: Sanford J. Ungar, *The Papers and The Papers* (New York: Columbia University Press 1989). Recent interest in military tribunals has yielded new accounts of the Supreme Court's decision in *Ex parte Quirin*, the case of the World War II German saboteurs: Louis Fisher, *Nazi Saboteurs on Trial: A Military Tribunal and American Law* (Lawrence: University Press of Kansas 2005); Michael Dobbs, *The Saboteurs: The Nazi Raid on America* (New York: Knopf 2004).

The issues of slavery, segregation and desegregation have also yielded notable analyses of individual cases: Don E. Fehrenbacher, *The Dred Scott Case: Its Significance in American Law and Politics* (New York: Oxford University Press 1978); Mark A. Graber, Dred Scott *and the Problem of Constitutional Evil* (Cambridge: Cambridge University Press 2006); Charles A. Lofgren, *The Plessy Case: A Legal-Historical Interpretation* (New York: Oxford University Press 1987); Richard Kluger, *Simple Justice: The History of Brown v. Board of Education and Black America's Struggle for Equality* (New York: Knopf 1976). A more recent contribution discusses one of the most famous cases on affirmative action as a remedy for racial discrimination or racial imbalance: Howard Ball, *The* Bakke *Case: Race, Education, and Affirmative Action* (Lawrence: University Press of Kansas 2000).

The reformulation of rights of criminal procedure during the Warren Court era has also given rise to a path-breaking account by the author of *Make No Law*: Anthony Lewis, *Gideon's Trumpet* (New York: Vintage 1989). And, finally, the issues of *Roe v. Wade* and other problems of modern "substantive due process" are also analyzed in several case studies. See, e.g., David J. Garrow, *Liberty and Sexuality: The Right to Privacy and the Making of* Roe *v.* Wade (Berkeley: University of California Press 1998); Eva R. Rubin, *Abortion, Politics, and the Courts:* Roe v. Wade *and Its Aftermath* (New York: Greenwood rev. edn. 1987). On earlier cases of "substantive due process," see, e.g., Paul Kens, *Lochner v. New York: Economic Regulation on Trial* (Lawrence: University Press of Kansas 1998).

It is fair to say, however, that these books on individual decisions of the American Supreme Court constitute only the tip of the iceberg of American works of this sort.

treatises rather than cases—and, more generally, on principles rather than their specific application—the absence of this genre of legal literature is perhaps not surprising.

But in a constitutional system like that of the Federal Republic of Germany, in which the individual case has now—in reality—become extremely important, it might be expected that this form of literature would become more popular among legal academics and political scientists. As far as I can tell, however, that has not yet happened on any substantial scale. There may be a few volumes on German cases by American writers, but the best-known of these—on the famous *Spiegel* affair of 1963—are primarily political studies, in which the Constitutional Court litigation figures at the margins or not at all.[7]

There are a few portents, however, suggesting that the situation may be starting to change. In 2005 a collection of historical and analytical essays appeared on the *Lüth* case, one of the most important decisions of the German Constitutional Court and the foundation of its doctrine on the freedom of expression.[8] And in the same year Werner Offenloch, perhaps the best-known—and most embattled—of the trial judges who decided the sit-in demonstration cases that we are about to consider, published a volume analyzing these cases from his point of view.[9] Judge Offenloch's thoughtful work —which, among other things, contains a previously unpublished opinion from his own court—is itself a significant historical docu-

[7] See David Schoenbaum, *The Spiegel Affair* (Garden City: Doubleday 1968); Ronald F. Bunn, *German Politics and the Spiegel Affair* (Baton Rouge: Louisiana State University Press 1968). For an elaborate political study of the *Spiegel* case in German—also with little comment on the opinion of the Constitutional Court—see Jürgen Seifert (ed.), *Die Spiegel-Affäre* (2 vols; Olten: Walter-Verlag 1966).

In the earlier literature, there are also a few collections of briefs, arguments, and other documents on specific German Constitutional Court cases, and some of these collections have interpretive introductions. See, e.g., Claus Arndt *et al.* (eds), *Der §218 StGB vor dem Bundesverfassungsgericht* (Heidelberg: Müller 1979) (Abortion Case); Dieter Blumenwitz (ed.), *Wehrpflicht und Ersatzdienst: Die Auseinandersetzung vor dem Bundesverfassungsgericht* (Munich: Olzog 1978) (Conscientious Objectors Case); Günter Zehner (ed.), *Der Fernsehstreit vor dem Bundesverfassungsgericht. Eine Dokumentation des Prozeßmaterials* (2 vols; Karlsruhe: Müller 1964–1965)(Television Case).

[8] Thomas Henne and Arne Riedlinger (eds), *Das Lüth-Urteil aus (rechts-) historischer Sicht: Die Konflikte um Veit Harlan und die Grundrechtsjudikatur des Bundesverfassungsgerichts* (Berlin: BWV 2005): For the *Lüth* case itself, see 7 BVerfGE 198 (1958).

[9] Werner Offenloch, *Erinnerung an das Recht. Der Streit um die Nachrüstung auf den Straßen und vor den Gerichten* (Tübingen: Mohr Siebeck 2005).

ment of this episode of legal and constitutional development in Germany.

Perhaps these works are preliminary signs of a new development in the examination and analysis of German constitutional law. Perhaps not. But in any event, I hope that the present volume may suggest that sustained case studies can add another dimension to the understanding of constitutional problems—not just in the United States but in Germany, and perhaps other systems, as well.

Chapter 1

# The anti-missile demonstrations

## The protests and their context

In a particular patch of land in Mutlangen, a small town near Stuttgart Germany, a casual visitor would find little out of the ordinary now. On an autumn evening not too long ago, a lone power shovel stood in the fields and two large bunkers, covered over with earth and grass, lay empty or had been converted to serve modest ends. One of the bunkers, for example, provided shelter for a flock of sheep and acted as a storage bin for bales of straw. On that cool autumn evening, the purple outline of the "Swabian Alb"—the high Swabian plateau—was visible against the sky.

It was a peaceful moment, and for a visitor it was difficult to imagine that, just a few years earlier, this quiet field contained the main repository of deadly Pershing II nuclear missiles in Germany and that, as a result, it was the scene of almost continuous protests by members of the German peace movement. In most cases, these demonstrations at Mutlangen were limited to a handful of protestors—normally less than a hundred participants at a time, engaging in a quiet form of civil disobedience. But, on occasion, crowds of demonstrators swelled to several thousands, blocking truck and tank traffic traveling up the main road to the Pershing missile base.

Little evidence of this tumultuous history remained in those tranquil fields by the end of the 1990s. Yet considerable commotion of a different sort was evident upon a return visit shortly thereafter; builders were constructing large suburban houses and quaint winding roads on a large tract of adjacent field—the historic Mutlangen Meadow (*Mutlanger Heide*)—and this development threatened to expand into the territory of the former missile base itself. Perhaps the people of Mutlangen were happy enough to erase some last traces of their town's conspicuous role in the history of the Cold War.

Not too many miles away—on the high Swabian plateau itself—the village of Großengstingen (Big Engstingen) lies amid an idyllic setting of forests and fields. (The even tinier village of Kleinengstingen—Little Engstingen—nestles on a slope nearby.) On the hillside above Großengstingen, a narrow road leads through pine forests into a deserted complex of concrete buildings. On a spring day in 2000, a visitor to this quiet spot could hear little more than the call of birds; massive white clouds drifted across a pale blue sky.

The deserted complex was an odd sight with its watch-towers looming over two empty bunkers—once repositories of Lance short-range nuclear missiles, but now (it is said) the home of nocturnal bats. The traces of previous military habitation were few: a large blue board with hooks for perhaps 40 keys—carefully labeled, but now completely empty—lay abandoned on the ground. On a metal shelf, an American soldier had used a felt-tipped pen to write an obscene note to the Soviet troops who he thought might be coming one day. At the inner gate of the base, someone had erected a large hand-painted sign that proclaimed: "Memorial Site: Battlefield of the Cold War, 1945-1991."

The outer gate of the complex, at the foot of the hill at Großengstingen, was also the scene of dramatic sit-down demonstrations, leading to hundreds of arrests. The demonstrations at Großengstingen were in general earlier than those in Mutlangen. Indeed, these protests were among the first sit-down demonstrations in Germany against NATO nuclear missiles.

## The sit-down blockades and the "double-track" decision

### *Protesting the Lance missiles—Großengstingen*

The demonstrations against the Lance missiles at Großengstingen began with a small blockade in July 1981, in which 13 protestors chained themselves to the entrance of a nearby German army barracks.[1] Following this modest beginning, the protests in Großengstingen reached their high point in the summer of 1982 with a series of demonstrations that extended over an entire week and involved approximately 700 participants, who had come from several parts of Germany and abroad. Because accommodation was scarce in this

[1] This demonstration, as well as its historical background, will be described in greater detail below.

somewhat remote rural area, organizers of the week-long protest established five "Tent Villages" in fields borrowed from local farmers, and they arranged with the fire departments from surrounding towns to keep the "villages" supplied with water.

The organization of the 1982 Tent Village protests involved considerable complexity.[2] The hundreds of demonstrators were organized on the basis of so-called "affinity groups" (*Bezugsgruppen*)—closely knit associations of up to 15 protestors, typically drawn together by friendship or common political views. Bearing fanciful—but pointed—names such as Termite, Nettle, and Grain of Sand,[3] approximately 50 "affinity groups" formed the basic units of the 1982 Tent Village demonstrations.

Typically, the blockades of the Tent Village protestors followed rotations of six-hour shifts. During each six-hour period, three affinity groups sat before the gates of the Lance missile base—supported by back-up groups in case the police cleared the area by arresting demonstrators and carrying them away. The demonstrators were generally cleared twice a day—when provisions for the base, or soldiers relieving those on duty, were transported into the compound. All in all, at least 400 protestors were arrested during the week of the Tent Villages in the summer of 1982.[4]

In this protest, and in many later anti-missile protests, strict non-violence was an absolute requirement. Before the demonstrations began, the protestors participated in joint "trainings"—this supposed English plural was taken over directly into German—in the theory and practice of non-violence. Indeed, participation in a weekend training session was a requirement for participation in the Tent Village demonstrations.

In these and later "trainings," the central purpose was to help protestors internalize the principles of non-violence, so that their

[2] At the outset, the organizers issued a "handbook" for participants, outlining the goals and structures of the demonstration, along with practical tips for life in the Tent Villages: Schwerter zu Pflugscharen Gross Engstingen, *Handbuch: Sommer '82* [Handbook-1]. After the demonstrations a second Handbook was issued, recapitulating the high points of the week, along with evaluation and criticism: Schwerter zu Pflugscharen Gross Engstingen, *Handbuch 2: Blockade Aktion '82—Auswertung* [Handbook-2]. The organizers also published a comprehensive collection of press reports on the demonstration: *Presse Spiegel–Sommeraktion 82 Gross Engstingen* [*Presse Spiegel*].

[3] *Presse Spiegel*, 62 (Badische Zeitung).

[4] Handbook-2, 12.

resistance would remain passive even if they were confronted with the violent acts of others. In the trainings, for example, participants were sometimes divided into two groups for the purposes of playing the roles of protestors and "police officers." They were then required to confront each other at close quarters in order to simulate and understand the tensions that each side might face in a real confrontation. In this way the organizers sought to ensure that this large demonstration of hundreds of protestors would remain non-violent even in the face of provocations.[5]

The "trainings" in non-violence, and the use of affinity groups, were influenced by similar preparations for American demonstrations against planned atomic power plants at Seabrook New Hampshire in 1979 and Diablo Canyon California in 1981.[6] Of course, the practice of training participants in non-violence goes back to the American civil rights movement of the 1950s,[7] and to the passive resistance organized by Mahatma Gandhi decades earlier; moreover, it is said that the idea of affinity groups originated in Republican military units in the Spanish Civil War.[8] Yet the immediate inspiration for these methods of organization was the massive protests against nuclear power plants in the United States and Germany, and this is

5 See, e.g., *Presse Spiegel*, 66 (Tages Anzeiger); cf. Ute Finkh and Inge Jens (eds), *Verwerflich? Friedensfreunde vor Gericht*, 11, 14–15 (Munich: Knaur 1985) [*Verwerflich?*].

6 See generally Robert Cooney and Helen Michalowski (eds), *The Power of the People: Active Nonviolence in the United States*, 224–27 (Philadelphia: New Society Publishers 1987) (affinity groups and mandatory non-violence training at Seabrook; affinity groups at Diablo Canyon).

7 See, for example, Martin Luther King's description of "teaching sessions to school the people in non-violent techniques" at a church in Montgomery Alabama, following the Montgomery bus boycott of 1955:

> We lined up chairs in front of the altar to resemble a bus, with a driver's seat out front. From the audience we selected a dozen or so "actors" and assigned each one a role in a hypothetical situation. One man was driver and the others were white and Negro passengers. Both groups contained some hostile and some courteous characters. As the audience watched, the actors played out a scene of insult or violence. At the end of each scene the actors returned to the audience and another group took their place . . . Often a Negro forgot his nonviolent role and struck back with vigor; whenever this happened we worked to rechannel his words and deeds in a nonviolent direction.
>
> (Martin Luther King, Jr., *Stride Toward Freedom: The Montgomery Story*, 163 (New York: Harper 1958))

8 Handbook-1, 31.

only one of the several ways in which the anti-missile protests were influenced by these slightly earlier environmental demonstrations.[9]

In the German protests the affinity groups played a particularly important role, and they made their decisions—for example, whether or not to take part in an illegal blockade—based on the principle of unanimity. The affinity groups were particularly crucial because they offered individual protestors an intimate and reliable refuge within a huge and otherwise anonymous demonstration—with its attendant anxiety in the face of possible injury or arrest. As the planning Handbook for the 1982 Tent Village protests put it:

> [In the affinity groups] we can largely avoid the anonymity, insecurity and feelings of isolation [that are present], above all, in the case of [protests] with numerous participants. Here we can find a basis of trust, which would make it possible for individuals to express their anxieties and show their feelings.[10]

In the 1982 protest at Großengstingen, coordination among the affinity groups was maintained through a complex system of councils linking the five Tent Villages which—because of the difficulty of finding farmers willing to allow use of their land—were located as far as 10 miles from the missile site itself.

[9] A particularly direct American influence was the September 1981 "People's Blockade" at the Diablo Canyon nuclear power plant site in California. Like its successor in Großengstingen, this demonstration included affinity groups, training in techniques of non-violence, and a "tent city." See Eugene Phillips and Wayne Saroyan (eds), *Blockade: Direct Action at Diablo Canyon* (Halcyon, CA: Imaginary Press 1981); Interview with Uwe Painke, Tübingen, 24 September 1999. In the preparations for the 1982 Tent Village blockades at Großengstingen, the organizers circulated a letter containing, among other things, a report on the blockade at Diablo Canyon, which had taken place the previous autumn. Handbook-2, 31.

[10] Handbook-1, 31; see also Interview with Wolfgang Müller-Breuer, Leichlingen, 24 July 2002. Unless otherwise noted, all translations in this volume are those of the author.

A planning handbook for the American Seabrook demonstrations of 1979 sets forth a similar explanation:

> Affinity groups allow for individual autonomy within the larger organization. In large groups, individuals tend to lose their identity. It is easier for most people to express their opinions clearly, in trust, among friends rather than in a large group of unknown people.
>
> (*"Let's Shut Down Seabrook!": Handbook for Oct. 6, 1979 Direct Action Occupation*, 7)

In the course of the Großengstingen protests, participants often tried to engage soldiers and bystanders in conversation about the goals of the blockade. Although military personnel on duty had strict orders not to fraternize with the protestors, off-duty soldiers in street clothes would occasionally appear at the blockade to discuss the issues. Furthermore, numerous "blockade tourists"—students, neighboring farmers, even a representative of the conservative political party, the CDU—came around for "passionate discussion" about "atomic rockets and disarmament, balance of weapons and non-violent resistance."[11] The period of the Tent Village demonstrations also involved "music programs, films, theater and [literature] readings."[12] On at least one occasion balloons, decorated with painted doves of peace, were released over the missile base.[13]

The week-long demonstration of the Tent Villages at Großengstingen ended with a one-hour "die-in"—a blockade by all 700 participants, accompanied by singing, meditation and 20 minutes of silence. At its conclusion, this dramatic protest had done little to affect the deployment of nuclear missiles. Yet it remained in the history of the protest movement as the first large-scale example of civil disobedience directed against nuclear missiles in Germany, and it had a significant effect on the form of subsequent blockades in Mutlangen.[14]

Indeed the organizers were aware that they were developing a new form of anti-nuclear protest for the Federal Republic—intentionally adopting, as we have seen, American forms of protest.[15]

## *NATO's "double-track" decision and the coming of the Pershing missiles*

The Lance short-range missiles, which were the focus of protest at Großengstingen, had been stationed in Germany since 1976. But in late 1983—somewhat more than a year after the protest of the Tent Villages—the Lance missiles were joined by new NATO nuclear rockets which many Germans believed seriously threatened the

[11] *Presse Spiegel*, 93 (Weser-Kurier); see also ibid., 89 (Badische Tageszeitung).

[12] *Verwerflich?*, 12.

[13] *Presse Spiegel*, 39 (Südwest Presse).

[14] Schlupp, "Mutlangen—ein Bild aus vielen Einzelteilen," in *Mutlanger Erfahrungen: Erinnerungen und Perspektiven* (Friedens- und Begegnungsstätte Mutlangen e.V. 1994), 4.

[15] *Presse Spiegel*, 62 (Badische Zeitung).

country's very survival. This development resulted from Cold War jockeying for strategic position among the great nuclear powers.

In the 1970s, the Soviet Union decided to "modernize" its nuclear forces in Europe by deploying intermediate-range SS-20 nuclear rockets. With a range of hundreds of kilometers, these missiles were directed toward targets in Western Europe. The SS-20s possessed improved accuracy and mobility and were equipped with multiple warheads.[16]

In a speech in 1977, German Chancellor Helmut Schmidt expressed alarm at the dangers posed in the deployment of the SS-20s,[17] and NATO planners came to view this Soviet move as a serious threat to the parity of forces between East and West. In response, the American and West German governments and the other NATO foreign ministers reached a so-called "double-track" decision at their meeting in Brussels in December 1979—confirming a plan that had been outlined by the leading NATO heads of government at a meeting in Guadeloupe some months earlier.[18] According to this plan, the United States would negotiate with the Soviet Union, at arms talks in Geneva, for the purpose of achieving a reduction in the number of Soviet missiles. But if this first "track" proved unsuccessful, NATO would move to a second "track"—deployment of American middle-range rockets in western Europe.[19]

[16] 66 BVerfGE, 39, 41 (1983); 68 BVerfGE, 1, 46 (1984); 2 Dennis L. Bark and David R. Gress, *A History of West Germany: Democracy and its Discontents 1963–1988*, 308–9 (Oxford: Blackwell 1989) [Bark and Gress]; Zbigniew Brzezinski, *Power and Principle: Memoirs of the National Security Advisor 1977–1981*, 307 (New York: Farrar Straus Giroux, rev. edn 1985).

Writing in later memoirs, Mikhail Gorbachev characterized the deployment of the SS-20 missiles as "an unforgivable adventure" resulting from "pressure" exerted by the Soviet "military-industrial complex." Mikhail Gorbachev, *Memoirs*, 443–44 (New York: Doubleday 1996).

[17] v. Münch, "Rechtsfragen der Raketenstationierung," 1984 NJW, 577; see Jürgen Busche, *Die 68er: Biographie einer Generation*, 125–26, 136–37 (Berlin: Berlin Verlag 2003).

[18] Helmut Schmidt, *Menschen und Mächte*, 232–34 (Berlin: Siedler 1999).

[19] 2 Bark and Gress, 308–20, 400–8; Alice Holmes Cooper, *Paradoxes of Peace: German Peace Movements since 1945*, 127–30 (Ann Arbor: University of Michigan Press 1996); Werner Offenloch, *Erinnerung an das Recht. Der Streit um die Nachrüstung auf den Straßen und vor den Gerichten*, 1–18 (Tübingen: Mohr Siebeck 2005).

Within NATO, the initial negotiations on the "double-track" plan evoked considerable personal tension between Chancellor Schmidt and U.S. President Carter. See Jimmy Carter, *Keeping Faith: Memoirs of a President*, 534–38 (New York: Bantam 1983); Brzezinski, 307–11, 461–63; Schmidt, 224–66.

By November 1983, the negotiations in Geneva had proven fruitless, and NATO shifted to the second "track" of its decision. Acting in concert with the West German government and the other NATO powers, the United States stationed hundreds of middle-range "Cruise" missiles in Great Britain, Italy, and West Germany. Moreover, in November 1983—after a resolution of support by the West German Parliament (Bundestag)—the United States began its deployment of 108 "Pershing II" missiles in West Germany, primarily at a special camp in the small town of Mutlangen.[20]

To many in Germany, the deployment of the Pershing II missiles seemed to present particular dangers. From their West German bases, these NATO rockets could reach territory controlled by the Soviet Union in eight to twelve minutes. The extremely short duration of this flight seemed to raise the serious possibility that, in case of a crisis, the Soviet Union might resort to a preventive strike in order to neutralize the threats of a first strike from the Pershing missiles.[21] Indeed, this danger was heightened by the assumption that the Soviet missiles themselves were the Pershings' principal targets.

Moreover, the short duration of the flight seemed to increase the risk of a mistaken Soviet reaction. If Soviet radar erroneously indicated that Pershing missiles had been launched, there would be little time to check the accuracy of this conclusion before the Soviets might fire their own nuclear rockets in order to protect them from being destroyed by the supposed strike.[22] Many Germans believed, therefore, that the stationing of these missiles increased the likelihood that Germany would become a nuclear battleground.

Furthermore, some members of the German peace movement assessed the presence of the Pershing missiles in even more alarming

[20] 68 BVerfGE, 43–44; 2 Bark and Gress, 407; Lloyd Jensen, *Bargaining for National Security: The Postwar Disarmament Negotiations*, 204 (Columbia: University of South Carolina Press 1988); see generally ibid. at 190–210; Jeffrey Herf, *War by Other Means: Soviet Power, West German Resistance, and the Battle of the Euromissiles*, 196–216 (New York: Free Press 1991). The Bundestag resolution of November 1983 followed an earlier parliamentary resolution, adopted in 1981, approving NATO's double-track decision. See 66 BVerfGE, 45.

In addition to Mutlangen, Pershing II missiles were also stationed in Ulm and Heilbronn. Südwestpresse, 7 October 1986, reprinted in Volker Nick *et al.* (eds), *Mutlangen 1983–1987: Die Stationierung der Pershing II und die Kampagne Ziviler Ungehorsam bis zur Abrüstung*, 106 (Mutlangen: 1993) [*Mutlangen 1983–1987*].

[21] 66 BVerfGE, at 47, 51.

[22] Ibid., 51; see also 68 BVerfGE, 34–35.

terms. In their view, American policy had shifted ominously in the early 1980s under President Reagan: instead of the previous goal of deterring all atomic war—through the doctrine of mutually assured destruction—these writers believed that American planners now thought that the West could win a nuclear conflict on European soil. Under this view, the United States could fight a nuclear war in Europe and avoid a threat to its own territory—a strategy that would drastically increase the danger to Germany and the rest of Europe.[23] As evidence for their view, members of the German peace movement cited a new American military document—Field Manual No. 100-5, 20 August 1982—which announced that "conventional, nuclear and chemical weapons" could be integrated in a future European war; in October 1981, moreover, President Reagan publicly suggested the "'conceivability' of a winnable, limited nuclear war."[24]

Members of the peace movement also argued that the NATO "double-track decision" and the deployment of the Pershing II missiles were part of an American drive toward a "first strike" capability.[25] Moreover, the President of the United States had sole authority to fire the Pershing missiles, and therefore this system delegated "the decision over the annihilation of the Federal Republic to a foreign power."[26] As a result, the opponents argued, the fate of the

[23] Herf, *War by Other Means*, 127–34, 175; cf. Gray and Payne, "Victory is Possible," *Foreign Policy*, No. 39, 14–27 (summer 1980). See generally Cooper, 143–48.

[24] Mushaben, "Grassroots and *Gewaltfreie Aktionen*: A Study of Mass Mobilization Strategies in the West German Peace Movement," 23 *Journal of Peace Research*, No. 2, 141, 142 (1986). A similar thesis was also put forth in an influential book by a well-known SPD politician. See Erhard Eppler, *Die tödliche Utopie der Sicherheit* (Reinbek bei Hamburg: Rowohlt 1983); see also Habermas, "Ziviler Ungehorsam —Testfall für den demokratischen Rechtsstaat. Wider den autoritären Legalismus in der Bundesrepublik," in Peter Glotz (ed.), *Ziviler Ungehorsam im Rechtsstaat*, 45–47 (Frankfurt/M: Suhrkamp 1983) [*Ziviler Ungehorsam im Rechtsstaat*].

[25] See Lutz, "Sind Erstschlagsfähige Nuklearwaffen Verfassungswidrig?," 38 Frankfurter Hefte, No. 9, 17–28 (1983). For discussion, see Offenloch, *Erinnerung*, 14–18. See also Huber, "Die Grenzen des Staats und die Pflicht zum Ungehorsam," in *Ziviler Ungehorsam im Rechtsstaat*, 114–15; Schüler-Springorum, "Strafrechtliche Aspekte zivilen Ungehorsams," in ibid., 95 ("Hardly anyone [*wohl niemand*] seriously denies anymore" that the Pershing rockets are first strike weapons.) But see v. Münch, 1984 NJW, 580 (denying this).

[26] Schlotter, "Die Stationierung von Pershing II und Cruise Missiles in der Bundesrepublik Deutschland. Überlegungen zur verfassungsrechtlichen Beurteilung," 31 January 1984, 17 (essay submitted by peace researcher Dr. Peter Schlotter to Federal Constitutional Court).

German nation had been removed from German hands. This alienation of authority—the opponents argued—violated the general constitutional requirement that German statehood be preserved.

### *The judicial challenge to the Pershing missiles*

As an initial measure of protest against these perceived dangers, members of the peace movement challenged the deployment of the Pershing II and Cruise missiles in two cases in the Federal Constitutional Court.[27] They were aided by the Greens, an environmental movement that had been organized as an official political party in 1980 and had entered Parliament in 1983.[28]

The first of these cases was filed immediately before the Pershing rockets were due to arrive in Mutlangen in the autumn of 1983. Declaring that the missiles would threaten a nuclear war in Germany, nine university professors and others sought an order to stop the deployment. Indeed the missiles were so dangerous, the complainants argued, that the imminent deployment would violate their right to life and bodily integrity, protected by Article 2(2) of the Basic Law—the West German Constitution.[29] At the very least, they maintained, an express statute of Parliament would be necessary if these crucial rights were to be threatened in this manner. No such statute, however, had been enacted.[30]

Moreover, in the protestors' view, the potential use of these rockets for a first strike constituted a violation of Article 26(1) of the Basic Law, which prohibited preparations for aggressive war.[31] This central provision of the post-war West German Constitution incorporated the doctrine of the 1946 Nuremberg judgment against major Nazi officials, which imposed severe penalties for "crimes against peace." Indeed, the protestors argued, the stationing of the rockets presented a threat of atomic catastrophe and thus also

[27] For a detailed description of the Constitutional Court and its jurisdiction, see Chapter 3.

[28] See Gerd Langguth, *The Green Factor in German Politics: From Protest Movement to Political Party* (trans. Richard Straus), 12–21 (Boulder, CO: Westview Press 1986); see also 2 Bark and Gress, 340–43.

[29] 66 BVerfGE 39, 46–47, 49–51, 53–55 (1983). For the text of Article 2(2) GG, as well as other relevant provisions of the Basic Law, see Appendix.

[30] 66 BVerfGE, 48, 51. As noted, the Bundestag had adopted a resolution "supporting" the deployment, but this approval was not in the official form of a statute.

[31] Ibid., 48.

violated human dignity which was protected by Article 1(1) of the Basic Law.[32] Finally, the complainants argued, the stationing represented an undue alienation of German sovereign rights and violated international law.[33]

In its first *Pershing* decision the Constitutional Court sidestepped these arguments and refused to issue an order against the deployment. Instead, the Court found that the complaints were "impermissible" because in reality they were not (and could not be) directed against the proper government officials. The Court pointed out that any threat to petitioners' life, bodily integrity, and human dignity actually came from atomic missiles that might be launched against Germany by the *Soviet* government. But—the Court emphasized—it was only authorized to hear complaints directed against actions of the *German* government.

Perhaps the German government had increased the danger of nuclear war by allowing Pershing and Cruise missiles to be stationed on its territory; and in some cases at least, a constitutional claim could be based on a risk of a future injury.[34] Yet whether the danger of nuclear war was actually increased—and, if so, by how much—was not the sort of decision that could be accurately assessed by the judiciary. Rather, risks and dangers of this kind must be assessed by the political organs of government.[35] As several commentators have pointed out, this argument seems to invoke something very similar to the American "political question" doctrine. The Court also found that stationing the Pershing rockets in West Germany, for the purposes of deterrence, would not violate general principles of international law.[36]

In a similar decision a year later—after the Pershing II missiles had been deployed—the Court again declined to limit the government's discretion on these matters. In an action brought by the parliamentary caucus of the Greens Party, the Court found that the executive branch of government was entitled to decide on

[32] Ibid.

[33] Ibid., 53.

[34] Ibid., 57–58. Indeed, the Constitutional Court had previously considered risks of future dangers in cases involving the regulation of nuclear power plants. See, e.g., 49 BVerfGE, 89 (1978) (Kalkar).

[35] 66 BVerfGE, 58–62.

[36] Ibid., 64–65. See v. Münch, 1984 NJW, 581. For commentary on this decision, see Hansjörg Reichert-Hammer, *Politische Fernziele und Unrecht*, 162–65 (Berlin: Duncker & Humblot 1991).

deployment, without the statutory approval of Parliament.[37] Indeed, to require parliamentary approval for this governmental action would allow Parliament to invade "central decision-making areas (*Gestaltungsbereiche*) of the executive."[38]

Of course, permitting the United States to deploy nuclear weapons in Germany seemed to represent a partial transfer of German "sovereignty"—particularly because the American president would ultimately decide on whether the missiles would be fired. If this were a new transfer of sovereign powers to an international organization (NATO), a new statute of Parliament would be required.[39] But the Court found that this was actually not a new transfer of sovereign powers but only a new development within the original grant of those powers to NATO. The Court emphasized that the executive, which made this decision, possessed a degree of democratic legitimation that was equal to that of Parliament. Moreover, Parliament retained a large measure of constitutional control over the executive in any case.[40]

These judicial challenges—although ultimately unsuccessful—

[37] 68 BVerfGE, 1 (1984). In this case, the Greens Party caucus was allowed to assert the constitutional rights of Parliament against claimed infringement by the executive. This type of proceeding is known as *Organstreit* or "dispute between governmental organs" and is specifically authorized by the Basic Law: Art. 93(1)(1) GG; see also Chapter 3. The Greens Party petition was therefore "permissible"—in contrast with the petition in the first *Pershing* case, filed by private individuals—but the case was limited to questions of the allocation of power between Parliament and the executive. See 68 BVerfGE, 65–66, 69–74.

[38] Ibid., 80–89. See Art. 59(2) GG.

[39] See Art. 24(1) GG.

[40] 68 BVerfGE, 89–111.

Unlike the first *Pershing* case, this decision drew one vigorous dissent. Judge Ernst Gottfried Mahrenholz argued that the threat posed by the missiles was so grave and unique that legislative approval was required—both as a new transfer of sovereign power and as a new international obligation. Cf. Art. 24(1)GG; Art. 59(2)GG. Mahrenholz noted the complainants' view that the Pershing II missiles increased the risk of a first strike and an accidental nuclear war, and that American planners now held that the West could prevail in a war. More generally, Mahrenholz insisted that Parliament must make all "essential decisions" and complained that the Court had shifted the constitutional balance in the direction of the executive. 68 BVerfGE, 111–32.

For selections from the *Pershing Missile* cases in English, see Donald P. Kommers, *The Constitutional Jurisprudence of the Federal Republic of Germany*, 155–60 (Durham: Duke University Press, 2d edn 1997). For commentary on both of the *Pershing* cases, see Offenloch, *Erinnerung*, 101–10.

were emblematic of the great controversy that the stationing of the Pershing rockets had evoked in Germany. Members of the peace movement seemed to have particular cause for disappointment because—due to the jurisdictional doctrines of the Constitutional Court—the tribunal did not fully consider several central challenges to the stationing of the missiles: the claim of undue danger to life and bodily integrity in possible violation of Article 2 (2), and the argument that the deployment violated Article 26 GG because the Pershings were first-strike weapons and therefore implements of aggressive war. These significant constitutional questions, therefore, remained undecided on the merits.[41]

Of course, the methods of protest available to the peace movement were not limited to the filing of this judicial challenge. Indeed, following the double-track decision in 1979, protestors organized massive demonstrations, and they revived the tradition of anti-war Easter Marches that had been common in the 1960s.[42] In 1980, moreover, protestors issued the "Krefeld Appeal," a petition that sought the exclusion of American nuclear weapons from Central Europe. Drafted by Gert Bastian, a former Bundeswehr general who

41 Germany was not the only country in which protestors challenged the presence of American missiles on constitutional grounds during this period. In 1983 a Canadian peace group sued to prohibit tests of American Cruise missiles in Canada, claiming a violation of "the right to life, liberty and security of the person" contained in Section 7 of the Canadian Charter of Rights—a claim that very closely resembled a principal argument of the complainants in the first of the German *Pershing Missile* cases. The Canadian Supreme Court dismissed the action on the grounds that the protestors could not possibly prove that these tests of unarmed Cruise missiles would result in a violation of anyone's life, liberty or security. The claim that the tests might make Canada a nuclear target and increase the chances of nuclear war were too speculative to countenance. *Operation Dismantle v. the Queen*, [1985] 1 S.C.R., 441. For commentary, see Michael Mandel, *The Charter of Rights and the Legalization of Politics in Canada*, 74–81 (Toronto: Thompson, rev. edn 1994).

In a somewhat later decision the German Constitutional Court also rejected a challenge to the stationing of American chemical weapons in the Federal Republic—evincing a willingness to defer to governmental choices on military and defense matters similar to that shown in the *Pershing* cases. Again Judge Mahrenholz dissented, arguing that the German government had violated its obligation to protect life (Art. 2(2)GG) by failing to implement adequate defenses against a catastrophic release of poisonous gas. 77 BVerfGE, 170 (1987).

42 See generally Rob Burns and Wilfried van der Will, *Protest and Democracy in West Germany: Extra-Parliamentary Opposition and the Democratic Agenda*, 205–29 (New York: St. Martin's Press 1988).

had joined the peace movement, this appeal ultimately attracted more than five million signatures.[43] Moreover, in October 1981, organizers mobilized 300,000 protestors for an anti-missile demonstration in Bonn. At the time, this was "the largest demonstration in German history," and it marked the point at which "the peace movement re-emerged as a vehicle of mass protest."[44] Indeed, the peace movement of the 1980s came to be "the largest mass movement in the history of the Federal Republic."[45]

In October 1983—shortly before the Pershing II missiles were to be deployed—the number of protestors at another huge demonstration in Bonn was said to have reached 500,000. On the same day, approximately 200,000 demonstrators formed a human "peace chain" which extended over 108 kilometers—between the headquarters of the American army in Stuttgart and the projected Pershing missile base at the American Wiley Barracks in Neu-Ulm.[46]

But neither the judicial challenges nor the massive protests in the autumn of 1983 succeeded in delaying the deployment of the Pershing II missiles. Accordingly, with the deployments of 1983—following the NATO double-track decision of 1979—the focus of the anti-nuclear blockades shifted from the Lance missile base in Großengstingen to the Pershing rocket depot in Mutlangen.

### *Protesting the Pershing missiles—Mutlangen*

The Mutlangen demonstrations extended, with some interruptions, over a period of approximately four- and-a-half years—from Easter 1983 until late 1987 when Presidents Reagan and Gorbachev signed a treaty that resulted in the dismantling and removal of the Pershing

[43] Ibid., 207–9, 225. On the Krefeld Appeal and Gert Bastian, see, e.g., Uwe Wesel, *Die verspielte Revolution: 1968 und die Folgen*, 293–94 (Munich: Blessing 2002); Offenloch, *Erinnerung*, 21–22.

[44] Burns and van der Will, 211.

[45] Wesel, *Die verspielte Revolution*, 292.

[46] FAZ, 24 October 1983, 2; Günther Gugel, *Wir werden nicht weichen: Erfahrungen mit Gewaltfreiheit*, 114–16 (Tübingen: Verein für Friedenspädagogik 1996).

An exhibition at the Historical Museum of Baden-Württemberg in the summer of 2004 displayed dramatic overhead television footage of the "peace chain," showing the demonstrators, with linked hands, dancing in huge "sine waves" along the Autobahn. The catalog of the 2004 exhibition, which focused on the demonstrations against the Pershing II missiles, contains a photograph of the scene. See *Zerreißprobe Frieden: Baden-Württemberg und der NATO-Doppelbeschluss. Katalog zur Sonderausstellung im Haus der Geschichte Baden-Württemberg* (2004), 7.

II missiles a year later.[47] Perhaps the high point of the Mutlangen protests was reached during a four-week period in September and October 1986—the so-called "Blockade Autumn"—when the organizers maintained an almost constant series of sit-down demonstrations near the missile base.[48] Previously the organizers had concerted their activities in a small "press cabin" (Pressehütte) in Mutlangen, but after Blockade Autumn they purchased a house in Mutlangen in order to maintain a constant presence near the rocket storage area.[49]

Unlike intercontinental ballistic missiles stationed in the United States, Pershing II missiles were not designed to remain stationary targets of a feared hostile attack.[50] Rather, the Pershing II missiles could be moved from place to place on motorized transporters, and the American army periodically took the rockets on "maneuvers" in the forests around Mutlangen. Accordingly, a particularly dramatic confrontation occurred in May 1987 when about 50 protestors—many of them older people who had lived through World War II—found the Pershing missiles in the forest and blocked their movement for a period of several hours.

A participant's report of the episode reflects the mixture of quixotic imagination and earnest religiosity that often characterized these demonstrations:

> [W]e saw three Pershing II [rockets] . . . lying under camouflage netting on their transport vehicles. . . . We placed a wooden cross of branches in the middle and prepared a religious service—a religious service in the middle of three Pershings, surrounded by American soldiers. We sang mostly English songs, someone

47 Treaty on the Elimination of Intermediate-Range and Shorter-Range Missiles, signed 8 December 1987; 1657 U.N.T.S., 2. See Herf, *War by Other Means*, 219.
On the removal of the Pershing missiles in 1988, see Manfred Laduch *et al.*, *Mutlanger Heide. Ein Ort macht Geschichte*, 104–10 (Schwäbisch Gmünd: Remsdruckerei 1990) [*Mutlanger Heide*]. See also *Mutlangen 1983–1987*, 48–49.

48 See *Mutlangen 1983–1987*, 94–107; on the blockades, see generally Offenloch, *Erinnerung*, 22–34.

49 The house in Mutlangen was named after Carl Kabat, an American priest who had engaged in anti-missile protests in Germany. In 1985, a United States district court had sentenced Kabat to 18 years in prison for damaging a Minuteman II missile silo site in Missouri. *United States v. Kabat*, 797 F.2d 580 (8 Cir. 1986). See *Mutlangen 1983–1987*, 53; Cooney and Michalowski, 234. Carl Kabat House remains in the hands of the remnants of those who were active in the anti-missile protests in Mutlangen.

50 See, e.g., 68 BVerfGE, 103.

> played a Bach cantata on a Flügelhorn, we translated . . . the Lord's prayer [into English]—at which a soldier took off his helmet. . . .
>
> We—that is to say, particularly the older generation—spoke with the . . . soldiers. . . . The men and women [of our group] spoke of their experiences under National Socialism and in World War II, and of their understanding of our personal responsibility for maintaining peace—in contrast with the obedience [to the regime, which was prevalent] in Nazi Germany. . . . We carried on a lively discussion with [the American commander] about the duty of obedience to government and the responsibility to human rights and to our conscience—about civil disobedience, non-violence and fascism.[51]

This stand-off lasted for about four hours—until the protestors were finally carried away by the police.

The dramatic blockade of missiles on maneuvers in the forest was, however, the exceptional case. As at Großengstingen, the more typical demonstration consisted of small groups of individuals—frequently no more than 10 or 15 persons; that is, one "affinity group"—who sat down in front of the main gate in order to block the route of a truck or convoy that sought to enter the missile base. Typically, the protestors would remain peacefully sitting or standing in the road until—after the ritual warnings to disperse—they were carried away by police.

Many of these demonstrations were conducted routinely by members of the peace movement who happened to be in the area—but other protests had special themes or characteristics. Some demonstrations, for example, were organized to represent particular geographical regions or religious groups, and some represented occupational groups such as weavers or physicians.[52] Some protestors celebrated their birthdays by inviting friends to a "birthday blockade," and there was a Mothers Day blockade in May 1987; similarly, on at lest two occasions there were "mother and child" blockades.[53] In August

[51] *Mutlangen 1983–1987*, 142–43.

[52] Ibid., 116–18; Interview with Uwe Painke, Leonberg, 20 July 2003.

[53] *Mutlangen 1983–1987*, 114–15; Hanne Narr, "Mutterstagsblockade—Mutlangen 1987," in Komitee für Grundrechte und Demokratie, e.V., *Ziviler Ungehorsam: Traditionen, Konzepte, Erfahrungen, Perspektiven*, 109–16 (Sensbachtal 1992) [*Ziviler Ungehorsam*].

1985, the peace movement proclaimed a special series of "Days of Civil Disobedience" to mark the 40th anniversary of the dropping of the first atomic bomb.[54] On Christmas Eve 1985 a prayer service, held outside the gate of the missile depot, turned into a blockade when police officers tried to pass through the gate.[55]

Certainly the best publicized of the demonstrations were the "Celebrity Blockades" (*Prominentenblockaden*) of 1983 and 1985 in which well-known figures, such as the writers Heinrich Böll and Günter Grass, played an important role.[56] Indeed, the first "Celebrity Blockade," on a hot day in September 1983, may well have been a watershed event which propelled the movement of civil disobedience into the consciousness of many citizens across the Federal Republic.[57]

The theme of anti-Nazism and the monitory example of World War II also played an important role in the demonstrations. In May 1987, for example, an "anti-fascist blockade" included former concentration camp prisoners and others persecuted by the Nazi regime;[58] moreover, as we have seen, in so-called "senior blockades" older people spoke of their experiences under Nazism. As one participant indicated, the senior blockades had a reconciling effect for younger protestors who may have been suspicious of their elders' actions in the Nazi period.[59]

54 Rems-Zeitung, 10 August 1985. See also Hanne and Klaus Vack (eds), *Mutlangen—unser Mut wird langen!* (Sensbachtal: Komitee für Grundrechte und Demokratie e.V., 6th edn 1988), 35 (statement of Martin Singe); ibid., 75 (statement of Dorothee Sölle).

55 Gmünder Tagespost, 27 December 1985.

56 *Mutlangen 1983–1987*, 108–13.

57 Interview with Klaus Vack, Sensbachtal, 22 July 2002; Albertz, "Erinnerung an die Prominentenblockade," in *Mutlanger Erfahrungen*, 3; Schlupp, in ibid., 4. See also Burns and van der Will, 224–25; Wesel, *Die verspielte Revolution*, 294.

58 *Mutlangen 1983–1987*, 127.

59 Ibid., 132. The suspicion of the younger generation had its counterpart in feelings of guilt or shame expressed by older demonstrators. See, e.g., *Unser Mut*, 54 (remarks of Mutlangen protestor Helga Einsele, born in 1920): "I belong to the generation that for a whole lifetime has not gotten over the fact that it did not sit on the tracks when the [German] trains rolled into the Rhineland in 1934, into Austria in 1938, and into Poland in 1939." See also the remarks of the theologian Norbert Greinacher, a member of an "affinity group" that was largely composed of older protestors: "The generation of my parents has been properly reproached with the fact that they were generally silent in the face of the inhumanities of the [Nazi]

There were also classical music blockades. On 15 September 1986, 120 musicians formed a symphony orchestra and performed a "blockade concert" in front of the main gate of the missile base, including works by Bach, Schubert, and Beethoven. This symphonic concert was followed by small groups of musicians performing chamber music outside the main gate, and the chamber concert was followed, in turn, by a choral concert and more chamber music, continuing into the night.[60] In the words of the organizers, this blockade was a symbol of the "life-affirming aspects of our culture", which took place at the rocket depot—"the symbol of the aspects and tendencies of [our] culture that are hostile to life."[61] One of the "blockade concerts" featured Schubert's *Unfinished Symphony*, in which a dwindling number of remaining musicians continued to play as their colleagues were carried away by police.[62] A certain "Freifrau" Droste zu Vischering issued a call to all "persons with famous names" (*namenhafte Leute*) to assemble for an aristocrats' blockade (*Adelsblockade*).[63]

Finally, in the sort of action that would seem unthinkable in England or the United States, 20 West German judges participated in a judges' blockade—a sit-down demonstration as an act of civil disobedience in front of the missile base in Mutlangen. This block-

regime. I have firmly decided not to remain silent, but to lift my weak voice—again and again—against this atomic madness." *Verwerflich?*, 40.

For recollections of the "senior blockades" see also Elisa Kauffeld, "Erfahrungen einer Seniorin," in *Ziviler Ungehorsam*, 118–20: "There they sat, the old, the fragile, the war victims with crutches—in front of the rocket convoy. . . . A church group had brought a large wooden cross, which stood wavering on the street between the sitting [demonstrators]." See also Sibylle Grüninger and Anne Frommann (eds), *"Wo diese schweigen, so werden die Steine schreien": Seniorinnen und Senioren für den Frieden* (Mössingen-Talheim: Talheimer 1989) (courtroom statements by participants in the senior blockades); *Nie wieder Krieg: Dokumentation Seniorenblockade und Manöverbehinderung Mai 1987* (Mutlangen 1987) (documentation of the 1987 senior blockade).

60 Thomas Schmidt and Barbara Rodi (eds), *Lebenslaute: 1 Konzertblockade, 15 September 1986, schöpferische widerstand in Mutlangen: eine dokumentation*; see also Rems-Zeitung, 16 September 1986.

61 *Mutlangen 1983–1987*, 130. For recollections of this concert blockade see also Kauffeld in *Ziviler Ungehorsam*, 120–21: "It was not only the friends of disarmament who were enthusiastic and thoughtful listeners. Also the U.S. soldiers, who were keeping watch over the machinery of death, heard the sounds of Mozart's harmonies and were visibly moved."

62 Interview with Klaus Vack, Sensbachtal.

63 *Mutlangen 1983–1987*, 126.

ade, which took place "in the icy stillness of a cold winter day" in January 1987, became a *cause célèbre* in the German press and in the professional literature.[64] The participating jurists declared that this was "an act of solidarity with hundreds of fellow citizens who have been charged by prosecutors and convicted by judges—precisely because of such a blockade."[65] The judges argued that the stationing of the missiles contravened the West German Constitution—as a violation of human dignity, the right to life and bodily integrity, and various provisions intended to preserve peace.[66] Some of the protesting judges were prosecuted for this blockade, but hundreds of other judges, prosecutors, and lawyers signed statements in their support.[67]

## The historical background of the sit-down demonstrations: 1968 and the development of political protest in the Federal Republic

### *Early protests against rearmament*

When the protests against nuclear missiles began at Großengstingen in 1981, they were the latest manifestations of a more general movement of political dissent that had been directed against armament and feared militarization in Germany since the early days of the Federal Republic. In the 1950s, for example, demonstrators had organized marches and other protests against German rearmament and the inclusion of the Federal Republic in NATO, the western military alliance. Later in the same decade, demonstrators protested plans to arm German troops with tactical nuclear weapons, acting under the aegis of an umbrella organization called Campaign against

[64] Rudolph, "Blockierende Richter—eine Herausforderung für den Rechtsstaat?", 1988 DRiZ 131. See also *Die Richter-Blockade-Mutlangen 12 Jan. 1987* (Dr. Helmut Kramer, Wolfenbüttel) (documentation of the blockade and its aftermath); Heinrich Hannover, *Die Republik vor Gericht 1975–1995*, 319–32 (Berlin: Aufbau 1999); *Mutlanger Heide*, 156–62; Walter Schmitt Glaeser, *Private Gewalt im politischen Meinungskampf*, 60, 130 (Berlin: Duncker & Humblot, 2nd edn 1992).

[65] *Mutlangen 1983–1987*, 154.

[66] The judges could at least plausibly take this position, because the Constitutional Court had not passed on the merits of these arguments in rejecting constitutional challenges to the stationing of the Pershing II missiles. See p. 23 above.

[67] See Hannover, 332. But the Federal Administrative Court upheld an official "warning" directed toward judges who had signed a similar statement. 78 BVerwGE, 216 (1987).

Nuclear Death (*Kampf dem Atomtod*).[68] Opponents sought to conduct advisory plebiscites or referenda on nuclear armament in the Länder, but the Constitutional Court prohibited these efforts on the grounds that they invaded the area of defense policy which was exclusively confined to the federal government under the Basic Law.[69]

These early anti-nuclear protests paralleled similar activity taking place at the same time in England, such as the mass Aldermaston Marches, which began in 1958, and other early projects of the Campaign for Nuclear Disarmament (CND).[70] Indeed, in its origins the German "Easter March" movement of the early and mid-1960s was "modeled after the [CND] marches in England" and "included people of various political opinions, social backgrounds, and ages, all united in their opposition to 'the bomb'."[71] But, in any event, these early German protests were rather ill-organized and generally small—in comparison, at least, with the massive demonstrations of the anti-missile movement of the 1980s.[72]

### *The student movement of 1968*

The sit-down protests in Mutlangen and Großengstingen were also an outgrowth of political forces released by the explosive student movement of 1968, a movement that was directed toward fundamental political and social change—in Europe generally and Germany in particular. During this period the prevailing silence of the Adenauer era was irrevocably broken, and the student generation condemned

[68] See generally 1 Bark and Gress, 272–91, 366–72, 386–91, 399–410, 459–60; Kielmansegg, "The Origins and Aims of the German Peace Movement," in Walter Laqueur and Robert Hunter (eds), *European Peace Movements and the Future of the Western Alliance*, 319–21 (New Brunswick: Transaction 1985); Ruud Koopmans, *Democracy from Below: New Social Movements and the Political System in West Germany*, 86–87 (Boulder, CO: Westview Press 1995). Plans to arm the *Bundeswehr* with nuclear weapons were eventually abandoned. Wesel, *Die verspielte Revolution*, 291.

[69] 8 BVerfGE, 104 (1958); 8 BVerfGE, 122 (1958). See also Chapter 5.

[70] See James Hinton, *Protests and Visions: Peace Politics in Twentieth-Century Britain* (London: Hutchinson 1989).

[71] Cooper, 99. Moreover, later examples of civil disobedience in England—such as the women's vigils of the 1980s, protesting the stationing of Cruise missiles on Greenham Common—were contemporaneous with the sit-down protests at Großengstingen and Mutlangen. See, e.g., Caroline Blackwood, *On the Perimeter* (London: Heinemann 1984).

[72] See, e.g., Cooper, 25–81.

their parents' complicity in the Nazi regime and what the students perceived as an attempt to restore traditional social structures in Germany after World War II. Indeed, in the protest movements that followed—including the anti-war and anti-nuclear movements—a bitter reaction against the Nazi era and anxiety about a possible revival of German militarism were never far from the surface.[73]

In 1968, the student revolt took concrete form in protests against the American role in the Vietnam War—which was supported by the Federal Republic—as well as protests against the regimes of oppressive leaders in the Third World, such as the Shah of Iran and Moise Tschombe of the Congo. But the more theoretical positions of the protestors—developed in "teach-ins" and other demonstrations at the German universities—sought the reconstitution of society and politics for the purpose of dismantling traditional hierarchical structures and achieving greater social and economic equality.

Toward this end, the revolutionary leader Rudi Dutschke proposed a "long march" through traditional West German institutions.[74] According to this plan, members of the student movement would gradually find their way into important positions in various areas of German public life and, in this manner, transform the basic characteristics of political and social structures. In the view of one observer, the idea of the long march "combined the elan of Mao Tse-tung's original long march through the Chinese countryside with the con-

[73] The past few years have seen an extraordinary wave of memoirs, analyses and other accounts of the student movement of 1968 in Germany, and its aftermath. See, e.g., Jürgen Busche, *Die 68er: Biographie einer Generation* (Berlin: Berlin Verlag 2003); Ingrid Gilcher-Holtey, *Die 68er Bewegung: Deutschland—Westeuropa—USA* (Munich: Beck 2001); Wolfgang Kraushaar, *1968 als Mythos, Chiffre and Zäsur* (Hamburg: HIS 2000); Oskar Negt, *Achtundsechzig: Politische Intellektuelle und die Macht* (Göttingen: Steidl 1995, 2001); Uwe Wesel, *Die verspielte Revolution: 1968 und die Folgen* (Munich: Blessing 2002); Carole Fink, Philipp Gassert and Detlef Junker (eds), *1968: The World Transformed* (New York: Cambridge University Press 1998).

In these accounts, the student leader Rudi Dutschke remains—as he was then—a particular focus of attention. See, e.g., Gretchen Dutschke, *Wir hatten ein barbarisches, schönes Leben. Rudi Dutschke—eine Biographie* (Munich: Knaur 1998); Rudi Dutschke, *Jeder hat sein Leben ganz zu leben: Die Tagebücher 1963–1979* (Gretchen Dutschke, ed.; Köln: Kiepenheuer & Witsch 2003); Rudi-Marek Dutschke, *Spuren meines Vaters* (Köln: Kiepenheuer & Witsch 2001).

For earlier analyses of the period, see, e.g., Ronald Fraser (ed.), *1968: A Student Generation in Revolt* (New York: Pantheon 1988).

[74] See, e.g., Rudi Dutschke, *Mein langer Marsch: Reden, Schriften und Tagebücher aus zwanzig Jahren*, 15 (Reinbek bei Hamburg: Rowohlt 1980); Kraushaar, 81–88.

viction that revolution in the West would be the consequence of long-term changes in consciousness, rather than of violence and terrorism by armed vanguards."[75]

Nonetheless, the student protests were accompanied by eruptions of violence on both sides of the divide. A notable example was the death of a student, Benno Ohnesorg, who was shot by police in June 1967 during protests in Berlin against a visit by the Shah of Iran. Rudi Dutschke, also, was shot and seriously wounded by a lone gunman.

In early 1968, the student movement mobilized opposition against a package of constitutional amendments and federal legislation that authorized the curtailment of civil and political rights in the case of emergency.[76] The protestors viewed this legislation "as a relapse into an authoritarian past and an acute danger to democracy,"[77] as well as "the ultimate abdication by parliament of its role as a watchdog of government."[78] Yet this unsuccessful campaign of opposition marked one of the last efforts of the organized student movement in Germany. After a series of defeats, its umbrella organization, the SDS, was finally dissolved in early 1970.[79] The movement left little behind in the way of concrete governmental changes, but nonetheless it had altered the historical and political consciousness of many in the Federal Republic.

After the failure of the student movement, some members of the "68 generation" despaired of political change and moved into the deadly violence of terrorist organizations, such as the Red Army Fraction (RAF) and the Baader-Meinhof group.[80] Others sought a radical political solution with the founding in 1968 of a new West German Communist Party (DKP)—to replace the historic German Communist Party (KPD) which had been banned by the Constitutional Court in 1956. Small splinter groups also offered refuge under the banner of Marx, Trotsky, or Mao.[81]

But many others took a more moderate route, joining the mainstream peace movement and founding the German ecological

[75] Herf, *War by Other Means*, 83.

[76] For analysis of these measures, see Note, "Recent Emergency Legislation in West Germany," 82 *Harvard Law Review* 1704 (1969).

[77] Cooper, 87; see also ibid., 106.

[78] Burns and van der Will, 11.

[79] See Wesel, *Die verspielte Revolution*, 109.

[80] Ibid., 182–91, 257–67; Schmitt Glaeser, *Private Gewalt*, 34–36.

[81] Wesel, *Die verspielte Revolution*, 160–68; Busche, 118–19.

movement, including the political party of the Greens. Yet—notwithstanding these developments—the peace movement itself was largely quiescent from the end of 1968 until the late 1970s when the "double-track" decision of NATO impelled its rejuvenation.[82]

When the German peace movement was revived in the late 1970s, one of the central issues that it had to confront was *die Gewaltfrage*—the "question of force."[83] Some voices argued that the goal of peace was so important that the use of force was justified in its pursuit.[84] But the mainstream of the peace movement—as well as the largely overlapping ecological movement—firmly held that the use of force was not justified.[85] Indeed, a rejection of the use of force was seen as the major distinction between the mainstream peace movement and its more radical counterparts.

### The 1970s: decade of environmental protest

Yet even though the peace movement was inactive in the 1970s, a "culture of protest" evolved in other areas during that period, and these developments formed a basis for the great peace demonstrations of the following decade.[86] During the 1970s, for example, the ecological movement engaged in massive protests which were directed particularly against the construction of nuclear power plants. In 1975, during the first series of these demonstrations, 28,000 protestors occupied a construction site at the planned nuclear plant at Wyhl in southwest Germany—and ultimately the construction was halted.[87]

Thereafter, the "inspiring success of the activists in Wyhl" evoked an unprecedented "wave of anti-nuclear protest."[88] Demonstrations

[82] Cooper, 118; Interview with Klaus Vack, Sensbachtal.

[83] See generally Sternstein, "Die 68er und die Gewaltfrage," 2001 Wissenschaft und Frieden (W&F), No. 2, 47.

[84] See generally Manfred Bissinger (ed.), *Günther Anders: Gewalt—ja oder nein* (Munich: Knaur 1987).

[85] See, e.g., Leinen, "Ziviler Ungehorsam als fortgeschrittene Form der Demonstration," in Peter Glotz (ed.), *Ziviler Ungehorsam im Rechtsstaat*, 26–27 (Frankfurt/M: Suhrkamp 1983) [*Ziviler Ungehorsam im Rechtsstaat*]; Glotz, "Am Widerstand scheiden sich die Geister", in *Ziviler Ungehorsam im Rechtsstaat*, 12–13.

[86] Cooper, 118.

[87] Andrei S. Markovits and Philip S. Gorski, *The German Left: Red, Green and Beyond*, 102–3 (New York: Oxford University Press 1993); Koopmans, 158–63; see also Wesel, *Die verspielte Revolution*, 251–54.

[88] Koopmans, 163.

against the building of an atomic power plant at Brokdorf in northern Germany involved considerable violence, but these protests also eventually led to an important decision of the Constitutional Court on the constitutional rights of assembly.[89] The Brokdorf protests were ultimately unsuccessful, but demonstrations in the late 1970s at Gorleben in northern Germany led to the cancellation of a nuclear reprocessing plant there.[90]

In another notable environmental protest which reached its zenith in late 1981, thousands of demonstrators sought unsuccessfully to prevent the construction of a new runway at the Frankfurt Rhein-Main Airport—a huge project that involved the destruction of many acres of forest.[91] Finally, an even larger series of sustained demonstrations was launched in the mid-1980s against a planned atomic reprocessing plant at Wackersdorf in Bavaria (the successor of the abandoned project in Gorleben). Ultimately, this plant was not built.[92]

Many of these political demonstrations were legal and indeed constitutionally protected. But they became illegal when, in some instances, demonstrators abandoned peaceful protest and engaged in violence or sought to "occupy" private lands.

In neither case, however, did these earlier demonstrations represent examples of non-violent civil disobedience. Indeed, up until the 1980s, organized non-violent civil disobedience was not well known as a tactic of political discourse or influence in Germany; rather, "the theory and practice of civil disobedience was developed elsewhere."[93] In the context of the protests at Mutlangen, the famous German novelist Heinrich Böll remarked: "Demonstrating and blockading . . . are in the best Anglo-Saxon tradition. When we demonstrate and blockade, therefore, our actions are very American

[89] See Markovits and Gorski, 103–4; Koopmans, 163–66. For discussion of the Court's *Brokdorf* decision, see Chapter 3.

[90] Koopmans, 163–70. Plans for a nuclear waste storage facility at Gorleben, however, were realized. In response, sit-down protests and other demonstrations directed against shipments of nuclear waste material to this facility at Gorleben continue up to the present day. See, e.g., FAZ, 13 November 2003, 5.

[91] See 32 BGHSt, 165 (1983); 82 BVerfGE, 236 (1990) (Schubart case). In the course of this protest, opponents built and occupied a "hut village" in the forest near the airport site for about a year. Koopmans, 179–88.

[92] Ibid., 207–10. See also Epilogue.

[93] Huber, "Die Grenzen des Staats und die Pflicht zum Ungehorsam," in *Ziviler Ungehorsam im Rechtsstaat*, 111.

—not anti-American—although they are directed against the American rockets."[94] Similarly, the German philosopher Jürgen Habermas declared: "The present [anti-missile] protest movement affords a chance—for the first time—to make civil disobedience comprehensible, even in Germany, as an element of a mature political culture."[95]

Thus, the stationing of nuclear rockets afforded the first important occasion for the development of this particular technique of political protest in Germany.[96]

[94] Böll, in ibid., 144. See also Hannah Arendt, "Civil Disobedience," in *Crises of the Republic* (San Diego: Harcourt Brace 1972), 83: "[A]lthough the phenomenon of civil disobedience is today a world-wide phenomenon . . . it still is primarily American in origin and substance."

[95] Habermas, "Ziviler Ungehorsam—Testfall für den demokratischen Rechtsstaat. Wider den autoritären Legalismus in der Bundesrepublik," in *Ziviler Ungehorsam im Rechtsstaat*, 32.

[96] The protests at Großengstingen and Mutlangen also drew upon a considerable international history of sit-down demonstrations—which had taken various forms, depending upon the specific political, economic and social context. For example, following methods that were also in use in Europe, American labor unions in the 1930s developed the technique of the sit-down strike in various industrial settings. Most notably, the United Automobile Workers union employed this method with considerable success in the great Flint and Detroit sit-down strikes of the later 1930s. See, e.g., Henry Kraus, *The Many and the Few* (Los Angeles, CA: Plantin Press 1947); Murray Kempton, *Part of Our Time: Some Ruins and Monuments of the Thirties*, 330–79 (New York: Modern Library 1998); Joel Seidman, "*Sit-Down*" (New York: League for Industrial Democracy 1937).

The purpose of this sit-down technique—really an occupation of the factory—was to prevent employers from resuming production with "replacement workers" in the absence of the striking employees. A union song of that era caught the rough-and-ready flavor of this form of industrial action—which was indeed rather different from that of the later anti-missile demonstrations: "Sit down, just take a seat, Sit down, and rest your feet, Sit down, you've got 'em beat. Sit down! Sit down!" Reprinted in Seidman, 9 (words and music by Maurice Sugar). The history of these strikes, however, was indeed known in a general way to the organizers of early anti-missile sit-down blockades at Großengstingen. Interview with Uwe Painke, Leonberg, 20 July 2003.

In the early 1960s the civil rights movement, following scattered precursors in earlier decades, engaged in widespread "sit-in" demonstrations to protest segregation of lunch counters and restaurants in the American South and in the border states. See, e.g., Peter Irons, *The Courage of Their Convictions*, 131–52 (New York: The Free Press 1988). These protestors generally followed the doctrine of non-violent resistance, as developed by Mahatma Gandhi and as employed by Martin Luther King in the Montgomery Bus Boycott. See, e.g., *Reporting Civil Rights Part I: American Journalism 1941–1963*, 431–52 (New York: Library of America 2003). In contrast with the sit-down labor strikes, the civil rights sit-ins

## The philosophical background: Satyagraha and civil disobedience

Certainly, the action of the protestors at Großengstingen and Mutlangen were considered by their proponents—and by their opponents—as a form of civil disobedience. As such, the protests fell within two overlapping but conceptually distinct traditions of direct action: the quasi-religious tradition of Satyagraha or non-violent resistance—as espoused and developed by Mahatma Gandhi—and a more explicitly political tradition of civil disobedience that has been analyzed and refined in recent years by eminent philosophers such as John Rawls and Jürgen Habermas. Although many acts of political resistance may—as here—partake of both traditions, the underlying concepts, purposes, and justifications of the two traditions are distinct in important ways.

were often intended as direct violations of specific unjust laws, and thousands of demonstrators were arrested for trespass. The Supreme Court reversed several of these convictions, but it never decided whether the use of trespass laws to enforce racial discrimination by private property owners is a form of unconstitutional state action. Paulsen, "The Sit-In Cases of 1964: 'But Answer Came There None'," 1964 Supreme Court Review 137. The enactment of the Civil Rights Act of 1964 rendered this question moot by prohibiting racial discrimination in hotels, restaurants, and other places of public accommodation.

Various forms of sit-in demonstrations and blockades were employed in the Berkeley "Free Speech Movement" of 1964–1965—evidently inspired by students who had returned from civil rights organizing in the American South. Fraser (ed.), *1968: A Student Generation in Revolt*, 89–99; Wesel, *Die verspielte Revolution*, 84–86. In October 1965, a sit-in demonstration at the office of a draft board in Ann Arbor Michigan was an early example in a long series of such demonstrations of civil disobedience in protest of the American role in the Vietnam War. Cohen, "Law, Speech, and Disobedience," in Hugo Adam Bedau (ed.), *Civil Disobedience: Theory and Practice*, 165–77 (New York: Pegasus 1969) [*Civil Disobedience: Theory and Practice*].

Sit-in demonstrations—directly inspired by students from Berkeley and the American civil rights movement—were also common in Berlin and elsewhere in the German students' movement of the late 1960s and in the early 1970s. These protests frequently took the form of the occupation of classrooms or offices in universities. See Wesel, *Die verspielte Revolution*, 25, 48, 66, 110–13, 177–78, 209. In the 1970s sit-in blockades were employed—as we have seen—to protest against nuclear power plants in the United States, and these efforts had a direct influence on the organizers of the sit-down blockades in protest of the Pershing II rockets in Germany.

### *Satyagraha and the religious form of civil disobedience: Gandhi and King*

Many of the theorists of the German anti-nuclear movement saw themselves as carrying on a tradition of non-violent or passive resistance as developed in the works of Gandhi and Martin Luther King. The Gandhian tradition, known as Satyagraha or "firmness in adhering to truth,"[97] requires non-violence, even in resistance to the most oppressive regimes. In this way, Gandhi taught, the prevailing authorities of the state may be convinced of the rightness of the protestors' cause—largely through the moral force of their example and the religious power of their suffering.[98] In essence, it is an appeal to the *conscience* of the prevailing community.[99]

Accordingly, the non-violence of the resistance must be preserved under all circumstances, even when serious injury or death might be the result—as was not infrequently the case in Gandhi's time. Martin Luther King, who was a follower of Gandhi in important respects, also emphasized the persuasive moral force of suffering. In this connection, King urged that southern segregationists should be addressed in the following manner:

> We will match your capacity to inflict suffering with our capacity to endure suffering . . . [W]e will soon wear you down by our capacity to suffer. And in winning our freedom we will so appeal to your heart and conscience that we will win you in the process.[100]

Moreover, in the eyes of Gandhi and King, non-violence was even

[97] M.K. Gandhi, Hind Swaraj *and Other Writings* lxxvii, ed. Anthony J. Parel; (Cambridge: Cambridge University Press 1997).

[98] See, e.g., Stanley Wolpert, *Gandhi's Passion: The Life and Legacy of Mahatma Gandhi*, 71, 74, 233 and *passim* (New York: Oxford University Press 2001). According to Gandhi, " 'civil disobedience is . . . based upon an absolute efficiency of innocent suffering'," and he "believed that it is through suffering voluntarily undergone that the *satyagrahi* melts the heart of his opponent and opens 'the eyes of his understanding.' " Accordingly, "The *Satyagrahi* strives to reach the reason through the heart." Vinit Haksar, *Civil Disobedience, Threats and Offers: Gandhi and Rawls*, 5, 8, 10 (Delhi: Oxford University Press 1986), quoting M.K. Gandhi, *Non-Violent Resistance* (New York: Schocken 1967), 172, 191.

[99] King, *Stride Toward Freedom*, 216.

[100] Ibid., 217. At the outset of the civil rights movement, King recalled that it "was in this Gandhian emphasis on love and non-violence that I discovered the method for social reform that I had been seeking." Ibid., 97.

more than a form of persuasion in a social struggle: it was an entire religious way of life. According to Gandhi, the practice of Satyagraha requires "true faith in religion . . . In other words, he who leaves everything to God can never know defeat in this world."[101] Such a practice requires a high degree of self-abnegation in all aspects of life. Indeed, a Satyagrahi "gives no thought whatever to his body,"[102] "he must be indifferent to wealth," and he "is obliged to break away from family attachments."[103] Moreover, in the scale of self-abnegation and risk of death, "[f]asting is a satyagrahi's last resort."[104] In his life Gandhi exemplified the practice of these precepts, and—to a less encompassing degree—King struggled to do so as well.

Gandhi also laid down rules for the "volunteers" who were to engage in Satyagraha or non-violent resistance. In some respects those rules anticipated the principles developed in the "trainings" for the anti-missile protestors.[105] Gandhi particularly emphasized that opposing forces—such as the police—were not to be treated in a hostile manner and that it "must be our resolve to win [opponents] over by courteous behavior."[106] In Gandhi's view a Satyagrahi "does not wish for the destruction of his antagonist . . . but has only compassion for him."[107] Indeed, Gandhi maintained that an individual

> has a duty to resist an unjust law, because it is a hindrance to the pursuit of truth *not only for the resister but also for the legislator or oppressor*. . . . [Thus] one disobeys an unjust law out of a reverence for the moral personality of the opponent.[108]

101 Gandhi, "Who Can Offer Satyagraha," in 9 *The Collected Works of Mahatma Gandhi*, 227 (Delhi: Publications Division, Ministry of Information and Broadcasting, Government of India 1963).

102 Ibid., 225. Gandhi viewed Socrates as a forerunner of Satyagraha in this respect. Raghavan Iyer (ed.), *The Essential Writings of Mahatma Gandhi*, 310 (Delhi: Oxford University Press 1991).

103 9 *The Collected Works of Mahatma Gandhi*, 225–26.

104 Wolpert, 253.

105 Gandhian training, however, was in general considerably broader, focusing on instruction and training for an entire life. Painke, "Trainings für Gewaltfreiheit: Ein historischer Streifzug," in Christian W. Büttner *et al.* (eds), *Politik von unten: Zur Geschichte und Gegenwart der Gewaltfreien Aktion*, 171 (Berlin: Gewaltfreie Aktion 1997).

106 Iyer (ed.), *The Essential Writings of Mahatma Gandhi*, 314–15.

107 Ibid., 310.

108 Leys and Rao, "Gandhi's Synthesis of Indian Spirituality and Western Politics," in J. Roland Pennock and John W. Chapman (eds), *Political and Legal Obligation*, 449 (New York: Atherton 1970) (emphasis added).

Similarly, Martin Luther King thought that an important goal of civil disobedience must be reconciliation—"not the humiliation or defeat of the opponent, but the winning of the enemy's friendship and understanding."[109] This tenet was related to King's view that "*agápe*"—a disinterested love for all, including one's enemies—stood "at the center" of the principle of non-violence.[110] A similar precept was illustrated in the German sit-down demonstrations—as the protestors frequently sought to engage the NATO soldiers in discussions and conversations, seeking to explain the purpose of their protest.[111]

Non-violent resistance may be employed—as it was by Gandhi and King—against widespread oppressive regimes. Often these acts of resistance may be a violation of prevailing law. Yet, strictly speaking, non-violent resistance may not always require or entail a violation of law. In the case of many civil rights demonstrations in the American South, for example, the protestors' actions may have been termed illegal by southern police officials; but in many instances the protests were ultimately upheld as legal by the American Supreme Court or other federal courts. For example, the "Freedom Rides" of the early 1960s—racially integrated bus trips through the American South—may have violated segregation doctrines of certain American states, but their legality was protected under superior federal law.[112]

[109] William D. Watley, *Roots of Resistance: The Nonviolent Ethic of Martin Luther King, Jr.*, 114 (Valley Forge: Judson 1985).

[110] Ibid., 124. See also Martin Luther King, Jr., "Letter from Birmingham City Jail," in Bedau (ed.), *Civil Disobedience: Theory and Practice*, 78 ("One who breaks an unjust law must do it *openly*, *lovingly*") (emphasis in original).

[111] Indeed, this form of discussion with the soldiers was prominently encouraged in the civil disobedience "trainings" of the German peace movement. Interview with Wolfgang Sternstein, Stuttgart, 10 July 2002.

[112] Alexander M. Bickel, *The Morality of Consent*, 96–97 (New Haven, CT: Yale University Press 1975). Cf. Storing, "The Case Against Civil Disobedience," in Hugo Adam Bedau (ed.), *Civil Disobedience in Focus*, 86–87 (London: Routledge 1991) [*Civil Disobedience in Focus*]. Yet at least some theorists of the German anti-missile movement believed that action should be considered "civil disobedience" if it was classified as illegal by one part of government—for example, the police—even if at a later point the protest might be found to be legal by the courts or some other branch of government. Interview with Volker Nick, Mutlangen, 18 July 2003.

## *The political form of civil disobedience: Rawls and Habermas*

On the other hand, the more political concept of civil disobedience—in most definitions—actually does require the violation of law. By violating the law, the demonstrators seek to add particular weight and drama to a protest against a measure or action that is claimed to be unjust. This is basically a political measure; "religious or pacifist conceptions are not essential."[113]

In this more political view, civil disobedience is a heightened form of speech that plays a role in democratic political dialogue in times of crisis. It occupies a position between legally protected political speech (distribution of handbills; marches with parade permits, etc.) and violent resistance—but it is considerably closer to the former. Of course, civil disobedience involves illegal action. But the protestors demonstrate their adherence to the legal system in general by breaking the law in public, and by being manifestly willing to accept the corresponding punishment. In this respect they follow a model with an ancient pedigree—extending at least as far back as the refusal of Socrates to escape imprisonment and death in the *Crito*.[114]

Modern theorists have emphasized that civil disobedience of this form is only possible in the context of a regime that is fundamentally democratic and just, in most respects.[115] Indeed, the regime may be only, or principally, unjust in the measure or measures being resisted through civil disobedience. Accordingly, in this view, civil disobedience is an attempt by the minority to convince the majority

113 Rawls, "Definition and Justification of Civil Disobedience," in *Civil Disobedience in Focus*, 116.

114 The requirement of publicity in civil disobedience has equally venerable roots. In Plato's *Apology*, Socrates declares that he would continue his public policy of constant questioning, even if forbidden by the state. Moreover, in the *Crito*, Socrates rejects his friend's plea that he escape Athens by stealth—even though he could thereby avoid death—at least in part because of the secrecy and deception that this course would involve. In Sophocles' *Antigone*, moreover, Antigone rejects her sister's plea that she disobey the law in secret. Instead, Antigone insists on all possible publicity for her disobedient act—burying the body of her brother in violation of the edict of the King.

But for an interesting argument discounting the requirements of publicity and punishment in civil disobedience, see Ronald Dworkin, "Civil Disobedience and Nuclear Protest," in *A Matter of Principle*, 114–15 (Cambridge, MA: Harvard University Press 1985).

115 See, e.g., Rawls, in *Civil Disobedience in Focus*, 103; Habermas, in *Ziviler Ungehorsam im Rechtsstaat*, 39.

that the measure being protested is a violation of fundamental principles that both the majority and the minority accept; it is the attempt of the minority to recall the majority to the basic principles of the polity.[116]

Accordingly, the violation of law may be seen as part of a political conversation with the majority of the electorate, in which the act of civil disobedience is intended to underscore the importance that the minority attaches to the issue in question. Certainly, civil disobedience may be more effective than more traditional forms of expression in conveying the intensity of the minority's view on the subject.[117] In some ways, accordingly, civil disobedience could be viewed as an extension of the right of political assembly because it performs, in a more dramatic manner, the basic function of contributing to democratic political dialogue.[118]

In some instances, moreover, civil disobedience can actually serve as a protection of the state's constitution itself. It can serve this "stabilizing" function by recalling the government to constitutional principles that it has unlawfully abandoned.[119] This function of civil disobedience can be particularly important in those circumstances in which the judiciary—invoking the "political question" doctrine or otherwise—refuses to enforce certain constitutional principles.[120] Thus civil disobedience might be most clearly justified

[116] See Rawls, in *Civil Disobedience in Focus*, 105–6; Habermas, in *Ziviler Ungehorsam im Rechtsstaat*, 39–41; Cohen, "Civil Disobedience in a Constitutional Democracy," 10 *The Massachusetts Review*, No. 2, spring 1969, 211, 217–18.

See also Dworkin, in *A Matter of Principle*, 105: Persons engaged in civil disobedience do not seek "any basic rupture or constitutional reorganization. They accept the fundamental legitimacy of both government and community; they act to acquit rather than to challenge their duty as citizens." According to Martin Luther King, therefore, a person engaging in civil disobedience "is in reality expressing the very highest respect for law." King, in Bedau (ed.), *Civil Disobedience: Theory and Practice*, 78–79.

[117] See Bickel, 100–1.

[118] See Leinen, in *Ziviler Ungehorsam im Rechtsstaat*, 23–28.

[119] Rawls, in *Civil Disobedience in Focus*, 114–15; Huber, in *Ziviler Ungehorsam im Rechtsstaat*, 118 (citing E. Küchenhoff).

See also Habermas, in ibid., 40–41 (civil disobedience actually protects legitimacy). Habermas also suggests that civil disobedience is all the more justified if—as in the case of the stationing of the Pershing rockets—a perhaps irreversible decision is to be taken by a government with a narrow parliamentary majority that would afford "insufficient democratic legitimacy" for the gravity of the decision. Ibid., 50.

[120] See Arendt, in *Crises of the Republic*, 80–82.

in instances—such as the American involvement in the Vietnam War, or German permission for the stationing of the Pershing rockets—in which the courts failed to consider all constitutional questions on the merits, or avoided deciding the constitutional issues at all.

In a just society, it has been argued, the government might well refrain from prosecuting acts of civil disobedience—or at least mitigate or suspend the punishment for such protests.[121] And in the specific German context, one opponent of civil disobedience has acknowledged that the constitutional principle of "proportionality" would allow the government to "close its eyes" to certain "direct actions of a demonstrative character," such as sit-down protests for short periods.[122]

The protestors who engaged in sit-down demonstrations at Großengstingen and Mutlangen partook of both of these traditions. Many considered themselves to be followers of Gandhian principles, and an influential theoretician of the movement, Wolfgang Sternstein, devoted much of his scholarly career to the study of Gandhi's works.[123] Moreover, in general, the German peace movement from its beginning was always influenced by a strong religious component.[124] Yet, in reality, the more political ideas of civil

121 See Rawls, in *Civil Disobedience in Focus*, 118; Dworkin, in *A Matter of Principle*, 114; Dworkin, "On Not Prosecuting Civil Disobedience," *New York Review of Books*, 6 June 1968, 14. See also Hughes, "Civil Disobedience and the Political Question Doctrine," 43 *New York University Law Review* 1, 3–4 (1968).

In the American context, one dissenting appellate judge has taken a similar position: non-violent civil disobedience "is engrained in our society and the moral correctness of political protestors' views has on occasion served to change and better our society. . . . In these circumstances, the courts . . . have ordinarily acted with a degree of restraint as to the severity of the punishment, recognizing that, although legally wrong, the offender may carry some moral justification for the disobedient acts." *United States v. Kabat*, 797 F.2d 580, 601 (8 Cir. 1986) (Bright, J., dissenting).

122 Wassermann, "Zur Rechtsordnung des politischen Kampfes in der verfassungsstaatlichen Demokratie", 1984 JZ, 263, 265. Another German legal philosopher has gone further and argued for a limited legal right to non-violent resistance, when the traditional requirements of civil disobedience are met and the protest is directed against "grave injustice" and remains within the limits of proportionality. Ralf Dreier, in *Ziviler Ungehorsam im Rechtsstaat*, 60–69.

123 See, e.g., Sternstein, "Gandhi—eine Herausforderung für unsere Zeit," in Mahatma Gandhi, *Für Pazifisten* (trans. Sternstein; Münster: Lit 1996).

124 Cooper, 39–48, 163–74.

disobedience seem to have played at least an equally important role.[125]

Considerable discussion surrounded the question of whether the anti-missile protests could be viewed as civil disobedience in the strict sense—because many protestors argued that the law under which they were being prosecuted actually did not apply to their demonstrations.[126] Accordingly, these protestors did not acknowledge the illegality of their acts. In any case, when in 1987 the superpowers seemed to be reaching an agreement that would lead to the withdrawal of the missiles, the campaign leaders ceased organizing sit-in protests against the Pershing II missiles—following the principle that civil disobedience is permissible only when no other means of eradicating the perceived injustice appears to be at hand.[127]

### *Other forms of civil disobedience: Thoreau, etc.*

Other forms of civil disobedience probably also played a role in the anti-missile sit-down demonstrations. For example, arguments in the pioneering essay of Henry David Thoreau on civil disobedience seem to fall into yet another category of writings on this subject.[128] Unlike Gandhi or King, or the political protestors posited by Rawls and Habermas, Thoreau did not seem to be primarily interested in persuading the government to change its course of action—either by virtue of the religious or moral force of his possible suffering or through more secular political dialogue. Rather, Thoreau was principally interested in following the requirements of his own conscience by disassociating himself completely from particular evils

[125] For good examples, see Vack, *Unser Mut*, 27–34 (remarks of protestor Andreas Buro, analyzing civil disobedience as a "process of societal education"); *Verwerflich?*, 58 (remarks of protestor Inge Jens emphasizing civil disobedience as a method of achieving public discussion on the questions raised by the stationing of the missiles); Hartmut von Hentig, *Arbeit am Frieden*, 206–26 (Munich: Carl Hanser Verlag, 2nd edn 1987) (protest at Mutlangen directed toward creating popular movement for constitutional amendment).

[126] See Chapter 2.

[127] *Mutlangen 1983–1987*, 66. Cf., e.g., Habermas, in *Ziviler Ungehorsam im Rechtsstaat*, 42; Huber, in ibid., 117.

[128] See Henry David Thoreau, "Civil Disobedience," in *Walden and Civil Disobedience* (New York: Penguin 1983).

that he found intolerable—slavery and the Mexican–American War.[129]

Thus the (often) isolated disobedient, acting in response to the calls of individual conscience and not particularly concerned with social or governmental reaction, may fall within another category of civil disobedience. Elements of this view were doubtless held by those German sit-down demonstrators who believed that a failure to protest the Pershing II rockets would lend tacit support to a murderous, or potentially murderous enterprise—and would thus repeat their parents' or grandparents' failure to resist the Nazi regime. For them, conscience required opposition to the missiles whether or not this form of protest had any real prospect of success.[130]

There is one final form of civil disobedience that should also be mentioned. Some leaders of the German peace movement may well have hoped that constant demonstrations might actually impede the maintenance and possible use of the missiles in Germany and thus

129

> Must the citizen ever for a moment, or in the least degree, resign his conscience to the legislator? Why has every man a conscience, then? . . . It is not a man's duty, as a matter of course, to devote himself to the eradication of any, even the most enormous wrong; he may still properly have other concerns to engage him; but it is his duty, at least, to wash his hands of it, and, if he gives it no thought longer, not to give it practically his support.
>
> (Thoreau, 387, 393)

This interpretation of Thoreau's essay is cogently presented by Hannah Arendt, in *Crises of the Republic*, 59–60. Yet, in emphasizing Thoreau's quest to satisfy his own conscience, Arendt may have unduly neglected other aspects of "Civil Disobedience." In certain passages, for example, Thoreau seems to suggest that acts of disobedience might change the minds of the governors or bring the governmental apparatus to a standstill. See, e.g., Thoreau, 396–99, 408–9.

Notwithstanding possible differences in emphasis or approach, Thoreau had a significant influence on later theorists of non-violent civil disobedience, such as Gandhi and King. See Watley, 48 (King); Parel, "Editor's Introduction," in *Hind Swaraj*, xlvi ("Thoreau remained a source of life-long inspiration for [Gandhi]"). Indeed, the individual who violates the law in response to the claims of conscience seems to be more closely related to the religious protest of Gandhi and King than to the more purely political approach of theorists like Rawls and Habermas.

The example of Thoreau was also well known to members of the German peace movement. See Vack, *Unser Mut*, 77–78 (remarks of Mutlangen protestor Dorothee Sölle).

130 For this reason, some have argued that the sit-down demonstrations might be protected by the German constitutional guarantee of freedom of conscience. See Reichert-Hammer, 122–26. But see Offenloch, *Erinnerung*, 112 (discussing decision of screening committee of Constitutional Court rejecting a similar argument).

lead to their removal. In Ronald Dworkin's phrase, this would be a "non-persuasive" use of civil disobedience—because its effect would be achieved by the administrative inconvenience caused by the blockades, rather than by political or religious arguments or convictions operating on the minds or consciences of the relevant NATO governments. According to Dworkin, a "non-persuasive" strategy "aims not to change the majority's mind, but to increase the cost of pursuing the program the majority still favors, in the hope that the majority will find the new cost unacceptably high."[131] Indeed, some of the protest leaders at Mutlangen seem to have hoped for such a result and thus, to that extent, this form of civil disobedience may have played a role in the anti-missile sit-down demonstrations.[132]

## The Jens–Offenloch debate

The status of the sit-down demonstrations as examples of civil disobedience—and the political implications of these actions, as so conceived—were vigorously discussed in the academic and popular literature of the time, and various political parties took positions on the issue.[133] Moreover, on one particularly remarkable occasion these issues broke out into public debate in open court. The protagonists in this controversy were Walter Jens, a well-known Professor of Rhetoric at the University of Tübingen, and Judge Werner Offenloch,

131 Dworkin, in *A Matter of Principle*, 109. Indeed, Gandhi himself entertained such ideas upon occasion—although they seemed to deviate substantially from his principal view that the power of suffering could actually change the minds of the oppressors. Haksar, 3.

132 Theorist Wolfgang Sternstein declared, for example, that "the final goal of non-violent resistance is to make it impossible, through massive resistance, for the injustice chosen by the majority to be carried out," *Presse Spiegel*, 158 (Der Spiegel); and another protest leader, Klaus Vack, proclaimed that it was the "goal" of the movement "to shut down the rocket bases by means of sit-down demonstrations." Bissinger (ed.), *Gewalt—ja oder nein*, 84. See also Dworkin, in *A Matter of Principle*, 111–13.

Some leaders of the anti-missile protests may also have hoped that the large number of resulting prosecutions would ultimately cause a breakdown in the courts and the legal system. See, e.g., Südwestpresse, 7 October 1986, reprinted in *Mutlangen 1983–1987*, 106.

133 The Greens, for example, argued that civil disobedience could be legitimate and desirable under the proper circumstances, while the conservative CDU/CSU completely rejected its use. See Karpen, " 'Ziviler Ungehorsam' im demokratischen Rechtsstaat," 1984 JZ, 249. For the German academic literature on the subject, see, e.g., 73 BVerfGE, 206, 233 (1986).

one of the most active and prominent of the judges in the Criminal Court (Amtsgericht) of Schwäbisch Gmünd, the court with jurisdiction over sit-down blockades taking place in the nearby town of Mutlangen.

## *Jens' address to the Court*

In January 1985, after participating in several demonstrations in Mutlangen, Walter Jens appeared before the Criminal Court in Schwäbisch Gmünd. Jens was a well-known literary figure in Germany, and a noted controversialist and debater for many left-wing causes. He had participated in blockades as part of an "affinity group" from Tübingen named after Gustav Heinemann, a progressive president of the Federal Republic from 1969 to 1974.[134] Specifically, Jens was prosecuted for his participation in a blockade organized by the "Affinity Group Gustav Heinemann" in Mutlangen on 24 June 1984. Interestingly, Jens was not prosecuted for his earlier participation in the important Celebrities' Blockade (*Prominentenblockade*) of September 1983; apparently, the authorities were unwilling to arrest and prosecute the well-known individuals who were assembled on that occasion.[135]

In his trial in Schwäbisch Gmünd, Jens delivered an address to the

[134] The "Affinity Group Gustav Heinemann" was somewhat unusual in that the average age of its 11 members was close to 50—considerably older than most of the generally youthful sit-down protesters. See *Verwerflich?*, 13.

Gustav Heinemann's career had particular relevance for these demonstrations because in 1950 he had resigned from Chancellor Adenauer's cabinet in protest over plans for German rearmament. Cooper, 39–40. It has been said that Heinemann's resignation initiated the German anti-war movement of the 1950s. Wesel, *Die verspielte Revolution*, 291.

In his own work, Jens considered himself to be the representative of a

> radical-democratic, civil-progressive, liberal and humanistic tradition following the model of Gustav Heinemann. [This tradition is] the unloved and rejected inheritance of persons of the Enlightenment, Jacobins and the revolutionaries of 1848. [The recovery of this tradition] is essential at a moment when the conservatives in our country more openly than ever seek to re-create the hierarchical state.
>
> (Walter Jens, *Republikanische Reden* 9 (Munich: Kindler 1976))

For Jens' rhetorical attack on the stationing of the Pershing II missiles, see "Appell in letzter Stunde," in Walter Jens (ed.), *In letzter Stunde: Aufruf zum Frieden*, 7–26 (Munich: Kindler 1982).

[135] See, e.g., Burns and van der Will, 224–25; *Verwerflich?*, 48 (remarks of Inge Heckhausen).

Court that displayed his considerable rhetorical powers. Because of Jens' prominence, his remarks on that occasion were printed in the highly respected newspaper, the *Frankfurter Allgemeine Zeitung*.[136]

The first part of Jens' published address outlined the reasons that led him to engage in a sit-down demonstration and his words could therefore be viewed as an exposition seeking to justify civil disobedience. The first of Jens' arguments invoked the political justification for civil disobedience along the lines of Rawls and Habermas. Jens declared that he protested at Mutlangen because he wanted to contribute to a public dialogue—"here and today"—which would resemble the public dialogue that took place in the 1950s "on a high level and with a maximum sense of responsibility." As Jens' audience would certainly have understood, this "public dialogue" of the 1950s focused on German rearmament and the question of whether a German army should be equipped with tactical nuclear weapons.[137] Without dramatic acts of civil disobedience today, Jens implies, there would be no full public debate analogous to the debate that earlier accompanied Germany's re-emergence as a military power.

Jens shared the belief of many in the German peace movement that the American government was intending to fight World War III with nuclear weapons on the continent of Europe—a strategy that would sacrifice Germany but could thus preserve the territory of the United States. Indeed, citing the new Defense Department documents Field Manual FM 100–5 and Air Land Battle 2000, Jens declared that "the offensive strategy of the Americans holds . . . that preparation for a war of aggression is [now] opportune." But—Jens continued—even though there is a difference between preparation and action, such planning in itself would violate Article 26 of the Basic Law, which prohibits wars of aggression and actions that

[136] FAZ, 29 January 1985, 23. Jens' address to the Court is reprinted in *Verwerflich?*, 61–66. This volume also contains addresses to the Court by other members of the "Affinity Group Gustav Heinemann," as well as lawyers' arguments and related material.

In his book, Judge Offenloch—commenting only briefly—does not dwell on Jens' address before his court; but Offenloch does assert that the published version of Jens' remarks is "in nuance" different from the address as it was actually delivered. Offenloch, *Erinnerung*, 50.

[137] See generally Cooper, 25–81. Due to its high quality, the rearmament debate in Parliament in 1956 has been called "one of the finest hours of postwar German democracy." David Schoenbaum, *The Spiegel Affair*, 233–34 (Garden City, NY: Doubleday 1968).

appear suited to the purpose of destroying the "peaceful coexistence of nations." In these remarks Jens—along with many other adherents of the German peace movement—seemed to follow the view of Rawls and Habermas that civil disobedience may be a method of recalling the populace to the basic principles of the constitution. In this instance, these were principles of peaceful international conduct that had been part of the Basic Law from the beginning, incorporating fundamental teachings of the Nuremberg Charter.

In contrast, certain other references in Jens' remarks mirrored the religious tone of many other peace demonstrators. In an interesting manner, Jens placed these religious references in the context of an invocation of solidarity with individuals believed to be working for peace in East Germany. Jens expressed solidarity with "my friends in [East Germany], who consider themselves Christians and Socialists" and, at a slightly later point, he declared: "I wanted, with my friends, to give a quiet sign—'we are still here, you brothers and sisters in Christ, cheerful socialists in [the East German cities of] Magdeburg, Halle, Greifswald, Rostock!' " In these passages, Jens also seemed to be invoking what might be called the national interest of all Germans against a feared attempt to make both East and West Germany into a nuclear battleground.[138]

Jens also invoked the memory of Nazi atrocities—and, seemingly, the claims of conscience—by declaring that his actions were intended to show sympathy with the Soviet Union in which 20 million people had been killed by Hitler's troops, and in which people are now afraid because " 'our' Pershings" are directed against them. Thus, in a dramatic statement, Jens sought to combine general aspects of the theory of civil disobedience with commentary on concerns arising from specific events in Germany considered against the background of the German past.[139]

In the second part of his speech, Jens addressed a requirement in the relevant statute that actions of the demonstrators must be "reprehensible" in order to be subject to punishment. Jens vigorously denied that the sit-down demonstrations met this test. Jens' stirring

[138] Indeed, here we might catch a glimpse of a form of German nationalism that some analysts have seen as an important (albeit secondary) attribute of the German peace movement of the 1980s. See, e.g., Herf, *War by Other Means*, 139–40.

[139] Further, Jens objected to the practice of arresting ordinary "anonymous" protestors, while "prominent" demonstrators and members of certain powerful groups could engage in blockades without being subjected to prosecution—a state of affairs that violated the principle of equality before the law.

peroration on this point will be examined in greater detail in the next chapter.

## Judge Offenloch's response

Four days after Walter Jens delivered his address, Judge Werner Offenloch of the Criminal Court in Schwäbisch Gmünd found Jens guilty and sentenced him to a fine of 3,000 German Marks. Judge Offenloch's judicial opinion, also reprinted in the *Frankfurter Allgemeine Zeitung*, sought to respond to certain of the points made by Professor Jens.[140] In addition to the more strictly juristic argumentation of the opinion, Judge Offenloch made one central philosophical point. Although Jens had not used the precise formulation, it seemed to Offenloch that arguments such as those of Jens sought to weigh the protestors' claims of a "higher legitimacy" against the state's claims of "legality"—with the result that "higher legitimacy" should prevail. But as a judge—Offenloch continued—he was "obligated to legality." Indeed, according to Offenloch, "such a contrast between legitimacy and legality is suited—there is a historical example—to prepare the way for the totalitarianism that we both reject."

In this reference to "legality," "legitimacy," and "the totalitarianism that we both reject," Judge Offenloch was evoking a famous political argument of the eminent legal theorist of the Weimar period, Carl Schmitt—whose discussion of the opposition of legitimacy and legality might indeed have eased the way for Nazi ideology in Germany. Indeed, Schmitt himself became the Nazi regime's chief legal advisor for a time, and he seems never to have renounced his views of this period, even after the end of World War II.[141]

By this reference, Offenloch implies that the maintenance of strict

[140] FAZ, 1 February 1985. For Judge Offenloch's more general analysis of the views of the anti-missile protestors, drawn from various speeches before the courts, see Offenloch, *Erinnerung*, 45–52.

[141] Judge Offenloch did not mention Carl Schmitt by name in his opinion, but he had Schmitt in mind when he referred to "legality" and "legitimacy." Interview with Judge Werner Offenloch, Schwäbisch Gmünd, 19 July 2001. Moreover, this reference was easily understood by German readers. See, e.g., Reifenrath, in *Frankfurter Rundschau*, 30 January 1985, reprinted in *Verwerflich?*, 191. Cf. Habermas in *Ziviler Ungehorsam im Rechtsstaat*, 38 ("A lot of mischief has been made with the paired concepts Legality/Legitimacy"). For recent evaluations of Carl Schmitt's work and career, see, e.g., Mark Lilla, *The Reckless Mind: Intellectuals in Politics*, 49–76 (New York: New York Review of Books 2001); Jan-Werner Müller,

"legality" acts to preserve the rule of law, whereas the argument for a higher "legitimacy" that might prevail against legality opens the way for a disregard of the law that could lead to dictatorial regimes. Perhaps Judge Offenloch's implicit point was that blockades and similar techniques were not limited to people seeking peace: if they are tolerated, they could also be employed by forces on the ominous right wing of German politics for the purpose of leading the German government back toward totalitarian structures of the past.

Offenloch sought to underscore this point by arguing that there were particular dangers in a point of view that was absolute and did not contemplate the possibility that the other side might be correct—and he implied that the peace protestors held such a point of view. Offenloch deplored the rage with which—in his opinion—the anti-missile protests had been conducted, and he read a letter, received that very morning, comparing him to a judge on the Nazis' notorious "People's Court" and suggesting that he himself be chained to a Pershing missile.[142]

Offenloch maintained that these techniques were different from the "Anglo-Saxon so-called civil disobedience, which presupposes a precisely limited violation of rules and accepts the legal sanctions." Offenloch concluded with the following general observation:

> The meaning of history can surely not be that it should vanish in atomic death—but also not that it would become the prey of political totalitarianism—all the more so because the latter certainly cannot guarantee that the former will be avoided.

This argument sounds a somber note—in a specifically German context—for those theorists who may assume that civil disobedience and related doctrines invariably represent a progressive movement in jurisprudence and political thought. Indeed, this aspect of the debate

*A Dangerous Mind: Carl Schmitt in Post-War European Thought* (New Haven, CT: Yale University Press 2003); Ellen Kennedy, *Constitutional Failure: Carl Schmitt in Weimar* (Durham, NC: Duke University Press 2004).

For similar criticism of the German peace movement on the grounds that it sought to elevate "legitimacy" over "legality," see Walter Schmitt Glaeser, *Private Gewalt im politischen Meinungskampf*, 20 (Berlin: Duncker and Humblot, 2nd edn 1992).

142 Evidently not all adherents of the German peace movement followed the admonition of Martin Luther King that even opponents should be treated "lovingly."

attracted the attention of an eminent outside observer, the famous sociologist and political scientist Ralf Dahrendorf, who commented on the Jens–Offenloch exchange in a newspaper article and then later in a book on political theory.

Although Dahrendorf was a friend of Walter Jens, Dahrendorf concluded that Judge Offenloch had the better argument in this exchange. Indeed, Dahrendorf commended Offenloch for supporting the safeguards of official legality against what might be considered the law of the streets. On the substance of the debate, Dahrendorf concluded:

> Whoever invokes a supposedly higher judgment against the statutory law—a judgment that nullifies the law that is in effect—also opens the floodgates (unintentionally but nonetheless effectively) to lawlessness. Whoever believes that he can ignore the laws—because he possesses the spirit of good—thus abandons the most important weapon against those who do the same thing in the name of the spirit of evil.[143]

## The sit-down cases: the facts

These aspects of history and political theory, then, form the background of the anti-missile sit-down demonstrations of the 1980s—including, in particular, the sustained protests at Großengstingen and Mutlangen. Against this background, we will follow the course of three specific criminal cases arising from these events. These cases—two from Großengstingen and one from Mutlangen—form only a small fraction of the thousands of prosecutions arising from the anti-missile blockades. But they are among the very few that

[143] *Die Zeit*, 12 September 1986, *Politik*, 4; see also Ralf Dahrendorf, *Law and Order*, 134–35 (Boulder, CO: Westview Press 1985). On Dahrendorf, see generally Ralf Dahrendorf, *Über Grenzen: Lebenserinnerungen* (Frankfurt/M: Fischer Taschenbuch 2004).

Many German legal academics and other writers adopted a similar skeptical position on the question of civil disobedience—often employing arguments similar to those of Dahrendorf. For a sampling of the vast literature, see Isensee, "Rechtsbewußtsein im Rechtsstaat," in Wolfgang Fikentscher *et al.*, *Wertewandel, Rechtswandel*, 17–40 (Gräfeling: Resch 1997); Karpen, "Ziviler Ungehorsam im demokratischen Rechtsstaat," 1984 JZ, 249, 256: Civil disobedience undermines "general confidence in the efficacy of the legal order"; it leads to "the delegitimization of the essence of the state . . . A calculated violation of the legality of the constitutional order is, in the last analysis, a blow against its legitimacy."

ultimately reached the Federal Constitutional Court and resulted in important constitutional decisions. By following the facts and, later, the arguments and results of these cases, we can see how the German legal system—and, to a significant extent, the German state itself—sought to handle this sharp domestic challenge to a central pillar of NATO's foreign policy in the Cold War. At the same time we will also see how the courts struggled to handle the claims of civil disobedience within the traditional structures of criminal and constitutional law.

### *Großengstingen, July 1981—Wolfgang Müller and Hansjörg Ostermayer*

One of the very first sit-down blockades protesting NATO nuclear rockets took place in Großengstingen in July 1981. This blockade was organized by adherents of "Non-Violent Action" (*Gewaltfreie Aktion*), a pacifist protest group that had been involved for some years in demonstrations against nuclear power plants. Among the organizers of the protest was Wolfgang Müller, a student of political science from the Free University in Berlin, who was working at the time as an intern with a peace group in Tübingen.

Müller had a substantial history in the peace movement. In 1979, for example, he and other members of "Cornpoppy" (*Klatschmohn*)—a sub-group of Non-Violent Action in Berlin—had traveled to the United States in order to meet with American peace groups, including a visit to protestors at the Seabrook Nuclear Plant in New Hampshire. A major purpose of the visit was to examine the concept of "affinity groups"—a form of organization that had been employed in the United States and, as we have seen, later came to be an essential aspect of peace protests at Großengstingen and elsewhere in Germany.

On the Sunday evening before the Großengstingen demonstration, Müller and several members of "Non-Violent Action" gathered for a brief meeting in Tübingen to discuss the nature of the coming protest. This meeting was not a formal "training"—such as later came to be required for participation in the 1982 Tent Village demonstrations; there had been a more formal "training" earlier in the weekend. Nonetheless, there was instruction on such matters as how one should hold oneself to avoid injury when being carried away by the police. On this evening, Hansjörg Ostermayer, a student of history and German literature at Tübingen University—and a conscientious objector to military service—also decided to join the protestors.[144]

The next morning, Müller, Ostermayer, and several others drove 20 kilometers from Tübingen to Großengstingen. The group assembled before the Eberhard Finckh Barracks, the German army base near the Lance missile depot, which had been the subject of several "Easter March" demonstrations in the past.[145]

At about 8:30 a.m. Müller, Ostermayer, and 11 others chained themselves together in front of the main gate of the barracks. The chain was wound around each protestor's waist and attached to each participant by a padlock. The ends of the chain were then padlocked to two metal posts—one on each side of the road.[146] Thirteen people were wrapped in the chain, while another 10 protestors stood on the sidelines for moral support, holding banners and distributing leaflets. Soon a heavy rain began to fall, but the protestors held a small press conference. Southwest Radio, a major German channel, also broadcast a report.

At first, the German army (*Bundeswehr*) officials reacted mildly to this protest. Indeed, one of the *Bundeswehr* officers emerged from the barracks with coffee for the demonstrators.[147] The protestors had informed officials of the pending demonstrations and had distributed leaflets in Großengstingen on the preceding day, outlining their plans for the demonstration. The leaflets declared that, at all times, "every citizen is as helplessly exposed to an atomic

144 Many of the details recounted in this section are drawn from the following sources: Interviews with Hansjörg Ostermayer, Tübingen, 13 April 2000, 27 July 2004; Interview with Wolfgang Müller-Breuer, Leichlingen, 24 July 2002; Jugendkammer des Landgerichts Tübingen, Judgment of 6 September 1982, II Ns 62/82 [LG Tübingen Opinion]; Wolfgang Müller, *Die gewaltfreie Blockade des Atomwaffenlagers bei Großengstingen/Alb im Sommer 1982: Deutsches Modell einer Kampagne zivilen Ungehorsams?* (Müller's Diploma Dissertation at the Free University of Berlin, July 1983).

Upon his marriage in 1987, Wolfgang Müller changed his name to Wolfgang Müller-Breuer, and so for events after that date his married name will be used.

145 Colonel Eberhard Finckh, after whom the barracks were named, had been an officer under the Nazis, but he had assisted in the uprising against Hitler on 20 July 1944 and was executed by the Nazi regime. See Peter Steinbach and Johannes Tuchel (eds), *Lexikon des Widerstandes 1933–1945*, 57–58 (Munich: Beck, 2nd edn 1998).

146 *Der Spiegel*, 25 March 1985, 177. See also Günther Gugel and Horst Furtner, *Gewaltfreie Aktion*, 4 (Tübingen: Verein für Friedenspädagogik e.V. 1983), which contains a photograph showing the demonstrators in the chain.

147 *Der Spiegel*, 25 March 1985, 178.

blast as we in our chains [will be] to the police and to the military police."[148] With this early warning, the army was able to open an alternate route into the barracks in order to avoid the protestors' blockade.

From time to time the chain was unlocked to allow a certain change of personnel. Later in the day, more protestors arrived from Tübingen as word spread about the demonstration in Großengstingen. The new arrivals brought sleeping bags and mulled wine for the demonstrators, as well as dry clothing in light of the rainy weather.[149] Some of the protestors discussed their goals with the German soldiers and with the commander of the barracks.[150] Generally the scene remained calm. But at one point a military vehicle approached the protestors at high speed, braking only at the last minute, indicating to those in the chain that there was indeed some danger in what they were doing.

As night approached, some of the protestors in the chain became discouraged by the lack of response from the army and argued that the protest should be abandoned. But other voices prevailed and the protestors—Müller and Ostermayer among them—remained in the chain overnight.

At about 9:00 the next morning, the officials decided to act. According to Müller, the base commander had become "visibly annoyed" that the demonstrators were still there.[151] Numerous police officers arrived in Volkswagen buses, and an official gave three warnings, requesting that the protestors disperse. When the demonstrators failed to comply, the police cut the chain with large wire-cutters, extracted Müller, Ostermayer, and the other protestors, and carried them over to the police buses. The removal of the demonstrators occurred in a non-violent, indeed almost ritualized manner, with two police officers carrying each protestor. As they had been taught on the evening before the demonstration, or in earlier "trainings," the protestors crossed their arms over their chests and held themselves in a manner that made them easy to carry without injury.

Once in the police buses the protestors showed their identity cards, which they had deliberately brought with them in order to acknowledge personal responsibility for their acts. After the police officers

148 Ibid., 177; Müller, 11.
149 Interview with Wolfgang Müller-Breuer, Leichlingen.
150 LG Tübingen Opinion, 6.
151 Müller, 12 ("*sichtlich verärgert*").

recorded this information, Müller, Ostermayer, and the other protestors were free to go.

Although the demonstrators would eventually face criminal prosecution, nothing happened for approximately nine months. Yet, notwithstanding this judicial inactivity, news of the chain demonstration at Großengstingen spread, and this encouraged peace activists in undertaking more of such blockades.

## *Großengstingen, May 1983—Gunhild Beuter, Wilfried Braig, Eva-Maria Moch, and Thomas Moch*

The chain blockade at Großengstingen in July 1981 was welcomed by the German peace movement and, as we have seen, it led the way for the organization of the Tent Village blockades in the summer of 1982.[152] Thereafter, however, protest activity at Großengstingen returned to a more sporadic and leisurely pace.

In the spring of 1983 Volker Nick, an active member of the German peace movement—perhaps seeking to reinvigorate protests at the Lance missile site—placed an advertisement in a newspaper in Tübingen, under the heading "Who will blockade with us?" The advertisement called for protestors to take part in a renewed series of non-violent blockades of the missile base at Großengstingen on 9 May 1983. The specific purpose of the blockades would be to show that the peace movement was not intimidated by the numerous criminal trials of sit-down demonstrators—from the Tent Village protests of 1982—which were then taking place in the nearby town of Münsingen.[153]

A dramatic handbill that announced and publicized the proposed new blockades laid particular emphasis on the protestors' view that Germany was threatened with imminent nuclear annihilation—especially in light of the pending deployment of the Pershing II missiles:

> [We are outraged] that in [the Münsingen trials] the court so little understands that the probability of our total extermination has increased immeasurably—and in the autumn will likely rise dramatically again, perhaps for the last time . . .

[152] See generally Handbook-1, 16.

[153] In all, more than 300 criminal trials for *Nötigung* arose out of the 1982 Tent Village protests. Interview with Judge Thomas Rainer, Münsingen, 8 July 2004.

> Without courageous and drastic steps by each of us, atomic war cannot be prevented—[as was the case with] fascism fifty years ago, and the war that it caused. For us, this is clear: we must continue to resist our atomic death, [in ways that are] always new and always different. Non-violent blockades are an appropriate means of taking our first steps in this direction.[154]

Among the protestors who appeared in front of the missile base at Großengstingen on the morning of 9 May 1983 were four members of a tightly knit "affinity group"—Eva-Maria Moch, her brother Thomas Moch, Gunhild Beuter, and Wilfried Braig. The four had met as fellow students in Tübingen, and Beuter and the Mochs had taken part in the Tent Village demonstrations at Großengstingen in summer 1982. Braig had not participated in the Tent Village protests, but he had taken part in notable demonstrations against the planned nuclear power plant in Brokdorf, and he also demonstrated against construction of a nuclear renovation facility in Wackersdorf.[155]

During the tent city demonstrations of 1982, Beuter and the Mochs had not been among those who had actually blockaded the gate to the missile base. For Eva Moch, the 1982 gathering was more in the nature of a "peace camp" where members of their group could discuss methods for pursuing and living a non-violent life.[156] But they did decide to take part in a blockade in May 1983, when they read Volker Nick's newspaper advertisement calling for renewed demonstrations. According to their later trial testimony, Eva Moch and Gunhild Beuter took this step out of a sense of helplessness because their earlier actions, such as handing out leaflets, had remained without success.[157] For his part, Wilfried Braig thought that there was a real possibility of atomic war in 1983.[158]

On 9 May 1983, the sit-down protests were organized in successive

[154] See Christian Eichhorn *et al.*, "Gewaltfreier Widerstand gegen Atomwaffen," April/May 1983.

[155] Interview with Wilfried Braig, Tübingen, 25 July 2002.

[156] Interview with Eva Moch, Freiburg im Breisgau, 13 July 2004.

[157] Hanns-Michael Langner, summary of trial in LG Tübingen [Trial Summary], 6 February 1987, 7–8. Indeed, this experience paralleled the experience of the peace movement itself, which went through phases of petitions and demonstrations, before turning toward the use of civil disobedience. Leinen, in *Ziviler Ungehorsam im Rechtsstaat*, 23.

[158] Interview with Wilfried Braig, Tübingen.

shifts. At mid-day the gate was blockaded twice, and the blockading protestors were removed by the police. But, as their shift had not come up, Beuter, Braig, and the Mochs were not among these groups. Indeed, the four had some disagreements with the main group of the peace movement—they wanted to remain more anarchistic and autonomous. According to one observer, the four approached the impending blockade with a degree of gaiety that may have grated on the sensibilities of the more totally earnest members of the group.[159] In any case, Beuter, Braig, and the Mochs sought to remain in their own separate blockade.[160]

Finally, late in the afternoon of 9 May, Beuter, Braig, and the Mochs took their places, with one other person, outside the gate of the missile base in Großengstingen. Beuter and Thomas and Eva Moch had painted their faces white—perhaps to symbolize the possibility of death in atomic war and also "as in the theater" to indicate that they were acting as symbols for many other individuals.[161] A few supporters stood nearby, and a police cameraman made a video film of the proceedings.[162]

While they were sitting outside the gate, Gunhild Beuter was startled to see a rank of soldiers aiming their rifles at the protestors from an adjoining field—but the rifles were not fired. It turned out that a group of soldiers on exercises had been ordered to imagine that the demonstrators were invaders of the base.[163]

At about 5:30 p.m., a German army truck, with provisions for the base, approached the gate and stopped before the protestors. When the protestors refused to obey three warnings to leave, they were carried away by police. As in the case of Müller and Ostermayer, this event followed a ritualized pattern on both sides. Although Beuter, for example, had feared that the process might be rough, there was no violence or injury. The defendants were taken to police vehicles, stationed a kilometer away in the woods, for booking.[164]

Although the protests and removal of these four demonstrators

159 Interview with Uwe Painke, Leonberg, 20 July 2003.

160 Ibid.; Interview with Wilfried Braig, Tübingen.

161 Ibid.

162 Amtsgericht Münsingen, Protokoll über die Hauptverhandlung in öffentlicher Sitzung, 2 Cs 413–416/83, 31 October 1984, 6; Trial Summary, 5 February 1987, 1–2.

163 Interview with Gunhild Beuter, Tübingen, 14 April 2000; Interview with Wilfried Braig, Tübingen; Interview with Eva Moch, Freiburg.

164 Landgericht Tübingen, Judgment of 16 February 1987, Gesch. Nr. 2 Ns 27/85 u.a., 10–11.

seemed like a routine incident in the long course of the anti-missile demonstrations, this particular case was to follow a path of extraordinary complexity in no less than five German courts. Moreover, it would yield a significant appellate decision and would ultimately result in the Constitutional Court's most important judgment in the sit-down demonstrations cases.

### *Mutlangen, February 1984—Luise Scholl*

As we have seen, the blockades at Großengstingen were among the first sustained exercises of civil disobedience against the stationing of nuclear missiles in Germany; yet these demonstrations were followed by even larger and more sustained blockades at the depot of the NATO Pershing II missiles in the small Swabian town of Mutlangen. Thousands of protestors were arrested outside the gates of the missile depot in Mutlangen.

One of the demonstrators arrested at such a blockade, rather late in the evening of 7 February 1984, was a freelance artist and sculptor by the name of Luise Scholl. Scholl had often participated in demonstrations and blockades in Mutlangen. During the day, she worked in the nearby town of Schwäbisch Gmünd, and she often traveled the few kilometers to Mutlangen in the evening to take part in the demonstrations. Scholl was an active and engaged member of the German peace movement, who felt deeply threatened by the presence of the rockets. In January 1984—shortly before her arrest—she wrote a bitter and despairing letter to a local newspaper:

> I hope that the population will finally wake up. But I can scarcely believe in such a thing anymore. They have learned nothing from the past. Apparently they are not shocked by wars and by the atom bomb over Japan. How can one live on the earth with such people? It is awful.[165]

To the judge in her case she wrote:

> I and EVERYTHING have the right to live. It is a crime to obliterate humanity and the earth. There is no law that allows the annihilation of humanity and of the earth. And everyone

[165] Waiblinger Kreis-Zeitung, 14 January 1984.

> who does not resist this madness assumes part of the guilt. Everyone—including the judges[166]

Scholl's arrest on this February night in 1984 was to be the first of three arrests arising from her participation in blockades at the missile depot.[167]

The blockade on the night of 7 February 1984 was apparently somewhat spontaneous. As an American truck convoy neared the gates of the depot, several protestors decided that they would stand in the street to block its passage.[168] On this occasion, Luise Scholl made clear that she was more determined than some of her colleagues. As the police officers read the accustomed warning to clear the street, seven of the ten demonstrators did disperse in order to make way for the American vehicles. But Scholl and two other protestors remained standing in the street, causing an interruption of traffic that lasted between five and ten minutes.[169] Scholl did not wish to be carried away by the police, and therefore, when the police came to arrest participants in the blockade, she went along with them voluntarily to be booked. In this way she became one of the many hundreds to be arrested at the main gate in Mutlangen.

Thus the cases of Müller and Ostermayer, the Mochs and their colleagues, and Luise Scholl were three sets of cases drawn from the myriad prosecutions of persons arrested for blockades protesting the NATO nuclear missiles in Germany. In many respects, these stories are little different from those of thousands of other sit-down demonstrators whose cases were eventually decided in the German judicial system. Yet these stories are nonetheless of particular interest, because in each of these cases, the process initiated by these events wended its way through the German criminal courts, and then came to be decided ultimately by the highest court in Germany for constitutional matters—the German Constitutional Court.

[166] Letter of 5 August 1984, from Luise Scholl to Judge Wolfgang Krumhard.

[167] See Gmünder Tagespost, 12 August 1987.

[168] Appellate Brief in *Revision* Process on behalf of Luise Scholl, 28 December 1984 (Rechtsanwalt Alfred Hinderer), Ns 260/84–10; 3KV 177/84, 9.

[169] Landgericht Ellwangen, Judgment of 19 November 1984, 4–5.

# Chapter 2

# The sit-down blockades in the criminal courts

## Introduction: the rule of law and the German Criminal Code—a comparative perspective

When the sit-down demonstrators from Großengstingen and Mutlangen were arrested by the police, their cases moved from reality on the streets into the specialized and somewhat artificial realm of the law. The fate of those who had acted to blockade NATO bases was now to be decided within specially constructed legal categories.

But why was it necessary to proceed in this manner? Why was it not possible for a judge, or even a police officer or other executive official, simply to address the protestors along the following lines: "You have done something particularly heinous: You have interfered with the smooth running of the state and with the functioning of NATO, a treaty organization that is essential for the independence of the Federal Republic of Germany, and we can justifiably punish you for doing these things, without further ado?"

The answer to this question lies, of course, in the idea of the rule of law, or—as it is known in its German version—the *Rechtsstaat*, the state that functions according to law. The central idea of the rule of law is basic to an understanding of modern democracy: according to this idea, it is not only the citizens who are limited by the power of the state; rather the state itself is also bound by a network of statutory and constitutional rules.

Among the most fundamental principles of the rule of law is the doctrine of non-retroactivity. According to this doctrine, the state cannot punish a person for committing a crime unless it acts according to a general rule adopted by the legislature or courts *before* the crime is committed. Only in this way can a person know whether he or she is committing a forbidden act.

This principle is of central importance because it preserves the citizens from the terror that may arise (and has often arisen) in dictatorial regimes, when the citizens do not know what acts are forbidden.[1] The principle also tends to prevent the governors from punishing people they dislike—for political or personal reasons—on the basis of offenses designed specifically to punish those individuals. Moreover, the application of the rule to the individual case must be undertaken by a judge or jury in a court. That, at least, is the theory—the ideal against which the reality must be measured.

In Germany, France and other continental countries, the use of comprehensive legal codes may have brought the idea of the rule of law to a higher degree of theoretical perfection than has been achieved in England and the United States. Indeed, well into the twentieth century, criminal law in the Anglo-American world principally took the form of judge-made "common law" or case law, which had been developed over decades or centuries.[2] In more recent decades, much of the criminal law in the Anglo-American systems has been transferred into statutory form, whether enacted by the state legislatures or Congress (in the United States) or by various parliaments (in Great Britain and the commonwealth jurisdictions).

Yet the idea of the "code" in the European sense is something more than a collection of disparate statutes on specific problems enacted at various times. Rather, the European idea of the code is that all the rules of a single large body of law—such as the criminal law—should be contained in one comprehensive and systematic legal text, conceived and promulgated as a unified whole, which in theory should provide the answer to all questions concerning that area of

1 See Quint, "The Border Guard Trials and the East German Past—Seven Arguments," 48 *American Journal of Comparative Law* 541, 561 and n. 53 (2000). See generally Herbert L. Packer, *The Limits of the Criminal Sanction*, 71–102 (Stanford, CA: Stanford University Press 1968); Jeffries, "Legality, Vagueness, and the Construction of Penal Statutes," 71 *Virginia Law Review* 189 (1985).

2 As late as the mid-twentieth century, some common law courts still engaged in the creation of new criminal offenses without legislative participation, although by this period these cases were controversial—and rare. *Shaw v. Director of Public Prosecutions*, [1962] A.C. 220; *Commonwealth v. Mochan*, 177 Pa. Super. 454, 110 A. 2d 788 (1955). See, e.g., H.L.A. Hart, *Law, Liberty and Morality*, 6–12 (Stanford, CA: Stanford University Press 1963); Packer, 91; Jeffries, 71 *Virginia Law Review*, 194 n.13.

law.[3] Codes in this sense are still rather exceptional in the Anglo-American legal world—although the Model Penal Code (issued in 1962 as a proposal by the American Law Institute) represents a notable American step in this direction.[4] The Uniform Commercial Code and the Federal Rules of Evidence are similar undertakings in other areas of American law.

The first of the great modern European codes was the French Civil Code of 1804, which was drafted with the personal participation of Napoleon Bonaparte. The French Criminal Code followed in 1810.[5]

Shortly after the enactment of the Napoleonic Civil Code, some theorists urged that a civil code should be adopted in Germany as well. For most of the nineteenth century, however, these proposals were rejected under the influence of an opposing "historical school" of thought, led by the eminent scholar Friedrich Carl von Savigny. Savigny argued that a code should not be formulated until the history of German law (including its Roman law components) had been thoroughly investigated; after this painstaking historical research, the "essential principles" of German law could be distilled and "eventually systematically restated."[6] Accordingly, the German Civil Code was not adopted until the very end of the nineteenth century: it was enacted into law in 1896 and went into effect in 1900.

The German Criminal Code, the *Strafgesetzbuch* (or *StGB*), was adopted some years earlier—immediately after the first German unification in 1871. The German Code was based on a criminal code that had been adopted in Prussia in 1851, although it was also significantly influenced by the French Code of 1810. In its original form, the German Code of 1871 was based primarily on Kantian concepts of blame and retribution. After World War II, however,

[3] See John Henry Merryman, *The Civil Law Tradition*, 26–33 (Stanford, CA: Stanford University Press, 2nd edn 1985); William Seagle, *The Quest for Law*, 277–98 (New York: Knopf 1941).

[4] See generally Markus D. Dubber, *Criminal Law: Model Penal Code*, 1–31 (New York: Foundation 2002).

[5] The Criminal Code was the fifth and last of the Napoleonic codes, enacted between 1804 and 1810. It replaced a transitional penal code of 1791 which was adopted in the early period of the Revolution. Ancel, Introduction, in *The French Penal Code*, 1–13 (American Series of Foreign Penal Codes, No. 1, 1960); Tomlinson, Introduction, in *The French Penal Code of 1994*, 1–25 (American Series of Foreign Penal Codes, No. 31, 1999). See also Jean-Louis Halpérin, *The French Civil Code*, 6, trans. Tony Weir (Abingdon: UCL Press 2006).

[6] Merryman, 30–31.

scholars began to seek the inclusion of revisions reflecting more modern goals of rehabilitation and treatment, and a major revision of the Criminal Code in 1975 satisfied some of these demands. Yet notwithstanding more than a century of legislative revision and great political upheavals, several of the Code's original provisions remain in effect today—although perhaps somewhat amended in detail.[7]

## Coercion (*Nötigung*) under the German Criminal Code

### *The principle of legality*

When the demonstrators in Mutlangen and Großengstingen were arrested, they could undoubtedly have been convicted of a minor administrative offense under the Assemblies Law (*Versammlungsgesetz*), a federal statute regulating demonstrations and similar matters.[8] Article 15 of the Assemblies Law permits the police to dissolve an assembly which has not been "registered" (*angemeldet*) or which directly endangers public security or order; and an individual who disobeys such an order is subject to an administrative fine.[9]

Many participants in the sit-down demonstrations conceded that they were subject to this kind of administrative penalty. But an administrative procedure of this sort does not result in a conviction under the Criminal Code, the fine is not considered a criminal penalty, and the offense does not give rise to a criminal record. Rather, this offense is classified as a "violation of order" (*Ordnungswidrigkeit*), which occupies a position similar to that of a minor traffic offense in the United States. Less concretely—but nonetheless of very great importance to many defendants—an administrative fine

7 See Schröder, Introduction, in *The German Penal Code of 1871*, 1–14 (American Series of Foreign Penal Codes, No. 4, 1961); Wise, Editor's Preface, and Jescheck, Introduction, in *The Penal Code of the Federal Republic of Germany*, xiii–xvi, 1–24 (American Series of Foreign Penal Codes, No. 28, 1987). See generally "Symposium: The New German Penal Code," 24 *American Journal of Comparative Law* 589 (1976). Subsequent revised versions of the German Criminal Code have been issued in 1987 and 1998. See Jescheck, Introduction, in *The German Penal Code*, xxxiii–lxxi (American Series of Foreign Penal Codes, No. 32, 2002).

8 Gesetz über Versammlungen und Aufzüge (VersG), of 24 July 1953, as amended.

9 VersG §29 (1)(2).

of this type is generally not regarded as ethically reprehensible in German society.[10]

But in the sit-down demonstration cases, the government's prosecutors were apparently not satisfied with this form of tap on the wrist. Rather they thought that the demonstrators should be prosecuted under a criminal provision that would reflect what was, in their minds, the seriousness of the demonstrators' actions and, perhaps, the resulting danger to the state.

Moreover, German law is said to be governed by the "principle of legality" (*Legalitätsprinzip*). This doctrine holds that if there is enough evidence to prosecute a defendant under a section of the Criminal Code, the prosecutor must proceed with the charges in most instances.[11] In theory at least, therefore, the German prosecutors had little discretion to decline to proceed under the Criminal Code if there was adequate evidence to establish an offense.[12]

[10] See generally Fritjof Haft, *Strafrecht Allgemeiner Teil*, 6 (Munich: Beck, 8th edn 1998); Jürgen Baumann *et al.*, *Strafrecht Allgemeiner Teil*, 44–47 (Bielefeld: Giesek-ing, 10th edn 1995). See Gesetz über Ordnungswidrigkeiten (OWiG), of 24 May 1968, as amended, §113.

[11] StPO §152. See generally, Herrmann, "The Rule of Compulsory Prosecution and the Scope of Prosecutorial Discretion in Germany," 41 *University of Chicago Law Review* 468 (1974); Langbein, "Land Without Plea Bargaining: How the Germans Do It," 78 *Michigan Law Review* 204 (1979). It is said that this doctrine grew out of ideas of equality espoused by the French Revolution. Damaška, "Structures of Authority and Comparative Criminal Procedure," 84 *Yale Law Journal* 480, 503 n.52 (1975).

[12] The German Criminal Code, however, does contain some exceptions to the "principle of legality." In the case of lesser offenses (*Vergehen*), for example, the prosecutor may sometimes refrain from prosecution "if the actor's guilt would be viewed as minor and no public interest exists in favor of the prosecution" StPO §153 (I). But this provision for exceptional cases might not justify mass non-prosecution of an entire class of defendants—such as the sit-down demonstrators. Interview with Senior Prosecutor (*Oberstaatsanwalt*) Peter Rörig, Stuttgart, 9 July 2003; but see Schüler-Springorum, "Strafrechtliche Aspekte zivilen Ungehorsams," in Peter Glotz (ed.), *Ziviler Ungehorsam im Rechtsstaat*, 93–94 (Frankfurt/M: Suhrkamp 1983) (suggesting such a possibility). See Herrmann, 41 *University of Chicago Law Review*, 484–89; John H. Langbein, *Comparative Criminal Procedure: Germany*, 98–100 (St. Paul: West 1977).

Even after the trial has begun, prosecutors may offer to dismiss the charges if the defendant agrees to pay a sum to the treasury or to a charitable organization. See StPO § 153a; Herrmann, "Bargaining Justice—A Bargain for German Criminal Justice?," 53 *University of Pittsburgh Law Review* 755, 757–60 (1992). But typically when such a possibility was offered in the missile protest cases, the defendants refused to agree, fearing that to do so would be to admit guilt and wishing in any

## *The offense of* Nötigung

Accordingly, the sit-down demonstrators from Mutlangen and Großengstingen were charged with a violation of §240 of the German Criminal Code—which provides a fine or prison sentence for the crime of *Nötigung* or "coercion."[13] In essence, this offense punishes a person who uses force (or certain other means) to coerce someone to do something against his or her will.

This is a well-known offense in Germany. Indeed, in basic principle, this provision had been present in the German Criminal Code at the time of its adoption in 1871, and similar prohibitions were even found in the criminal statutes of independent German states before unification and the adoption of the national code.[14]

case to put forth their views in open court. Interview with Prosecutor Richard Hörz, Ellwangen, 24 July 2003; see also Küchenhoff, "Rüstungsgegner vor Gericht," in Christoph Butterwegge *et al.* (eds), *Kriminalisierung der Friedensbewegung: Abschreckung nach innen?* (Köln: presseverlag ralf theurer 1985), 34–47.

In the past, some commentators have argued that stringent limitations imposed on prosecutorial discretion in Germany contrast sharply with considerably broader discretion that prevails in the United States. Yet recent scholarship has found that German prosecutors now actually wield considerable discretionary authority—under StPO §§ 153 and 153a, and otherwise. Julia Fionda, *Public Prosecutors and Discretion: A Comparative Study*, 133–71 (Oxford: Clarendon Press 1995). Moreover, practitioners and other experts confirm that the pressure of business in the German criminal courts has evoked widespread plea bargaining—so that, according to some, the ideology of the legality principle has now become an "illusion." FAZ, 17 September 2003, 12.

On the current importance of plea bargaining in Germany, see generally Dubber, "American Plea Bargains, German Lay Judges, and the Crisis of Criminal Procedure," 49 *Stanford Law Review* 547, 549–50 (1997); see also Herrmann, 53 *University of Pittsburgh Law Review*, 755. On plea bargaining or its "analogues" in France, see Frase, "Comparative Criminal Justice as a Guide to American Law Reform," 78 *California Law Review* 542, 626–47 (1990).

13 Technically, the protestors were charged with "coercion [*Nötigung*] in combination with [other persons]" under §§ 240 and 25 of the Criminal Code. Apparently prosecutors also considered charging the protestors with serious security offenses, such as "anti-constitutional sabotage" (StGB §88) or "coercion of constitutional organs" (StGB §106), but these charges were ultimately not pursued. See Schüler-Springorum, in *Ziviler Ungehorsam im Rechtsstaat*, 84–85.

14 See Achim Bertuleit, *Sitzdemonstrationen zwischen prozedural geschützter Versammlungsfreiheit und verwaltungsrechtsakzessorischer Nötigung*, 76–80 (Berlin: Duncker & Humblot 1994). The offense of "*Notigung*" made its first appearance in the Prussian General State Law (*Allgemeines Landrecht*) of 1794. Bertuleit, 73–76, 81; see also Hruschka, "Die Nötigung im System des Strafrechts," 1995 JZ, 737,

In contrast, however, even the name of this offense will most likely be unfamiliar and puzzling to American or English readers. Indeed, there is no crime exactly like this in most Anglo-American jurisdictions—although the penal laws of a certain number of American states do contain a rather narrow and generally obscure offense, also called "coercion."[15] There is no corresponding provision in French law either; but similar provisions are present in the criminal codes of countries closer to the German tradition, such as Austria and Switzerland.[16] Accordingly—for better or for worse—the offense of *Nötigung* has been called "a specifically German contribution to international legal culture."[17]

The underlying philosophical theory of this offense is that each person should enjoy a maximum degree of freedom of the will and that certain serious attempts to interfere with that freedom require punishment under the criminal law. According to one eminent scholar of German criminal law, the offense of *Nötigung* may be viewed as a measure of the "late Enlightenment" that was directed toward extending the freedom of the individual against other individuals. While American and French theorists

737–38 and nn. 7–10. Attempts have also been made to link the offense of *Nötigung* to the offense of *crimen vis*—a general offense directed toward preserving security and order—in the common law of crimes, influenced by Roman law, that preceded codification in Germany. Recently, however, this connection has been sharply rejected by some scholars. See generally Arndt Sinn, *Die Nötigung im System des heutigen Strafrechts*, 43–44 (Baden-Baden: Nomos 2000); Jakobs, "Nötigung durch Gewalt," in Hans Joachim Hirsch *et al.* (eds), *Gedächtnisschrift für Hilde Kaufmann* (Berlin: de Gruyter 1986), 792–96; Bertuleit, 61–72.

15 See, e.g., N.Y. Penal Law §§135.60 (Coercion in the second degree); 135.65 (Coercion in the first degree). See also Model Penal Code §212.5 (Criminal Coercion).

16 See, e.g., Herbert Tröndle, *Antworten auf Grundfragen*, 195–96 (Munich: Beck 1999).

17 Amelung, "Sitzblockaden, Gewalt und Kraftentfaltung," 1995 NJW, 2584.

In German law the offense of coercion is closely related to the offense of extortion or blackmail. See StGB §253 (*Erpressung*). The key difference is that extortion requires that the defendant (or a third person) has received property or other enrichment as a result of the coercive activities. This requirement is not present in the general offense of *Nötigung*. For a similar distinction in American law, see *Scheidler v. National Organization for Women, Inc.*, 537 U.S. 393 (2003). In the German Criminal Code the crime of rape or "sexual coercion" also follows, in part, the structure of the general *Nötigung* statute. See StGB §177. More generally, §240 is placed among a series of provisions—such as certain forms of kidnapping—that criminalize deprivations of individual freedom. See StGB §§232–241a.

> were creating basic rights in order to secure civil liberty against the state, the authors of the Prussian General State Law of 1794 created the first criminal (*strafbewehrte*) prohibition of *Nötigung*, in order to protect this liberty against threats originating from society itself.

But notwithstanding its liberal origins—this author continues—the criminal offense of *Nötigung* was soon overtaken by "anti-liberal" amendments and interpretations. The result is that "today we have a criminal offense for the protection of civil freedom that was formulated in an anti-liberal spirit—a self-contradiction."[18]

That is at least one skeptical view of the history. On the other hand, however, many other commentators have reached the conclusion that the offense of *Nötigung* is a crucial bulwark of order in a society threatened by chaos and potential breakdown. Certainly, as we will see, the provision came to be widely used against political protestors in a time of social stress.

### *Nötigung: examining the text*

As is generally the case in legal analysis, however, a summary statement of a legal provision—along with general remarks about its background and history—can only furnish little more than an introduction to any serious examination of a particular problem. Indeed, the reality of a legal issue is very often more complicated than it may seem at the outset. Accordingly, we must undertake a task that is often essential for understanding a provision of the criminal law: we must engage in a careful examination of a complicated and not very clear legal text. Specifically—in order to understand the problems of the anti-missile protest cases—we must work our way carefully through the precise wording of the *Nötigung* provision in the German Criminal Code.

Such a careful verbal examination may seem to be a distraction from the broader political and philosophical principles that often lie behind seemingly mundane legal provisions. But we must always remember the basic principle of the rule of law, which requires that an individual may be punished only according to a legal rule that is set down in advance. When we bear this principle in mind, we will

[18] Amelung, 1995 NJW, 2584–85.

understand that a careful examination of the statute—the legal rule itself—must begin our investigation of this problem.

Section 240 of the German Criminal Code—the provision that the Mutlangen and Großengstingen sit-down demonstrators were charged with violating—reads as follows:

(1) Whoever illegally [*rechtswidrig*] coerces another person, through force [*Gewalt*] or by the threat of a substantial evil, to undertake an action, to allow something to happen, or to omit to do something, will be punished by up to three years imprisonment or by a fine, or, in particularly serious cases, by imprisonment from six months to five years.
(2) An act is illegal [*rechtswidrig*] if the application of force or the threat of the evil, for the purpose of achieving the intended end, is to be viewed as reprehensible [*verwerflich*].
(3) An attempt [to commit the above offense] is also punishable.

When we seek to apply this complex text to the case of the demonstrators, we see that not all of the language is necessary in our case. For example, the phrase in section (1) that penalizes coercion "by the threat of a substantial evil" refers largely to statements that the defendant would do something unpleasant *in the future*—and not to *present* coercive acts. In any event, the courts have generally disregarded this language in the sit-down cases and have concentrated, rather, on the provision requiring the use of "force." The phrases covering coercion "to undertake an action" or "to allow something to happen" also seem irrelevant because the demonstrators—in blocking the progress of trucks or other vehicles in or out of the missile bases—were rather seeking to *stop* something from happening.

Therefore a shortened version of the text, which focuses on the language that is relevant to our problem and omits irrelevant language, could read as follows:

(1) Whoever illegally [*rechtswidrig*] coerces another person, through force [*Gewalt*] . . . to omit to do something, will be punished by [imprisonment or a fine.]
(2) An act is illegal [*rechtswidrig*] if the application of force . . . for the purpose of achieving the intended end, is to be viewed as reprehensible [*verwerflich*].

The next important point to notice is that section (2) is really little more than a definition of one of the crucial terms in section (1): "illegally" or, in German, "*rechtswidrig*." Under section (2) an act is "illegal" for the purposes of section (1) if the use of force under the circumstances is "reprehensible" (*verwerflich*).

From the position of the ordinary reader, or ordinary language, the substitution of "reprehensible" for "illegal" may not seem to move us toward greater clarity; but as we will see, it is an essential step in the legal analysis.

So, for the moment, taking only small liberties, we could further condense the section as follows:

> Whoever *reprehensibly* coerces another person, through *force* . . . to omit to do something, will be punished by [imprisonment or a fine] [emphasis added].

This, then, is the essence of the legal provision under which the Großengstingen and Mutlangen demonstrators were charged.

But how does it apply to those protestors?

## The *Nötigung* statute and the sit-down demonstrations

A reader who is unfamiliar with the interpretation of this provision by the German courts may seriously question that this provision is applicable to the sit-down protestors at all.

To help us with this problem, let us try to imagine the central type of case which the provision was intended to cover. A clear violation of the provision might arise, for example, if Arthur did not want Bill to sign a legal document in Mary's favor and therefore beat Bill with a large club until he agreed not to sign the document. Here, the beating clearly constitutes Arthur's use of "force" in order to "coerce" Bill to "omit to do something" (signing the document). Moreover, we could readily agree that this act of forcible coercion, in its context, is "reprehensible."

Yet when we turn from our easy case of coercion by beating and try to apply the statutory language to the demonstrations of the sit-down protestors, we encounter two serious problems.

The *first* problem is that the text requires that the defendant act with "force" (*Gewalt*). Yet, unlike Arthur who violently beats Bill in the example above, the sit-down protestors were following the dictates of passive resistance—as developed by Gandhi and Martin Luther King. As individuals who did nothing more than sit peacefully in the street, they vigorously denied that they were using "force" at all. Indeed, they argued, they were employing the opposite of force.[19]

*Second*, the text requires that the defendants' actions be considered "reprehensible" under the circumstances. Yet the protestors argued that they were acting from the best of motives and with the most praiseworthy of intentions: they were trying to save humanity from the catastrophe of nuclear war. How could such an action be viewed as "reprehensible"?[20]

These, then, were the two central problems that confronted the prosecution of the anti-nuclear sit-down demonstrators for the crime of *Nötigung* under StGB §240: How could it be said that a few passive resisters sitting in the street were using "force" against the massive trucks and military vehicles that they confronted, and how could it be said that their well-intentioned—if possibly mistaken—actions were "reprehensible"?

In examining the position of the German criminal courts, let us address each of these questions separately.

## §240(I): The "spiritualization" of the concept of "force"

As we saw above, a very clear case of the use of "force" in the *Nötigung* statute might be Arthur's beating Bill to coerce him not to sign a legal document favorable to Mary. The underlying value being protected is that an individual's (Bill's) freedom of will—including, of course, the person's freedom to act in accordance with that will—must not be impaired by forcible actions.

Yet at a very early point, the German courts began a process that substantially diluted the requirement that the coercion be undertaken

[19] For example, at his trial for *Nötigung* in January 1985, the well-known theologian Norbert Greinacher declared: "It is also incomprehensible to me that I could be accused of the use of force [*Gewalt*] . . . I cannot imagine anything in the world that is more peaceful than our completely non-violent demonstration." Ute Finckh and Inge Jens (eds), *Verwerflich?: Friedensfreunde vor Gericht*, 40 (Munich: Knaur 1985). See also Hanne and Klaus Vack (eds), *Mutlangen—unser Mut wird langen!* (Sensbachtal: Komitee für Grundrechte und Demokratie e.V. 1986), 37 (remarks of protestor Martin Singe) (Demonstrators are acting in the non-forcible tradition of Thoreau, Gandhi and King).

[20] For a particularly vigorous statement of this objection—by a prominent figure in the German peace movement—see below.

with "force." Indeed, the courts began to concentrate more on the underlying principle of freedom of the will and somewhat muted the requirement that "force"—at least in the sense of physical force—be applied. As one author put it, the courts shifted "more and more from the exercise of physical strength on the part of the actor" to the requirement that there be a "compulsive effect on the victim."[21]

Repeating a process that often occurs in the judicial development of law, this "shift" in doctrine started with cases rather close to the common idea of physical "force" and then moved into less closely related areas. It is sometimes said that certain continental systems are based entirely on statute and have only a weak concept of judicial precedent—if, indeed, they have any such concept at all. But the history of these sit-down cases—among many others—shows that, in the interpretation of codes and other statutes, the German legal system can act in a manner that is not very different from the case-law development of Anglo-American common law courts.

Even before the founding of the Federal Republic—remember that §240 had been in the Criminal Code since 1871—the highest court of the German Empire (the "Imperial Court" or *Reichsgericht*) found that the firing of warning shots to impel someone to do something could be considered the use of "force" under §240.[22] Although this act seems to be very close to the use of force in the commonly understood physical sense, the important thing for future development was that the coercive effect of the act did not come from actual physical force applied to the victim through bodily contact, but rather from the weakening of the victim's will through terror caused by the shots. So, starting here, the weakening of the will that resulted from a physical act that did not involve contact with the victim—pulling the trigger, discharging the shots into the air—became effectively equivalent, in some instances, to the application of forcible acts to a person's body through unmediated physical contact.[23]

A further development along these lines occurred in a very early post-World War II case in which a thief tried to trick a woman to submit to an anesthetic so that he could steal her possessions.

[21] Brohm, "Demonstrationsfreiheit und Sitzblockaden," 1985 JZ, 501, 504.

[22] 60 RGSt, 157 (1926).

[23] In another early case, decided in 1911, the *Reichsgericht* found that *Nötigung* had been committed by members of a large crowd that blocked the passage of pallbearers endeavoring to enter a cemetery. The pallbearers were carrying the coffin of a person who had committed suicide, and the persons in the crowd believed—for

Although this case did not involve the *Nötigung* law, but rather a theft statute that also employed the word "force," later cases seemed to view the word "force" as being equivalent in both provisions. In the anesthetic case also, the Court found that "force" was being used—here, again, principally because the victim's will was being weakened or interfered with. As long as the thief sought to achieve this end, it did not matter that he had employed only a minimal amount of physical exertion. This result reflected the perception that "in the general affairs of life, the application of pure physical force increasingly becomes subordinate to the employment of other forces of nature."[24]

In a similar case of the same period a defendant, who had "moral or religious" objections to a well-known film (*Die Sünderin* or The Sinner), protested against a showing of the film by detonating devices with noxious vapors which drove patrons from the theater.[25] The BGH found that the defendant could be convicted of *Nötigung*—presumably under the assumption that the effect of these vapors

religious reasons—that the deceased should not be buried in consecrated ground. 45 RGSt 153 (*Sargträger*).

In some ways this case resembles the cases of the sit-down demonstrators. Yet the crowd in this case presented a massive physical barrier to the further movement of the pallbearers, as well as the implicit threat of actual violence if the pallbearers should attempt to move forward—factors that are not present in the typical case of a small group of demonstrators sitting down in front of military trucks or vehicles. See, e.g., Altvater, "Anmerkung," 1995 NStZ, 278, 281.

24 1 BGHSt, 145, 147 (1951).

This case was decided by the highest West German court for criminal and civil matters, known as the *Bundesgerichtshof* or BGH. Because this court stands at the apex of the criminal and civil justice systems in Germany, it is sometimes referred to in English as the Federal Supreme Court. The BGH should be carefully distinguished, however, from the Federal Constitutional Court, which is supreme in matters of constitutional interpretation but generally has no authority over the interpretation of the "ordinary" civil and criminal law. The Constitutional Court is discussed in detail in Chapter 3.

25 In *Die Sünderin*, for the first time in post-war German history, an actress—Hildegard Knef—appeared nude on the screen. This apparition triggered major perturbations in West German society. For reflections on this unexpected reaction, see Hildegard Knef, *The Gift Horse*: *Report on a Life*, 243–45, trans. D. Palastanga (New York: McGraw-Hill 1971): "The film was attacked from the pulpit, rent asunder by the clergy, shown amid clouds of tear gas. . . . Having [lived outside of Germany after World War II and therefore having] missed the formative years of moral renaissance, Wirtschaftswunder, and a society striving to reinstate virtue and order, I completely failed to grasp that stable currency, regular nourishment, and heated bedrooms had returned hand in hand with a prudery of the most insipid and nauseating sort, ignoring and disclaiming recent history."

was equivalent to "force," even though his actual expenditure of bodily energy was minimal.[26] On the other hand, the noxious vapors clearly had some sort of actual physical effect on the victims.[27]

Any possible requirement of physical contact for a forcible *Nötigung* was further diminished in notable cases from the early 1960s which applied §240 to obstreperous drivers. In one case the defendant—blowing his horn, flashing his lights, and driving at more than 90 kilometers per hour—remained within six feet of a preceding driver in the passing lane for at least two kilometers, until the preceding driver finally relinquished the lane. Finding that the defendant had exercised "force" (*Gewalt*) under §240, the court remarked that significant bodily exertion is not essential; rather, the important criterion is the compulsion exerted on the victim. Moreover, in traffic, influences "of a physical and psychological type cannot be distinguished from each other."[28]

These cases, which focused on the effects of certain acts on the mental state of the victim—the person being "coerced"—set the scene for the important *Laepple* decision in 1969.[29] This case is crucial for our problem, because in that opinion the BGH found that certain sit-down blockades could constitute the use of "force" under §240 StGB.

The facts of the *Laepple* case seemed to reflect an early phenomenon of the German student movement; and the resulting decision

[26] 5 BGHSt, 245 (1953).

[27] In another case of the early years of the Federal Republic—a case that is indeed a sort of Cold War relic—the BGH found that the feared use of certain strikes could cause the "forcible" overthrow of the government. In reaching this conclusion, the Court was not finding that the strikers would actually use physical strength against the bodies of government personnel. Rather, the cessation of economic and other activity caused by the strike would have such a powerful effect on the minds of duly elected officials that they would relinquish control of the government; 8 BGHSt 102 (1955). Here again, the broad interpretation of the term "force" or "forcible" in a quite distinct statute was found to have a bearing on the interpretation of "force" in the *Nötigung* statute.

[28] 19 BGHSt, 263, 265 (1964). For a similar case of the same period, see also 18 BGHSt, 389 (1963) (*Nötigung* found when a driver proceeded slowly in front of another vehicle for some kilometers, changing lanes when necessary to prevent the other driver from passing him).

[29] 23 BGHSt, 46 (1969). For commentary on this case, see, e.g., Ott, "Anmerkung," 1969 NJW 2023; Eilsberger, "Die Kölner Strassenbahnblockade," 1970 JuS 164; Altvater, 1995 NStZ, 281; Werner Offenloch, *Erinnerung an das Recht. Der Streit um die Nachrüstung auf den Straßen und vor den Gerichten*, 94–101 (Tübingen: Mohr Siebeck 2005).

of the BGH was issued in an atmosphere of political tension and generational conflict that characterized the period in which it was decided.[30] Protesting an increase in streetcar fare, a group of students staged a mass "sit-down strike," blocking streetcar traffic at two important points in the city of Cologne. Some protestors were dispersed by mounted police and high-pressure hoses. In the prosecution of demonstration leaders, the BGH declared that the students who sat on the tracks "coerced (*nötigten*) the streetcar drivers with force (*Gewalt*) to stop their vehicles." The Court reached this conclusion even though the students "did not stop the streetcars through the direct application of physical strength, but rather—expending only minimal physical energy—[they] set in motion a *psychologically-determined process*."[31]

In the Court's view, the "psychologically-determined process" seemed to arise from the streetcar drivers' fear of the consequences —to the demonstrators and perhaps to themselves—if they failed to halt their vehicles. Thus, through this psychological pressure, the use of "force" was present, even though there was no purely physical process of coercion like the beating of Bill by Arthur in our example above.

In cases of this kind, the Court stated, the crucial issue is the amount of "weight" to be attributed to this psychological effect. When persons sit on the streetcar tracks, they are applying "irresistible" coercive pressure, because the driver must stop to avoid committing manslaughter. The effect of this pressure is "further increased through the simultaneous massed incursion of many persons onto the tracks."[32] In this decision, therefore, the BGH cleared the way for sit-down demonstrations and blockades to be viewed as constituting "forcible" coercion under §240 of the Criminal Code. Under the language of the decision, however, there might possibly be room to argue that the principle applied only to "mass" sit-down demonstrations.

In any case, the *Laepple* decision confirmed that a certain kind of coercive effect may constitute "force" under §240, even though the weakening of the will is not accomplished by physical action directly applied to the body of the victim (the "coerced" streetcar driver). Psychological pressure resulting from the expenditure of a small amount of physical energy—for example, the amount of energy

[30] See Eilsberger, 1970 JuS, 165.

[31] 23 BGHSt, 54 (emphasis added).

[32] Ibid.

needed to walk to the streetcar tracks and sit down upon them—will be enough to qualify as "force" (*Gewalt*) under §240.

This development in the interpretation of §240 is frequently referred to as the "spiritualization" (*Vergeistigung*) of the concept of force.[33] In any case, the *Laepple* decision led to the conclusion that the persons who were sitting in the street, in order to stop traffic from entering the missile bases, were exercising "force" under §240(I). Thus when the anti-nuclear sit-in cases began to come to the courts in the early 1980s, the doctrine of the *Laepple* case provided a readily available argument that could be used against the protestors.[34]

[33] Although the "psychological" argument of *Laepple* is generally recognized as the basis for the judicial extension of § 240(I), some writers contend that the common meaning of the word "force" includes sit-down blockades—without the necessity of referring to psychological factors. In this view, "force" includes the creation of any hindrance (such as a blockade) that itself can only be removed through the use of physical force. See, e.g., Tröndle, *Antworten auf Grundfragen*, 193–95; cf. also Offenloch, "Geforderter Rechtsstaat," 1986 JZ, 11, 12; Calliess, "Der strafrechtliche Nötigungstatbestand und das verfassungsrechtliche Gebot der Tatbestandsbestimmtheit," 1985 NJW, 1506.

At the other end of the spectrum, a few lower courts rejected the "spiritualized" definition of "force" altogether and consequently acquitted sit-down protestors. According to these courts, the statutory requirement of "force" in StGB §240(I) required an application of actual physical force that was directly experienced as such by the victim. See, e.g., Decision of AG Frankfurt/M, 26 July 1985, 1985 StV, 462. See generally Frankenberg, "Passive Resistenz ist keine Nötigung: Untergerichte wider die herrschende Rechtsprechung zu §240 StGB," 1985 KJ, 301.

[34] Indeed, in another politically charged case of the period—after the *Laepple* decision, but before the anti-missile sit-down cases came to the courts—the BGH seemed to dilute the requirement of "force" even further. BGH, Decision of 8 October 1981, 1982 NJW, 189. In this case student protestors yelled, sang, whistled, and played loud instruments in order to prevent lectures from taking place at the University of Heidelberg. Some of the students were convicted of coercion by "force" under §240—even though the lectures were not impeded by any physical barrier. Quoting the *Laepple* decision, the BGH found that the instructors would experience the loud noise as a form of pressure that was "not only mental, but also physical." But if the effect on the instructors had arisen from the *content* of the students' speech instead of the loudness of the noise—if, for example, students had interrupted the lectures with calls to have a discussion—the Court indicated that these interjections might not have constituted "force" under §240.

This case evoked a lively exchange of views on whether noise could justifiably be interpreted as "force" under StGB §240(I). See Köhler, "Vorlesungsstörung als Gewaltnötigung?," 1983 NJW, 10; Brendle, "Lärm als körperliche Einwirkung—Gewaltbegriff und Einheit der Rechtsordnung," 1983 NJW, 727; Köhler, "Nochmals: Vorlesungsstörung als Gewaltnötigung?," 1983 NJW, 1595.

## §240(II): What sort of "force" is "reprehensible"?

### The background of §240(II)

But even if we accept the view that the sit-down demonstrators were using "force" under §240(I)—under the broad "spiritualized" interpretation put forth by the BGH—we have seen that the protestors could not be convicted unless their actions were also found to be "reprehensible" under §240(II). Recall that, in the full statement of §240(II), the act of coercion is not illegal unless "the application of force . . . for the purpose of achieving the intended end, is to be viewed as reprehensible."[35]

But what is the meaning of the term "reprehensible" in this context? It is a term that is often used in ordinary speech, but what does it mean when it is transported into the language of the criminal code? Perhaps we can best approach this opaque and difficult term if we first examine its function in the broader purpose of the provision, as well as the history of its original insertion into the statutory prohibition of *Nötigung*.

#### THE FUNCTION OF §240(II)

First, we should understand that §240(II) basically functions as a statutory "corrective," since it is evident that if §240(I)—the first section of the provision—remained in effect without further limitation, it could be dangerously and excessively broad.[36] Indeed, §240(I)—viewed alone—might well cover actions that everyone would

[35] §240(II) is actually rather anomalous in the German Criminal Code. Ordinarily, German criminal law follows three steps in deciding whether a defendant should be convicted. The first inquiry is whether the basic elements of the offense—the required actions and intent—are present (*Tatbestandsmässigkeit*). In the second step, the Court then determines whether any general defenses—such as necessity or self-defense—make the acts justifiable and therefore not "illegal" (*Rechtswidrigkeit*). Finally, in the third step, the Court decides whether this particular defendant is excused because of some individual incapacity, such as insanity (*Schuld*). See, e.g., Eser, "Justification and Excuse", 24 *American Journal of Comparative Law* 621, 625–27 (1976).

The peculiarity of §240(II) is that it adds a novel aspect to the second step of the procedure—the determination of illegality (*Rechtswidrigkeit*). If the act is not "reprehensible," the act is justified and the defendant cannot be convicted—even though this special justification goes beyond the traditional factors of justification generally provided in the Code. See, e.g., 35 BGHSt, 275–76.

[36] See, e.g., ibid.; cf. 2 BGHSt, 194, 195–96 (1952).

agree should not be criminalized. For example, if George held Rodney's arm to prevent Rodney from impetuously stepping into dangerous traffic, that would clearly be the use of "force" by George to "coerce" Rodney into "omitting" the perilous "action" of stepping into traffic. Accordingly, George's act would seem to satisfy the requirements for criminality set forth in §240(I).

Yet everyone would certainly agree that such a benevolent and praiseworthy act of "coercion" should not be criminalized. Accordingly, George's act could be saved from criminality by a finding that the act—although coercion by "force" under §240(I)—was not "reprehensible" under §240(II). Section 240(II), therefore, serves to screen out innocuous—or indeed beneficial—acts that fall within the definition of §240(I) and thus might be found to be criminal in the absence of the requirement that the action must be "reprehensible."

### THE HISTORY OF §240(II)

This, then, is the present function of §240(II). But its history is a bit more complicated and tortuous; indeed, its history introduces a distinctly ominous note in the development of this provision of German criminal law. Section 240(II) was added to the Criminal Code in 1943, together with a provision that expanded §240(I) to include "threats of a substantial evil." Previously, the "threats" covered by §240(I) were limited to "threats" to commit a criminal act, and thus the extension of this provision to include coercion by "threats" of any substantial evil—whether criminal or not—represented a significant increase of coverage. Accordingly, this broad expansion of §240(I) made it clear that some corresponding limitation—to be furnished in the new §240(II)—was required.

But of course the year 1943, when these changes were made, was deep in the Nazi period. Accordingly, the original version of §240(II) reflected the language of Nazi ideology. In the original 1943 version of §240(II), "coercion" would be illegal only if it was contrary to "the healthy feelings of the people" (*gesundes Volksempfinden*). This was a code expression, frequently found in Nazi statutes and documents, which was intended to encompass views approved by Nazi ideology, such as "Aryan racial purity" and so on.[37] After World War II, the occupation government of the Allies prohibited the

[37] See generally Ingo Müller, *Hitler's Justice: The Courts of the Third Reich*, 68–81, trans. Deborah Lucas Schneider (Cambridge, MA: Harvard University Press 1991).

application of this phrase in German criminal statutes. But through a questionable process of interpretation, the BGH continued to apply §240 (II), in its original form, until well into the 1950s.[38]

Finally in 1953, the West German Parliament amended §240(II) and inserted the word "reprehensible" (*verwerflich*) to replace "contrary to the healthy feelings of the people."[39] Yet some writers argued that this amendment had little real effect, calling it a "negligible cosmetic adjustment."[40] Certainly, for a considerable period, criminal court judges continued to explain the term "reprehensible" through the use of formulas that strikingly resembled the discarded language of the Nazi period.[41] In any event, even after this change, the scope of §240 remained considerably broader than it had been before 1943.[42] Accordingly, after World War II, this expanded provision encountered considerable resistance and criticism as a result of its broad and undetermined scope.[43]

### *§240(II) in the criminal courts*

In light of the vague and open-ended nature of the requirement of "reprehensible" action, it is not surprising that the German courts have advanced a number of differing views on the meaning of §240(II). In an early decision, for example, the BGH proposed what seemed to be a narrow definition of the word "reprehensible," restricting illegality to only very clear cases.[44] The Court declared that for a finding of illegality the act, under all the circumstances, must be "clearly so offensive [*anstößig*] that, as a harsh [*gröberer*] attack on another's freedom of decision, it requires correction through the means of the criminal law." According to the Court, this test required "a heightened degree of ethical disapproval."[45]

[38] Calliess, 1985 NJW, 1510–11; 1 BGHSt 84 (1951); see 1 BGHSt, 13 (1951).

[39] Drittes Strafrechtsänderungsgesetz, 6 August 1953, BGBl I, 742.

[40] Calliess, 1985 NJW, 1506.

[41] See, e.g., 17 BGHSt, 328, 331–32 (1962) ("justice-feelings of the people" [*Rechtsempfinden des Volkes*], "the general convictions of the people" [*die allgemeine Volksüberzeugung*]). Cf. 5 BGHSt, 254 (1953).

[42] Calliess, 1985 NJW, 1506.

[43] Ibid., 1507. See also Kaufmann, "Der BGH und die Sitzblockade", 1988 NJW, 2581, 2582: "Is it possible to describe an offense (*Unrecht*) much more vaguely than with the word 'reprehensible'?" See also Roellecke, "Bio-Recht oder die Sanftmut von Gesäß-Protestierern," 1995 NJW, 1525, 1526.

[44] 17 BGHSt, 328 (1962).

[45] Ibid., 332.

But a few years later in the crucial *Laepple* case—the case of the Cologne streetcar protest—the BGH seemed to swing in a different direction. Invoking the history that we have reviewed above, the *Laepple* court noted that §240(II) was introduced in order to provide a limit on illegality for certain coercive *threats*—that is, threats of a "substantial evil." But, the court argued, §240(II) was not introduced to limit illegality for the coercive use of "*force*" which is covered by a separate clause of §240(I). Accordingly, if "force" was used—rather than threats—no further limitation was necessary. The result of this reasoning was that if the defendant was found to have used "force" under §240(I), the act would ordinarily be "reprehensible" under §240(II), without anything more.[46] Together with the *Laepple* court's notable dilution of the requirement of "force," this argument implied a significant expansion of the offense of *Nötigung*.

Interestingly, the Constitutional Court in the first of its *Nötigung* cases—a decision that we will examine in Chapter 4—called this stern interpretation into question.[47] But a few months before this opinion was handed down, the BGH itself had already backed away from its remarks on "reprehensible" action in the *Laepple* case. Instead, the BGH adopted a more neutral or open position, finding that—even when "force" was present under §240(I)—the "reprehensible" nature of the act must be determined by a balancing of all the circumstances of the specific case.[48] Under such an open-ended test, the result in any particular case might well depend upon the nature of the factors that could permissibly be taken into account in the course of this balancing.

What were the factors, then, that could be taken into account in making this determination in the cases of the sit-down demonstrators? What were the factors that could be considered in deciding whether their acts were "reprehensible"? Certainly, the answer to this question could have an important bearing on the ultimate position that civil disobedience would hold in German criminal law.

As the German peace movement vigorously argued, a full consideration of the anti-war goals of the sit-down demonstrators would

[46] Only in exceptional cases could "special circumstances" change this result. 23 BGHSt, 55.

[47] 73 BVerfGE, 206, 254–56 (1986).

[48] See 34 BGHSt, 71, 77 (1986). For commentary on this decision, see Hansjörg Reichert-Hammer, *Politische Fernziele und Unrecht*, 28–30 (Berlin: Duncker & Humblot 1991); Jakobs, "Anmerkung," 1986 JZ, 1063; Offenloch, *Erinnerung*, 132–36.

lead to the conclusion that this form of civil disobedience could not be viewed as "reprehensible." Indeed, in a number of opinions in the late 1980s, certain criminal courts found that, even if the sit-down protestors were using "force" under §240(I), the protestors were not acting "reprehensibly" under §240(II) because the purpose of their actions was directed toward the common good—that is, toward preserving humanity from the catastrophe of nuclear war.[49]

Of course, the protestors' immediate goal ("*Nah-Ziel*") was to block the entrances of the missile bases—and this use of "force" counted against them on the question of "reprehensible" action. But their ultimate goal or motive ("*Fern-Ziel*") was to preserve humanity, and that was a laudable goal that counted heavily in their favor. According to some courts, when the "immediate goal" and the "ultimate goal" were balanced against each other, the laudable ultimate goal carried sufficient weight to prevent the entire act from being considered "reprehensible." Some of these opinions contained interesting reflections on the requisite process of interpretation when a word from moral language is employed in a statutory text.

For example, one State Appellate Court (OLG) declared:

> When a rule of criminal law—like §240(II) of the criminal code—refers to moral values . . . it is necessary to take into account everything that influences the ethical judgment . . . [F]or the moral sense, there is obviously a difference whether an action serves ends that should be disapproved or whether it seeks a goal that, in itself, is worthy of respect . . . [A]n action that, in itself, is oriented toward the common good—even if it may possibly rest on an error—should be evaluated differently as an ethical matter than an action that is determined by selfish goals.[50]

Another State Appellate Court concurred:

> The required balancing . . . cannot be limited to the question of the direct goals that the actor sought to achieve . . .; rather, for a comprehensive evaluation of his conduct it is necessary to ask whether the actor was pursuing . . . broader goals and what kind of goals these were: the [judgment] of the conduct of the actor cannot remain uninfluenced by whether this ultimate goal . . .

49 For an overview of these cases, see Reichert-Hammer, 33–36.

50 OLG Zweibrücken, Judgment of 28 August 1987, 1988 NJW, 716, 717.

> was sustained by motives that were worthy of approval, and a feeling of responsibility for the common good, and therefore could be evaluated positively.[51]

Although a number of lower courts adopted this view in the 1980s, the BGH put an end to arguments of this kind in a highly controversial decision in 1988.[52] In this opinion the BGH declared that, in the balancing required to determine whether "forcible" actions are "reprehensible" under §240(II), the "ultimate goals" of the protestors—goals such as the pursuit of world peace—are not to be taken into account.[53] The BGH claimed that it had maintained this position since 1953 when, in the famous "Sinner" (*Sünderin*) case, it declared that the courts should focus only on "the action that is the subject of coercion. It is without importance, on the question of [reprehensible conduct], what broader goals the defendant . . . sought to achieve."[54]

The word "reprehensible" in §240(II) is a word drawn from common language, without any technical legal meaning. But with its 1988 decision, the BGH in effect began to establish a special legal meaning for this word—a meaning that, in certain contexts, might well deviate from its meaning in ordinary speech. In deciding whether a particular action was "reprehensible," an ordinary speaker would probably not adopt a general rule that completely excluded any particular aspect of the action—such as the motive of the act or its ultimate goal or purpose. As this word is used in the context of a legal

51 OLG Oldenburg, Judgment of 14 September 1987, 1987 StV, 489, 490 (sit-down demonstration protesting construction of nuclear power plant). For similar views, see OLG Köln, Judgment of 22 July 1986, 1986 NJW, 2443 (blockade in protest of Pershing II rockets). But for differing views in appellate decisions of the period, see 1988 NJW, 718 (BayObLG); 1988 NJW, 720 (OLG Koblenz).

52 35 BGHSt, 270 (1988). For commentary on this important case, see Roggemann, "Der Friede—ein Strafrechtsgut wie jedes andere?," 1988 JZ, 1108; Kaufmann, "Der BGH und die Sitzblockade," 1988 NJW, 2581; Arzt, "Anmerkung," 1988, JZ, 775; Reichert-Hammer, 36–37, 48–64; Schmitt Glaeser, "Politisch motivierte Gewalt und ihre 'Fernziele'," 1988 BayVBl, 454; Eser, "Irritationen um das 'Fernziel'. Zur Verwerflichkeitsrechtsprechung bei Sitzblockaden," in Bernhard Töpper (ed.), *Wie würden Sie entscheiden? Festschrift für Gerd Jauch*, 35–53 (Munich: Beck 1990); Herbert Tröndle, "Sitzblockaden und ihre Fernziele," in *Antworten auf Grundfragen*, 229–56 (Munich: Beck 1999); Offenloch, *Erinnerung*, 155–60.

53 According to the Court, however, these goals may be taken into account in determining the severity of the punishment.

54 5 BGHSt, 245, 246 (1953); for the "Sinner" case, see above, pp. 72–73.

structure, however, it begins to be influenced by the requirements of that structure and to take on characteristics that would most likely play no particular role in determining its usage in ordinary speech.[55]

Thus, in concluding that the ultimate goal of the demonstrators could not be taken into account in a finding of whether actions were "reprehensible" under §240(II), the BGH emphasized that the specific statutory structure of §240 required this resolution.[56] Indeed, the Court also argued that, as a matter of principle, the German criminal law ordinarily relied on "externally recognizable objective circumstances"—rather than subjectively held ultimate goals or motives—to establish a defense that would justify actions that would otherwise be illegal.[57]

Moreover, the BGH doubted whether there were criteria for assessing the value of the "ultimate goal," and it declared that the commonly urged distinctions between private "selfish" goals (low value), and goals "oriented to the public interest" (high value), are notoriously difficult to draw.[58] Here the Court invokes another criterion—a modicum of precision or foreseeability—which the Court believes is required by the nature of the legal system but which might not play any particular role in the determination of usage in ordinary language.

Finally—according to the opinion of the BGH—a finding that the sit-down protests were legal would raise "the danger of a radicalization of political debate." Opposing groups would also engage in legalized blockades, which could "open the floodgates for serious impairment of domestic peace."[59] This final argument suggests that, if legalized, the method of sit-down demonstrations could easily be employed by right-wing as well as by pacifist or left-wing groups; and it seems intended to call to mind the political street battles of the last years of the Weimar period—a specter that is rarely far from the

[55] For a discussion of a similar phenomenon in Anglo-American law, see Holmes, "The Path of the Law," 10 *Harvard Law Review* 457 (1897).

[56] 35 BGHSt, 275–76.

[57] Ibid., 278–80. But for criticism of this argument, see Eser, in *Festschrift für Gerd Jauch*, 46–47.

[58] 35 BGHSt, 280–82. Of course the distinction would be equally difficult to draw in the context of sentencing—where the Court does acknowledge that its use would be permissible. Indeed, the Constitutional Court has itself employed such a distinction in a long line of cases concerning the freedom of expression. See, e.g., 7 BVerfGE, 198 (1958) (*Lüth*); but see Schmitt Glaeser, 1988 BayVBl, 457–58 (arguing that the distinction should be abandoned in all areas).

[59] 35 BGHSt, 282.

surface in discussions of the right of assembly and demonstration in the Federal Republic.

Many German commentators approved this important decision of the BGH,[60] but others found it questionable to distinguish between "immediate goals" and "ultimate goals" as the BGH had done.[61] Certainly, the goal of world peace is recognized as a basic value in several provisions of the German Constitution and laws, and several authors argued that this value deserved more weight than the BGH had accorded to it. Another well-known German scholar suggested that the BGH, in deciding this case, could have been animated by its disapproval of the protestors' political goals.[62]

Yet even after the BGH excluded the protestors' "ultimate" goals from consideration, a balancing of other factors continued to result in occasional acquittals in these cases. According to the State Appellate Court (OLG) in Stuttgart, a number of other factors—more specifically related to the blockades or the protestors themselves—could still be taken into account in the requisite balancing. These included, for example, the length and intensity of the blockade; whether protestors had given the authorities warning of a particular blockade; whether an alternative route was available for the entry or exit of vehicles; and "the psychological situation of the [defendant], his actual anxieties, cares and the necessities of his conscience." Apparently, the uncertainty of these factors eventually led to the reluctance of some judges to convict defendants in these trials for *Nötigung*.[63]

60 See e.g., Arzt, 1988 JZ, 775; Tröndle, in *Antworten auf Grundfragen*, 229 (a "classical showpiece [*Kabinettstück*]" of appellate jurisprudence); Schmitt Glaeser, 1988 BayVBl, 454. See also Baumann, "Demonstrationsziel als Bewertungsposten bei der Entscheidung nach §240II StGB?," 1987 NJW, 36.

61 Roggemann, 1988 JZ, 1108. Moreover a handful of lower courts—citing principles of judicial independence—rather extraordinarily refused to adhere to this decision of the BGH. See Otto, "Strafbare Nötigung durch Sitzblockaden in der höchstrichterlichen Rechtsprechung und die Thesen der Gewaltkommission zu §240 StGB," 1992 NStZ, 568 and n.2; LG Zweibrücken, Judgment of 1 June 1989, 1989 StV, 397. On the lower courts' reactions, see generally Reichert-Hammer, 38–41.

62 Kaufmann, 1988 NJW, 2582.

63 Offenloch, "Der Richter als Organ der Strafverfolgung?," in Ludwig Häsemeyer *et al.* (eds), *Rechtsprechung heute—Anspruch und Wirklichkeit*, 49, 51–56 (Frankfurt/M: Peter Lang 1996); see also Offenloch, "Die Erosion traditoneller Standards der Rechtsprechung durch das Bundesverfassungsgericht am Beispiel der Behandlung von Sitzblockaden aus Anlaß der Nachrüstung," in Martin Gutzeit and Markus Reimann (eds), *Liber Discipulorum: Dankschrift für Günther Wiese* (Weinheim: GOR-Verlag 1996).

### *The reaction of the peace movement and Jens' peroration*

Notwithstanding occasional acquittals, however, the result in most of these cases was that if "force" was found under §240(I) of the Criminal Code, the protestor's action was also found to be "reprehensible" under §240(II). This judicial conclusion drew sharp reaction from members of the peace movement who believed that their actions were far from reprehensible because their intention was the promotion of peace.

This position was perhaps put most effectively—and in any event most sharply—by Walter Jens, Professor of Rhetoric in Tübingen, in the closing passages of his address to Judge Offenloch in the court in Schwäbisch Gmünd.[64] These passages also clearly illustrate the underlying connection, in the minds of many of the peace demonstrators, between the suppression of blockades against nuclear missiles and authoritarian concepts of the Nazi period. Jens' remarks also furnish an interesting commentary on the growing difference between the word "reprehensible" in its ordinary sense and in its "legal" sense as interpreted by the German courts.

In the final portion—the peroration—of his address, Professor Jens first commented on the motives and character of the demonstrators themselves and the tradition in which they were acting.[65] Jens argued that to use the word "reprehensible" with respect to the sit-down demonstrations would be "a moral disqualification of people who are acting from honorable motives in the spirit of Albert Schweitzer [and] Martin Luther King"—and he ironically suggested that if this was the Court's real view, it should also ensure that "in the future, the Martin Luther King passages in our anthologies should be printed with a footnote: 'This man acted reprehensibly according to the jurisprudence of the Federal Republic.' "

Continuing in this ironic vein, Jens asked whether the sit-down demonstrations are "reprehensible—as malicious murder is reprehensible?" He pointed out that, according to the dictionary, a reprehensible person is "wicked and dissolute". "And—this is monstrous!" Jens continued:

> They want to apply *such* [a concept] to us [the demonstrators]:

[64] See Chapter 1.

[65] The following passages of Professor Jens' peroration are drawn from FAZ, 29 January 1985, 23; reprinted in *Verwerflich?*, 61–66.

> indeed, where are we living then? Still in the day before yesterday [that is to say, in the Nazi period]—as the transparent camouflage-translation of the phrase "healthy feelings of the people" [*gesundes Volksempfinden*] seems to indicate? (In the Third Reich: "healthy feelings of the people"; today: "reprehensible". Now as then, there is manifested the same Good/Evil pattern of a jurisprudence that is far [removed] from the Enlightenment.) Inciting peace as a reprehensible act: Someone should have painted such a terrifying picture for me in 1945, after our country was freed from Fascism—I would have declared that the person was crazy!

Jens continued by reflecting on the relationship between the term "reprehensible" and the constitutional system of the Federal Republic of Germany. Indeed, Jens denied that the word "reprehensible" was "appropriate in a state ruled by law," and particularly not in Germany, whose Basic Law "is obliged to preserve the dignity of every person." "But," Jens continued, "precisely this Basic Law is eroded at its core, when the formula 'reprehensible'—in the context of honorable endeavors for peace—becomes a threatening formula of an authoritarian state . . ."

Once more adopting an ironic mode, Jens questioned whether it could be called "reprehensible" to engage in "ten minutes of demonstrating for peace" in front of the munitions camp at Mutlangen, which is a "storehouse of weapons that contain . . . annihilation for now and forever." Is it really reprehensible to "attempt to help promote a little engine trouble on the way to the abyss"? Indeed, Jens concluded by emphasizing the similarity that he saw between the current statutory requirement of "reprehensible" action and the earlier Nazi formula which this term had replaced. In dramatic words, Jens declared: "I am afraid that the evil spirit of the 'healthy feelings of the people'—the evil spirit of a totalitarian jurisprudence—is celebrating here its belated and evil triumph."

In sum, Jens' peroration before the Criminal Court in Schwäbisch Gmünd seemed to capture two central aspects of the self-conception and political views of many of the anti-missile protestors. First and foremost, they saw themselves as continuing the tradition of nonviolent protest that had a long and honorable pedigree in the United States and India, although perhaps not yet in Germany. Second, they saw the government's prosecution of the Pershing missile protestors as containing elements, at least, of a form of repression that bore a relationship to repressions of the Nazi past. For Jens and certainly for many other demonstrators, therefore, the application of the term "reprehensible" to their actions seemed both inaccurate and ominous in its implications.

## The Großengstingen and Mutlangen cases in the criminal courts

With this background in understanding the offense of "coercion," let us now return to the individual cases of the Großengstingen and Mutlangen demonstrators and examine the fate of these specific prosecutions in the German criminal courts. We will see that, while these three cases reach similar conclusions, each set of trials presents its own distinctive issues and characteristics.[66]

### *Großengstingen—Müller and Ostermayer*

At the conclusion of Chapter 1, we saw that the first Großengstingen demonstration came to an end when the police cut the padlocked chain and carried the protestors away from the gate of the Eberhard Finckh Barracks. The police arrested Wolfgang Müller, Hansjörg Ostermayer, and the 11 other protestors, but they were then released to await their trials approximately nine months later.

Since some of these demonstrators were under the age of 21, their first trial was held in a Juvenile Court [*Jugendschöffengericht*] in the town of Reutlingen at the foot of the high Swabian plateau. Here something happened that was rather unusual—but not completely unknown—in cases of this kind. After an emotional hearing before a packed courtroom,[67] the defendants were acquitted.

[66] It may be worth noting at this point that the German judiciary is composed of five separate systems of courts. The largest and most important of these systems is composed of the "ordinary" civil and criminal courts—the courts whose opinions we will be examining in this chapter. In addition, there are separate court systems for administrative law, employment law, social security law, and tax law. In addition to these parallel systems—and clearly set apart from them—is the Federal Constitutional Court, whose jurisdiction is limited principally to the decision of constitutional questions (see Chapter 3). Moreover, most states also have state constitutional courts devoted primarily to the decision of state constitutional questions. Conversely, the court systems of the "ordinary" law are not authorized to decide the constitutionality of federal or state statutes.

[67] *Südwest Presse-Schwäbisches Tagblatt*, 3 April 1982.

What sort of court was it that acquitted Müller, Ostermayer, and the other protestors? To address this question, let us step back for a moment and examine some of the salient characteristics of German and continental criminal procedure in general. At the outset, we must understand that criminal procedure in most continental legal systems is quite different from that familiar in the Anglo-American world. To an English or American observer, perhaps the most striking difference is that criminal trials in Germany are not conducted before a separate jury of 12 (or sometimes six) citizens who decide on guilt or innocence—after hearing the judge's instructions on the applicable legal principles. Rather, most of the cases that we will be examining in this book were either tried before a single judge, or by a panel composed of a single judge and two "lay judges" or *Schöffen*.[68]

The "lay judge" is a common figure in German criminal trials and on the European continent in general. Unlike Anglo-American jurors who are selected for a single trial or a similar short period, the German *Schöffen* are appointed by local governmental units for four-year terms. Although they are chosen from the general population, their selection may sometimes reflect the influence of the local political parties.[69] The judges and the *Schöffen* vote together on the question of innocence or guilt and on the appropriate penalty (if any) in a unified process of deliberation: each member has one vote, and a two-thirds vote is necessary for conviction.[70] In this way there is an admixture of popular participation in many criminal trials, without the full institutional complexities of the Anglo-American jury.[71]

Moreover, the continental trial does not proceed in the "adversarial" method of Anglo-American courts, with evidence being elicited from witnesses through questioning by lawyers. Instead, a

68 In one instance, we will also see that the case was tried by three judges sitting together with two lay judges or *Schöffen*.

69 For discussion of the process of selecting the lay judges, see Langbein, "Mixed Court and Jury Court: Could the Continental Alternative Fill the American Need?", 1981 *American Bar Foundation Research Journal* (ABFRJ) 195, 206–8.

70 Strafprozeßordnung (StPO) §263. The Strafprozeßordnung is the German Code of Criminal Procedure, which is the procedural counterpart of the German Criminal Code (StGB). The Criminal Code sets forth the substantive definitions of criminal offenses, while the Code of Criminal Procedure contains the procedural rules for carrying out a criminal prosecution and trial.

71 Indeed, this procedure is the residue of experiments with an English-style jury system that spread from France into Germany after the French Revolution. Langbein, 1981 ABFRJ, 197–98.

"presiding judge" generally asks the questions, based on a file or dossier prepared in advance by the prosecution and the police. Accordingly—although they can participate in cross-examination and deliver a final statement—the lawyers ordinarily play a rather passive role at trial. Further, in another striking contrast with Anglo-American procedure, the defendant or defendants generally testify at the very beginning of the trial; moreover, the defendant may personally participate in questioning witnesses during the course of the proceeding.[72]

Finally, it should be noted that most German judges—indeed, continental judges in general—differ significantly from Anglo-American judges in education, training and experience. Instead of being appointed or elected to judicial office after a substantial legal career—as in the Anglo-American world—the German judges are career officers selected principally by competitive examination at the conclusion of their legal training. A young judge may then advance through the judicial ranks, subject to careful review and evaluation by senior judges and by the state or federal Ministries of Justice.[73] Accordingly, the judicial office in Germany has distinct bureaucratic

[72] Langbein, *Comparative Criminal Procedure*, 65. For a classic account of German criminal trials by an English observer, see Sybille Bedford, *The Faces of Justice: A Traveller's Report*, 101–201 (New York: Simon & Schuster 1961). For a more recent critical report, see Fletcher, "A Trial in Germany," 18 *Criminal Justice Ethics* 3 (winter/spring 1999). For a famous author's detailed description of a German criminal trial in a satirical novel, see Heinrich Böll, *Ende einer Dienstfahrt* (Köln: Kiepenheuer & Witsch 1966).

The French procedure for criminal trials presents an interesting contrast to both the German and American systems. For illuminating analyses of French criminal trials—conducted before three judges and nine jurors, who deliberate together with equal votes and the requirement of a two-thirds vote for conviction—see McKillop, "Anatomy of a French Murder Case," 45 *American Journal of Comparative Law* 527 (1997); Renée Lettow Lerner, "The Intersection of Two Systems: An American on Trial for an American Murder in the French *Cour d'Assises*," 2001 *University of Illinois Law Review* 791. On French criminal procedure, see generally Frase, 78 *California Law Review* 542.

Although a juvenile court in the United States may have certain features that more closely resemble the continental system—for example, there is ordinarily no jury in American juvenile proceedings—the features of the German legal system outlined above are generally present both in juvenile and adult trials. Indeed, the juvenile courts in this case in effect treated the defendants as adults. See LG Tübingen, Judgment of 6 September 1982, II Ns 62/82 [LG Tübingen, 6 September 1982], 11.

[73] See Meador, "German Appellate Judges: Career Patterns and American–English Comparisons," 67 *Judicature* 16 (1983); Langbein, *Comparative Criminal Procedure*, 59–60.

qualities which may result in more focused and perhaps less flexible views on the law. That is, at least, the consensus of several observers.[74]

In Reutlingen, the protestors' case was heard by a single judge and two jurors or *Schöffen*. Although it might be surmised that the *Schöffen* are often compliant and follow the wishes of the professional judge,[75] such a relationship of subordination evidently did not prevail in the case of Müller, Ostermayer, and the other Großengstingen demonstrators. Rather in this case, the two *Schöffen* apparently outvoted the professional judge—in any case the Court found the protestors innocent, presumably on the grounds that their conduct was not "reprehensible" under §240(II).[76] Accordingly, the defendants were acquitted in the first trial court.

If this had been an ordinary trial court in the United States this acquittal would almost certainly have ended the matter. The constitutional right against double jeopardy, contained in the Fifth Amendment of the American Constitution, guarantees that a person will not be tried twice for the same offense. In the interpretation of the American Supreme Court, this provision prohibits the prosecution from appealing an acquittal in a criminal case. Only the defendant may appeal from a criminal judgment—in the event of a conviction.[77]

[74] See, e.g., Clark, "The Selection and Accountability of Judges in West Germany: Implementation of a *Rechtsstaat*," 61 *Southern California Law Review* 1795, 1820 (1988).

[75] See, e.g., Dubber, 49 *Stanford Law Review*, 565, 581–91; Casper and Zeisel, "Lay Judges in the German Criminal Courts", 1 *Journal of Legal Studies* 135 (1972).

[76] Counsel for the defendants believed that the two lay judges favored acquittal and outvoted the single professional judge. Interview with Karl Joachim Hemeyer, Tübingen/Mutlangen, 24 September 1999. This view was also held by others in the peace movement. See Volker Nick *et al.*, *Mutlangen 1983–1987: Die Stationierung der Pershing II und die Kampagne Ziviler Ungehorsam bis zur Abrüstung*, 197 (Mutlangen 1993). The precise grounds of acquittal were not clearly stated in the judgment.

[77] It has been clear since the 1960s that the United States Constitution prohibits the prosecution from appealing (or otherwise challenging) a judgment of acquittal in either a state or a federal criminal case. *Fong Foo v. United States*, 369 U.S. 141 (1962); *Benton v. Maryland*, 395 U.S. 784 (1969). The Supreme Court has rejected contrary views on this question, endorsed by eminent American judges in an earlier period. See *Kepner v. United States*, 195 U.S. 100, 134–37 (1904) (Holmes, J., dissenting); *Palko v. Connecticut*, 302 U.S. 319 (1937) (Cardozo, J.). The American prohibition of double jeopardy applies to juvenile trials as well, although its rigor has been relaxed somewhat within the juvenile court system. *Breed v. Jones*, 421 U.S. 519, 534–35 (1975); *Swisher v. Brady*, 438 U.S. 204 (1978).

Germany also has a constitutional right against double jeopardy. Article 103(3) of the German Basic Law declares that no one should be punished twice for the same offense. Although the text of this provision only forbids double *penalties*, it is generally understood that the provision also prohibits a second trial after a defendant has been acquitted.[78] But, in contrast with the rule in the United States, the prosecution in Germany *is* entitled to appeal a criminal acquittal to a higher court. It is only after all such appeals have been exhausted—and the defendant has been "finally" acquitted—that a defendant secures the right not to be tried again for the same offense.[79]

In sum, it appears that the German system has adopted the view that a single judicial case, including all appeals on both sides and resulting new trials, constitutes only one "jeopardy"—a view that was once put forth in the United States by Justice Holmes in a dissenting opinion.[80] In any event, the prosecution followed this procedure and appealed the acquittal in the cases of Müller, Ostermayer, and the other defendants in the Großengstingen chain demonstration case.

Following the acquittal in the Juvenile Court in Reutlingen, therefore, the prosecution appealed to the juvenile section of the State Court (*Landgericht*), which was located in Tübingen, an ancient university town not far from Reutlingen. This appeal took the form of what the German law calls a "*Berufung*"—a procedure in which the higher court retries the entire case and makes a new decision on all legal and factual issues.[81] In the Tübingen State Court, a tribunal of greater status than the court in Reutlingen, the

[78] 3 Ingo von Münch (ed.), *Grundgesetz-Kommentar*, 685 (Munich: Beck, 2nd edn 1983); Theodor Maunz, Günter Dürig *et al.*, *Grundgesetz-Kommentar* Art. 103 (3) Nr. 126 (Munich: Beck) (Dürig, 1960).

[79] Indeed, even after such a "final" acquittal, it is possible that—in relatively rare instances—a defendant's case could be reopened in the event of certain types of newly discovered evidence. StPO §362.

[80] *Kepner v. United States*, 195 U.S. 100, 134–37 (1904). For discussion, see Langbein, *Comparative Criminal Procedure*, 84–86. The German position on this question seems to accord with the general view on the continent. See Damaška, 84 *Yale Law Journal*, 491.

[81] StPO §§312–332. See generally Nigel G. Foster, *German Legal System and Laws*, 225–26 (London: Blackstone, 2nd edn 1996); Werner F. Ebke and Matthew W. Finkin, *Introduction to German Law*, 443 (The Hague: Kluwer 1996); Langbein, *Comparative Criminal Procedure*, 82–84. In the *Berufung* procedure, witnesses may be heard again and new evidence introduced. StPO §323.

*Berufung* procedure was heard by a panel of three judges and two *Schöffen*.[82]

At the conclusion of this retrial, the State Court found the protestors guilty and reversed the earlier acquittal.[83] According to the Court, when the defendants chained themselves together and locked the chain to a post, they exercised "psychological force" (*psychisch ausgeübte Gewalt*) against the German army drivers who had to go out of their way to reach a side door of the Eberhard Finckh Barracks.[84] Moreover, the Court declared, the constitutional right of freedom of assembly did not protect persons who intentionally direct force against others.[85]

The Court also found that the protestors' exercise of "force" was "reprehensible" under §240(II). Of course the protestors' goal—to seek new recruits who would help promote worldwide disarmament—was "worthy of respect and not reprehensible." But the use of a blockade to further that end was not justified, because the goals could have been achieved by less disruptive means. Yet, although the protestors were found guilty, the Court considered their engagement for world peace as a mitigating factor in determining their punishment, and the protestors received fines ranging from 300 to 600 German Marks.

These fines—as well as the other fines levied in the sit-down cases—were determined by an ingenious system, based on a Scandinavian model, that had been introduced in the 1975 revision of the German Penal Code. In this system, the judge imposes a fine of a certain numbers of "days" measured by the severity of the offense, in light of relevant aggravating and mitigating factors. The total fine is then calculated by multiplying the number of "days" by the amount of the defendant's daily earnings (or the amount that the defendant could earn if employed at his or her level of occupational skill). In this way, individual fines are calculated in part according to a defendant's income and ability to pay.[86]

As their next and final step in the criminal court system, Müller and Ostermayer appealed to the State Appellate Court

[82] This expanded court traditionally heard *Berufung* proceedings in some cases, but it has subsequently been abolished for appeals of lesser offenses such as *Nötigung*.

[83] LG Tübingen, 6 September 1982.

[84] Ibid., 9–10.

[85] Ibid., 10.

[86] See StGB §§40, 43; Ebke and Finkin, 406–7. A similar system is also found in the French Penal Code of 1994. See Tomlinson, Introduction, in *The French Penal Code of 1994*, 12 and n.43.

(*Oberlandesgericht*) in Stuttgart, the capital of the state of Baden-Württemberg. This was an appeal on questions of law alone, a procedure known in Germany as "Revision."[87] In a summary order, however, the appellate court rejected the defendants' claims.

At this point, then, the defendants' conviction was final in the criminal court system, and payment of their fines was due to the state. On point of principle, however, Müller refused to pay his fine. The Criminal Code provides that, in case of failure to pay, the defendant's fine will be converted into a number of days of imprisonment equal to the number of the days upon which the fine was calculated. The result was that Müller was required to spend five days in jail.[88]

## Großengstingen—Beuter, Braig and the Mochs

At the end of Chapter 1, we also saw that Gunhild Beuter, Wilfried Braig, and Eva-Maria and Thomas Moch were arrested after their sit-down demonstration in Großengstingen late in the afternoon of 9 May 1983. A few weeks later these four protestors received a "penal order" (*Strafbefehl*)—a judgment issued by the prosecutor in Tübingen, and signed by a judge, finding the defendants guilty of *Nötigung* and imposing a fine. If the protestors had not responded within a specified period, the result would have been a summary criminal conviction for each defendant. But the protestors did file an objection, and so the case went to trial.[89]

[87] StPO §§333–58. On this procedure see generally Langbein, *Comparative Criminal Procedure*, 83–84; Merryman, 41.

[88] Interview with Wolfgang Müller-Breuer, Leichlingen, 24 July 2002.

[89] Prosecutions for lesser criminal offenses are often commenced by penal order in Germany, and this summary criminal process was employed in many of the sit-down demonstration cases—although the protestors generally contested the orders, as did Beuter, Braig, and the Mochs. Interview with prosecutor Richard Hörz, Ellwangen, 24 July 2003. On "penal orders" see generally StPO §§ 407–11; Dubber, 49 *Stanford Law Review*, 559–60; Felstiner, "Plea Contracts in West Germany," 13 *Law & Society Review* 309 (winter 1979); cf. Frase, 78 *California Law Review*, 645–47 (penal orders in France).

The possible advantage of a penal order for a defendant is that the maximum penalties are limited, and the defendant can avoid the cost, uncertainty and publicity of trial. Accordingly, the uncontested penal order is rather like the American guilty plea—which is otherwise unavailable in Germany. Cf. Langbein, *Comparative Criminal Procedure*, 96–98. The German penal order was challenged as violating the right to a hearing contained in Article 6 of the European Convention of Human Rights, but the procedure was upheld by the European Court of Human

Accordingly, in October 1984, these four protestors found themselves before the criminal trial court (*Amtsgericht*) in Münsingen—as had hundreds of Großengstingen sit-down demonstrators before them. Indeed, because of its jurisdiction over the adjacent area of Großengstingen, the local court in this tiny town on the high Swabian plateau had become known throughout Germany as the location of the first long series of these *Nötigung* trials. Each of these trials, more than 300 in all, was held before the sole criminal court judge in Münsingen—Judge Thomas Rainer.[90]

When the four protestors arrived at the court on the first day of trial, everything seemed calm. But as the trial went on and achieved a degree of notoriety, police began to surround the building, and officers were stationed in the courtroom—out of fear that these controversial trials could give rise to disruptions.[91] The courtroom was full.

Although the *Nötigung* cases were criminal prosecutions, many defendants in these trials did not have lawyers to represent them. The rules applicable to the lowest German criminal court—the *Amtsgericht*—do not generally require that defendants be represented by counsel.[92] Moreover, there is no constitutional rule that would require the state to provide counsel for indigent defendants in these courts.

Beuter, Braig, and the Mochs were impecunious university students, and they may well not have been able to pay a lawyer.[93] Moreover, a German regulation, adopted a few years earlier in reaction to claimed abuses by lawyers in certain terrorist trials, strengthened a rule prohibiting a lawyer from representing more than one person in a group that allegedly had acted together.[94] But, for this purpose, all persons who blockaded a particular site in a single day were

Rights. *Hennings v. Germany*, European Court of Human Rights, Judgment of 16 December 1992, No. 68/1991/320/392.

For more serious offenses in Germany, prosecution is commenced when the prosecutor files a "complaint" (*Anklage*), a formal charging document. See Langbein, *Comparative Criminal Procedure*, 8–10.

90 See *Verwerflich*?, 12; Interview with Judge Thomas Rainer, Münsingen, 8 July 2004.

91 Interview with Hanns-Michael Langner and Siegfried Nold, Tübingen, 24 March 2004; Interview with Wilfried Braig, Tübingen, 25 July 2002.

92 See Frase and Weigend, "German Criminal Justice as a Guide to American Law Reform: Similar Problems, Better Solutions?," 18 *Boston College International and Comparative Law Review* 317, 324 (1995).

93 Interview with Wilfried Braig, Tübingen.

94 StPO §146; see Uwe Wesel, *Die verspielte Revolution: 1968 und die Folgen*, 275 (Munich: Blessing 2002).

considered to have been acting together. Therefore, each defendant would require a separate lawyer, and it was most unlikely that enough willing lawyers could be found to fill this need.[95]

At Tübingen University, however, one of Gunhild Beuter's housemates was Siegfried Nold, a law student who was sympathetic to the peace movement. Accordingly Nold, together with his friend Hanns-Michael Langner, agreed to act for two of the defendants. But at the time of the trial in Münsingen, Nold and Langner were not yet full-fledged lawyers. Rather they were so-called *Referendare*: they had finished their academic law courses and passed their "First State Examinations," but they were still engaged in the period of practical training that was required before they could take the "Second State Examination" and become fully qualified jurists.[96] Because Nold and Langner were still in this preparatory stage, Judge Thomas Rainer of the Münsingen Court admitted them specially to act in these cases only.

In previous sit-down cases, lawyers had frequently adopted a strategy of repeating arguments that made a certain political point but that had proven unsuccessful in court. For example counsel asserted that protestors should be acquitted because the stationing of the nuclear missiles in Germany was unconstitutional. These arguments were quickly rejected and the defendants, with few exceptions, were speedily convicted.

But probably because Nold and Langner came to these cases with a fresh view, they adopted a different strategy and made novel—although perhaps equally quixotic—arguments. For example, they

[95] Interview with Hanns-Michael Langner, Horb, 6–7 January 2000.

[96] As in most countries of the world, legal education in Germany is an undergraduate study. (The United States is the major exception to this rule.) After a period of academic work that can last from three to five years, or sometimes even longer, an aspiring law student must take an examination that is prepared by the state—and not by the university ("First State Examination"). If successful, the candidate becomes known as a *Referendar* and pursues several periods of practical training—covering a total of approximately two-and-a-half years—in the office of a prosecutor, a judge, or a private practitioner, among other possibilities. Then, upon the passage of a "Second State Examination," the candidate becomes a "full jurist" capable of entering legal practice or becoming a prosecutor or a judge. Candidates may often reach 30 years of age (or more) before this long process is completed. See, e.g., Brunnée, "The Reform of Legal Education in Germany: The Never-ending Story and European Integration," 42 *Journal of Legal Education* 399 (1992); Reimann, "Legal Education in the United States and in Germany: Lessons for Korea?," 41 *Seoul Law Journal* 293 (2000).

argued that the determination of whether the blockades were "reprehensible" under §240(II) required an assessment of the views of society on this question: therefore, they maintained, the courts must commission public opinion polls to guide them in deciding this issue.[97] The defendants also sought to recuse Judge Rainer for bias—on the grounds that he had uniformly convicted defendants in the past (in an "assembly-line" manner) on evidence similar to the evidence presented in this case.[98] One of counsel's motions apparently so perplexed Judge Rainer that he suspended proceedings for a week in order to consider the arguments—before he denied the motion.

By the beginning of an extraordinary fourth day of trial, Judge Rainer, who was perhaps exhausted by the great flood of *Nötigung* cases, apparently tired of the novel arguments of these earnest *Referendare*. In a startling move, Rainer withdrew permission for Nold and Langner to appear as advocates, claiming that they had delayed the proceedings through unjustified motions and were, at present, incapable of presenting a defense according to the rules.[99]

This abrupt action naturally evoked considerable anxiety on the part of the defendants, who were now completely without legal representation—although Nold and Langner continued to sit in the courtroom as spectators. The defendants requested time to find new counsel, but this motion was denied. The defendants then asked the court to appoint counsel for them, but this motion was also denied, on the grounds that they had had a year to prepare for the case and could have understood the issues through newspaper accounts.[100] The four protestors were accordingly required to proceed without counsel.[101]

[97] Interview with Hanns-Michael Langner, Horb.

[98] Interview with Wilfried Braig, Tübingen.

[99] *Schwäbisches Tagblatt*, 10 November 1984; Amtsgericht Münsingen, Protokoll über die Hauptverhandlung in öffentlicher Sitzung, 2 Cs 413–416/83, 9 November 1984, 2 [Münsingen Protocol].

[100] *Schwäbisches Tagblatt*, 10 November 1984; Münsingen Protocol, 9 November 1984, 2–4.

[101] In an American criminal trial, the sudden removal of counsel would most likely result in a mistrial or—at the very least—a continuance to allow the defendants to seek new counsel. On the other hand, the current doctrine of the Supreme Court might not require that the state provide counsel for defendants who—like these four protestors—were ultimately sentenced to pay a fine rather than serve a prison sentence. *Alabama v. Shelton*, 535 U.S. 654 (2002); *Scott v. Illinois*, 440 U.S. 367 (1979); *Argersinger v. Hamlin*, 407 U.S. 25 (1972). The judge's willingness to proceed immediately in this case without defense counsel may reflect, among other things, the generally less important position of lawyers in continental criminal trials.

In a closing argument, the defendant Thomas Moch noted that, as a medical student, he viewed the blockades as a form of "preventive medicine" against the medical emergency of atomic war. In case of such an emergency, Moch continued, all of "your moral values" that are being protected by atomic weapons "would go to the devil!" Moch also declared that people must fight for freedom rather than beg for it.[102]

Thereafter, the trial was swiftly concluded. The defendants were convicted of *Nötigung* and each was sentenced to pay a fine of between 225 and 375 Marks. In his opinion Judge Rainer found that the defendants had exercised "irresistible psychic compulsion" against the occupants of the army truck that had halted before their blockade. This use of "force" under §240(I) was also "reprehensible" under §240(II): if the defendants' message had failed to win adherents, "this failure does not justify seeking to attract the desired attention through criminal acts."[103]

The next step in the process was an appeal to the State Court (*Landgericht*) in Tübingen. As in the case of Müller and Ostermayer, this first appeal took the form of a "*Berufung*" under German law—a proceeding in which the higher court hears the evidence again and makes a new decision on both facts and law. This appeal was heard more than two years after the defendants' convictions in Münsingen.[104]

Again, two of the defendants were represented by Hanns-Michael Langner and Siegfried Nold—now, after two years, appearing as full-fledged lawyers.[105] At this trial—as in Münsingen—the prosecution was somewhat embarrassed by its inability to find the German army truck driver who had been "coerced" to come to a stop by the

102 *Schwäbisches Tagblatt*, 10 November 1984; Reutlinger General-Anzeiger, 12 November 1984.

103 Amtsgericht Münsingen, Judgment of 9 November 1984, 2 Cs 413–416/83.

104 This substantial delay resulted, at least in part, from the wish of the judge in Tübingen to wait for a pending decision of the Federal Constitutional Court. In this decision—as we will see in Chapter 4—the Court found that all factors and circumstances must be taken into account in order to determine whether an act is "reprehensible" under §240(II) StGB. Interview with Judge Ernst-Günther Grebe, Tübingen, 12 April 2000.

105 In conformity with the rule prohibiting representation of multiple defendants, Nold represented Gunhild Beuter, and Langner represented Eva Moch. Defendants Thomas Moch and Wilfried Braig were, therefore, without formal representation.

defendants' blockade in 1983.[106] But the prosecution argued that the absence of this witness did not really matter because the driver had been accompanied by his superior and it was this superior's "will" that had actually been interfered with by the blockade.

In their statements before the court, Eva Moch and Gunhild Beuter emphasized the sense of hopelessness that they felt in confronting the nuclear missiles. Trained as a family therapist, Ms. Beuter also noted that the anxiety produced by the missiles had a profound effect on children. Wilfried Braig recalled conversations in which his father discussed his participation in World War II. Braig remarked that his father "could not explain his participation to me. . . . The majority decision of that period is now considered reprehensible. It is precisely that [fact] that gives me a right to resistance now." Moreover, because of a period of military service, "I know about the senselessness of atomic weapons. Therefore I felt like a small wheel in a machine—and was also trained that way. But I did not want to give in to that anymore." Again drawing on his role as a physician, Thomas Moch emphasized that atomic war would mean the "total collapse of all social and societal infrastructure within hours."[107]

Interestingly, in this *Berufung* procedure in Tübingen—as in the first trial of Müller and Ostermayer in Reutlingen—the defendants were acquitted by a court composed of one judge and two lay judges (*Schöffen*). According to a newspaper account, this was the first acquittal in 450 *Nötigung* cases in Tübingen.[108]

In a nuanced opinion, Judge Ernst-Günther Grebe first found that the defendants had exercised "force" under §240(I). Employing the approved "spiritualized" or "de-materialized" concept of force, Grebe noted that producing a "psychic inhibition" can be as effective as bodily compulsion—as the defendants had indeed intended.[109]

On the other hand, Judge Grebe found that the four defendants had not acted "reprehensibly" under §240(II). Emphasizing that this determination required a balancing of all of the factors, Grebe noted that the defendants had participated in one short blockade, involving only a small group of protestors. Moreover, the blockade had been

[106] See, e.g., Landgericht Tübingen, Judgment of 16 February 1987, Gesch.-Nr. 2 Ns 27/85 u.a. [Grebe Opinion], 12–13.

[107] The material in this paragraph is drawn from Hanns-Michael Langner, summary of trial in LG Tübingen, 6 February 1987, 7–11.

[108] *Die Tageszeitung* (taz), 18 February 1987.

[109] Grebe Opinion, 14–15.

announced in advance, so that officials could have opened alternative routes of access. The importance of these factors was made clear in a companion case in which the same court convicted a separate defendant, Michael Sonne, because he had participated in three blockades in a two-hour period, with a larger number of protestors. Moreover, Sonne's blockades had not been announced in advance.[110]

The prosecution immediately appealed this acquittal to the State Appellate Court (OLG) in Stuttgart in a "Revision" procedure which —as we have seen—involves review of questions of law only.[111] But in Stuttgart there was an unexpected development. The OLG noticed that Judge Grebe's opinion had also taken into account the protestors' "ultimate goals", for the purpose of showing that their actions were not reprehensible because they were "unselfish and directed solely to the welfare of the entire populace."[112]

Rejecting this approach, the OLG reversed the acquittals. The Court suggested that, if the motives or ultimate goals of the defendants could be taken into account, the multiplicity of such possible factors might make §240 unconstitutionally vague.[113] On the question of whether the defendants' actions were "reprehensible," the court also stated:

> Whoever restricts the freedom of action of another citizen, in order to inform the public about his political views, quite intentionally makes these citizens into a mere tool, into an object of his action. Accordingly, he shows contempt for their human dignity. Intolerance that finds its expression in the negation of the freedom of the will of other citizens should be [considered to be the sort of] illegality that is worthy of criminal punishment, and not simply a violation of administrative law.[114]

The OLG acknowledged, however, that other State Appellate Courts—from Cologne, Düsseldorf, and Zweibrücken—had come to a different conclusion on the question of whether the protestors' ultimate goals could be taken into account.[115] Because there was a

110 Grebe Opinion, 16–21.
111 OLG Stuttgart, Judgment of 17 December 1987, 4 Ss 361/87.
112 Ibid., 6; see Grebe Opinion, 17.
113 OLG Stuttgart, Judgment of 17 December 1987, 10.
114 Ibid.
115 Ibid., 15; see, e.g., OLG Köln, Judgment of 22 July 1986; 1986 NJW, 2443.

division of opinion among the State Appellate Courts, the OLG was required to invoke a special procedure and seek the opinion of the Federal Supreme Court (BGH)—the highest criminal court—on this issue.[116]

Accordingly, the BGH was called upon to decide whether, as a matter of law, the protestors' "ultimate goal" could be taken into account in reaching a decision on the "reprehensible" nature of the defendants' action under §240(II). It was in this case—as we have seen—that the BGH found that the "ultimate goal" could *not* be taken into account in determining whether the blockade was "reprehensible," although it *could* be taken into account in deciding the severity of a defendant's punishment.[117]

When the OLG Stuttgart received this opinion from the BGH, it reversed Judge Grebe's opinion of acquittal and returned the case, for a new trial, to a different panel of the State Court in Tübingen.[118] This time, therefore, the case was not to be heard by Judge Grebe, but rather by Judge Hans Jürgen Freuer of the Tübingen State Court.

When the trial before Judge Freuer was concluded, the panel—again consisting of one professional judge and two lay judges or *Schöffen*—retired to an adjacent room to consider its decision. Thereafter, the defendants and their lawyers reported that they could hear sustained loud argument from behind the closed doors—unusual conduct that seemed to suggest heated disagreement between the *Schöffen* and the judge on the proper disposition of the case. According to one of the defendants, when the judge and the *Schöffen* returned to the courtroom, one of the *Schöffen* was crying.[119]

In the end, the four defendants were convicted. Indeed, they were not only found guilty of *Nötigung*, as a result of their own sit-down demonstration; they were also convicted of complicity with other sit-down protestors of the same day, because the four defendants had

[116] See § 121(2) *Gerichtsverfassungsgesetz* (GVG). The GVG is the federal statute that establishes the German court system (except for the Federal Constitutional Court) and regulates the jurisdiction of the various courts. According to § 121(2), if a State Appellate Court (OLG) wishes to "deviate" from a decision handed down by another OLG, it must transmit the matter to the BGH for final determination.

[117] 35 BGHSt, 270 (1988); see above, pp. 81–83.

[118] OLG Stuttgart, Judgment of 23 June 1988, 4 Ss 361/87.

[119] Interview with Wilfried Braig, Tübingen; see also Interview with Hanns-Michael Langner and Siegfried Nold, Tübingen, 24 March 2004.

stood at the side of the road to lend moral support to the other demonstrators.[120]

On the other hand—in what appeared to be the sign of a compromise—the fine was set at the lowest possible amount, and the state was required to pay a portion of the costs. Interestingly, the Court also remarked that it had been willing to dismiss the action because it had been pending for such a long time. But the prosecutor had been unwilling to give the required approval.[121]

In his opinion, Judge Freuer first found that the defendants were exercising the requisite "force." The Court then proceeded to a balancing of all relevant factors—except the "long-term goals" of the protestors—to determine whether the action was "reprehensible." The Court found that the action was reprehensible because it had lasted for an entire day, there had been several obstructions of ingress and egress, and substantial police action had been necessary to clear the protestors from the street. Moreover, because the driver and his accompanying officer obviously had no influence on the stationing of the Lance missiles at Großenstingen, the protestors were "consciously" using the soldiers as "mere tools . . . in order to inform the public about their political views." That type of activity constitutes a "disregard of the human dignity of the affected soldiers."[122]

The OLG Stuttgart summarily affirmed the conviction,[123] and the case—after precisely six years had elapsed from the date of the defendants' protest at Großengstingen—was ready for a petition to be filed in the Constitutional Court.

## *Mutlangen—Luise Scholl*

About five months after her arrest at the blockade in Mutlangen on 7 February 1984, Luise Scholl appeared before Judge Wolfgang Krumhard in the criminal court (*Amtsgericht*) of Schwäbisch Gmünd. As was true of all judges in the *Amtsgericht*, Judge Krumhard sat alone, without accompanying lay judges.

Encircled by a turreted medieval wall, Schwäbisch Gmünd is a pleasant town located four kilometers from Mutlangen, near the

[120] LG Tübingen, Judgment of 19 October 1988, Gesch.-Nr. 1 (2) Ns. 27–30/85 [Freuer Opinion], 11–12.

[121] Freuer Opinion, 19. See StPO §153a.

[122] Freuer Opinion, 15–16; see also 92 BVerfGE, 1, 6 (1995).

[123] OLG Stuttgart, Judgment of 9 May 1989, 4 Ss 119/89.

edge of the high Swabian plateau. Trials of hundreds of Mutlangen demonstrators took place in the small courthouse of this town, and its judges acquired a certain temporary fame as a result of these events. One of the best known of the judges in Schwäbisch Gmünd was Werner Offenloch whose debate with Walter Jens on civil disobedience was discussed in Chapter 1.

In her trial before Judge Krumhard, Luise Scholl was convicted of *Nötigung* in violation of §240 of the Criminal Code. She was sentenced to a fine of 400 Marks (20 days times 20 Marks per day).[124] In his opinion, Judge Krumhard remarked that under §240(I) the use of "force" may arise "through an effect produced without the use of bodily strength—for example through the blocking of a right of way." Moreover, Scholl's blockade was "reprehensible" under §240(II)—apparently because it was part of a systematic series of similar blockades, as the defendant well knew.[125]

124 AG Schwäbisch Gmünd, Judgment of 28 June 1984, 5 Cs 568/84–16.

125 Interestingly, at a somewhat later date—in early 1987—Judge Krumhard had a change of heart on the question of "reprehensible" conduct. After the Constitutional Court emphasized in 1986 that all circumstances must be balanced under §240(II), Judge Krumhard concluded that most sit-down blockades were not "reprehensible," and therefore he began to hand down routine acquittals in these cases. Krumhard noted that thousands of respectable citizens had taken part in the anti-missile demonstrations and that the press was generally favorably disposed toward these protests. Accordingly, the demonstrators' actions no longer met with the general disapproval necessary for a finding that they were "reprehensible" under §240 (II). See Heinrich Hannover, *Die Republik vor Gericht: 1975–1995*, 325–26 (Berlin: Aufbau 1999); Reichert-Hammer, 33. But the five other judges in Schwäbisch Gmünd continued their almost uniform practice of convicting defendants in such cases. According to one official, this lack of uniformity had "a negative effect on the legal consciousness of the populace." *Mendener Zeitung*, 28 February–1 March 1987. In any case, however, these acquittals were subject to reversal upon appeal. Interview with prosecutor Richard Hörz, Ellwangen, 24 July 2003.

In what was to be her third trial before Judge Krumhard—for later sit-down blockades—Luise Scholl was accordingly acquitted because this trial took place in 1987 after Krumhard's "change of heart." But Judge Krumhard's change of heart had not yet occurred when he convicted Scholl in her first trial in 1984 and in a second trial in 1986. *Mendener Zeitung*, 28 February–1 March 1987.

Ultimately, however, Judge Krumhard did not fully persist in his new, more lenient course. In light of the BGH decision of May 1988—which prohibited a judge from taking the "ultimate goals" of the protestors into account in assessing whether a blockade was "reprehensible"—Judge Krumhard again handed down a conviction in a notable demonstration case involving the peace movement theoretician Wolfgang Sternstein. Although a second change of direction would re-establish unity among the judges, Krumhard expressed some uneasiness concerning this conviction. *Rems-Zeitung*, 28 November 1988.

Judge Krumhard also rejected the argument that Scholl's actions were justified as a result of self-defense or "emergency" under sections 32 or 34 of the Criminal Code. In German law—as in the United States—these justifications may include not only protection of oneself, but also emergency action to protect third persons and other public interests.[126] Accordingly, the anti-missile protestors sometimes argued that civil disobedience was necessary in order to combat what they saw as the overwhelming danger of nuclear war. Nonetheless, the court rejected these defenses because, under the German Criminal Code, they provide a justification for a response to a *present* danger only. In Krumhard's view—a view widely held in the literature—any danger posed by the missiles was not a "present" danger because nuclear annihilation was not shown to be imminent; therefore the sit-down protests could not be justified under these provisions.[127]

[126] See generally Eser, "Justification and Excuse", 24 *American Journal of Comparative Law* 621, 631–35 (1976).

[127] For general discussion of this defense in the context of the missile protest cases, see Offenloch, 1988 JZ, 16–17. See also Reichert-Hammer, 161–211; Thomas Laker, *Ziviler Ungehorsam: Geschichte—Begriff—Rechtfertigung*, 228–36 (Baden-Baden: Nomos 1986).

In American law also, the appellate courts have rejected the defense of "necessity" in civil disobedience cases on similar but not always identical grounds. Some cases have indeed denied the defense on the grounds that the feared danger was not "immediate" or "imminent"—as in Luise Scholl's case. See, e.g., *State v. Dorsey*, 118 N.H. 844, 395 A.2d 855 (1978) (occupation of construction site of nuclear power plant at Seabrook); *Commonwealth v. Berrigan*, 509 Pa. 118, 501 A.2d 226 (1985) (trespass in defense plant and destruction of missile components).

Other American courts have held that necessity is not present in civil disobedience cases because the alternative of litigation or legal political protest always remains open. For example, in the case of a protestor who damaged an MX nuclear missile, the Court remarked:

> Those who wish to protest in an unlawful manner frequently are impatient with less visible and more time-consuming alternatives. Their impatience does not constitute the "necessity" that the defense of necessity requires . . . [Indeed, there] "are thousands of opportunities for the propagation of the anti-nuclear message: in the nation's electoral process; by speech on public streets, in parks, in auditoriums . . . to name only a few." . . . The availability of this option prevents [defendant] from raising the necessity defense.

*United States v. Dorrell*, 758 F.2d 427, 431–32 (9 Cir. 1985); see also *United States v. Kabat*, 797 F.2d 580, 590–92 (8 Cir. 1986).

In the MX protest case, the Court also noted that there was no reasonable likelihood that the acts of civil disobedience would bring about the intended results, including a "reduction in the risk of nuclear war." Dorrell, 758 F.2d,

Luise Scholl—who, as we have seen, was a prolific correspondent on these issues—responded with a letter to Judge Krumhard, vigorously disputing the judge's conclusion that there was no question of imminent emergency or self-defense. Among other things, her letter vividly portrayed the fears of many of the demonstrators. Scholl wrote:

> It is the greatest case of self-defense that has ever existed, because my life—and all life—is threatened to the greatest degree. It is a lie that there is no present danger. There are already enough persons who have been killed or contaminated, contamination of the earth and the sea, enough children born dead—through atomic testing. The rockets are constantly being driven here and there through towns and villages. If there is a short circuit . . . there will be thousands of people killed. And then the Court says that there was no present danger? . . . I assume that you know that the technology is not 100 per cent certain, that there

433–34; see also *United States v. May*, 622 F.2d 1000, 1008 (9 Cir. 1980); Kabat, 797 F.2d at 592. More generally, the Court remarked:

> To accept [the defendant's] position would amount to recognizing that an individual may assert a defense to criminal charges whenever he or she disagrees with a result reached by the political process. [But the necessity defense was not designed to] excuse criminal activity intended to express the protestor's disagreement with positions reached by the lawmaking branches of the government. To [find] otherwise would . . . force the courts to choose among causes they should make legitimate by extending the defense of necessity.

Dorrell, 758 F.2d at 432. See also *United States v. Schoon*, 971 F.2d 193 (9 Cir. 1991) (excluding necessity defense, as a matter of law, in many civil disobedience cases).

Finally, defendants in American civil disobedience cases have sometimes raised defenses that are based on treaties or on the general principles of international law. But, as with the claims of necessity, these international law defenses have not fared well in the appellate courts. May, 622 F.2d at 1009–10; Kabat, 797 F.2d at 590; *State v. Marley*, 54 Hawaii 450, 467–69, 473–77 (1973).

In contrast with the appellate decisions, however, juries in American trial courts have sometimes acquitted defendants who have argued that their acts of civil disobedience were impelled by "necessity." But these decisions are ordinarily not included in the official case reports, and they have "little precedential value." Lippman, "Reflections on Non-Violent Resistance and the Necessity Defense," 11 *Houston Journal of International Law* 277, 297 (1989); Levitin, "Putting the Government on Trial: The Necessity Defense and Social Change," 33 *Wayne Law Review* 1221, 1222–24 and n.12 (1987).

> are continually short circuits of some sort, that there are continually computer errors of some sort, and that human beings do not act in accordance with reason—otherwise they never would have manufactured weapons, and never such weapons of mass destruction. And then the Court says that there was no present danger?[128]

Scholl's conviction in 1984 was swiftly upheld in a *Berufung* proceeding in the State Court (*Landgericht*) in the town of Ellwangen. A professional judge and two lay judges found that "force" under §240(I) does not require the application of bodily strength; rather, force may arise "from any action that influences the will of an individual and impels that will in a particular direction." The American truck driver had no choice but to follow the will of Scholl and the other persons who blocked the street because, if he had not stopped, he would have made himself criminally liable for "bodily injury or even manslaughter."[129]

The State Court also found that Scholl's actions were "reprehensible" under §240(II). The long-term goal of the demonstrators—the abolition of nuclear missiles—did not justify "participation in a long-lasting blockade that was directed toward significantly impeding and disturbing the service activities of the U.S. Army." Indeed, the victims of the blockade—the truck drivers—could personally have done nothing to assist the defendant in achieving her goal of nuclear disarmament. Moreover, in any requisite weighing of values under §240(II), the defendant's intended goals cannot be taken into account because the Court is not permitted to give preference to particular political views.

The conviction was affirmed, without opinion, by the State Appellate Court (*Oberlandesgericht*) in Stuttgart.[130]

In this way, the cases of our three sets of defendants—Müller and Ostermayer; Beuter, Braig, and the Mochs; and Luise Scholl—came to an end in the German criminal courts. In some cases, the possibility of a further appeal in the highest court for criminal and civil

[128] Letter from Luise Scholl to Judge Krumhard, 5 August 1984.

[129] LG Ellwangen, Judgment of 19 November 1984, NS 260/84–10: 3 KV 177/84, 7.

[130] OLG Stuttgart, Judgment of 18 February 1985, 3 Ss(14) 18/85; referring to its decision of 31 January 1985–3 Ss756/84.

cases—the *Bundesgerichtshof* (BGH) or Federal Supreme Court—would have been possible, but in our three cases there was no such possibility. These cases had been commenced in a lower criminal court, and each defendant had already had a *Berufung* (in the State Court) and a *Revision* (in the State Appellate Court)—all the appeals that German law ordinarily allows.

Accordingly, the lawyers for these convicted defendants came to the end of the line in seeking any possible relief in the "ordinary" German courts. Their single remaining alternative in the German system was to file a Constitutional Complaint in the German court for constitutional matters—the Federal Constitutional Court.

Chapter 3

# The sit-down blockades in the Constitutional Court:

## The Court and the arguments

When the convictions of Müller, Ostermayer, and the other protestors from Mutlangen and Großengstingen were affirmed in the criminal courts, the way was free for their cases to move to the German Constitutional Court. At this point we leave the realm of the "ordinary" criminal process. For in the Constitutional Court, the judges would no longer consider the questions of coercion, force, and "reprehensible" acts as part of the interpretation of the "ordinary" law—the German Criminal Code. Rather, the Court would concentrate on the question of whether punishment of these protestors for *Nötigung* was consistent with the Basic Law (Constitution) of the Federal Republic of Germany.

In other words, at this point the case moved from the general realm of the "ordinary" criminal statutes into the realm of constitutional law—and from the realm of the ordinary criminal court system into the jurisdiction of a separate court for constitutional questions.

### The Federal Constitutional Court

One of the great innovations of the Basic Law of 1949, the Federal Constitutional Court has become a crucial governmental organ of the Federal Republic of Germany.[1] It alone has the authority to find

[1] A recent two-volume collection of essays celebrates the fiftieth anniversary of the founding of the Constitutional Court in 1951. Peter Badura and Horst Dreier (eds), *Festschrift 50 Jahre Bundesverfassungsgericht* (Tübingen: Mohr Siebeck 2001). For systematic commentary on the Court and its procedures, see, e.g., Klaus Schlaich and Stefan Korioth, *Das Bundesverfassungsgericht: Stellung, Verfahren, Entscheidungen* (Munich: Beck, 5th edn 2001). Some recent works by former justices provide

that statutes of Parliament are unconstitutional, and it also plays an important role in drawing the constitutional lines of separation between other organs of government.

With a few exceptions, the jurisdiction of the German Constitutional Court is generally limited to the decision of constitutional issues. In this respect, it is unlike the Supreme Court of the United States which, in addition to its authority to decide constitutional questions, is also the supreme interpreter of federal statutory law—such as federal criminal statutes, the Social Security Act and the Internal Revenue (tax) code. Indeed, the German Constitutional Court is primarily based on a pattern—devised in Austria in the 1920s by the famous legal philosopher Hans Kelsen—which places the Constitutional Court apart from the system of the "ordinary" civil, criminal, and administrative court systems. Another significant forerunner was the German *Staatsgerichtshof* of the Weimar period, a special court that was intended to supervise the allocation of authority among the other governmental units.[2]

The creation of a separate and distinct Constitutional Court was based in part on the fear that the "ordinary" judges would not possess the range of experience and intellectual self-confidence that would be needed to stand up to the other branches of government when necessary. In Germany and other continental countries, the "ordinary" judges have traditionally occupied a position which is viewed as rather closer to that of civil servants than to the more

a unique perspective on the Court and its doctrine. Jutta Limbach, *Das Bundesverfassungsgericht* (Munich: Beck 2001); Jutta Limbach, *"Im Namen des Volkes": Macht und Verantwortung der Richter* (Stuttgart: Deutsche Verlags-Anstalt 1999); Roman Herzog, *Strukturmängel der Verfassung? Erfahrungen mit dem Grundgesetz* (Stuttgart: Deutsche Verlags-Anstalt 2000); Dieter Grimm, *Die Verfassung und die Politik* (Munich: Beck 2001).

For a pioneering work on the Federal Constitutional Court in English, see Donald P. Kommers, *Judicial Politics in West Germany: A Study of the Federal Constitutional Court* (Beverly Hills, CA: Sage 1976). For other standard English sources, see Donald P. Kommers, *The Constitutional Jurisprudence of the Federal Republic of Germany* (Durham, NC: Duke University Press, 2nd edn 1997); David P. Currie, *The Constitution of the Federal Republic of Germany* (Chicago, IL: University of Chicago Press 1994). See also Rinken, "The Federal Constitutional Court and the German Political System," in Ralf Rogowski and Thomas Gawron (eds), *Constitutional Courts in Comparison: The U.S. Supreme Court and the German Federal Constitutional Court* (New York: Berghahn 2002).

2 See Donald Kommers, *The Federal Constitutional Court*, 2 (Washington: American Institute for Contemporary German Studies 1994).

independent position of the Anglo-American judiciary.[3] Even so, federal law requires that a minority of the Constitutional Court judges be drawn from the highest courts of the "ordinary" judiciary; in this way, a certain degree of expertise and background in the "ordinary" law will remain directly available to the Court.[4]

Although the main outlines of the structure and jurisdiction of the Constitutional Court are set forth in the Basic Law,[5] many of the details of the Court's structure, composition, and procedure are actually contained in a Law Concerning the Federal Constitutional Court, enacted by the West German Parliament in 1951 and amended frequently thereafter.[6] In a similar way, the Constitution of the United States contains some general guidelines for the United States Supreme Court, but most of the details of its actual structure and jurisdiction are set forth in congressional legislation.

The judges of the Constitutional Court are appointed for 12-year terms by the Federal Parliament, which consists of the *Bundestag* (the directly elected parliamentary assembly) and the *Bundesrat* (a legislative council composed of representatives of the state governments). Eight of the 16 judges are chosen by the *Bundesrat*, and eight are appointed by a committee of the *Bundestag*. The terms are made non-renewable, to avoid the danger that a judge might be tempted to tailor his or her decisions for the purpose of securing reappointment. This method represents an interesting alternative to the lifetime appointments that are required by the Constitution of the United States for the federal judiciary; and there is currently some debate in the United States over whether a method of non-renewable appointments for a term of years—as in the German system—might have important advantages over the current American method.[7]

The Constitutional Court Act also requires that the judges be

3 See, e.g., John Henry Merryman, *The Civil Law Tradition*, 34–38 (Stanford, CA: Stanford University Press, 2nd edn 1985); cf. Chapter 2 above. In Germany, for example, the "ordinary" judiciary is under the general supervision of the federal and state ministries of justice—organs of the executive branch.

4 Limbach, *Das Bundesverfassungsgericht*, 23.

5 See Arts 93–94, 100 GG.

6 *Gesetz über das Bundesverfassungsgericht*, of 11 August 1993, as amended [BVerfGG]. For convenience this statute will be referred to as the Constitutional Court Act.

7 For a recent contribution to this debate, see Burbank, "Alternative Career Resolution II: Changing the Tenure of Supreme Court Justices," 154 *University of Pennsylvania Law Review* 1511 (2006).

chosen by a special majority of two-thirds of the *Bundesrat* or of the *Bundestag* committee.[8] Because it is unlikely that a political party in Germany will attain such a majority, this method has the effect of requiring that both major parties concur on each appointment. As a result, it is most unlikely that an individual with extreme or aberrational views—either on the left or on the right—will be appointed to the Court. On the other hand, it is inevitable in such a system—as in the quite different system of the United States—that political considerations will play a significant role in the elaborate negotiations surrounding the choice of Constitutional Court judges.[9]

The Constitutional Court sits in two panels or "senates," each of which is composed of eight judges. Cases are allocated to the senates according to their subject matter: roughly speaking, most cases involving issues of Basic Rights are confided to the First Senate, while most issues of federalism and governmental structure fall within the jurisdiction of the Second Senate. Yet, in order to equalize the burden of the caseload, certain areas of individual rights—for example, asylum, immigration, and citizenship cases—have been reallocated to the Second Senate.[10]

As we will see, the presence of an even number of judges in each senate may lead to difficulties due to the possibility of an even split in the Constitutional Court. On the other hand, the presence of an even number of judges in each senate means that (ordinarily) no statute will be declared unconstitutional by a one-vote margin. A more decisive margin of five to three is required, because the Constitutional Court Act makes clear that no statute or governmental action may be found unconstitutional by an equally divided vote.[11] Some German scholars suggest that legislative decisions should not

[8] BVerfGG §§ 6,7.

[9] See Limbach, *Das Bundesverfassungsgericht*, 24–25; Kommers, "Autonomy versus Accountability: The German Judiciary," in Peter H. Russell and David M. O'Brien (eds), *Judicial Independence in the Age of Democracy: Critical Perspectives from around the World*, 148–150 (Charlottesville: University Press of Virginia 2001); Uwe Wesel, *Der Gang nach Karlsruhe. Das Bundesverfassungsgericht in der Geschichte der Bundesrepublik*, 205–10 (Munich: Blessing 2004). For sharp criticism of the political method of choosing the Constitutional Court judges, see Rolf Lamprecht, *Zur Demontage des Bundesverfassungsgerichts*, 189–91 (Baden-Baden: Nomos 1996).

[10] Limbach, *Das Bundesverfassungsgericht*, 20–21. See also Kommers, *Constitutional Jurisprudence*, 16–18.

[11] BVerfGG §15(4).

be invalidated by a one-vote margin, and that avoiding such a possibility is a distinct advantage of this system.[12]

## The Basic Law

The main role of the Constitutional Court is to interpret the Basic Law of the Federal Republic of Germany and to enforce it, when necessary, against statutes of Parliament and acts of the executive and of the "ordinary judiciary." Adopted in 1949, the Basic Law was designed as a liberal western constitution, in reaction to the lawlessness and tyranny of the Nazi regime. It was drafted primarily by German scholars and politicians, but its drafting was initiated, and in some respects influenced, by the United States and the other western occupation powers.

The fundamental concepts and many of the provisions of the Basic Law were drawn from Germany's first republican charter, the Weimar Constitution of 1919. Indeed, in some respects, the Basic Law may be viewed as an attempt to redraft the Weimar Constitution in a way that would eliminate some of the problematic aspects of that document.[13] The Basic Law also drew—often indirectly—on the so-called Pauls Church Constitution of 1849, a document that was adopted by a constituent assembly in Frankfurt in the wake of the Revolution of 1848. The Pauls Church Constitution was drafted with high hopes, but when the revolution failed, this ambitious constitutional proposal never went into effect.

Written to confront modern problems, the Basic Law of 1949 is considerably longer and more detailed than the spare and elegant eighteenth-century Constitution of the United States. Yet many of the problems that the Basic Law was designed to resolve are the familiar issues of liberal constitutionalism. The Basic Law organizes the structures of the German federal government—the Parliament, the executive, and the national courts—allocates authority to these organs, and regulates the relationship among them. Like the United States—but unlike, for example, France—Germany has a *federal* system, possessing not only a national government but also 16 constituent states or *Länder*. Accordingly, the Basic Law also regulates the

[12] See Roellecke, "Bio-Recht oder die Sanftmut von Gesäß-Protestierern," 1995 NJW, 1525, 1526.

[13] See, e.g., Kommers, *Federal Constitutional Court*, 5.

relationship among the *Länder* and between the national government and the states.

In some of its structural sections, the Basic Law sets forth provisions of considerable detail, conferring constitutional status on issues that are regulated only by statute in the United States. For example, the Basic Law contains complex provisions on the distribution of tax revenue among the federal government and the states—provisions that have no counterpart in the United States Constitution.[14] The Basic Law also has provisions that were intended to regulate the circumstances in which German armed forces may be employed.[15]

Pride of place in the Basic Law belongs to a long and sometimes carefully qualified listing of Basic Rights of the individual. Drawn in part from the Weimar Constitution and the Universal Declaration of Human Rights of 1948, this catalogue of guarantees is found at the beginning of the constitution—a decision that was intended to emphasize the primacy of individual rights, in contrast with the massive deprivation of those rights under the Nazis. Many of the Basic Rights have parallels in the Constitution of the United States and in other important human rights instruments. For example, rights of free speech and free press are quite prominent in both constitutions and in the human rights instruments—as are rights of criminal procedure, such as the guarantee against double jeopardy.[16]

Although these Basic Rights apply primarily against the national and state governments, many of the rights may also apply—in a somewhat diluted or "indirect" form—against private individuals and groups.[17] An important provision of the Basic Law also declares that the Federal Republic of Germany is a "social" state, indicating that the government is obligated to provide a certain reasonable level of welfare benefits to its citizens.[18] Although this provision is

[14] See Arts 106, 107 GG; Dam, "The American Fiscal Constitution," 44 *University of Chicago Law Review* 271 (1977); Larsen, "States Federal, Financial, Sovereign and Social. A Critical Inquiry into an Alternative to American Financial Federalism," 47 *American Journal of Comparative Law* 429 (1999). In general, these constitutional provisions are intended to help equalize the income of the states, and therefore the standard of living of their inhabitants.

[15] Arts 87a, 24 (2), 26 GG.

[16] Moreover, the rights set forth in the German Basic Law are similar to some guarantees in the almost contemporaneous European Convention on Human Rights, promulgated in 1950 by the Council of Europe: 312 U.N.T.S., 221.

[17] See generally Quint, "Free Speech and Private Law in German Constitutional Theory", 48 *Maryland Law Review* 247 (1989).

[18] Art. 20(1) GG.

summary in form, it has played a role of some significance in the jurisprudence of the Constitutional Court. As a document whose origins lie in a considerably earlier era, the Constitution of the United States contains no similar rights to social welfare.[19]

In contrast with the Weimar and Pauls Church constitutions, the Basic Law has been a major success: it is highly respected by most citizens and is carefully considered in parliamentary debates and in the course of governmental decision-making. Certainly, the strong interpretative role of the Constitutional Court—giving concrete (and enforceable) meaning to the general phrases of the Basic Law—has contributed significantly to the success of the constitutional document itself.[20]

## Constitutional rights and the sit-down demonstrations: Articles 8 and 103(2)

Of the numerous constitutional guarantees contained in the Basic Law, two are particularly important for our consideration of the cases of the anti-missile blockades. In the Constitutional Court, the protestors argued that these two constitutional provisions invalidated their convictions—even though the convictions had been upheld by appellate courts in the criminal court system.

### *Article 8 GG*

The first of the constitutional provisions invoked by the protestors was Article 8 of the Basic Law, which guarantees the freedom of assembly. This right is essential in the broader structure of freedom of expression and democratic political choice, as it extends the right of a public forum to those who may not have access to the press or television and may have to rely on public association in the streets in order to communicate their views. Indeed, as significant (and sometimes chaotic) political demonstrations have become prominent in

19 Compare Michelman, "Foreword: On Protecting the Poor Through the Fourteenth Amendment," 83 *Harvard Law Review* 7 (1969), with *DeShaney v. Winnebago County Dept. of Social Services*, 489 U.S. 189 (1989).

20 See generally Dieter Grimm, "Das Grundgesetz nach 50 Jahren," in *Die Verfassung und die Politik*, 295–324.

German political life, Article 8 has assumed an increasingly important role.[21]

Indeed, Article 8 has a position of substantially greater independence than the corresponding provision of the American First Amendment, which guarantees "the right of the people peaceably to assemble, and to petition the government for a redress of grievances." In the United States, this specific provision has receded into the background, and issues of political assembly are ordinarily resolved under the general "speech" guarantee of the First Amendment. But Article 8 of the Basic Law retains its own important and distinct role.

Article 8 follows a common pattern—often seen in modern constitutions—in which the first section of a constitutional provision sets forth a broadly stated right, but the second section then authorizes certain (possibly quite substantial) limitations or qualifications of that right.

Article 8 of the Basic Law reads as follows (emphasis added):

(1) All Germans have the right of *peaceful and unarmed* assembly, without a requirement of registration or a requirement that permission be received.
(2) For assemblies *in the open air*, this right may be *limited* by statute or on the basis of a statute.

If the protestors' sit-down demonstrations are viewed as "peaceful and unarmed" assemblies, the protests might potentially enjoy some protection under section 1 of Article 8. Yet the right of assembly "in the open air" has indeed been very significantly "limited" by statute, as contemplated by the second section of Article 8. In 1953, Parliament enacted a comprehensive Assemblies Law (*Versammlungsgesetz*) for this purpose, and central provisions of that statute authorize the police to dissolve certain assemblies which have not been registered in advance (*angemeldet*) or which "directly endanger security or order."[22] It was this provision that authorized the police to arrest

[21] For general discussion of Article 8 of the Basic Law, see, e.g., Hansjörg Reichert-Hammer, *Politische Fernziele und Unrecht*, 135–49 (Berlin: Duncker & Humblot 1991). Quite similar provisions were contained both in the Weimar Constitution of 1919 and in the Pauls Church Constitution of 1849. See WRV Art. 123; Paulskirchenverfassung Art. VIII §161.

[22] *Gesetz über Versammlungen und Aufzüge (Versammlungsgesetz)*, of 24 July 1953, as amended, §§14–15.

the sit-down demonstrators, setting the scene for their prosecution for the criminal offense of *Nötigung*.

Yet, even with such a limiting statute, the Court generally requires that the values of freedom of assembly in Article 8(1) must be weighed against the strength of the limiting factors present in the individual case—in order to determine whether the specific restriction of the freedom of assembly is constitutionally justified. Therefore, some scope remained for constitutional arguments in favor of the sit-down protestors under Article 8.

### *Article 103(2)GG*

The second important constitutional guarantee advanced by counsel for the protestors was Article 103(2)GG. This provision is not found in the listing of Basic Rights at the beginning of the constitution. Rather, like some other important procedural rights, Article 103(2) appears in a later section on the judiciary. Nonetheless, this provision forms a central element of the rule of law and thus represents a crucial constitutional guarantee.[23] A provision of perhaps deceptive brevity, Article 103(2) states in full:

> An act may be punished only if its criminality was determined by statute before the act was committed.

As an aspect of the rule of law, this provision serves two functions. First and most prominently, it prohibits Parliament from enacting what is known as retroactive criminal legislation—that is, a statute which makes an act criminal *after* the act has been committed. As noted in Chapter 2, a rule that would permit retroactive legislation would allow a government to pursue its political opponents by criminalizing their acts after the acts were committed—something that has often occurred in dictatorial regimes. Such a method could terrorize citizens who would never know in advance what acts would

[23] Indeed, this provision, in almost identical words, was contained in the Weimar Constitution, and similar provisions were included in earlier criminal codes in the German states. See WRV Art. 116; Helmken, "Dekorporierung des Gewaltbegriffs versus verfassungsrechtliches Bestimmtheitsgebot," in Freia Anders and Ingrid Gilcher-Holtey (eds), *Herausforderungen des staatlichen Gewaltmonopols: Recht und politisch motivierte Gewalt am Ende des 20. Jahrhunderts*, 143 (Frankfurt/M: Campus 2006).

be criminal.[24] The Constitution of the United States has similar provisions, which prohibit the federal government and the states from enacting *ex post facto* laws or passing legislative judgments of individual criminality, known as bills of attainder.[25]

But Article 103(2)GG has another aspect as well. The requirement that the criminality of the act must be determined "by statute" indicates that the definition of the crime must be established not by the courts but by the legislature, the organ that most directly represents the people. This requirement therefore rejects the possibility of the sort of common law crimes that, until recently, were prevalent in the Anglo-American legal world—and that still exist to some extent in several common law jurisdictions.

Of course, any statutory text set down by the legislature must be interpreted by the courts. But German scholars agree that the principle of the rule of law, as embodied in Article 103(2), prohibits the courts from departing too drastically from the statutory text itself. It was this aspect of Article 103(2) that was most clearly at issue in the sit-down demonstration cases. Counsel for the protestors argued that the criminal courts' extension of the word "force" (*Gewalt*) to cover their passive and completely peaceful conduct went beyond any plausible meaning of the statutory text.[26] In its relationship to the requirement of statutory certainty, this argument bears some similarity to the American constitutional doctrine prohibiting unduly vague statutes, which violate general guarantees of due process of law.[27]

In sum, then, these two provisions of the Basic Law—Article 8, guaranteeing freedom of assembly, and Article 103(2), requiring a clear statutory definition of criminal offenses as an aspect of the rule of law—formed the principal constitutional bases on which the cases of the sit-down protestors were argued in the Constitutional Court.[28]

24 See Quint, "The Border Guard Trials and the East German Past—Seven Arguments," 48 *American Journal of Comparative Law* 541, 561 and n. 53 (2000).

25 U.S. Const. Art. I, §§ 9 and 10.

26 See Chapter 2.

27 See, e.g., *Lanzetta v. New Jersey*, 306 U.S. 451 (1939).

28 Another constitutional provision invoked by the protestors was Article 26 GG, which prohibits preparation or planning of aggressive war—a constitutional incorporation of the doctrine of the Nuremberg Trials. As we saw in Chapter 1, some commentators argued that the NATO Pershing II missiles were in reality "first-strike" weapons, and therefore the stationing of the weapons violated that constitutional prohibition. If the stationing was unconstitutional, the protestors maintained, civil disobedience undertaken in protest would not be illegal. Arguments of this kind were contained in some briefs filed in the Constitutional

The Court confronted these issues in two major decisions—the first in 1986, and the second in 1995. Among the litigants in the 1986 case were two sets of protestors whose cases we have followed through the ordinary courts: Wolfgang Müller and Hansjörg Ostermayer—participants in the 1981 chain demonstration that initiated the anti-missile sit-down protests in Großengstingen—and Luise Scholl who took part in a sit-down demonstration in Mutlangen in 1984. Gunhild Beuter, Wilfried Braig, and Eva and Thomas Moch—whose cases we have also followed—were the litigants in the 1995 decision of the Constitutional Court.

## The 1986 case—the Constitutional Complaints

After the criminal courts had upheld the convictions of Müller, Ostermayer, and Luise Scholl, their lawyers sought review in the Constitutional Court by filing a form of petition known as a "Constitutional Complaint."

Any person may file a Constitutional Complaint in the Constitutional Court—and indeed the assistance of a lawyer, while certainly advisable, is by no means necessary. The Complaint must charge that the petitioner has been "injured by public authority," through the infringement of a constitutionally guaranteed right.[29] Ordinarily, a

Court and were also advanced in the criminal courts. See Offenloch, "Geforderter Rechtsstaat," 1986 JZ, 11, 14. But in decisions handed down before the Court's *Nötigung* decisions, the Constitutional Court refused to interfere with the stationing of the Pershing II missiles (see Chapter 1). Thereafter, arguments based on Article 26 and similar constitutional provisions played no further role in the Court's opinions, although those arguments did not completely disappear from constitutional debate on the subject.

[29] Art. 93(1)(4a)GG; BVerfGG §90ff. See generally Limbach, *Das Bundesverfassungsgericht*, 36–48; Kommers, *Federal Constitutional Court*, 12–13; Rinken, in *Constitutional Courts in Comparison*, 66–69.

Originally, the Constitutional Complaint was authorized by statute but was not contained in the Basic Law itself. In 1969, however, the Basic Law was amended to provide explicit authorization for the Constitutional Complaint. This change was part of an attempt to strengthen the "legal position of the citizen", in compensation for certain potential limitations on civil rights contained in emergency legislation of the same period. As noted in Chapter 1, this emergency legislation had evoked some of the most bitter protests of the 1968 students' movement. See Dieter Dörr, *Die Verfassungsbeschwerde in der Prozeßpraxis*, 6–9 (Cologne: Schmidt, 2nd edn 1997); see also Herzog, *Strukturmängel der Verfassung?*, 132.

litigant must exhaust all possibilities of review in the "ordinary" courts before seeking redress in the Constitutional Court. In Chapter 2, we saw that Müller, Ostermayer, and Luise Scholl had fully satisfied that requirement.

The device of the Constitutional Complaint is not the only method by which a case may come to the Constitutional Court: for example, one of the German states (*Länder*) or one-third of the Bundestag members may challenge a federal statute in the Court, and one "organ" of government may in effect sue another organ for infringement of its governmental powers.[30] In these respects, the jurisdiction of the Constitutional Court is significantly broader than that of the United States Supreme Court in constitutional cases. In the United States, challenges to a federal statute by members of Congress, and suits by one organ of government against another for infringement of its powers, have frequently been found "nonjusticiable" matters that cannot be decided by the Supreme Court or any other federal court.[31]

In any event, the Constitutional Complaint—which in most cases raises claims that are similar to the traditional "case or controversy" of American doctrine—remains by far the most commonly used method of review in the German Constitutional Court. Thousands of Complaints are filed annually,[32] but the Constitutional Court—even with its two senates—generally decides fewer than 50 cases per year in full-fledged opinions. Accordingly, the Court employs preliminary screening committees (each composed of three justices) to determine which complaints should be decided by the full Court.[33] But even with these committees, the growing number of Constitutional Complaints continues to pose serious practical problems for

[30] Art. 93(1)(1), (2)GG. Indeed, one of the challenges to the stationing of the Pershing missiles—discussed in Chapter 1—employed the latter method of access to the Court. This case was commenced by the parliamentary caucus of the Greens Party, which claimed that the executive had infringed the authority of Parliament by allowing the missiles to be stationed in Germany without statutory approval: 68 BVerfGE, 1 (1984).

[31] See, e.g., *Raines v. Byrd*, 521 U.S. 811 (1997); *Goldwater v. Carter*, 444 U.S. 996 (1979).

[32] Limbach, *Das Bundesverfassungsgericht*, 38; Dörr, 4–6.

[33] See generally Kommers, *Constitutional Jurisprudence*, 18–20; Quint, "Leading a Constitutional Court: Perspectives from the Federal Republic of Germany," 154 *University of Pennsylvania Law Review* 1853, 1862–63 (2006).

the Court.[34] Indeed, the overwhelming number of Constitutional Complaints may eventually oblige the Court to adopt a system of discretionary review like the certiorari jurisdiction of the United States Supreme Court.[35]

The Großengstingen and Mutlangen demonstrators were not the only parties in the 1986 *Nötigung* case in the Constitutional Court. In addition to Müller and Ostermayer from Großengstingen and Luise Scholl from Mutlangen—whose cases we followed in Chapters 1 and 2—there were six other Constitutional Complainants. One of these, for example, was Thomas Spörer, a university employee who had participated in one of the Tent Village blockades in Großengstingen in August 1982. Another Complainant was Karl Wenning, a social education worker who, on Easter Sunday 1983, helped blockade the American Wiley Barracks in Neu-Ulm, Bavaria, a prospective stationing depot for Pershing missiles.

The Court also heard the cases of Wolfgang Howald, a labor court judge, and Michael Geywitz, a university student, who marked the third anniversary of the NATO double-track decision by helping to blockade the Patch Barracks in Stuttgart-Vaihingen—the command center of U.S. forces in Europe, from which (it was thought) the Pershing missiles might someday be launched. Finally, there were

[34] See, e.g., Lamprecht, *Zur Demontage*, 193–97. In accordance with the principle that every petitioner deserves a decision on the merits, the screening committees have no authority to reject a Constitutional Complaint on discretionary grounds. Rather, if it acts unanimously, a committee may dismiss a Complaint that is clearly unfounded and, in certain cases, it may summarily uphold a Complaint that is clearly justified. Only in cases of doubt is the Complaint referred to the full senate for decision. The decisions of the screening committees are unreviewable, however, and some observers fear that the committees may sometimes decide cases that should actually be referred to the full senate. The decisions of the screening committees are not ordinarily published in the Court's official reports, but excerpts are sometimes found in German law journals. Moreover, a new series of reporters has begun to publish selected opinions of the screening committees: 1–6 BVerfGK, *Kammerentscheidungen des Bundesverfassungsgerichts. Eine Auswahl* (Verein der Richter des Bundesverfassungsgerichts 2004–2006).

In another layer of complexity, the full senate applies some additional screening procedures after receiving the Complaints from the screening committees. See Heun, "Access to the German Federal Constitutional Court," in *Constitutional Courts in Comparison*, 136–39; see also ibid., 133–35; Kommers, *Constitutional Jurisprudence*, 19.

[35] Rinken, in *Constitutional Courts in Comparison*, 68. For the American certiorari procedure, see generally, e.g., William H. Rehnquist, *The Supreme Court: How It Was, How It Is*, 263–69 (New York: Quill 1987).

two other complainants from the demonstrations in Mutlangen. The first was an accountant whose protest in December 1983 marked the fourth anniversary of the double-track decision. The second was Heinz-Günter Lambertz, a local government official (*Kreisamtmann*) who took part in a large demonstration which blocked a convoy of American vehicles on a snowy evening in December 1983.

Thus, in all, the Court heard nine Constitutional Complaints in the 1986 *Nötigung* case. Of course this number represented only a small fraction of the thousands of people who had been arrested and convicted under §240 of the Criminal Code for their participation in the sit-down demonstrations.

## The 1986 case—the constitutional arguments of the parties

What were the arguments that were made by the protestors—and their opponents—in the Constitutional Court? As noted above, these fall into two parts—the arguments based on freedom of assembly under Article 8 of the Basic Law and those based on the rule of law as embodied in Article 103(2).

Let us examine each of these sets of arguments in turn.

### *Article 8 and the freedom of assembly*

#### *The Constitutional background and the Brokdorf decision*

When the Constitutional Court reached the problem of the sit-down protests in 1986, it was acting against the background of its greatest decision on the question of demonstrations and the constitutional freedom of assembly—a case that it had decided in 1985, just one year earlier.[36] Involving issues that were closely related to the concerns of the sit-down demonstrators, this case arose from massive protests against the construction of an atomic power plant at the town of Brokdorf in northern Germany.[37]

[36] 69 BVerfGE, 315 (1985).

[37] See Chapter 1. See generally Hans-Jürgen Benedict, *Ziviler Ungehorsam als christliche Tugend*, 58–91 (Frankfurt/M: Athenäum 1989).

For commentary on the *Brokdorf* decision, see, e.g., Frowein, "Die Versammlungsfreiheit vor dem Bundesverfassungsgericht," 1985 NJW, 2376; Schenke, "Anmerkung," 1986 JZ, 35; Fritz, "Stellung nehmen und Standpunkt bezeugen—Behinderung als Mittel zum aufklärenden Protest," in Willy Brandt *et al.* (eds), *Ein*

In February 1981, between 50,000 and 100,000 protestors convened in a huge demonstration at the gates of the construction site in Brokdorf. Although most of the protestors were peaceful, some "autonomous groups" engaged in violence. Moreover, the protestors were acting in violation of a court order against the demonstration, which was based in part on the organizers' failure to "register" their plans with the authorities.

In an opinion that remains its basic statement on freedom of assembly, the Constitutional Court declared that the lower court's blanket prohibition of the demonstration was unconstitutional. Applying the balancing procedure that is typical in speech and assembly cases, the Court found that a narrower prohibition might have been constitutional under some circumstances, but a total prohibition of the demonstration at Brokdorf violated the freedom of assembly contained in Article 8 of the Basic Law.

At the outset of the *Brokdorf* opinion, the Court engaged in a thoughtful general discussion of the function of demonstrations—emphasizing the democratic importance of the freedom of assembly guaranteed by Article 8 of the Basic Law.[38] According to the Court, demonstrations have a physical nature, in which a point of view is not necessarily communicated by the traditional method of argumentation. Rather, demonstrations involve "diverse forms of common action [and] non-verbal forms of expression," and their principal purpose may be to attract attention to a particular point of view rather than to provide a reasoned articulation of that view.[39]

According to the Court, the right of assembly protects "dissenting minorities" in particular: in "Anglo-American" law, for example, the right of assembly vindicated popular sovereignty and furthered the citizen's "active participation in the political process."[40] But, more than that, the right of assembly also represents an aspect of the free development of the individual personality—"because the demonstrator proclaims his viewpoint [through] his physical presence,

*Richter, ein Bürger, ein Christ: Festschrift für Helmut Simon* (Baden-Baden: Nomos 1987); Uwe Wesel, *Der Gang nach Karlsruhe. Das Bundesverfassungsgericht in der Geschichte der Bundesrepublik*, 288–91 (Munich: Blessing 2004); Jörg Menzel (ed.), *Verfassungsrechtsprechung*, 372–79 (Tübingen: Mohr Siebeck 2000) (Katharina Pabel).

38 69 BVerfGE, 342–47.

39 See ibid., 343, 345.

40 Ibid., 343.

completely in public, and without the interposition of the media." Ideally, "demonstrations are the joint bodily concretization of opinions: on the one hand, the participant experiences a community with others and the reinforcement of his opinions. On the other hand, by his mere presence . . . the participant takes a position (in the true sense of the word) and bears witness to his point of view", with respect to those outside the demonstration.[41] At some points in this complex and philosophical discussion, the Court almost seemed to express a sense of solidarity with the demonstrators.

Against this background, the Court went on to add some pointed remarks about the specific importance of freedom of assembly in the German political system. Indeed, the Court suggested that a bureaucratic political system—presumably like that of the Federal Republic—could not adequately function in the absence of demonstrations. The Court noted that the "formation" of the democratic "political will" depends not only on votes at elections, but also on other forms of influence. Large corporations and the mass media can wield this influence, but the individual citizen feels "powerless" in contrast.[42] Accordingly, collective popular influence through demonstrations may represent one way of redressing the balance.

Indeed, demonstrations may be particularly important in the German parliamentary system, which affords little opportunity for plebiscites and where power between elections is often exercised by a "bureaucratic apparatus." In this context, demonstrations may play a stabilizing role by assuring that all interests can participate. Indeed, these protests may act as an "early warning system" for political officials.[43]

These strong statements by the Court on the importance of freedom of assembly seemed to cast the *Nötigung* cases in a new and rather different light. After *Brokdorf*, it seemed possible that the justices might employ the principles of Article 8 in a manner that could favor the sit-down protestors.[44] And indeed, although the

[41] Ibid., 345.
[42] Ibid., 346.
[43] Ibid., 347.
[44] See, e.g., Kühl, "Sitzblockaden vor dem Bundesverfassungsgericht," 1987 StV, 122, 131; Fritz, in *Festschrift für Helmut Simon*, 410 and n. 29. But for criticism of the *Brokdorf* opinion on precisely these grounds, see Walter Schmitt Glaeser, *Private Gewalt im politischen Meinungskampf*, 80 (Berlin: Duncker & Humblot, 2nd edn 1992) (The "one-sided emphasis" on demonstrators' rights in *Brokdorf* could impair the struggle against the use of force); see also ibid., 81–99.

*Brokdorf* case came too late for consideration in many of the lawyers' briefs, the decision did play a significant role in the Court's opinion in the *Nötigung* cases in 1986.[45]

### *Freedom of assembly and civil disobedience—the briefs of the complainants*

The *Brokdorf* case might suggest, therefore, that the freedom of assembly of Article 8 GG could be employed in an argument that might favor the protestors' claims. Such an argument might take a number of possible forms. Put most strongly, the argument could assert that the sit-down blockades constituted a form of "assembly" that was fully protected by Article 8 and was therefore exempt from criminal punishment. For this argument to succeed, the Court would have to find that the sit-down demonstrations were a form of "peaceful" assembly under Article 8—notwithstanding a possible finding that they were "forcible" under §240 (II).[46] Moreover, the Court would have to find that—for some reason—the legislature's attempt to "limit" this form of demonstration, pursuant to Article 8 (2), would ultimately not prevail.

To many, however, this argument was so far-reaching that it seemed unlikely to be accepted by the Court. Rather, some lawyers for the protestors adopted a subtler form of the argument, in which the relationship of the sit-down blockades to Article 8 was said to bear on the question of "*Verwerflichkeit*"—the "reprehensible" nature of the protestors' acts as required by StGB

[45] It has been reported that Roman Herzog, Vice-President of the Constitutional Court and Chairman of the First Senate, "tipped the balance" in favor of the demonstrators in the *Brokdorf* case. Uwe Wesel, *Der Gang nach Karlsruhe. Das Bundesverfassungsgericht in der Geschichte der Bundesrepublik*, 216 (Munich: Blessing 2004). This news came as a considerable surprise to members of the peace movement and others, because a few years earlier Herzog, as Interior Minister of the State of Baden-Württemberg, had taken a hard line against political protestors (ibid., 217). An important figure in the history of the Constitutional Court, Herzog became President of the Court in 1987 and, in 1994, he was elected President of the Federal Republic of Germany. See generally Quint, "Leading a Constitutional Court: Perspectives from the Federal Republic of Germany," 154 *University of Pennsylvania Law Review* 1853, 1876–1877 (2006).

[46] Remember that Article 8(1) of the Basic Law guarantees "the right of *peaceful* and unarmed assembly" only (emphasis added). See above.

§240(II).[47] Under this argument, if the sit-down protests were *closely related* to activity that was protected under Article 8—even if the protests were not actually protected themselves—they could not in any event be viewed as "reprehensible" under §240(II).[48]

These arguments rested on a position, asserted by the Constitutional Court at a very early point in its history, that the Basic Rights exercise a degree of influence over all other areas of law—an influence that has a particularly strong impact on statutory terms of great generality, such as "contrary to good morals," or (as in our case) "reprehensible." This "influence" of the Basic Right often requires that the right be weighed or balanced against the state's countervailing interest in criminalization or other regulation, as a part of the process of statutory interpretation.[49] According to this argument, therefore, it could be the "influence" of Article 8 on the interpretation of the word "reprehensible" in §240(II) that might lead to a result favoring the protestors—rather than a finding that the protestors' actions were themselves constitutionally protected.

In a closely related argument, the protestors also asserted that since blockades and other forms of "civil disobedience", have been considered acceptable—or even praiseworthy—in the Anglo-American political tradition, these sit-down protests could certainly not be characterized as "reprehensible" under §240(II). According to counsel, only actions that would be deemed worthy of stern disapproval by right-thinking people may be classified as "reprehensible." But that cannot be the case here, because "persons of indisputable moral integrity and authority have called for [the protests] and have taken part in them."[50]

47 See, e.g., Constitutional Complaint filed on behalf of Thomas Spörer by Rechtsanwalt Wolfram Leyrer, Tübingen, 8 July 1984 [Constitutional Complaint Spörer/Leyrer], 13. See generally Chapter 2.

48 These arguments were bolstered by the invocation of additional constitutional guarantees, such as the protestors' freedom of expression (Article 5 GG), their right to life (Article 2 GG), and their freedom of conscience (Article 4 GG). Constitutional Complaint Spörer/Leyrer, 13–19; Constitutional Complaint filed on behalf of Karl Wenning by Rechtsanwälte Frank Niepel and Klaus D. Klefke, Munich, 27 February 1985 [Constitutional Complaint Wenning/Niepel and Klefke], 39; Reichert-Hammer, 122–26.

49 This technique was first employed in the famous *Lüth* case, decided by the Constitutional Court in 1958 (7 BVerfGE, 198); see Quint, 48 *Maryland Law Review*, 252–90.

50 Constitutional Complaint filed on behalf of Heinz-Günter Lambertz by Prof. Dr. Gerald Grünwald, Bonn, 13 March 1985 [Constitutional Complaint Lambertz/

Counsel for Müller and Ostermayer also claimed that the sit-down protests were a new form of constitutionally protected right of participation in democratic political processes. In a democracy, counsel argued, the methods of challenging governmental decisions remain "open" to continuing development.[51] Indeed, the history of labor unions and political parties shows that new political forms arise when the existing methods of citizens' political participation have proven to be insufficient. Because the citizen now feels "helplessly delivered over" to a dangerous armament policy, new techniques are needed to direct public attention to the government's violation of higher law.[52] As counsel for another protestor argued, the problem of the nuclear missiles was "of existential importance for the entire population" of the Federal Republic.[53]

Indeed, according to counsel, the German federal government has long sought to conceal the first-strike capabilities of the Pershing II rockets, as well as the new American strategy of waging nuclear war in central Europe, in furtherance of American interests. The peace movement had tried to raise the alarm in numerous traditional demonstrations and petitions. But because the movement lacks means of publicity that could even approach those available to its opponents, "sit-down demonstrations against the Pershing II [rockets] are necessary to counter the . . . misleading propaganda of the Federal Government."[54]

### *The governmental response*

In response to the Constitutional Complaints of the anti-missile protestors, written arguments were filed by the Federal Ministry of Justice, as well as by the Justice Ministries of Baden-Württemberg and Bavaria, the two states in which these prosecutions took place.

In its brief, the Federal Justice Ministry first cast doubt on whether Article 8 could protect the sit-down demonstrators at all.

Grünwald], 16–17. See also Constitutional Complaint Wenning/Niepel and Klefke, 24.

51 Brief filed in support of Constitutional Complaint of Wolfgang Müller and Hansjörg Ostermayer by Rechtsanwalt Karl Joachim Hemeyer, Tübingen, 22 May 1985 [Hemeyer Brief], 26.

52 Ibid., 34–35.

53 Constitutional Complaint Spörer/Leyrer, 15.

54 Constitutional Complaint Wenning/Niepel and Klefke, 32–35.

Article 8 covers "peaceful" assemblies only, but it was "questionable from the outset" whether sit-down blockades could be considered "peaceful" since, as several scholars have argued, the blockades "impair the freedom of action" of third persons and force the protestors' views on others.[55] In any case, the protestors' psychological pressure can lie "outside the limits of proper intellectual debate, [and] peaceful community life can be just as seriously—or even more seriously—injured by this pressure as by bodily force."[56]

But even if the demonstrations are classified as "peaceful," the weighing of values required by Article 8 section 2 would uphold the convictions nonetheless. The freedom of will of the blockaded truck drivers—and the freedom to put that will into effect—serve eminent constitutional values that are at least as weighty as the protestors' freedom of assembly. Perhaps if the demonstrations had been truly symbolic, they might not be considered "reprehensible." But these sit-down blockades were not purely symbolic. In one of the cases, for example, even a short blockade was part of a series of sit-down blockades that were repeated every hour over a nine-hour period.[57]

Turning specifically to the cases of Müller and Ostermayer, the Justice Ministry of Baden-Württemberg argued that the long duration of the Großengstingen chain blockade indicates that its social invasiveness outweighed the values of freedom of speech. Indeed, according to the Ministry, any goals of expression were achieved by the protestors' press conference on the first day at Großengstingen—but the blockade continued for many hours thereafter.[58]

[55] Brief of Federal Minister of Justice, 25 October 1985, 1004 E (3839), (3840) 434/85 [Federal Brief (1985)], 8–9.

[56] Ibid., 10. See also Brief of Federal Minister of Justice, 2 September 1983, 1004 E (3551) 441/83 [Federal Brief (1983)], 3.

[57] Federal Brief (1985), 11–13.

[58] Brief of Justice Ministry of Baden-Württemberg, 16 August 1983, 1004a–V/1942 [Baden-Württemberg Brief (1983)], 14–15. See Chapter 1. See also Brief of Justice Ministry of Baden-Württemberg, 7 August 1985, 1004a–V/1942 [Baden-Württemberg Brief (1985)], 2 (arguing that almost any blockade of a vehicle is "reprehensible" and not constitutionally protected).

The governmental briefs also rejected the argument that the protestors were exercising a constitutional right of resistance, protected under Article 20(4) GG. Article 20(4) does state that "all Germans have the right of resistance against anyone who undertakes to overthrow this constitutional order, if no other redress is possible." But this right applies only against forces that are trying to set aside the "free democratic basic order" of the Constitution—something that

In sum, according to the governmental briefs, Article 8 of the Basic Law provided no constitutional protection—whether direct or indirect—for the protestors' actions.

### *Article 103(2)GG and the interpretation of "force"*

Counsel for the protestors also argued that the "spiritualized" interpretation of the word "force" adopted by the criminal courts extended well beyond what was actually authorized by the *Nötigung* statute and therefore constituted a form of interpretation by analogy —a violation of the rule of law under Article 103(2).[59]

In this connection, counsel made particular efforts to distinguish the *Laepple* case—with its massive blockade of streetcar crossings—from what was claimed to be the more "symbolic" action of small numbers of protestors in the anti-missile sit-down cases.[60] Under this argument, the small and symbolic anti-missile blockades could not reasonably be viewed as the employment of "force"—even if the massive blockade in *Laepple* might reasonably be said to possess this quality.

For the purpose of emphasizing this point, counsel took pains to explain the precise symbolic meaning of the anti-missile blockades. For example, the Großengstingen chain blockade was "the symbolic portrayal of [our] actual helplessness in the face of atomic armament policy"—and also in the face of the power of the German army.[61] In another argument, counsel declared that an anti-missile blockade could be viewed as a "symbolic" temporary anticipation of a future

cannot be said of the truck drivers (or others against whom the blockades were directed), or of the Federal Government or NATO. Baden-Württemberg Brief (1983), 19; Federal Brief (1983), 3–5.

59 See, e.g., Constitutional Complaint Wenning/Niepel and Klefke, 14–22; Constitutional Complaint Spörer/Leyrer, 6–11.

60 According to one brief, for example, in the *Laepple* case "the sit-down demonstration actually had the character of a blockade because the entire traffic of the center of a big city was completely paralyzed for hours." In *Laepple*, moreover, the blockade was only protesting streetcar fares—whereas the anti-missile blockades sought to "protect the entire population of the Federal Republic from atomic annihilation." Constitutional Complaint Wenning/Niepel and Klefke, 18. See also Constitutional Complaint Spörer/ Leyrer, 16.

61 Constitutional Complaint filed on behalf of Wolfgang Müller and Hansjörg Ostermayer by Rechtsanwalt Karl Joachim Hemeyer, 5 May 1983, 10.

demilitarized society, sought by the demonstrators, in which "any military traffic is no longer thinkable."[62]

Noting that §240 StGB is designed to protect individual free will, counsel also argued that the free will being protected in these cases was not really the will of the blocked truck drivers, as the courts assumed. Because the drivers were carrying out military orders—rather than following their own desires—the "will" being thwarted by the blockades was actually that of higher military officials or the government. But §240 StGB is not intended to penalize coercion of the government. Other provisions of the criminal code—not at issue in these cases, and probably not applicable in any event—are intended to prohibit that sort of coercion.[63]

Counsel also advanced linguistic arguments to explain the problematic nature of the extended definition of "force" adopted by the criminal courts. Under the courts' extended definition—counsel argued—the famous non-violent protests of Gandhi would have to be defined as "force." But no one would think of using that word for Gandhi's actions—which were in fact much more confrontational than the protests involved in these cases. Indeed, if a newspaper reporter stated simply that demonstrators "used force" against military vehicles, a normal reader would believe that violent acts had been committed. But obviously, with respect to these protests, such a belief would be false.[64]

Upon occasion the exasperation of the peace movement and its lawyers comes through in passages of angry denunciation. With striking candor, for example, one of the Constitutional Complaints argued that the criminal court decisions seem to represent

> political justice, which criminalizes—and thus eliminates—political opponents through the formal means of the justice system. This is nothing new in the history of criminal justice . . . Naked power appears in the guise of the power to make definitions. Thus nonforcible actions become forcible actions. Nonforcible protest against the atomic annihilation of the entire population becomes a reprehensible act.

62 Constitutional Complaint Spörer/Leyrer, 17.

63 Constitutional Complaint Wenning/Niepel and Klefke, 10–12, 29; Hemeyer Brief, 9–10.

64 Constitutional Complaint Lambertz/Grünwald, 12.

Counsel's conclusion was that this form of judicial activity "must be denounced."[65]

As might be expected, the governmental briefs rejected the protestors' claims under 103(2) GG as well. According to the Justice Ministry of Baden-Württemberg, it is accepted that the extended interpretation of "force" is legitimate as "a necessary adjustment" to the methods of coercion "that have become common in recent times."[66] If an exaggerated statutory precision were required, "the laws . . . could no longer do justice to the great diversity of life or to the special problems of the individual case."[67] Accordingly, the "spiritualization" of the concept of "force" was "essential" in order to counter "newly appearing" forms of compulsion which impair the freedom of the will.[68] These repeated references to "newly appearing" or "more refined" forms of compulsion may well reflect the governments' urgent sense that §240 StGB must be extended to cover the activities of the "new social movements" of the 1960s and 1970s, including in particular the German peace movement.

## Arguments requested or solicited by the Court

In addition to the arguments presented by the actual parties to the litigation, the Constitutional Court's First Senate solicited the views and arguments of a range of other respondents.[69] These included the major German peace institutes, the five criminal law senates of the Federal Supreme Court (BGH), and two academic or judicial "experts" in the criminal law. In each case, these requests—and the responses—illuminate significant aspects of the German legal system.

[65] Constitutional Complaint Wenning/Niepel, 20–21; see also ibid., 26–27.

[66] Baden-Württemberg Brief (1983), 6. See also Federal Brief (1985), 7 (Courts' interpretation takes into account "ever more refined forms of modern compulsion").

[67] Baden-Württemberg Brief (1983), 2.

[68] Ibid., 3.

[69] Typically the names of outside respondents in a case before the Constitutional Court are proposed by the Reporter in that case. The official decision to issue the invitations, however, is made by the entire senate. Interview with retired Justice Helmut Simon, Karlsruhe, Germany, 7 July 2004.

### *Arguments of the German peace institutes*

At the time when the Court's First Senate requested the views of various German peace institutes in the *Nötigung* cases, these institutes had been in existence for only a few years. Indeed, the history of the German peace institutes reflects some of the important political tensions of the period.

This history began when West German Chancellor Willy Brandt collaborated with Federal President Gustav Heinemann, who had long been skeptical of Cold War armaments, to establish federal funding for the field of "peace research"—the study of methods to increase understanding among nations and to avoid war.[70] Supported by these new government funds, a number of academic institutes were established in the early 1970s for the purpose of pursuing this line of research. After the NATO double-track decision, the German peace institutes furnished a reservoir of expertise that could be marshaled against the numerous government and industry experts who favored expanded armaments and deployment of the Pershing missiles. Accordingly, in the decades of the 1970s and 1980s, members of the peace institutes turned out large numbers of widely read books and papers on these issues. In this way, the peace institutes became "centers for the campaign directed against the [double-track] decision."[71]

The work of the more radical wing of peace researchers, in Germany and elsewhere in Europe, relied on a specific—albeit controversial—analysis of the nature of force or violence in society. According to this view, various forms of economic, political, and

[70] Such a field had already been established before World War II in the United States, but in Germany this area of study did not exist until the post-war period.

Many of the details in this paragraph are drawn from Jeffrey Herf, *War by Other Means: Soviet Power, West German Resistance, and the Battle of the Euromissiles*, 83–97 (New York: Free Press 1991); and Alice Holmes Cooper, *Paradoxes of Peace: German Peace Movements since 1945*, 135–38 (Ann Arbor: University of Michigan Press 1996). See also Ulrich de Maiziere, "The Arguments of the German Peace Movement," in Walter Laqueur and Robert Hunter (eds), *European Peace Movements and the Future of the Western Alliance*, 339–55 (New Brunswick NJ: Transaction 1985) [*European Peace Movements*].

[71] Herf, "War, Peace, and the Intellectuals: The West German Peace Movement,", 10 *International Security*, No. 4 (spring 1986) 172, 193. But see also Jahn, "Friedensforschung und Friedensbewegung," in Reiner Steinweg (ed.), *Die neue Friedensbewegung. Analysen aus der Friedensforschung*, 146–65 (Frankfurt/M: Suhrkamp 1982) (chronicling some tensions between the peace researchers and the peace movement itself).

social oppression existing in modern industrial states actually represented a kind of permanently existing "structural force" or "structural violence," which disadvantaged those who were at lower levels on the economic or social scale.[72] According to some theorists, the posited existence of this form of "structural force" might be understood to justify violent or otherwise illegal countermeasures. Naturally, the more traditional jurists and political scientists considered the doctrine of structural force to raise particular dangers for the constitutional state.[73]

Although the eminent researchers who responded to the Court's request and filed material in the sit-down demonstration cases represented a more moderate wing of peace research, their contributions heavily favored the protestors. Dieter Lutz at the Peace Institute of Hamburg University—and "[o]ne of the most prolific of the counter-experts to emerge from peace research"[74]—argued vigorously against the constitutionality of the missile deployments.[75] In a complex and nuanced analysis, Lutz argued that although the Pershing II missiles (along with the accompanying Cruise missiles) did not possess a full first-strike capability, they must be viewed as "part of a future first-strike capability that is already emerging." Accordingly, the "peace commandment" (*Friedensgebot*) of the Basic Law—contained in Article 26 and other provisions—prohibits the Federal Republic from allowing the deployment of these weapons.[76]

Peter Schlotter of the Peace Research Institute Frankfurt emphasized the power and precision of the Pershing II rockets and the resulting danger of a preventive nuclear strike by the Soviet Union directed toward neutralizing those weapons.[77] Schlotter also argued that—in light of the history of Nazi aggression—Germany is

72 See, e.g., Johan Galtung, "Violence, Peace, and Peace Research," 6 *Journal of Peace Research* 167 (1969).

73 See, e.g., Schmitt Glaeser, "Politisch motivierte Gewalt und ihre 'Fernziele', " 1988 BayVBl, 454, 458–59; see also Walter Schmitt Glaeser, *Private Gewalt im politischen Meinungskampf*, 65–69 (Berlin: Duncker & Humblot, 2nd edn 1992).

74 Herf, *War by Other Means*, 92. On Lutz, see generally ibid., 63, 92–93, 127; Cooper, 140–42.

75 Lutz, "Sind erstschlagsfähige Nuklearwaffen verfassungswidrig?," 38 *Frankfurter Hefte*, No. 9, 17–28 (1983). This article, along with two others, was submitted by Lutz to the Constitutional Court.

76 Ibid.

77 Schlotter, "Die Stationierung von Pershing II und Cruise Missiles in der Bundesrepublik Deutschland. Überlegungen zur verfassungsrechtlichen Beurteilung," 31 January 1984.

bound by a particularly rigorous obligation to avoid increasing the danger of war. By allowing the American president to launch the missiles, however, the German government has "delegated the decision over the annihilation of the Federal Republic to a foreign power."[78]

The Court also received comments from Professor Theodor Ebert, a political scientist and prominent peace researcher at the Free University of Berlin; Ebert was also Wolfgang Müller's dissertation advisor at the University. In his well-known work Ebert, a follower of Gandhi, sought to develop a strategy of "social defense" or passive resistance to replace escalating armaments on the national level.[79]

Turning to issues of civil disobedience, Ebert emphasized the political and persuasive aspects of the sit-down demonstrations. According to Ebert, the protestors expect that their prosecution as well as other governmental measures against their non-violent action "will direct public attention, more strongly than in the past, toward the arguments of the protest groups."[80] Indeed, civil disobedience can assist the minority in educating the majority about the nature of constitutional rights. In many countries, for example, the exemption of conscientious objectors from military conscription began as a process of civil disobedience, and only later—after "a long process of education"—was this exemption absorbed into law adopted by the majority.[81]

In the sit-down cases, civil disobedience is exercised against majority decisions that the minority believes may have "fatal consequences that could never be rectified." Certainly, failure of the government's armament policy "could lead to the end of the Federal Republic as a viable industrial society."[82] Accordingly, the minority brings its complaint against the "hubris" of the majority. Because civil disobedience resolves "certain deficits in the democratic process" and

78 Ibid., 17.

79 See de Maiziere, in *European Peace Movements*, 343–44; see generally Thomas Laker, *Ziviler Ungehorsam: Geschichte—Begriff—Rechtfertigung*, 156–57 (Baden-Baden: Nomos 1986).

80 Ebert, "Verfassungsrechtliche Überlegungen zur Funktion von zivilem Ungehorsam: Stellungnahme zur Verfassungsbeschwerde von Wolfgang Müller und Hansjörg Ostermayer," 30 August 1983, 2.

81 Ibid., 3.

82 Ibid., 4.

can even lead to the building of new majorities, "it may not be classified as 'reprehensible' ".[83]

Ebert also turned his attention to the attempt to treat "non-forcible" action as though it actually involved "force". Indeed, "if such [non-violent] actions are reproached with being the application of 'psychic force'—in order to apply §240 to them—then the borderline between violent and non-violent actions, which is extraordinarily important for life in a community, is rendered indistinct."[84] Accordingly—as Martin Luther King remarked in his Letter from Birmingham Jail—if non-violent civil disobedience is subjected to "rigid" disapproval, there are most likely competing opposition groups that will go beyond civil disobedience and resort to real violence.[85]

Finally, the Court received comments from Alfred Mechtersheimer, a former German army officer and director of the Research Institute for Peace Policy in Starnberg.[86] Mechtersheimer focused attention on the "intensively discussed" question of whether the peace movement should confine itself to symbolic (i.e., non-violent) action. But if symbolic action—like the sit-down blockades—is treated as the criminal offense of coercion, that discussion would become "irrelevant" and the result could be "a radicalization and criminalization of the peace movement, with all of its consequences for the inner peace" of the Federal Republic. In sum, the courts "should not handle those forms of protest in which force against other persons has been scrupulously avoided . . . as though force had been intentionally applied."[87] Evidently speaking as a former

[83] Ibid., 7.

[84] Ibid., 8.

[85] Ibid., 12–13.

[86] On Mechtersheimer, see Andrei S. Markovits and Philip S. Gorski, *The German Left: Red, Green and Beyond*, 108 and 321–22 n. 153 (New York: Oxford University Press 1993). For a general statement of Mechtersheimer's views on nuclear armaments and the German peace movement, see Mechtersheimer, "Rüstungsverweigerung statt Rüstungskontrolle," in Walter Jens (ed.), *In letzter Stunde: Aufruf zum Frieden*, 79–99 (Munich: Kindler 1982). See also Mechtersheimer,"Einleitung," in Alfred Mechtersheimer (ed.), *Nachrüsten? Dokumente und Positionen zum NATO-Doppelbeschluss*, 11–20 (Reinbek bei Hamburg: Rowohlt Taschenbuch 1981); Mechtersheimer, "Einleitung," in Alfred Mechtersheimer and Peter Barth (eds), *Den Atomkrieg führbar und gewinnbar machen?*, 11–21 (Reinbek bei Hamburg: Rowohlt Taschenbuch 1983).

[87] Mechtersheimer and Reich-Hilweg, "Schriftliche Äußerung an das Bundesverfassungsgericht zur Verfassungsbeschwerde der Herren Wolfgang Müller und Hansjörg Ostermayer," 31 August 1983, 3.

military officer, Mechtersheimer also emphasized the contrast between the protestors' "non-forcible forms of behavior" and the role of the army—a "military apparatus of force" which is "organized, trained, and equipped in order to deal with [an opponent's] capacity for forcible destruction."[88]

### *Statements of panels of the Federal Supreme Court (BGH)*

In addition to the arguments of the peace institutes, the Constitutional Court invited the criminal law "senates" of the Federal Supreme Court—the highest criminal court—to file their views on the relevant legal issues. Indeed, it is not unusual for the Court to issue such an invitation when a Constitutional Complaint challenges a decision of the civil or criminal courts.[89] In following this course, the Constitutional Court indicates a need to be educated by the "ordinary" courts on their decisions concerning the relevant provisions of the civil and criminal codes. This practice acknowledges the independent role of the "ordinary" criminal courts and reflects the clear institutional distinction in the German system between constitutional law and the "ordinary" law.

Four of the five "criminal" senates of the BGH responded to the Court's invitation. These tribunals provided short statements that mainly reiterated the finding of the *Laepple* decision that if an action is "forcible" under § 240(I), then it is also "reprehensible" under § 240(II)—in the absence of "extremely unusual circumstances."[90] Denying that §240 is unconstitutionally broad, the Second Criminal Senate also emphasized that "the use of . . . undetermined concepts that must be filled in with a choice of certain values" is permitted even in the criminal law, as long as a result can be reliably obtained "through the use of customary methods of interpretation."[91] The Third Criminal Senate reported on its recent decision in the case of massive environmental demonstrations at the Frankfurt airport,

[88] Ibid., 4.

[89] See Geschäftsordnung des Bundesverfassungsgerichts §22 (4); cf. BVerfGG §82(4).

[90] See Chapter 2.

[91] Letter, dated 23 January 1984, from the Chief Judge of the Second Criminal Senate to the President of the Federal Supreme Court (BGH).

which led to criminal liability for *Nötigung* and breach of the peace under the Criminal Code.[92]

Although these brief communications contained few surprises, we will see in the next chapter that the remarks of one of the criminal senates of the BGH seems to have played a very important role in the second *Nötigung* decision of the Constitutional Court, decided in 1995.

## The criminal law "experts"

In another move that has no real counterpart in American legal practice, the Constitutional Court invited two "experts" (*Sachverständiger*) in criminal law to address the Court in the oral argument of the sit-down cases. These "experts" were not invited to present factual information about the peace movement or the technique of sit-down demonstrations. Nor were they asked to analyze civil disobedience as a philosophical concept. Rather, these "experts" were jurists or scholars who were evidently invited to address the Court on the issues of criminal law presented by the sit-down demonstrations.

Why did the justices think it worthwhile to invite these two "experts" on criminal law to address the Court? In the Supreme Court of the United States the justices are ordinarily content to rely on the legal knowledge of counsel arguing the cases as well as the research of their own law clerks—not to mention the considerable expertise that the justices themselves have built up over years of considering not only constitutional questions, but also the various statutory and common law issues that they confront in their diverse caseload.

Of course, interested persons or groups are frequently permitted to file arguments as "friends of the Court" (*amici curiae*) in cases in the American Supreme Court. But ordinarily these *amici* have themselves sought unanimous consent of the parties, or the Court's permission, to file their arguments.[93] Often, these briefs seek to present some new or special point of view, perhaps depending upon factual knowledge that might not be ordinarily available to the

92 Letter, dated 11 January 1984, from the Chief Judge of the Third Criminal Senate to the President of Federal Supreme Court (BGH). On the Frankfurt airport demonstrations, see Chapter 1.

93 Supreme Court Rule 37.

judges or to counsel.[94] On occasion, the Supreme Court may ask the Solicitor General to file a brief or participate in oral argument—even when the United States is not a party to the litigation—so that the Court may have the benefit of the government's views on a particular issue.[95] Yet it seems most unlikely that the Supreme Court would seek "expert" advice on the law itself in a constitutional case.

In contrast, the German Constitutional Court has sought this form of "expertise" on significant occasions. Perhaps in this case the judges believed that—in light of the importance placed upon specialization in the German legal world and the significant divide between constitutional law and the various branches of the "ordinary" law—the Court should hear the views of individuals who were clearly specialists in criminal law, an area in which most of the constitutional judges are, in theory at least, not experts.

In any case, the Court's two invited "experts" represented quite separate sides of the dispute. The first was Rolf-Peter Calliess, a professor of criminal law at the University of Hannover, who had recently published an article in a widely read journal, arguing in effect that the *Nötigung* convictions of the sit-in demonstrators should be reversed.[96] The second expert was a well-known judge and commentator on criminal law, Herbert Tröndle, who was co-author of the best-known and most widely used commentary on the German Criminal Code.[97] A vigorous opponent of the peace movement,

[94] See Supreme Court Rule 37(1). For a recent notable example, see Consolidated Brief of Lt. Gen. Julius W. Becton, Jr. *et al.*, as *amici curiae* in *Grutter v. Bollinger*, 539 U.S. 306 (2003); and *Gratz v. Bollinger*, 539 U.S. 244 (2003) (brief of retired military officers and others, arguing that affirmative action programs are essential for the adequate functioning of United States armed forces).

In an interesting contrast, there is no official procedure through which interested persons or groups can petition to present briefs or arguments as *amici curiae* before the German Constitutional Court. Interview with retired Justice Helmut Simon, Karlsruhe. In the 1986 *Nötigung* case, however, 28 university professors of criminal law did succeed in submitting a one-sentence statement to the Constitutional Court, declaring their belief that StGB §240 was unconstitutionally vague: 73 BVerfGE, 206, 239 (1986); see Letter, dated 20 January 1986, from Prof. Dr. Rolf-Peter Calliess to the First Senate of the Federal Constitutional Court.

[95] Similarly the Court may seek the views of state officials in appropriate cases. See Robert L. Stern, Eugene Gressman *et al.*, *Supreme Court Practice*, 468 (Washington D.C.: Bureau of National Affairs, 8th edn 2002).

[96] Calliess, "Der strafrechtliche Nötigungstatbestand und das verfassungsrechtliche Gebot der Tatbestandsbestimmtheit," 1985 NJW, 1506.

[97] Cf. Herbert Tröndle and Thomas Fischer (eds), *Strafgesetzbuch und Nebengesetze* (Munich: Beck, 49th edn 1999).

Tröndle was a strong supporter of the application of StGB §240 to the sit-down demonstrations.[98] We will have the opportunity to review the remarks of these "experts" when we examine the oral argument below.

## The attempt to remove Judge Simon

After the briefs and other written materials were filed, the Constitutional Court set 15–16 July 1986 as the dates for oral argument in a public hearing in these cases. But, in a dramatic development a few days before oral argument was to begin, the State of Bavaria—one of the opposing parties in the case—moved for the disqualification of one of the judges of the Constitutional Court. If a judge were to be disqualified, a replacement would be chosen by lot from the other senate of the Court.[99] Obviously, such a change in personnel could be crucial for the decision in a close case.

The judge in question was Helmut Simon, a jurist whose general political views were very far to the left of those of the conservative government of Bavaria, which had moved for his recusal. Indeed, according to a respected commentator, Judge Simon was "recognizably the leader" of the left wing of the Court's First Senate.[100]

98 On Tröndle, see generally Dreher, "Herbert Tröndle zum 70. Geburtstag," in Hans-Heinrich Jescheck and Theo Vogler (eds), *Festschrift für Herbert Tröndle zum 70. Geburtstag* (Berlin: de Gruyter 1989); Odersky, "Vorwort," in Herbert Tröndle, *Antworten auf Grundfragen*, V–VIII (Munich: Beck 1999).

99 BVerfGG §19 (4). This provision was adopted in 1986—not long before oral argument in the *Nötigung* cases—in order to make certain that the number of judges hearing a politically sensitive case could not be unduly lowered through recusal. See Schlaich and Korioth, 50.

100 Benda, "Helmut Simon—Bild eines Richters," in *Festschrift für Helmut Simon*, 27 (quoting Friedrich Karl Fromme). For example, Simon had dissented in the famous *Abortion Case* of 1975, in which the Court, finding in favor of the State of Bavaria, had declared that abortion must generally remain a criminal offense: 39 BVerfGE, 1 (1975). In another dissenting opinion of the same era, Simon supported a plan of democratic university reform that had emerged from the ideas of the left-wing student movement of 1968: 35 BVerfGE, 79, 148–70 (1973); see generally Uwe Wesel, *Die verspielte Revolution: 1968 und die Folgen*, 232–38 (Munich: Blessing 2002); David P. Currie, *The Constitution of the Federal Republic of Germany*, 233–37 (Chicago, IL: University of Chicago Press 1994).

Judge Simon was prominent in the affairs of the German Evangelical Church, and his views bear the influence of his strong religious beliefs. Simon was appointed to the Constitutional Court before the justices were limited to non-renewable 12-year terms; accordingly, Simon served on the Court for 18 years and

In its petition, the Bavarian government argued that Simon should be removed from this case because he had made statements that were favorable to the anti-missile sit-down protestors in a magazine interview and in published speeches. For example, Simon had expressed sympathy for persons who engaged in civil disobedience and suggested that it was "unbearable" that the anti-missile demonstrators could be "criminalized." Simon's remarks were made after sit-down cases had already been filed in the Constitutional Court.[101]

Accordingly, the State of Bavaria argued that Simon must be excluded from the panel, on the grounds of "apprehension of bias" (*Besorgnis der Befangenheit*) under the Constitutional Court Act.[102] To exclude Judge Simon on these grounds, the State would not have to prove actual bias; rather, Simon would be recused if "a party to the action, considering all of the circumstances in a reasonable manner," would have "grounds to doubt that the judge was impartial."[103]

Responding to these charges, Simon declared that he did not believe himself to be biased and that his remarks were general in form, avoiding any comment on the constitutionality or interpretation of the *Nötigung* statute. He also noted that public statements are protected by the constitutional right of free speech.[104]

In the case of a charge of "apprehension of bias" against a Constitutional Court judge—or even a request by the judge to recuse

was nearing the end of his tenure when the 1986 *Nötigung* case was decided. For a summary of Judge Simon's career, see Albers and Eckertz-Höfer, "Helmut Simon zum 80. Geburtstag," 2002 NJW, 41; see also Benda *supra*.

101 73 BVerfGE, 330, 332–33 (1986); Letter, dated 9 July 1986, from the Bavarian Minister of Justice to the Vice-President of the Constitutional Court as Chair of the First Senate, 1004-I-564/86, 3. See also Simon, "Fragen der Verfassungspolitik," in Peter Glotz (ed.), *Ziviler Ungehorsam im Rechtsstaat*, 99–107 (Frankfurt/M: Suhrkamp 1983). Moreover, Simon had called for a "consultative" plebiscite on the question of allowing the Pershing II rockets to be stationed in Germany. See Benda, in *Festschrift für Helmut Simon*, 28–29; Frankfurter Rundschau [FR], 17 February 1983, 14; FR, 6 June 1983, 1.

Even before the motion for his recusal in the sit-down cases, Judge Simon's outspoken remarks on the stationing of the Pershing missiles had drawn considerable attention (and criticism) in the popular press and in professional circles. For discussion, see Sendler, "Was dürfen Richter in der Öffentlichkeit sagen?," 1984 NJW, 689, 696-97.

102 See BVerfGG §19.

103 See 72 BVerfGE, 296, 297 (1986).

104 Letter, dated 10 July 1986, from Dr. Helmut Simon to the Chair of the First Senate of the Constitutional Court.

himself—the other seven members of the panel make the final decision.[105] This system contrasts sharply with the practice in the United States Supreme Court in which the justice himself or herself makes that determination. In the Nixon-era case of *Laird v. Tatum*,[106] for example, Justice Rehnquist (as he then was) cast the deciding vote to dismiss a challenge to a program of political surveillance by the U.S. Army—a program that Rehnquist himself had defended before a Senate subcommittee when he was an official of the Justice Department. Explaining his decision not to recuse himself, Rehnquist noted that many Supreme Court justices have participated in deciding legal issues on which they had expressed strong opinions before being appointed to the bench. According to Rehnquist, the fact that these views "may have been publicly articulated prior to coming to this Court" is nothing more "than a random circumstance that should not by itself form a basis for disqualification."[107]

105 BVerfGG §19. On the disqualification of Constitutional Court judges, see generally Schlaich and Korioth, 49–52; Donald P. Kommers, *Judicial Politics in West Germany: A Study of the Federal Constitutional Court*, 201–3 (Beverly Hills CA: Sage 1976); Rüdiger Zuck, *Das Recht der Verfassungsbeschwerde*, 335–41 (Munich: Beck, 2nd edn 1988); Hans Lechner and Rüdiger Zuck, *Bundesverfassungsgerichtsgesetz*, 137–42 (Munich: Beck, 4th edn 1996).

106 408 U.S. 1 (1972).

107 *Laird v. Tatum*, 409 U.S. 824, 836 (1972) (Memorandum of Justice Rehnquist); see generally 28 U.S.C. §455. In another well-known instance, Justice Black refused to recuse himself when his former law partner argued a case in the Supreme Court. See Rehnquist, *The Supreme Court*, 65–66; *Jewell Ridge Coal Corp. v. Local No. 6167, United Mine Workers of America*, 325 U.S. 897 (1945) (Jackson, J., concurring in denial of petition for rehearing).

In an interesting recent instance, Justice Antonin Scalia recused himself from a case considering a reference to God in the "Pledge of Allegiance" after he had criticized a Court of Appeals judgment in that case in a public speech: *New York Times*, 15 October 2003, A1; cf. *Elk Grove Unified School District v. Newdow*, 542 U.S. 1 (2004). In contrast, however, Scalia declined to recuse himself in a case in which Vice President Richard Cheney was an official party, even after it was disclosed that Scalia had participated in a duck-hunting expedition with Cheney after the Supreme Court had decided to hear the case. See *Cheney v. United States District Court*, 541 U.S. 913 (2004) (Memorandum of Justice Scalia). Of course the Supreme Court retains appellate power to determine whether a *lower court* judge acted properly in declining to recuse himself, in light of the applicable statutory principles. See, e.g., *Liteky v. U.S.*, 510 U.S. 540 (1994) (upholding refusal of district judge to recuse himself in a trial for destruction of property as a political protest at a military base).

In a further variation in high court practice, the English House of Lords recently vacated a decision of one of its own panels because of a non-judicial office held by

Yet the doctrine in Germany, also, tends to make involuntary recusal of a judge quite difficult, and in this case the Court rejected the motion to exclude Judge Simon.[108] In reaching this conclusion, the Court expressed its anxiety that an easier standard for exclusion would promote the use of such motions in an increased number of cases. In principle, judges may express views on public questions, and Judge Simon's remarks were made in the course of a discussion of "basic questions of politics, religion and ethics." Moreover, Simon's remarks did not specifically address the relevant constitutional questions. Indeed, notwithstanding his sympathy for the protestors, Judge Simon had acknowledged that civil disobedience might be subject to "considerable legal risks."[109]

In declining to exclude Judge Simon, the Court followed its practice in a number of significant earlier cases, in which it refused to exclude a member of the Court for having some sort of connection with the parties or the subject matter of the litigation, or for having spoken about the matters at issue.[110]

one of the panel's judges. The panel had decided by a three-to-two margin that the former Chilean dictator, Augusto Pinochet, could not claim "head of state" immunity as a bar to extradition for alleged crimes against humanity. The Lords set aside this decision because a judge on the panel was a director and chairman of a subsidiary of Amnesty International, an intervenor in the *Pinochet* case. *Regina v. Bow Street Metropolitan Stipendiary Magistrate and Others, ex parte Pinochet Ugarte* (no. 2), [2000] 1 AC 119. According to one seasoned commentator, this case "galvanized the issues relating to the independence of the judiciary and the separation of powers" in England. Stevens, "Judicial Independence in England: A Loss of Innocence," in Russell and O'Brien (eds), *Judicial Independence in the Age of Democracy*, 157.

108 73 BVerfGE, 330 (1986). For commentary on the decision, see Wassermann, "Zur Besorgnis der Befangenheit bei Richtern des Bundesverfassungsgerichts," in *Festschrift für Helmut Simon*, 81–93; see generally Sendler, 1984 NJW, 689; Tröndle, in *Antworten auf Grundfragen*, 239–41.

109 73 BVerfGE, 336–39.

110 See, e.g., 43 BVerfGE, 126 (1976) (Judge Benda not excluded from considering defamation action, even though he previously had a close parliamentary association with the plaintiff); 32 BVerfGE, 288 (1972) (Judge v. Schlabrendorff not excluded even though, in his previous career as a lawyer, he had argued that a newspaper now appearing before the Court had expressed a Nazi point of view); 46 BVerfGE, 17 (1977) (Judge Hirsch not excluded from a case considering penalties imposed on a "radical" teacher, even though Hirsch had repeatedly and publicly sought to "defend" and "explain" the Court's previous decision on "radicals").

In certain other instances, however, judges have indeed been excluded. In 1973, for example, Judge Joachim Rottmann was excluded from considering the constitutionality of the "Basic Treaty" between the Federal Republic and East Germany because of remarks that he had made in a private letter, expressing views that had a bearing on the merits of the case.[111] In an earlier decision, the eminent constitutionalist Judge Gerhard Leibholz was excluded from considering the constitutionality of a statutory program that provided government subsidies to political parties. Addressing a meeting of law professors, Leibholz had commended the legislation, and he had questioned the democratic credentials of some opponents of the program.[112]

But an overall view suggests that in recent years the Constitutional Court has become more reluctant to exclude judges for expressing political views of relevance to a pending case. Certainly, the Court's refusal to exclude Judge Simon seems difficult to distinguish from the earlier *Rottmann* and *Leibholz* cases, in which judges were excluded for expressing strong views about the issues or parties in question.[113] Indeed—although there may be exceptions—the Constitutional Court generally seems to be moving toward something like the American resolution of this problem. Thus in recent years, the Court has ordinarily accepted a judge's own request for recusal.[114] In the same period, however, the Court has most often rejected a motion for exclusion filed by a party in the case, where the judge apparently believes that he or she can participate fairly in the proceedings.[115]

111 35 BVerfGE, 246 (1973). In a slightly earlier decision the Court had declined to exclude Rottmann for similar—but somewhat less pointed—remarks made in a public speech (35 BVerfGE, 171 (1973)). See Richard Häußler, *Der Konflikt zwischen Bundesverfassungsgericht und politischer Führung*, 57–58 (Berlin: Duncker & Humblot 1994).

112 20 BVerfGE, 1 (1966); 20 BVerfGE, 9 (1966); cf. 20 BVerfGE, 26 (1966).

113 Accordingly, one might well agree with a former Constitutional Court president who remarked that the *Simon* decision was on the "borderline." Benda, in *Festschrift für Helmut Simon*, 29.

114 For example, in criminal cases against certain East German officials, the Court accepted the self-recusal of Judge Jutta Limbach because, as Justice Minister in Berlin, she had actively favored such prosecutions (91 BVerfGE, 226 (1994)). See also 95 BVerfGE, 189 (1997); 98 BVerfGE, 134 (1998); 88 BVerfGE, 1 (1992). Cf. 72 BVerfGE, 296 (1986).

115 See, e.g., 88 BVerfGE, 17 (1992) (Judge Böckenförde not excluded from decision of case on constitutionality of abortion legislation even though he had been a member of an anti-abortion group); see also 89 BVerfGE, 359 (1994); 101 BVerfGE, 46 (1999); but see 82 BVerfGE 30 (1990).

Interestingly, the Court has indicated that the circumstances under which one of its judges should be recused are narrower than the circumstances for recusal applicable in other courts.[116] Thus, a Constitutional Court judge may continue to sit in situations in which a judge of another court would be excluded from participation. Perhaps this narrower rule of exclusion recognizes the more frankly political nature of the Constitutional Court in comparison with the role of the "ordinary" judiciary.

## The special role of the Reporter

The exclusion of Judge Simon would have been particularly momentous in this instance, because he was designated to be the Reporter (*Berichterstatter*) in the *Nötigung* case.[117] As perhaps another reflection of the specialized nature of German law,[118] each case accepted for full consideration by the Constitutional Court is assigned to a "Reporter," who is the justice with particular expertise in the relevant area. Accordingly, as each new justice joins the Court, he or she is encouraged to develop particular fields of expertise so that, among the judges, the major constitutional areas will be covered.[119]

After a case has been accepted for consideration by the Court, the expert Reporter writes an initial memorandum—a so-called "Votum"—which forms the basis of the justices' consideration and discussion of the issues. The Reporter also generally writes the (unsigned) final opinion in the case—although that opinion is subject to close review and amendment by the other justices in conference. Moreover, the Reporter may bear the burden of questioning the participants if there is oral argument.[120] Overall, it seems likely that the Reporter's deep expertise—developed through years of immersion in a particular area—gives him or her a considerable advantage in influencing the outcome of the Court's decisions in that area.[121]

[116] 73 BVerfGE, 335–37; 35 BVerfGE, 171, 173–74. For disapproving commentary, see Wassermann, in *Festschrift für Helmut Simon*, 89–90 (characterizing this result as "grotesque").

[117] Benda, in *Festschrift für Helmut Simon*, 29.

[118] Cf. Kommers, *Federal Constitutional Court*, 26.

[119] See Quint, 154 *University of Pennsylvania Law Review*, 1860.

[120] Kommers, *Judicial Politics*, 180; Kommers, *Federal Constitutional Court*, 28.

[121] See, e.g., Zuck, "Gerechtigkeit für Richter Grimm," 1996 NJW, 361.

This system stands in considerable contrast to the practice in the United States Supreme Court—in which opinions are assigned by the Chief Justice, if he is in the majority, or by the senior majority justice if the Chief Justice is among the dissenters.[122] These assignments are frequently made in a manner that does not particularly take into account any special expertise. Rather—it has been argued—assignments often reflect numerous other factors, such as the wish to allocate work more or less evenly among the justices and to achieve efficiency in the disposition of cases, the desire to reward judicial allies with opinions in prominent cases, and even the strategic goal of seeking out justices whose opinions, in specified matters, most resemble the Chief Justice's own views.[123] Although it is true that some American justices occasionally develop a special expertise—particularly in the more arcane areas of the Supreme Court workload—the much more general assignment of opinions reflects the somewhat less compartmentalized nature of American legal practice in general.

## The oral argument

Three days after the motion to remove Judge Simon was denied, the Constitutional Court held oral argument in a public hearing in the case of the sit-down protestors. A capacity audience jammed the modern, glass-walled Constitutional Court building in Karlsruhe to hear these arguments. It may be worthwhile to pause for a moment at this point, because the hearing had numerous interesting and distinctive characteristics.

The first important point to mention is that oral argument in the German Constitutional Court is relatively infrequent, and it is particularly unusual in the case of Constitutional Complaints. Indeed, it is unlikely that there will be more than a handful of oral arguments—perhaps about eight—in any given year.[124]

122 Rehnquist, *The Supreme Court*, 296.

123 See generally Davis, "Power on the Court: Chief Justice Rehnquist's opinion assignments," 74 *Judicature* 66 (1990); Danelski, "The Influence of the Chief Justice in the Decisional Process of the Supreme Court," in Sheldon Goldman and Austin Sarat (eds), *American Court Systems: Readings in Judicial Process and Behavior*, 494–96 (New York: Longman, 2nd edn 1989); Rehnquist, *The Supreme Court*, 296–97.

124 "[O]f fifty reported decisions handed down in 1991, only eight were decided subsequent to oral hearings." Kommers, *Federal Constitutional Court*, 27; see also

Accordingly, a very high percentage of the cases decided by a full senate of the Court each year are decided solely on the paper record. Of course, this is another area in which the system in the German Constitutional Court stands in considerable contrast with the practice in high courts in the Anglo-American world. In the Supreme Court of the United States, for example, oral argument is heard in almost all cases that are decided with a full opinion. In recent years, therefore, the Supreme Court has heard approximately 85 to 90 oral arguments in each term.[125]

In the English appellate courts oral argument is also common, and "in the House of Lords, Britain's highest court . . . counsel may go on for a week or more."[126] Perhaps the German practice reflects

Kommers, *Judicial Politics*, 180 (there were 151 oral arguments between 1951 and 1971—an average of somewhat less than eight per year). Actually, 1986—the year of the first *Nötigung* case—was said to be a "record year," with ten oral arguments in the Constitutional Court. Gerhardt, "'Das Bundesverfassungsgericht . . .!' Variationen über einen Ruf," in *Festschrift für Helmut Simon*, 63–64.

According to the Constitutional Court Act, oral argument may be dispensed with if all parties agree. BVerfGG §25(1). Moreover, in the special case of Constitutional Complaints, the Court itself may dispense with oral argument, if the Court concludes that argument will not assist the proceedings and if the governmental parties agree: BVerfGG §94(5); see Oswald, "Verfassungsbeschwerde-Verfahren ohne mündliche Verhandlung?," 1972 ZRP, 114 (criticizing special treatment of Constitutional Complaints). In most instances, the parties do agree to dispense with oral argument—"often with the Court's encouragement." Kommers, *Judicial Politics*, 180. See also Schlaich and Korioth, 47–48.

125 In both the 2004 term and the 2005 term, for example, there were 87 oral arguments in the Supreme Court: 2006 Year-End Report on the Federal Judiciary, 9. This number represents a considerable decline from the much larger docket of the Court in past decades. See generally O'Brien, "The Rehnquist Court's Shrinking Plenary Docket," 81 *Judicature* 58 (1997). For example, in the 1986 term—the year in which the *Nötigung* cases were decided in Germany—175 oral arguments were held in the American Supreme Court. Annual Report of the Director of the Administrative Office of the United States Courts-1987, 135.

Although it might be theoretically possible for counsel in the Supreme Court to submit a case on the briefs without oral argument, such a course is frowned upon by the Court. Stern, Gressman *et al.*, 673–76.

126 Anthony Lewis, *Make No Law: The Sullivan Case and the First Amendment*, 128 (New York: Random House 1991). Indeed, in the Court of Appeal, the tribunal directly beneath the House of Lords, the "proceedings are almost entirely oral. . . . Barristers file only the barest minimum of written materials in preparation for the appeal. . . . Some appellate judges decline to read the written material before the hearing, preferring to hear the case entirely in court." Fred L. Morrison, *Courts and the Political Process in England*, 43 (Beverly Hills, CA: Sage 1973); but see Terence Ingman, *The English Legal Process*, 14 (London: Blackstone, 6th edn

the less active role played by lawyers in general in the German and continental systems. Similarly, it may be that English and American judges—schooled in a more vigorous tradition of advocacy—find oral argument more useful than do their German judicial counterparts.[127]

But the infrequency of oral argument in the German Constitutional Court also leads to some other interesting features. Because oral argument is relatively unusual, the Court can afford to devote substantial time and attention to it when it does occur. Accordingly, the oral argument in the 1986 *Nötigung* case occupied one full day and a significant part of a second day. This somewhat exhaustive procedure contrasts with the very short time—usually limited to one hour—allowed for oral argument in a case in the American Supreme Court.[128] For American observers, the German practice may seem to recall a more leisurely period in the history of the Supreme Court, when the Court had considerably less business, and oral argument in an important case—sometimes ornamented by famous orators such

1996) (indicating that in recent years there has been a modest increase in the amount of factual material and written arguments that the Court of Appeal judges are required to read).

[127] Compare, for example, Rehnquist, *The Supreme Court*, 273, 276: "Probably the most important catalyst for generating further thought [about a case] was the oral argument of that *case*"; with Kommers, *Judicial Politics*, 180: Several Justices of the German Constitutional Court "frankly admitted . . . that oral arguments are a waste of time, since in their view such arguments do not yield information not already in the printed record."

In this light, it is perhaps not surprising that oral argument in the Constitutional Court has been subject to criticism for its "ritualized" nature. Zuck, *Recht der Verfassungsbeschwerde*, 333; see also Gerhardt, in *Festschrift für Helmut Simon*, 65. By way of contrast, compare a seasoned observer's comments on the nature of oral argument in the American Supreme Court: "To observe [the justices] as they question counsel in the courtroom is to see an extraordinarily open process, unaffected, human . . . [T]he Court seems old-fashioned, small, personal. For the lawyers, oral argument is a direct opportunity to reach those nine minds—with an idea, a phrase, a fact. Not many cases are won at argument, but they can be lost if a lawyer is unable or unwilling to answer a justice's question." Lewis, *Make No Law*, 128.

[128] Susan Low Bloch and Thomas G. Krattenmaker, *Supreme Court Politics: The Institution and Its Procedures*, 512 (St. Paul: West 1994); Rehnquist, *The Supreme Court*, 274. The Supreme Court may allow somewhat longer arguments in cases of unusual importance, such as *United States v. Nixon* in 1974 (three hours) and *Bowsher v. Synar* in 1986 (two hours). Ibid.

as Daniel Webster—could go on for days and were great social occasions in Washington.[129]

Why were the sit-down cases chosen for oral argument? One can only speculate on specific reasons. Some observers believe, however, that the function of oral argument in the Constitutional Court is as much to foster a sense of legitimacy about its processes and decisions as directly to inform the Court about the legal arguments involved in any particular case.[130] Interestingly, even after decades, the need for assurances of the political legitimacy of German institutions may not have completely disappeared. Perhaps in this case—which arose from protests against the government and NATO on a central issue of foreign policy and involved (at least according to the protestors) the question of human survival—it might have seemed particularly important to give the convicted protestors the greatest possible leeway to present their views. From the standpoint of the demonstrators, in contrast, the oral argument might well have been seen as a continuation of the protest itself.

In light of the importance of the occasion, both sides in the dispute were represented by eminent advocates or high government officials. The Federal Justice Minister Hans Engelhard (a vigorous opponent of the sit-down demonstrators) delivered an oral argument —as did the Justice Ministers of Bavaria and Baden-Württemberg, the two German states in which the relevant sit-down demonstrations had occurred. Professor Josef Isensee, one of the most eminent of the German teachers of constitutional law, also presented an argument on behalf of the State of Bavaria.

Apparently still stung by the Court's refusal to exclude Judge Simon from the proceedings, Bavarian and federal government

[129] Bloch and Krattenmaker, 512; Rehnquist, *The Supreme Court*, 274–76. For example, the oral argument in *McCulloch v. Maryland* in 1819 lasted for nine days, and two of the lawyers—Pinkney and Martin—spoke for three days each. IV Albert J. Beveridge, *The Life of John Marshall*, 282–88 (Boston, MA: Houghton Mifflin 1919). In another extraordinary example, oral argument in the great post-Civil War case of *Ex parte Milligan*, 4 Wall. 2 (1866) lasted for seven days. See Harold Hitz Burton, "Two Significant Decisions: *Ex parte Milligan* and *Ex parte McCardle*," in Edward G. Hudon (ed.), *The Occasional Papers of Mr. Justice Burton* (Brunswick: Bowdoin College 1969), 122; William H. Rehnquist, *All the Laws but One: Civil Liberties in Wartime*, 118 (New York: Knopf 1998).

[130] Cf., e.g., Kommers, *Federal Constitutional Court*, 28 ("By listening patiently to extended arguments on behalf of the litigants, the Court lends legitimacy to its proceedings").

representatives repeatedly raised doubts about Simon's impartiality in the open hearing.[131] Indeed, portions of the oral argument, in general, were conducted with a "polemic stridency" that was unusual for the Constitutional Court.[132]

Representing the protestors, several experienced advocates delivered oral arguments. These included Karl Joachim Hemeyer, a seasoned peace movement lawyer who represented Wolfgang Müller and Hansjörg Ostermayer, the chain protest defendants from Groß-engstingen; Professor Wolfgang Däubler, an eminent opponent of the Pershing missile deployment,[133] who represented Wolfgang Howald, the protesting labor court judge; and Frank Niepel, another peace movement veteran, who appeared on behalf of the defendant Karl Wenning. In addition, Professor Gerald Grünwald, an eminent teacher and scholar of criminal law and former Rector of the University of Bonn, who had long been critical of statist trends in political justice, represented Heinz-Günter Lambertz;[134] Wolfram Leyrer represented the protestor Thomas Spörer; and Rainer Schmid represented the university student Michael Geywitz. In the oral argument Schmid, in particular, emphasized the significance of the recent *Brokdorf* decision—as well as the Court's other statements on the political role of minorities—for the proper understanding of the sit-down demonstration cases.[135]

The two court-appointed legal "experts" also delivered their arguments. Rolf-Peter Calliess argued that it was clearly a violation of the rule of law when the protestors' non-violent action was changed by judicial interpretation into its very opposite—impermissible

[131] *Süddeutsche Zeitung* (SZ), 17 July 1986; SZ, 16 July 1986; FAZ, 17 July 1986.

[132] SZ, 17 July 1986.

[133] See Wolfgang Däubler, *Stationierung und Grundgesetz* (Reinbek bei Hamburg: Rowohlt Taschenbuch 1983). On Däubler, see generally Colneric, "Vorwort", in Thomas Klebe *et al.* (eds), *Recht und soziale Arbeitswelt: Festschrift für Wolfgang Däubler zum 60. Geburtstag*, 5–7 (Frankfurt/M: Bund-Verlag 1999).

[134] On Grünwald, see generally "Geleitwort der Herausgeber," in Erich Samson *et al.* (eds), *Festschrift für Gerald Grünwald zum siebzigsten Geburtstag*, 835–41 (Baden-Baden: Nomos 1999).

[135] SZ, 16 July 1986.

Relations among counsel for the protesters were not always smooth. On the day after oral argument, a lawyer for the protestors sent a blistering letter to another of the group, claiming that the latter had spoken at excessive length and had alienated the Court by strident polemics and promises that the protestors would continue their civil disobedience, no matter what the Constitutional Court ultimately decided.

"force." He recommended a return to an older form of the *Nötigung* statute that only punished coercion by actual physical violence or by the threat of physical violence or other criminal activity.[136]

In his vigorous presentation, the expert Herbert Tröndle ridiculed this proposal, arguing that statutes such as that advocated by Calliess were "already considered outmoded when horse-driven streetcars were still running in Berlin."[137] Tröndle pointed out that sit-down demonstrations could be conducted just as well by radicals of the right, pursuing nationalistic goals, and argued that sit-down blockades were "intolerable attacks on the *entire* legal order, which strike *at the core* of our system of freedom."[138] A person who seeks exceptions for demonstrations with particular goals "has departed from the fundamental principles of a free system of law. For peaceful conformity to law [*Rechtsfrieden*] deserves unlimited protection."[139]

In a bitter attack on the peace movement, Tröndle assailed the "constant self-celebration of this so-called 'nonviolence'."[140] Tröndle went on to argue that the phrase "civil disobedience"

> is a non-thought [*Ungedanke*] in a democratic state under the rule of law . . . Whoever considers this phrase, originating in the struggle against colonial overlords, to be worthy of discussion in our society, has either not really understood the basic principles of the legal order of the rule of law, or is trying to get rid of those principles [*oder es geht ihm darum, sie auszuhebeln*].[141]

The rage of an older generation of conservative German jurists when confronted with various new phenomena of the peace movement seems well represented in these bitter remarks.[142]

Furthermore, in a move that would ordinarily be unheard of in the United States Supreme Court, one of the convicted protestors

136 The argument of Rolf-Peter Calliess is reprinted in full in *Frankfurter Rundschau* (FR), 5 August 1986.

137 Herbert Tröndle, *Antworten auf Grundfragen*, 197. Tröndle's argument before the Constitutional Court is reprinted in ibid., 191–204.

138 Ibid., 200 (emphasis in original).

139 Ibid.

140 Ibid., 201.

141 Ibid., 202.

142 For Tröndle's view of the full sweep of the courts' jurisprudence on StGB §240, see Tröndle and Fischer (eds), *Strafgesetzbuch*, 1291–1317.

himself argued before the Constitutional Court—in addition to the prolific arguments of the battery of lawyers. The speaker was the defendant Heinz-Günter Lambertz, a regional administrative official(*Kreisamtmann*), who seems to have been regarded by the defendants as the most fluent and articulate of their number. Instead of propounding legal arguments, Lambertz sought to describe for the Court his "motives, fears, and hopes." Lambertz recalled the first demonstration in which he had participated, and he cited a declaration of the World Council of Churches, stating that the stationing of atomic weapons was a crime against humanity.

Invoking a theme that had become common in the statements of the German anti-nuclear movement, Lambertz likened a failure to resist atomic weapons to the failure of his parents' generation to confront the Nazis' oppression of the Jews—a failure that "helped make Auschwitz possible." In this connection Lambertz—with a "trembling voice"[143]—reminded the Court of the words of an eminent German theologian (Dorothee Sölle) who had referred to the Pershing II rockets as "flying cremation ovens." Lambertz also quoted a dramatic passage from one of the leaflets circulated by the tiny White Rose resistance movement—university students who were executed by the Nazis during World War II. The White Rose leaflet urged the Germans to "[t]ear up the cloak of indifference that you have laid over your heart. Make a decision before it is too late." And, in this connection, Lambertz noted that a surviving sister of the executed White Rose anti-Nazi protestors was also among the demonstrators at Mutlangen.[144]

In one of his closing passages, Lambertz echoed a famous speech of Martin Luther King:

> I have this dream: Day and night thousands of citizens, men and women, sit on the streets of Overkill—without weapons, obviously defenseless, hoping that their strength will be irresistible. They do not yield . . . The police approach. I am afraid. [Will they] use their clubs, let loose the police dogs, employ high

[143] SZ, 16 July 1986, 1.

[144] Cf. Hanne and Klaus Vack (eds), *Mutlangen—unser Mut wird langen*! (Sensbachtal: Komitee für Grundrechte und Demokratie e.V., 6th edn 1988), 67–74 (remarks of Inge Aicher-Scholl).

> pressure hoses,[even] . . . draw their weapons, run us over? [Or] will they turn back in favor of life?[145]

One can imagine the irritation with which an American Chief Justice would have cut off such an apparently irrelevant use of the Court's time. But the Chairman of the First Senate, Roman Herzog, politely heard this presentation to the very end.

The oral argument contained other dramatic or contentious moments. The Bavarian Minister of Justice argued that a failure to punish sit-down demonstrations under §240 could lead the Federal Republic to a fate similar to that of the Weimar Republic, which failed because it was not able to control political criminality on the streets. In such a case, argued the Minister, "the state is in danger of sinking into chaos."[146]

On the other hand, counsel for one of the protestors declared that the stationing of the nuclear missiles was a "criminal policy because it allows for undifferentiated mass murder as part of a defense strategy." Moreover, counsel argued, President Reagan (whose actions in Nicaragua had recently been held to violate international law) "constituted an additional incalculable danger" because it was he who would have the ultimate decision on the use of the Pershing II missiles.[147]

Thus, in addition to the prolific legal debates, oral argument in the *Nötigung* cases also circled back to the main contending positions underlying any evaluation of civil disobedience. On the one hand, Lambertz and counsel for the protestors emphasized the view that the stationing of the missiles posed such a grave danger to humanity

[145] The complete speech of Heinz-Günter Lambertz before the Constitutional Court is set forth in Volker Nick *et al.*, *Mutlangen 1983–1987*: *Die Stationierung der Pershing II und die Kampagne Ziviler Ungehorsam bis zur Abrüstung*, 156–57 (Mutlangen: 1993) [*Mutlangen 1983–1987*]. For Lambertz's account of his protests in Mutlangen, see "Ich glaube an die Gewaltlosigkeit," in *Mutlanger Erfahrungen: Erinnerungen und Perspektiven*, 6–9 (Mutlangen: Friedens- und Begegnungsstätte Mutlangen e.V. 1994). For Lambertz's account of his trial before Judge Offenloch in Schwäbisch Gmünd, and his address to the trial court, see *Mutlangen 1983–1987*, 180–85. See also the contribution of Heinz-Günter Lambertz, in Manfred Bissinger (ed.), *Günther Anders: Gewalt–ja oder nein*, 62–63 (Munich: Knaur 1987).

[146] *Frankfurter Rundschau* (FR), 16 July 1986.

[147] FR, 16 July 1986 (quoting newspaper summary of counsel's remarks). See *Nicaragua v. United States*, International Court of Justice, 1986 I.C.J. 14.

that the sit-down demonstrations or similar non-violent resistance represented the only moral course. On the other hand, the opponents emphasized the importance of order and legality, without which—in their view—the very stability of political organization and the State would be seriously endangered.

Chapter 4

# The sit-down blockades in the Constitutional Court:

## The decisions of 1986 and 1995

### The decision of 1986—the convictions upheld

When the Constitutional Court's decision was announced in November 1986, the opinion came as something of a shock. The eight judges of the Court's First Senate were equally divided on most issues, and so the case ended as a 4–4 tie.[1] According to the Court's rule, no statute or other governmental act may be found unconstitutional by an equally divided vote.[2] The result, therefore, was that the

[1] 73 BVerfGE, 206 (1986); substantial portions of the opinion are translated into English in *Decisions of the Bundesverfassungsgericht—Federal Constitutional Court—Federal Republic of Germany*, Volume 2/Part II, 357–85 (Baden-Baden: Nomos 1998).

For commentary on this decision, see, e.g., Kühl,"Sitzblockaden vor dem Bundesverfassungsgericht," 1987 StV 122; Starck, "Anmerkung," 1987 JZ, 145; Otto, "Sitzdemonstrationen und strafbare Nötigung in strafrechtlicher Sicht," 1987 NStZ, 212; Meurer and Bergmann, "Gewaltbegriff und Verwerflichkeitsklausel," 1988 JR, 49; Prittwitz, "Sitzblockaden—ziviler Ungehorsam und strafbare Nötigung?," 1987 JA, 17; Werner Offenloch, *Erinnerung an das Recht. Der Streit um die Nachrüstung auf den Straßen und vor den Gerichten*, 136–55 (Tübingen: Mohr Siebeck 2005).

Both of the criminal law experts who addressed the Court in the oral argument also published extensive—and critical—commentaries on the decision. See Calliess, "Sitzdemonstrationen und strafbare Nötigung in verfassungsrechtlicher Sicht," 1987 NStZ, 209; Herbert Tröndle, "Sitzblockaden und ihre Fernziele," in *Antworten auf Grundfragen*, 229–56 (Munich: Beck 1999); see also Herbert Tröndle and Thomas Fischer, *Strafgesetzbuch*, 1291–1317 (Munich: Beck, 49th edn 1999).

For significant articles canvassing the issues shortly before the decision was handed down, see Brohm, "Demonstrationsfreiheit und Sitzblockaden," 1985 JZ 501; Calliess, "Der strafrechtliche Nötigungstatbestand und das verfassungsrechtliche Gebot der Tatbestandsbestimmtheit," 1985 NJW 1506; Wolter, "Gewaltanwendung und Gewalttätigkeit," 1985 NStZ 193.

[2] BVerfGG §15 (4). See Chapter 3.

protestors lost in most cases, and their convictions remained undisturbed.[3]

### *Anonymity and the Constitutional Court*

An interesting, and perhaps somewhat exasperating, aspect of the Constitutional Court's long opinion in the 1986 case is that the Court never reveals the identity of the four judges who voted on either side. Following the usual practice, the opinion had no signed author, but the text went on to state that four judges (not naming them) hold one opinion and that the remaining four judges (not naming them) hold a contrary view.[4] Indeed, the Court had employed this form of anonymity for some years in cases of equal division, even though its rules required that any concurring or dissenting opinion must be signed with the author's name.[5]

A four-to-four tie may also occur in the Supreme Court of the United States if one of the nine justices does not participate. In such a case, the votes of the individual justices also generally remain undisclosed, and the decision of the lower court—which could be for or against the constitutionality of a statute—is affirmed.[6] Moreover, in such cases no opinion is ordinarily issued on either side, and the decision has no precedential authority "for other cases of like character."[7]

But this rare instance of judicial anonymity in the Supreme Court contrasts sharply with ordinary practice in the American legal system, in which almost all judicial opinions—in the federal courts as

[3] Only one conviction was reversed—as noted below—due to an error in the opinion of the criminal court.

[4] All eight judges signed their names at the conclusion of the opinion in the customary manner.

[5] Starck, 1987 JZ, 145. For comment on this aspect of the opinion, see also Kühl, 1987 StV, 123; Tröndle, in *Antworten auf Grundfragen*, 234–39.

[6] See, e.g., *Lotus Development Corp. v. Borland International, Inc.*, 516 U.S. 233 (1996).

[7] *Durant v. Essex Company*, 7 Wall. (74 U.S.) 107, 113 (1868). Occasionally, however, justices have issued separate opinions in such cases. See, e.g., *Biggers v. Tennessee*, 390 U.S. 404 (1968) (Douglas, J., dissenting). On equal divisions in the American Supreme Court see generally Hartnett, "Ties in the Supreme Court of the United States," 44 *William and Mary Law Review* 643 (2002); Reynolds and Young, "Equal Divisions in the Supreme Court: History, Problems, and Proposals," 62 *North Carolina Law Review* 29 (1983). On "opinion delivery practices", see generally Kelsh, "The Opinion Delivery Practices of the United States Supreme Court 1790–1945," 77 *Washington University Law Quarterly* 137 (1999).

well as in the state systems—are clearly signed, or concurred in, by named judges. Indeed, in recent years Supreme Court opinions have disclosed, with almost pedantic exactitude, the specific sections or subsections in which each justice has joined.[8] Even in the infrequent cases of unsigned *per curiam* opinions, the presence or absence of signed concurrences or dissents adequately indicates which judges support the unsigned opinion. In any event dissents—and concurrences—play an essential role in the jurisprudence of the Supreme Court and other American courts.[9]

In the English high courts, the judges commonly state their views in separate "speeches"—a practice that represents an even more extreme assertion of judicial individuality.[10] The view of each judge is therefore clearly identifiable. But since there is no joint opinion for a majority of the Court, the "holding" of the case—what it actually tells us for the future—is sometimes difficult to piece together from the speeches of the individual judges. Separate or "seriatim" opinions of this sort were also common in the United States Supreme Court in its earliest days, until the fourth Chief Justice, John Marshall, insisted that an "opinion of the Court" be delivered and that, in most cases, he deliver it.[11] Indeed, recent developments suggest that even in England there may be a modest trend away from the seriatim style and toward "composite" opinions.[12]

But the practice in Germany and other continental legal systems is quite different from these American and English patterns. Apart from the Constitutional Court itself, all judicial opinions in Germany are unsigned in the official reports, and concurring or dissenting

[8] For one of many examples, see *City of Richmond v. J.A. Croson Co.*, 488 U.S. 469 (1989). For a rare variation—with certain similarities to the practice of the Constitutional Court in the 1986 *Nötigung* case—see *Ex parte* Quirin, 317 U.S. 1, 47–48 (1942).

[9] See generally William J. Brennan, Jr., "In Defense of Dissents," 37 *Hastings Law Journal* 427 (1986); Ruth Bader Ginsburg, "Speaking in a Judicial Voice," 67 *New York University Law Review* 1185 (1992).

[10] A similar practice is still followed, to a certain extent, in high courts of certain jurisdictions influenced by the English legal tradition, such as Canada and South Africa.

[11] See e.g., Brennan, 37 *Hastings Law Journal*, 432–34; ZoBell, "Division of Opinion in the Supreme Court: A History of Judicial Disintegration", 44 *Cornell Law Quarterly* 186, 192–95 (1959).

[12] Munday, " 'All for One and One for All'," 61 *Cambridge Law Journal* 321 (2002) (indicating, also, that one court—the Criminal Division of the Court of Appeal—uniformly employs "composite" opinions).

opinions are prohibited. Of course, a litigant would know the identities of the participating judges because the parties may receive a signed copy of the opinion. But an outside observer, reading a report of an opinion in the official collection of cases, would not even know the identity of the participating judges in almost all courts. Moreover, no one at all would know if there had been internal dissent within the panel.

The effective rule against dissents or concurring opinions—and the public anonymity of the judges—seems to reflect a continental ideology that perhaps remains even stronger in France today than it does in Germany. According to this view, the judge resembles a bureaucratic official whose task is to apply clear legal doctrine to a specific case in a syllogistic manner in order to obtain the only true "solution" to the legal problem. For those who hold this position, the presence of dissents could impugn the authority of the law by indicating that a court's decision might possibly be open to question.[13] Indeed, any recognition of judicial individuality—by allowing separate opinions, even if the ultimate vote remained unanimous—might tend in the same direction.

Accordingly, dissents and other separate opinions are prohibited in almost all German courts to this day. The one exception to this rule is the Federal Constitutional Court. Facing some insistent pressure on this point from the judges themselves,[14] the West German Parliament enacted a statute in 1970 allowing a judge of the Constitutional Court to express his or her separate views in a dissenting or concurring "special opinion" (*Sondervotum*).[15]

Yet even with this express statutory permission, the judges of the German Constitutional Court make considerably less use of separ-

[13] John Henry Merryman, *The Civil Law Tradition*, 121–22 (Stanford, CA: Stanford University Press, 2nd edn. 1985). For interesting comparative background on this issue, see Nadelmann, "The Judicial Dissent: Publication v. Secrecy," 8 *American Journal of Comparative Law* 415 (1959).

[14] Commencing in 1966 in the famous *Spiegel* case, the Second Senate of the Constitutional Court began to announce divided votes in its opinions, without disclosing the identity of the judges on either side. 20 BVerfGE 162 (1966); see Donald P. Kommers, *Judicial Politics in West Germany: A Study of the Federal Constitutional Court*, 195 (Beverly Hills, CA: Sage 1976); see also David Schoenbaum, *The Spiegel Affair*, 209 (Garden City: Doubleday 1968) (noting that the *Spiegel* opinion was "the first published dissenting opinion in German legal history").

[15] BVerfGG §30(2); see generally Kommers, *Judicial Politics*, 194–98; Roellecke, "Sondervoten," in 1 Peter Badura and Horst Dreier (eds), *Festschrift 50 Jahre Bundesverfassungsgericht*, 363–84 (Tübingen: Mohr Siebeck 2001). Indeed, the

ate opinions than do their counterparts on the American Supreme Court. According to a former President of the Constitutional Court, separate opinions were issued in considerably fewer than 10 percent of the cases decided by the Court between 1971 and 2000; and these opinions appear principally in cases that have been controversial in the legal profession or in society at large.[16]

The German Court's focus on unanimity—and the relative infrequency of dissenting opinions—seems to go together with a somewhat Olympian tone in which doubt is rarely betrayed and explanation of strongly stated conclusions is not always thought to be necessary. On the other hand, the sharp personal criticism of fellow judges—which has not infrequently made its way onto the pages of Supreme Court opinions in recent years—is virtually unknown in the German Constitutional Court.[17]

In any event, a certain continuing sense of discomfort on the score of separate, signed dissents may be suggested by the peculiar form of

SPD favored including authorization for dissenting opinions in the original Constitutional Court Act of 1951, but apparently the proposal was too revolutionary for that early period. See Rinken, "The Federal Constitutional Court and the German Political System," in Ralf Rogowski and Thomas Gawron (eds), *Constitutional Courts in Comparison: The U.S. Supreme Court and the German Federal Constitutional Court*, 62 (New York: Berghahn 2002). Professional and public opinion on this question seems to have changed "only in the mid-1960s with the beginning of the student revolution" and a call for a new form of "politically conscious judge, universal transparency, and the democratization of society." Roellecke, supra, 366.

16 Limbach, *Das Bundesverfassungsgericht*, 33–34. In contrast, only about 25 percent of cases in the United States Supreme Court are decided unanimously, without separate opinions. Kelsh, 77 *Washington University Law Quarterly*, 175; see also Rogowski and Gawron, "Introduction," in *Constitutional Courts in Comparison*, 11. Interestingly—but not surprisingly to an American observer—Justice Limbach concludes that the publication of separate opinions has caused no lasting injury to "the reputation or the authority" of the German Constitutional Court. Limbach, *Das Bundesverfassungsgericht*, 34.

In contrast, however, the practice in France fully adheres to the traditional continental style. As in Germany, there are no separate opinions—either concurring or dissenting—in the ordinary courts of the French legal system. But, more than that, there are no separate opinions or acknowledgments of dissent in the Conseil Constitutionnel—the special organ that passes on the constitutionality of certain statutes before their promulgation. Even so, it has been reported that unanimity has not always prevailed among the members of that tribunal. See John Bell, *French Constitutional Law*, 47 (Oxford: Clarendon Press 1992).

17 On trends toward incivility in the American courts, see Ginsburg, 67 *New York University Law Review*, 1194–98; Lacovara, "Un-Courtly Manners: Quarrelsome justices are no longer a model of civility for lawyers," *American Bar Association*

the opinion that we are about to examine. Thus, as recently as 1986, the judges preserved their anonymity, perhaps suggesting the continuing strength of the older tradition—at least in cases in which the Court was equally divided.[18]

## *§103(2)GG and the rule of law*

In its 1986 opinion, the Constitutional Court engaged in its most comprehensive examination of the issues raised by the sit-down blockades and the *Nötigung* statute. First, the Court considered fundamental arguments on the questions of vagueness and the rule of law in connection with the concept of "force" in §240(I) of the Criminal Code. Second, the Court examined the requirement that the defendant's action be "reprehensible" under §240(II) and considered arguments seeking to place the sit-down blockades and civil disobedience in the context of freedom of assembly and the right of expression.

The four-to-four split in the Constitutional Court ran through parts of both discussions.

### *Constitutionality of the* Nötigung *statute*

At the outset, the Court turned to the most sweeping argument of the protestors: the claim that the entire *Nötigung* statute was unconstitutional because it was overly vague—particularly in light of the breadth of the term "force" and the amorphous requirement that, for conviction, the defendant's act must be "reprehensible." Because of these infirmities, the protestors argued, the entire provision violated the requirement of certainty contained in Article 103(2)GG.[19]

A decision finding §240 unconstitutional on grounds of vagueness would have had profound consequences for German criminal law.

Journal (December 1994), 50; Wald, "The Rhetoric of Results and the Results of Rhetoric: Judicial Writings," 62 *University of Chicago Law Review* 1371, 1382–83 (1995).

For an unusual example of personal debate in the German Constitutional Court, see 104 BVerfGE 92 (2001). This case is discussed in the Epilogue.

18 But for a somewhat later protest case in which the Constitutional Court was split evenly but disclosed the names of the judges voting on each side, see 82 BVerfGE 236 (1990) (upholding a conviction for *Nötigung* and "breach of the peace" [StGB §125] in connection with environmental protests against construction at the Frankfurt airport).

19 73 BVerfGE, 236–39.

First, it would have invalidated what is seen in Germany as a very important criminal statute. Moreover, such a decision could also have had serious implications for many other sections of the German Criminal Code. For the hard truth is that—notwithstanding all attempts to achieve precision—many criminal statutes contain vague formulations and open-ended terms which must be clarified through judicial interpretation. Perhaps that is an inevitable result of attempting—through codification or otherwise—to cover innumerable specific events by means of statutes drawn in general terms. Indeed, at an earlier point in its history, the Constitutional Court had upheld—against attack on grounds of vagueness—the probably equally uncertain language providing criminal liability for "gross mischief" (*grober Unfug*).[20]

In any case, in one of the two unanimous sections of the opinion, the Court rejected the argument of vagueness and upheld the statute.[21] The Court conceded that, under Article 103(2)GG, criminal statutes must achieve a significant degree of concreteness—both in order to give adequate warning of criminal liability and also to assure that the basic decision on criminality is made by the legislature, rather than by the executive or by the courts. Nonetheless, statutes may include concepts that "particularly require interpretation by the judges," because the legislator must take into account the "multifarious nature of life."[22] Although this view emphasizes statutory clarity at the outset, it ultimately seems to accord substantial power to the judiciary in the making of policy in the criminal law.

Accordingly, the unanimous Court found that the term "force" in §240(I) was not unduly vague. Rather, it is a "linguistically understandable criterion" that is also found in many other sections of the Criminal Code. Although the term may be open to interpretation, that interpretation—when "oriented on the text and statutory purpose"—can be undertaken in an "adequately foreseeable manner."[23]

[20] 26 BVerfGE, 41 (1969). See Schroeder, "Die Bestimmtheit von Strafgesetzen am Beispiel des groben Unfugs," 1969 JZ 775. This minor crime, perhaps resembling the American offense of disorderly conduct, has subsequently been deleted from the German Criminal Code—although a similar provision remains a petty infraction subject to administrative penalty.

[21] For comment on this portion of the opinion, see Kühl, 1987 StV, 124–26; Prittwitz, 1987 JA, 27; Offenloch, *Erinnerung*, 138–41.

[22] 73 BVerfGE, 234–35 (quoting 71 BVerfGE, 108, 114).

[23] 73 BVerfGE, 237.

But the Court had considerably more difficulty with §240(II) which requires that, for conviction, the defendant's act must be "reprehensible." Indeed, this requirement had evoked "serious doubts" about its vagueness from the moment that it was inserted into the Criminal Code.[24] Moreover, although the term "reprehensible" is used in a few other places in the Code, it does not seem to have a well-developed history of interpretation such as that which grew up around the statutory concept of "force."

The Court acknowledged that the term "reprehensible" involves "social-ethical evaluations," and the result is that the ultimate determination of criminal conduct is "shifted to a substantial extent, to the judge in the individual case." Indeed, the highest criminal court—the BGH—had candidly declared that, in deciding whether specific conduct is "reprehensible," the judge actually steps into the legislature's role.[25] Even so, according to the Court, this degree of vagueness was acceptable—particularly because the requirement that the act be "reprehensible" was a "corrective" which limited the criminal liability that would otherwise arise under §240(I). Here the Court seems to be saying that if the definition of the offense under §240(I) was adequately clear, some greater degree of vagueness could be tolerated in a section whose entire function was to *reduce* the coverage of that adequately clear criminal liability, rather than to expand it.[26]

Moreover, the Court indicated that this general structure—in which unclear provisions limit clear provisions—had analogues in other sections of the Criminal Code. For example, the crucial code section that furnishes a justification for certain emergency actions (*rechtfertigender Notstand*) requires the judge to weigh the competing interests and determine whether the interest in the defendant's emergency actions substantially prevails (*wesentlich überwiegt*).[27] The Court implied that the vagueness of this justification or defense was acceptable because in effect it was an exception—favoring the defendant—from an adequately well-defined criminal offense of which the defendant would otherwise be guilty.

Although comparisons on this issue are difficult, it seems quite possible that American constitutional doctrine would not permit

[24] See Kühl, 1987 StV, 125–26.

[25] 73 BVerfGE, 238 (citing 2 BGHSt, 194, 195f. (1952)).

[26] 73 BVerfGE, 238–39.

[27] StGB §34. See also StGB §193.

criminality to turn on a decision of whether a court found particular action "reprehensible." The principle of undue "vagueness," as a constituent of due process of law, might well prohibit such a result.[28] Moreover, the Supreme Court has often applied this doctrine with special rigor in cases involving the freedom of speech or assembly.[29]

Indeed, this portion of the *Nötigung* opinion was subject to sharp criticism in the German literature. One critic, for example, suggested that the constitutional requirement of certainty was revealed to be little more than a verbal formula that allowed "permissive application in the individual case."[30] On the other hand, American criminal law certainly also contains concepts whose lack of specificity rivals that of the term "reprehensible" in §240(II) of the German Criminal Code—and, in many instances, these terms have not been the subject of successful constitutional challenge.[31]

In its general discussion of §240, the Constitutional Court did not consider whether the adoption of the statute's present structure in 1943 as a product of the Nazi regime—as well as the statute's incorporation of a central phrase of Nazi ideology (albeit later amended)—raised doubts about the provision's conformity with the fundamental principles of the Basic Law. At least one critic—indeed, one of the two "experts" who spoke at oral argument—has questioned whether the Court acted properly in considering the Nazi decree of 1943 to be the equivalent of democratic legislation. Rather,

28 See, e.g., *City of Chicago v. Morales*, 527 U.S. 41 (1999) (loitering statute); *Papachristou v. City of Jacksonville*, 405 U.S. 156 (1972) (vagrancy statute); *Lanzetta v. New Jersey*, 306 U.S. 451 (1939) ("gang").

29 See *Smith v. Goguen*, 415 U.S. 566, 573 (1974) (Statute providing criminal penalty for person who "treats contemptuously the flag of the United States" is unconstitutionally vague); see also Note, "The Void-for-Vagueness Doctrine in the Supreme Court," 109 *University of Pennsylvania Law Review* 67 (1960).

30 Prittwitz, 1987 JA, 27.

31 See, e.g., Model Penal Code §210.3(1)(b). Under this section, which has been adopted in New York and certain other jurisdictions, the crime of murder is reduced to manslaughter if the act was committed "under the influence of extreme mental or emotional disturbance for which there is reasonable explanation or excuse." On the definition of reasonableness under this section, the Model Penal Code commentary candidly remarks: "In the end, the question is whether the actor's loss of self-control can be understood in terms that arouse sympathy in the ordinary citizen. Section 210.3 faces this issue squarely and leaves the ultimate judgment to the ordinary citizen in the function of a juror assigned to resolve the specific case." *Model Penal Code and Commentaries, Part II*, 63 (Philadelphia: American Law Institute 1980). Interestingly, this provision might also be analyzed as a mitigating exception to the presumably well-defined offense of murder.

the history of §240 "could have raised the issue of whether a rule set down by a social-authoritarian state—in which the 'healthy feelings of the people' was [later] simply exchanged for the concept of 'reprehensibility'—is compatible with" the Basic Law's concept of freedom and the rule of law.[32] Similarly, as we saw in Chapter 2, the eminent professor of rhetoric, Walter Jens, declared—in his argument before the criminal court in Schwäbisch Gmünd—that the term "reprehensible" had become "a threatening formula of an authoritarian state" and retained echoes of Nazi doctrine.

### *Constitutionality of the interpretation of "force"—four-to-four split*

The Court's unanimity quickly broke down, however, when it turned from the general question of the constitutionality of the statute to the specific issue of whether the criminal courts' extensive *interpretation* of the term "force" (*Gewalt*) in §240(I) was consistent with the rule of law as embodied in Article 103(2)GG.[33] A finding of unconstitutionality on this point would not have invalidated the entire statute. But—by requiring a narrower concept of "force" in §240(I)—such a holding would have reversed the convictions of the sit-down demonstrators and significantly restricted the coverage of the crime of *Nötigung*.

After outlining the steps through which the criminal courts had "spiritualized" or "dematerialized" the concept of force,[34] the Court announced that it was equally divided on whether this interpretation was constitutional. On this point, therefore, no finding of unconstitutionality could be made.

#### THE VIEWS OF THE FOUR "PREVAILING" JUDGES

According to the four "prevailing" judges—the judges who voted to uphold the convictions—the criminal courts' broad interpretation of "force" (*Gewalt*) "did not overstep the boundaries of permissible interpretation" and therefore did not violate Article 103(2) of the

32 Calliess, 1987 NStZ, 210.

33 For discussion of this portion of the opinion and related issues, see, e.g., Kühl, 1987 StV, 127–30; Meurer and Bergmann, 1988 JR, 49–51; Otto, 1987 NStZ, 212–13; Prittwitz, 1987 JA, 27–28.

34 73 BVerfGE, 239–42. See Chapter 2.

Basic Law.[35] This expanded interpretation protects the freedom of will—in this case, the will of the blocked truck drivers—against effects that are "admittedly more refined, but similarly effective as the application of bodily strength." Yet even this expansion of the concept remains within the boundary of proper judicial interpretation—a boundary that is "marked by the possible meaning of the words" (*möglicher Wortsinn*).[36]

In reaching this conclusion, the four judges noted that the word "force" (*Gewalt*) in German is not limited to the application of physical strength. Indeed, the term *Gewalt* may be used to refer to abstractions, such as governmental "powers," or it may be employed metaphorically, as in the phrase "a forceful speech" (*gewaltige Rede*). In any case the outer boundary of interpretation is not exceeded if "force" is found to refer to "irresistible pressure" on the victim which involves "the employment of a certain . . . bodily energy"[37]—even though the amount of that energy may be trivial, as in the case of the sit-in demonstrations (which involved little more than the amount of energy needed to go into the street and then sit down on it).

Of course, lying behind this entire discussion of the proper scope of interpretation was the strict prohibition of the use of "analogy" in German criminal law—in reaction to the baneful use of this technique under the Nazi regime. Indeed, Nazi doctrine, as reflected in an amendment to the German Criminal Code in 1935, allowed criminalization even where no statute provided an offense—if the act was found to "merit punishment" according to the basic purpose of any criminal statute or according to "the healthy feelings of the people [*gesundes Volksempfinden*]."[38] This provision therefore accorded great power to the courts to create new criminal offenses in accordance with Nazi ideology. Conversely, a principal goal of the modern prohibition of analogy in German criminal law is to assure that basic decisions on criminality are made by the legislature with some clarity in statutes, rather than by the courts in the form of extensive interpretation.[39]

35 73 BVerfGE, 242–44.

36 Ibid., 242.

37 Ibid., 243.

38 See, e.g., Ingo Müller, *Hitler's Justice: The Courts of the Third Reich*, 74 (Cambridge, MA: Harvard University Press 1991).

39 The problem of analogy in criminal law—and its relationship with the doctrine of unconstitutional vagueness—has also been discussed by the American Supreme Court. See *Papachristou v. City of Jacksonville*, 405 U.S. at 168 and n.12 (noting the use of the principle of analogy in the criminal law of the Soviet Union).

Yet, the prevailing judges in the 1986 *Nötigung* case argued that the legislature had actually countenanced a broad interpretation of §240 by continuing to use the term "force" (*Gewalt*) and not replacing it by the narrower term *Gewalttätigkeit*—which clearly refers to physical violence only. In contrast, the narrower term "*Gewalttätigkeit*" is employed elsewhere in the Criminal Code—for example, in provisions criminalizing forcible resistance to governmental officials, and in certain provisions criminalizing trespass and disturbing the peace.[40]

### THE RESPONSE OF THE FOUR "DEFEATED" JUDGES

The four other judges rejected this position and found that the criminal courts' broad interpretation of "force" violated the constitutional prohibition of analogy in criminal law.[41] According to these judges, the protestors had acted "in a completely passive manner, therefore certainly without force." When the statute was enacted, no one could have foreseen such an extended interpretation as the one adopted by the criminal courts.[42]

The four judges noted that, according to the traditional view, force required "the elimination of resistance. . .through the application of physical strength."[43] When the BGH began to adopt a looser requirement—for example, in *Laepple*—there was immediate criticism. Indeed, the legal doctrine remained unstable—particularly because, at the same time that the BGH was expanding the interpretation of "force" in §240, the BGH retained a significantly narrower definition of "force" for offenses of rape or sexual coercion. Indeed, the BGH found that locking a victim in a closed room—certainly at least the equivalent of the deprivation of free will at issue in the sit-down cases—did not constitute the use of force for the purpose of proving sexual coercion.[44]

Although the four judges do not elaborate further on this point, this comparison seems to imply that the criminal courts have been acting in an unprincipled or discriminatory manner. The word "force" is expanded for the purpose of convicting left-wing demonstrators.

40 73 BVerfGE, 243–44. See StGB §113(2)(2), §§124ff.

41 73 BVerfGE, 244–47.

42 Ibid., 244.

43 Ibid., 244–45.

44 Ibid., 245; see 1981 NJW, 2204. For an attempted distinction of the two areas, see Altvater, "Anmerkung," 1995 NStZ, 278, 279.

But the same term is interpreted narrowly in a manner that will reduce convictions for an offense—rape or sexual coercion—that was designed primarily for the protection of women.

Moreover, the four judges suggest, if the extended interpretation were correct, there would have been no need to insert the phrase "by force" in §240(I) at all—because this interpretation seems broad enough to cover all forms of effective pressure and therefore would have been adequately conveyed by the verb "coerce" (*nötigen*) already present in the statute. But, on the contrary, the drafters included the phrase "by force" in order to limit the coverage of the statute to certain kinds of coercion only. If the result of such a limitation is that there are "gaps" in the statute, it is not up to the courts to close those "gaps" in a manner that "empties" the statute of its meaning.[45]

The four "defeated" judges also commented on the political context of the dispute. They noted that, according to the protestors, this was an area of "high political" controversy. In such cases, it was important that "violent acts" [*Gewalttätigkeiten*] be avoided and that "the line between violent and nonviolent behavior retain clear contours." But under the broad interpretation of "force," the state itself would contribute to a blurring of these conceptual lines. If that is to happen, the *legislature* should be responsible for such a decision—not the courts. This result is required by the prohibition of analogy in criminal law, which "strictly reserves" the definition of criminal norms to the legislator, as an aspect of the principle of democracy and the separation of powers.[46]

This important passage in the opinion of the four "defeated" judges may also have contained an oblique reference to a central dispute within the German peace movement itself.[47] The sit-down protestors were drawn from the majority wing of the peace movement, which insisted on strict non-violence—in contrast with a smaller group that countenanced and engaged in violent protest. As one of its central tenets, the non-violent wing sought complete separation from those willing to engage in violent acts. Therefore, an interpretation of Section 240 which indicated that the peaceful non-violent resisters had been exercising illegal "force" could lead to an unfortunate confusion of concepts—and perhaps to an actual increase in violent action itself.

In any case, the interpretation of "force" approved by the prevailing

[45] 73 BVerfGE, 245–46.

[46] Ibid., 246–47.

[47] See Chapter 3.

judges afforded a powerful weapon to political opponents of the sit-down demonstrators. By emphasizing that the protestors had been convicted of acting with illegal "force," the opponents could foster the impression that the sit-down protestors should be placed in the same political category as violent criminal groups, such as the Baader-Meinhoff gang.

The view of the four "defeated" judges would have avoided this result. Yet it is important to understand that this argument was based on the specific nature of the extended interpretation of "force" in the *Nötigung* statute. Even the four "defeated" judges acknowledged that the defendants' acts were properly considered to be a violation of the various administrative rules relating to traffic and political assemblies.[48]

## Article 8 and the right of assembly

### Sit-down demonstrations are not protected under Article 8

The Court then turned to a complex discussion of the constitutional effect of the rights of assembly and free expression. Again, the panel was equally divided in its ultimate decision, although it remained unanimous on some important preliminary issues.

The Court first unanimously acknowledged that the sit-down demonstrations fell within the general area of the freedom of assembly protected by Article 8(1) GG.[49] Although Article 8(1) guarantees a right of "peaceful" assembly only, the Court found that a non-violent sit-down protest can be viewed as "peaceful" under Article 8 GG—even if it qualifies as the exercise of coercive "force" under §240(I) StGB. Lack of "peacefulness" under Article 8(1) is a narrower concept than the use of "force" under §240(I): it is limited to dangerous behavior such as violence or aggressive actions against persons or things and does not include passive sit-down protests and the psychic force found to satisfy §240 (I) StGB.

This is a good example of a form of argument that is frequently encountered in legal discourse—in which quite similar words or formulae may have different meanings in light of the differing contexts in which they are found. This form of argument may be

48 73 BVerfGE, 244.

49 Ibid., 248–49. For commentary on the Court's discussion of Article 8 GG, see Kühl, 1987 StV, 130–33; Offenloch, *Erinnerung*, 141–45.

troublesome or even exasperating at times. Yet it is a reminder of the limitations of language which, unlike mathematics perhaps, is always dependent upon context, whether in legal discourse or elsewhere. Here the context is that of a quite extensive freedom of assembly, and the liberal spirit of the *Brokdorf* decision—decided only one year earlier—clearly animates this portion of the discussion.[50]

Yet, the protestors' victory on this preliminary point was short-lived. Even though the demonstrations fall within the protection of Article 8(1) GG, the unanimous Court found that these protests were ultimately *not* protected by Article 8 as a whole. This conclusion followed from section 2 of Article 8 which allows the legislature to impose restrictions even on "peaceful" outdoor assemblies that receive general protection under section 1. Of course, most demonstrations cause blockages and disturbance of traffic, which must be accepted as an inevitable side-effect if the right of assembly is to be preserved. But the unanimous Court concluded that Article 8(2) *does* allow the police to dissolve demonstrations whose very purpose and intent is to obstruct the passage of third persons and to arouse attention for the demonstrators' cause in that way. Furthermore, when the demonstration is legally dissolved, any constitutional protection "falls away" as well.[51]

This, then, is the crucial difference between the sit-down demonstrations at Mutlangen (and Großengstingen) and the protests against the nuclear plant at Brokdorf. The Brokdorf protest was not specifically directed at blocking a particular entrance or exit along a particular road; if traffic was indeed interrupted, the blockage was basically a by-product of the mass demonstration that was primarily directed at the dissemination of ideas in other ways. In the sit-down protests, in contrast, the blocking of traffic itself represented the principal purpose of the defendants' actions. Therefore the sit-down protests were ultimately not protected by Article 8.[52]

[50] Cf. Kühl, 1987 StV, 131. But for a lively exposition of the opposing view that a "forcible" blockade can never be considered a "peaceful" assembly under Article 8(1) GG, see Schmitt Glaeser, *Private Gewalt*, 105–8. For discussion of the *Brokdorf* case, see Ch. 3.

[51] 73 BVerfGE, 249–250; see generally VersG §15.

[52] But this apparently neat distinction may sometimes be extremely difficult to draw in practice. The organizers of a large traditional demonstration—whose ostensible purpose lies in conveying ideas through signs and parades—may believe that their cause is also furthered by the inevitable blockage of traffic that may result. See generally 32 BGHSt, 165 (1983) (mass demonstration at Frankfurt Airport).

### *Sit-down demonstrations not protected as "civil disobedience"*

The unanimous Court also found that the protests were not protected under a constitutional right of civil disobedience.[53] The Court noted that civil disobedience included the violation of legal rules as a method of calling attention to governmental decisions that might be disastrous or ethically illegitimate. According to its proponents, civil disobedience must not be directed toward actually paralyzing governmental functions, but rather toward a dramatic intervention in public debate. Moreover, it must be absolutely non-violent, undertaken in public, and consistent with general principles of proportionality. The Court also noted the protestors' view that civil disobedience had been developed in response to the "incompleteness" of the political process—"a view that immediately called forth associations with the *Brokdorf* decision of the Constitutional Court, in which the weaknesses of the political process were emphasized in quite a similar manner."[54]

In contrast, the opponents maintained that civil disobedience contravened the citizens' duty of domestic peace, violated the doctrine of equality, and disregarded the principle of majority rule which is crucial in a democracy.[55]

But the Court did not find it necessary to pursue these arguments more fully because it concluded—unanimously—that in any case the concept of civil disobedience could not justify intentional interference with traffic through sit-down protests, at least when the rights of third persons were impaired. Moreover—the Court noted—the entire purpose of civil disobedience is to underscore a political view by engaging in illegal action. Thus to argue that a

[53] 73 BVerfGE, 250–52. This section of the Court's opinion seems to be a response to the arguments of the Peace Research Institutes, and to the elaborate argument of Karl Joachim Hemeyer, the lawyer for the Großengstingen chain protestors Müller and Ostermayer. See Chapter 3. In this section, the Court also explicitly responds to a widely noted Memorandum (*Denkschrift*) of the German Evangelical Church which had discussed these issues. See *Evangelische Kirche und freiheitliche Demokratie: Der Staat des Grundgesetzes als Angebot und Aufgabe (Eine Denkschrift der Evangelischen Kirche in Deutschland)* (Gütersloh: Mohn 1985). For commentary on this section of the opinion, see, e.g., Kühl, 1987 StV, 133–34. See also Prittwitz, 1987 JA, 22–25.

[54] Kühl, 1987 StV, 133.

[55] 73 BVerfGE, 251.

context of civil disobedience should have the effect of *removing* illegality of the act would involve a form of self-contradiction.[56]

### *Article 8 and the requirement of "reprehensible" action*

#### BALANCING IS NECESSARY IN EVERY CASE

Yet these general findings that the sit-down demonstrators were not protected by Article 8 or by a general right of civil disobedience—reached by a unanimous panel—did not conclude the Court's opinion. Rather, the Court then focused on the specific role of §240(II)—the requirement that the defendant's action be "reprehensible"—in the structure of the offense of *Nötigung*.[57]

First, the unanimous Court found that this requirement played a role of *constitutional* importance. Since the broad terms of §240(I) might cover harmless or even praiseworthy forms of "coercion"—remember George holding Rodney's arm to restrain him from stepping out into dangerous traffic[58]—the requirement that the action be "reprehensible" in §240(II) serves the essential constitutional function of separating acts of coercion which should be made criminal from those which should not be the subject of such treatment. In so doing, §240 (II) embodies the crucial principle of proportionality in German constitutional law and the fundamental requirement that a criminal penalty must not exceed the degree of a defendant's guilt. This "corrective" function of §240(II) is particularly important in light of the extension of the coverage of §240(I) through the broad interpretation of the concept of "force" discussed above.[59]

Because §240(II) plays such a crucial constitutional role, it must not be subverted by the criminal courts. But the BGH did precisely that in the *Laepple* decision, when it held that if "force" was present under §240(I), it would automatically follow that the act was

[56] Ibid., 252.

[57] Ibid., 252–61. For commentary on this portion of the decision and the justices' treatment of §240 (II), see Kühl, 1987 StV, 134–36; Meurer and Bergmann, 1988 JR, 51–54; Prittwitz, 1987 JA, 28; Otto, 1987 NStZ, 213; Offenloch, *Erinnerung*, 146–49. See generally Otto, "Strafbare Nötigung durch Sitzblockaden in der höchstrichterlichen Rechtsprechung und die Thesen der Gewaltkommission zu §240 StGB," 1992 NStZ, 568, 571–73.

[58] See Chapter 2.

[59] 73 BVerfGE, 252–54.

"reprehensible" under §240(II)—a holding that virtually deprived §240(II) of any independent effect.[60]

Such an automatic conclusion might be justified if the defendant had engaged in a violent coercive attack. (Remember our case of Arthur beating Bill with a club to coerce him to sign a legal document.)[61] In such cases, the "reprehensible" nature of the act could be inferred directly from the use of this type of force alone.

But where the "force" in question is the psychological "spiritualized" force at issue in the cases of the sit-down protestors, such an automatic conclusion is not permissible. Rather, in such cases, an independent weighing of all of the circumstances of the case is required in order to determine whether the act is actually "reprehensible." This balancing is of constitutional importance, in light of the German constitutional principle that any penalization of an individual must be "proportionate" to the nature of his or her underlying act. Consequently, there is a constitutional violation if the criminal court does not undertake this weighing.[62]

Moreover, the justices found—unanimously—that the criminal court had not undertaken the required balancing in one of the nine cases on review. The Court therefore reversed the conviction of defendant Karl Wenning who had participated in a blockade of an American army base in Neu-Ulm on Easter Sunday 1983.[63] In revers-

[60] Ibid., 254; see Chapter 2.

[61] See Chapter 2.

[62] See 73 BVerfGE, 255–56. As noted in Chapter 2, the BGH had adopted a similar position in a case handed down a few months before the Constitutional Court's 1986 decision, thus departing from its earlier view in the *Laepple* case of 1969. See 34 BGHSt, 71 (1986). But the BGH decision rested on an apparent change of statutory construction, while the Constitutional Court found that balancing in these cases was constitutionally compelled.

For general discussion of the principle of proportionality in German constitutional law, see David P. Currie, *The Constitution of the Federal Republic of Germany*, 307–10 (Chicago, IL: University of Chicago Press 1994); Schlink, "Der Grundsatz der Verhältnismäßigkeit," in 2 *Festschrift 50 Jahre Bundesverfassungsgericht*, 445–65. For general discussion of balancing in free speech cases in German constitutional law, see Quint, "Free Speech and Private Law in German Constitutional Theory," 48 *Maryland Law Review* 247(1989).

[63] The Easter Blockades of 1983 were the culmination of a weekend of protests at the Wiley Barracks in Neu-Ulm—a potential location of Pershing II missiles. On the same weekend, major anti-missile demonstrations also took place in many other parts of Germany. The Easter Blockades of 1983 were "a modified version of the Easter Marches against nuclear armaments" of decades past. Thomas Laker, *Ziviler*

ing Wenning's conviction, the Court referred to several factors that might have been considered in the process of balancing. The Court noted, for example, that the protest took place on Easter Sunday, when there was less traffic than usual; that the duration and "intensity" of the blockade were slight; and that the blockade was announced in advance so that other methods of entry to the base could be arranged.[64] Because the criminal courts had not taken these mitigating factors into account on the question of "reprehensible" action, Karl Wenning's case was returned to those lower tribunals.[65]

*Ungehorsam: Geschichte—Begriff—Rechtfertigung*, 107 (Baden–Baden: Nomos 1986).

As in the Großengstingen Tent Village protests of the previous year (see Chapter 1), the Easter 1983 demonstrators in Neu-Ulm formed "affinity groups" and participated in "trainings" in methods of non-violence, which included discussion of the views of Mahatma Gandhi. Interview with Karl Wenning, Munich, 15 July 2002. Also as at Großengstingen, each affinity group sent a representative to sit in a general council of the demonstrators (*Sprecherrat*), which sought to find consensus among the affinity groups. Opinion of Amtsgericht Neu-Ulm, 6 May 1987, 2 Cs 14 Js 23383/83, 4.

In the preparatory handbook for the Easter Weekend Blockades, the authors remarked: "We can learn much from Gandhi's independence struggle in India, as well as from the civil rights movement of Martin Luther King. But we cannot simply transpose their actions and methods to another situation—rather, we are always challenged anew to act in a creative and imaginative manner." *Handbuch Gewaltfreie Aktion, Lichtblick Blockade Neu-Ulm, Ostern '83*, 8. Participation in these demonstrations involved some risk. On the first day of the protests, two demonstrators were seriously bitten by police dogs. *Dokumentation zur Blockade Ostern '83 in Neu-Ulm*, 30 (reproducing London *Times*, 2 April 1983).

On Easter Sunday 1983, Karl Wenning participated in the third blockade of the day, along with 200 other demonstrators. For this action, Wenning was convicted under §240 StGB and related provisions. But the opinion of the trial court contained no substantial discussion on the question of the "reprehensible" nature of Wenning's conduct. Instead, a conclusory passage merely declared that his conduct was to be viewed as reprehensible. Opinion of Amtsgericht Neu-Ulm, 18 July 1984, 2 Cs 14 Js 23383/83, 6–7. It was this conclusory portion of the criminal court's opinion that led to the reversal of Wenning's conviction by the Constitutional Court. (For an example of a similar reversal by a screening committee of the Court in a subsequent case, see Judgment of the 3rd Chamber of the First Senate, 14 February 1991, 1991 NStZ, 279.)

[64] 73 BVerfGE, at 256–57.

[65] On remand, the *Amtsgericht* in Neu-Ulm acquitted Wenning on the grounds that, in the circumstances, his action was not "reprehensible." On appeal (*Berufung*), the State Court in Memmingen upheld the acquittal on the grounds that—due to certain special circumstances of the case—it could not even be said that Wenning was exercising "force" that impaired the passage of military vehicles. The prosecution

## STRIKING THE BALANCE—ANOTHER FOUR-TO-FOUR SPLIT

In the final passages of the opinion, the Court turned to the cases of the other eight protestors. In these cases—unlike the *Wenning* case—the criminal courts had given some attention to the specific circumstances of the situation in determining that the sit-down blockades were "reprehensible." The Court was split four to four on the question of whether these courts, in handing down convictions, had reached a constitutionally permissible result.[66]

*The Constitutional Court and the "ordinary" courts* In this discussion, the judges were sharply divided on a question that has long been controversial in German constitutional law—the extent to which the Constitutional Court can review or overrule the *application* of constitutional balancing principles by the "ordinary" courts in civil and criminal matters. To understand this problem, we must always bear in mind that—unlike, for example, the Supreme Court of the United States—the German Constitutional Court is not a part of the "ordinary" civil and criminal court system and that it stands apart from that system. Accordingly, the Constitutional Court ordinarily plays no significant role in the routine interpretation of the civil or criminal law—even though that law is federal law in Germany.

In contrast, the United States Supreme Court, which is a part of the general system of federal courts, frequently decides questions of the interpretation of federal statutes, including federal criminal statutes, even when absolutely no issue of constitutional law is involved. Yet, the Supreme Court of the United States ordinarily does not have jurisdiction to decide questions of *state law*. Therefore, the relationship between the Supreme Court and the law of the states is rather similar to the role ordinarily occupied by the German Constitutional Court with respect to questions of German "ordinary" criminal or civil law—even though in Germany that law is federal law.

But the neat division of constitutional and "ordinary" law in Germany can sometimes become blurred. In a long line of cases, the Constitutional Court has found that the rules of civil law must be "influenced" by certain constitutional values; and the same doctrine

missed the deadline for filing a *Revision* procedure in the State Appellate Court, and therefore Wenning's acquittal became final.

66 73 BVerfGE, 257.

applies in certain criminal cases as well.[67] Specifically, in our anti-nuclear protestors' cases, we have seen that the *constitutional* doctrine of proportionality requires the criminal courts to balance all of the circumstances of the case, in order to determine whether the action is a "reprehensible" form of coercion. Moreover, at least four of the justices acknowledged that the constitutional value of freedom of assembly under Article 8 GG must also play a role—or have some influence—in this balancing, even if the actions of the defendants are not absolutely protected under Article 8.[68]

In cases of this kind, in which the constitution itself influences the interpretation of the "ordinary" civil or criminal law, what is the role of the Constitutional Court in reviewing the decisions of the "ordinary" civil and criminal courts? Should the Constitutional Court scrutinize the *result* reached by the ordinary courts in order to assure that the constitutional balancing has been properly undertaken and that adequate weight has been given to the constitutional "influence"? Or should the Constitutional Court say that, as long as the ordinary court adequately stated the relevant constitutional principles, the actual balancing of the interests is something to be done by the ordinary courts, and we will not intervene?[69]

In a sense, this question suggests a point of tension over the issue of whether the system of constitutional law or of the "ordinary law" is ultimately to be accorded the greater weight in cases of this kind. An insistence on the clear supremacy of constitutional law might require that the Court strictly review this balancing to determine whether the proper constitutional result has been achieved. In contrast, a decision to defer to the balancing undertaken by the criminal courts—as long as the correct constitutional principles have been mentioned by the criminal court—would seem to suggest deference to the greater expertise of the "ordinary" courts over their body of law and, ultimately perhaps, the greater importance of that body of doctrine.

Such a view may harken back to an earlier—but not too distant—era in which the civil and criminal codes (which in significant aspects find their origins in Roman law) were seen as the fundamental substance of the law; and constitutional law, a modern and in some

[67] 7 BVerfGE, 198 (1958) (*Lüth*); 12 BVerfGE, 113 (1961) (*Schmid-Spiegel*).

[68] See 73 BVerfGE, 259.

[69] For general discussion of this issue, see Quint, 48 *Maryland Law Review*, 308–14, 325–29.

circles suspect legal phenomenon, was viewed as superficial and quite possibly ephemeral—in any case not deserving the dignity of the older bodies of "ordinary" law. Deference to the criminal courts—as long as they have mentioned the correct constitutional principles—may also reflect the central importance of doctrine and principle in continental legal systems, in contrast with the lesser importance of the result in the individual case.[70]

It was precisely this point on which the judges of the Constitutional Court were equally divided, in the final passages of the 1986 decision. Four judges concluded that the Court should review the criminal courts' balancing on the question of the "reprehensible" nature of the actions. But the four "prevailing" judges argued that the balancing should be left to the criminal courts in most cases—as long as the lower court stated the proper constitutional principles to be applied in the balance.[71]

*The view of the four "defeated" judges* The four judges who sought closer review maintained that the demonstrators' goals must be taken into account as a possible counterweight to the obstruction of traffic that they had caused.[72] These included the protestors' immediate goal of attracting greater attention to their views, as well as the long-term goal of opposing what they saw as dangerous atomic armaments.

In taking the long-term goal into account, these judges argued, the courts would not be preferring certain political opinions over others. Rather, the courts would only be acknowledging that actions oriented toward public issues are of greater value than actions directed toward selfish financial interests—a view that the Court has frequently advanced in balancing cases related to the freedom of

70 Ibid., 310–12.

71 73 BVerfGE, 257–61. By way of comparison, it is clear that the Supreme Court of the United States feels itself free to reverse state court decisions on the grounds that correct constitutional principles require a specific result and that the state court did not reach that result in the particular case. See, e.g., *New York Times v. Sullivan*, 376 U.S. 254, 284–92 (1964). Certainly, the Supreme Court does not consider itself at all precluded from reviewing a state court decision on a federal constitutional issue merely because the state court has repeated the correct constitutional formula. On the other hand, the constitutional doctrine of the Supreme Court frequently takes the form of rules that are somewhat more precise than the open-ended balancing tests favored by the German Constitutional Court in speech and assembly cases.

72 73 BVerfGE, 257–60.

expression.[73] By including the requirement of "reprehensible" action in Section 240(II), the legislature intended that the courts undertake an ethical evaluation of the protestors' actions; accordingly the courts may not ignore the protestors' motivation, which is "one of the most important circumstances for such an evaluation."[74]

As perhaps the most interesting aspect of their argument, the four "defeated" judges then concluded that if the strict requirements of civil disobedience were met—public symbolic protest, non-resistance to police arrests, etc.—these demonstrations could *not* generally be characterized as "reprehensible" coercion. According to the four judges, this conclusion resulted in part from the impact of Article 8 GG—providing a constitutional right of assembly—on the interpretation of the word "reprehensible" in §240(II).

The judges also noted that the use of "force" remained at its lowest level in these cases, and that in some instances the protestors had been specifically trained in the capacity for non-violence. In this light, "the mere circumstance that the obstruction is intended as a means of informative protest—and not accepted merely as an unavoidable side effect of a demonstration—cannot be sufficient" to classify a sit-down blockade as "reprehensible."[75] The judges did acknowledge, however, that an exception might be made in aggravated circumstances—for example, if a blockade impeded the progress of an ambulance or obstructed traffic in a "particularly intensive" manner. Accordingly, the cases should be remanded to the lower courts to determine whether any aggravating circumstances were present.

In light of the remarks of these four judges, we may be able to review the Court's position on the constitutional role of civil disobedience with some perspective. The Court held unanimously that there was no constitutional right to civil disobedience: therefore, actions that are otherwise illegal may be punished under the criminal law even though they satisfy the most stringent definition of persuasive civil disobedience.

On the other hand, four judges took the position that civil disobedience does occupy a certain position of constitutional importance—in a more indirect manner. If a criminal statute provides for a defense or justification in general and open-ended terms—such as a

[73] 7 BVerfGE, 198, 212 (*Lüth*); 68 BVerfGE, 226, 232–33 (1984) (Sheriff in Black).

[74] 73 BVerfGE, 258.

[75] Ibid., 259.

provision removing criminal liability if a defendant's actions are not "reprehensible"—the law might require acquittal if the actions satisfied the definition of civil disobedience, at least in the absence of certain aggravating factors. This result could be achieved, in significant part, by virtue of the impact or "influence" of the constitutional guarantee of freedom of assembly on the interpretation of such an open statutory term.

Thus, although there is no fully protected right to civil disobedience, four judges argue that the Constitution might require that some general and open-ended statutes be interpreted to provide a defense to criminality for civil disobedience in some cases. Modest though this constitutional recognition of civil disobedience might be—and notwithstanding the fact that, as the view of the four "defeated" judges, it did not become the doctrine of the Constitutional Court—this step toward recognition of the constitutional status of civil disobedience certainly goes beyond any ideas that are current in American constitutional or criminal decisions.[76] As has been noted, the liberal spirit of the *Brokdorf* decision, which accorded extensive protection to the rights of demonstrators, seems to be particularly strongly represented in the opinion of the four "defeated" judges.

*The views of the four prevailing judges* Of course, the remaining four judges—whose views ultimately prevailed—reached quite a different conclusion on the role of the Constitutional Court in these cases.[77] These judges reiterated the general principle—often stated by the Court—that the interpretation and application of the rules of ordinary law is fundamentally a matter for the ordinary courts. Of course if a criminal court completely misunderstands a constitutional principle, then the Constitutional Court should intervene. Indeed, that is what happened in Karl Wenning's case, in which the criminal court had failed to engage in any independent weighing of the circumstances at all, in order to determine whether the

[76] For the generally hostile approach of the American appellate courts to defenses based on ideas of civil disobedience, see Chapter 2.

On the other hand, of course, the Supreme Court has frequently found that certain acts of defiance of local authorities were forms of protected speech under the First Amendment (or otherwise constitutionally protected) and therefore not strictly acts of civil disobedience at all. See, e.g., *Edwards v. South Carolina*, 372 U.S. 229 (1963); *Cox v. Louisiana*, 379 U.S. 536 (1965); *Peterson v. City of Greenville*, 373 U.S. 244 (1963).

[77] 73 BVerfGE, 260–61.

defendant's actions were "reprehensible" under StGB §240 (II). But if—as in the cases of the other protestors—the criminal courts undertook the required weighing of interests, the striking of the balance in the individual case "belongs to the typical tasks" that are confided to the criminal courts in deciding these cases. Accordingly, the Constitutional Court should not intervene in order to decide whether the weighing was properly done or to substitute its own assessment of the proper result.

Moreover, these four judges argued, the Constitution does not require the criminal courts to consider the protestors' ultimate goals in determining whether the blockades were "reprehensible" under §240(II). It was sufficient that these goals were taken into account in deciding the defendant's penalty, and indeed the criminal courts had done so—with the result that the defendants' fines in these cases were set at low amounts.[78]

Because, as we have seen, a judgment cannot be found unconstitutional by an equally divided vote, the protestors' convictions were upheld on this point as well.[79]

78 Ibid.

79 In a brief decision handed down a few months later, the Constitutional Court indicated that it was still equally divided on issues relating to the sit-down demonstrations. 76 BVerfGE, 211 (1987). The Constitutional Complainant in this case was Gert Bastian, a former German army general who had lost his command in 1980 because he criticized the planned deployment of the Pershing II missiles. Later that year Bastian was the author of the Krefeld Appeal, a petition opposing the presence of American missiles in Germany. See Chapter 1; see also Rob Burns and Wilfried van der Will, *Protest and Democracy in West Germany*, 208 (New York: St. Martin's Press 1998). A prominent theoretician of the peace movement, Bastian entered Parliament as a member of the Greens Party in 1983, but he left the Greens parliamentary caucus in January 1984, claiming that it had been "subver[ted] by extremists." Thomas R. Rochon, *Mobilizing for Peace: The Antinuclear Movements in Western Europe*, 4, 85 (Princeton, NJ: Princeton University Press 1988); Gerd Langguth, *The Green Factor in German Politics*, 18 (trans. Richard Straus; Boulder, Co: Westview Press 1986). For Bastian's commentary on the issues of the peace movement, see Gert Bastian, *Frieden schaffen! Gedanken zur Sicherheitspolitik* (Munich: Kindler 1983); Bastian, "Die Nachrüstungs-Lüge," in Walter Jens (ed.), *In letzter Stunde: Aufruf zum Frieden* (Munich: Kindler 1982), 27–62.

Bastian was convicted of *Nötigung* for participating in the Easter Sunday sit-down demonstration in 1983 at the American barracks in Neu-Ulm—the same demonstration that led to the trial of Karl Wenning. Because Bastian was a prominent figure in the peace movement, his presence was calculated to draw attention to the demonstrations; yet he was not regarded as a particular leader of the protest—

To many observers, this decision of the Constitutional Court in 1986 came as a great disappointment—not only because of the equal division of the judges, but also because the opinions seemed to be seriously lacking in clarity. According to one commentator, the prevailing views in the case "remain so imprecise and general that the reader gets the impression that the opinion does not actually express" the justices' underlying convictions.[80] Certainly, the case was open to varying interpretations. For example, the 1986 decision was followed in January 1987 by a sit-down blockade of about twenty German judges at the Pershing rocket depot in Mutlangen.[81] While, on the

because the affinity groups, in an egalitarian spirit, sought to avoid having leaders at all. Interview with Karl Wenning, Munich, 15 July 2002.

Although the Constitutional Court unanimously reversed Wenning's conviction in 1986, the Court in 1987 upheld Bastian's conviction by a four-to-four vote. Four judges found that the opinion of the criminal court "contained in several places clear elements of a weighing of values" in determining that Bastian's actions were "reprehensible" under §240(II)—whereas no such balancing had been undertaken in Wenning's case. The other four judges, however, denied that the proper balancing could be found in the opinion of the criminal court. As in the 1986 *Nötigung* case, the identity of the judges on either side was not disclosed.

In the *Bastian* case, the Constitutional Court unanimously declared that, because of the four-to-four split, the Court was making no decision on the constitutionality of applying §240 to these protestors. 76 BVerfGE, 216–17. This conclusion aroused the ire of some commentators, who maintained that a four-to-four vote was a decision *on the merits* that the challenged action was constitutional. See, e.g., Willms, "Ein Justizskandal neuer Art," FAZ, 14 August 1996, 8; but see Fritz, "Stellung nehmen und Standpunkt bezeugen: Behinderung als Mittel zum aufklärenden Protest," in Willy Brandt *et al.* (eds), *Ein Richter, ein Bürger, ein Christ. Festschrift für Helmut Simon* (Baden-Baden: Nomos 1987), 424–27. For discussion of the *Bastian* case, see Offenloch, *Erinnerung*, 152–55.

In the years following these events, Karl Wenning has worked as an actor and clown, performing in cabarets and in other settings, sometimes in shows for children. Among other things, he has presented a cabaret program about the sit-down blockades of the 1980s and their legal aftermath—using his own case as an example. Interview with Karl Wenning, 15 July 2002; see also Schwäbische Zeitung, 19 February 1992.

In contrast, Gert Bastian came to a considerably more problematic end. In 1992 Bastian and his partner Petra Kelly, an early leader of the Greens Party, were found shot to death in their apartment. It seems most likely that this was a case of murder and suicide by Bastian—although other theories (suicide pact, mysterious intruder) have occasionally been advanced. See, e.g., *New York Times*, 20 October 1992, A1; *New York Times*, 6 July 1995, B10 ("suicide pact").

[80] Otto, 1987 NStZ, 212. See also, e.g., Meurer and Bergmann, 1988 JR, 49 (criticizing the justices' discussion of "force" as "largely superficial").

[81] See Chapter 1.

one side, the federal justice minister declared that these judges had contravened the 1986 decision, the judges apparently invoked the same decision in responding that their actions were justified because the blockade was not "reprehensible" under the prevailing doctrine.[82]

In any event, the 1986 decision was attacked from both sides of the spectrum. One conservative critic, for example, deplored the Court's requirement that the "reprehensible" nature of the act be determined anew by a balancing in every case, taking all factors into account. According to this commentator, the stable judicial interpretation that had previously prevailed was thus replaced by a "completely open" concept that could be susceptible to influence by political views.[83] In contrast, one of the "experts" who appeared in the oral argument—a critic on the left—concluded that the wide difference in the interpretations of the judges proved, in itself, that §240 of the Criminal Code was unconstitutional: the divergent opinions showed that this statute opened the floodgates to various "contradictory and mutually exclusive interpretations."[84]

Finally, the other "expert" called before the Court—representing the more conservative position—launched a vigorous attack on Judge Simon, the judge who remained on the panel after surviving a challenge to his impartiality.[85] Because Simon was the "Reporter" (*Berichterstatter*) in the case, Tröndle held him responsible for the form of the opinion. Tröndle argued that the opinion was infused with the self-conceptions and even the language of the protestors.[86] Moreover—according to Tröndle—Simon showed his partiality in requesting briefs from a number of the peace institutes but not from the military or the Ministry of Defense.[87] In important passages, Tröndle argued, the opinion placed undue weight on the views of the four "defeated" justices, and the positions of the "prevailing" judges were given short shrift.[88]

[82] See Otto, 1987 NStZ, 212. Blockade supporters also favorably contrasted the resistance of these protesting judges with the notorious obedience of judges under the Nazi regime. See Heinrich Hannover, *Die Republik vor Gericht, 1975–1995*, 319–32 (Berlin: Aufbau 1999).

[83] Starck, 1987 JZ, 148.

[84] Calliess, 1987 NStZ, 209–10.

[85] See Tröndle, "Sitzblockaden und ihre Fernziele," in *Antworten auf Grundfragen*, 239ff.

[86] Ibid., 242. Cf. also Offenloch, "Der Streit um die Blockaden in rechts- und verfassungstheoretischer Sicht," 1992 JZ, 438–39 (Portions of the Court's 1986 opinion "read like a self-portrait written by the protestors themselves.")

[87] Tröndle, in *Antworten auf Grundfragen*, 241.

[88] Ibid., 245–46.

Amid this general unhappiness, there was an uneasy sense that this decision could not be the last word on the constitutional problems raised by the offense of *Nötigung*. In the minds of many, for example, some sort of legislative revision of §240 seemed to be necessary.

## Müller-Breuer and Ostermayer before the European Human Rights Commission

With the decision of the Constitutional Court in 1986, the case of Mutlangen demonstrator Luise Scholl, as well as the cases of the Großengstingen chain protestors Müller-Breuer and Ostermayer, appeared to have come to an end in the German courts. Yet there seemed to be one more possibility of legal redress, however remote. Müller-Breuer and Ostermayer filed a complaint before the European Commission of Human Rights.

### *European law and national law*

It will be worthwhile to pause for a moment at this step in the proceedings, because European institutions have assumed an important role in the legal systems of Germany and other European countries. Unlike the case in the United States—where the domestic legal system still remains basically self-contained—litigants and judges in European countries must always bear in mind that there is a European legal system that is in some ways "superior" to domestic institutions. Indeed, the European legal system may sometimes override national rules of law and judicial decisions.

The chief component of the European legal system is the law of the European Union, including the extensive economic law of the European Communities. Although EU law is not directly applicable in our case, there is another important component of the European system that does have a bearing here. This is the law developed by the institutions of the Council of Europe under the European Human Rights Convention.[89]

The European Human Rights Convention was issued in 1950 and

[89] European Convention for the Protection of Human Rights and Fundamental Freedoms, 4 November 1950, 312 U.N.T.S., 221, E.T.S., 5, as amended.

It is also worth noting that, in the future, the authority of the European Union to enforce European constitutional rights within the member states may be significantly expanded under a possible future constitution for the European Union.

has now been signed and ratified by 46 European countries, including many states of the former Soviet bloc. The Convention binds the signatory states to a basic level of human rights and establishes institutions to enforce that obligation. In 1986, when the first *Nötigung* case was decided by the Constitutional Court, an individual claiming a violation of the Convention could file a complaint in the European Commission of Human Rights, and the case might later proceed to the more august European Court of Human Rights. More recently, the Commission has been abolished, and the European Court of Human Rights has been re-established with expanded jurisdiction.[90] Now, the full court—or a screening committee of its judges—adjudicates all individual complaints under the Convention.

The precise relationship between the European Convention and the domestic legal system varies from country to country. In some European countries the Convention is a source of law directly enforceable by national courts; in other countries, however, that is not the case.[91] In the United Kingdom, for example, an international treaty plays no role in the national legal system unless a Statute of Parliament gives it that effect. But for many years there was no such statute with respect to the European Human Rights Convention. As a result, an individual who prevailed against the United Kingdom in the European Court of Human Rights was dependent upon the enactment of a parliamentary statute for redress.

In 1998, however, Parliament enacted the Human Rights Act, which made the European Convention a part of United Kingdom law. Under the Act, all judges must interpret Statutes of Parliament in a manner that conforms with the Convention. If a statute cannot be interpreted to avoid a conflict with the Convention, the judges must issue a "declaration of incompatibility" and refer the matter to a cabinet minister for possible swift action in Parliament to amend the statute. An important open question is whether the British judges will vigorously enforce this form of quasi-constitutional human rights law in a legal culture that has traditionally been dominated by theories of parliamentary supremacy.

The Federal Republic of Germany was also an early signatory of

[90] Protocol No. 11 to the Convention for the Protection of Human Rights and Fundamental Freedoms, restructuring the control machinery established thereby, Strasbourg, 11 May 1994, E.T.S., 155.

[91] See generally Mark W. Janis *et al.* (eds), *European Human Rights Law: Text and Materials*, 448–50 (Oxford: Clarendon Press 1995).

the European Human Rights Convention, and a statute of Parliament incorporated the Convention into domestic law in 1952. Yet this step was of considerably less importance in Germany than it would have been in the United Kingdom—because the guarantees of the Convention largely coincide with constitutional rights already protected in Germany by the Basic Law. The "ordinary" courts may be required to interpret statutes in conformity with the Convention, but the German Constitutional Court has ruled that it has no jurisdiction to invalidate statutes or other governmental actions on the ground that they violate the European Convention.[92] Accordingly, if an individual who claims a violation of the Convention does not receive a favorable judgment from an "ordinary" court, the principal remaining avenue of redress for violations of the Convention is to secure a judgment in the European Court of Human Rights (or, previously, the Commission) and to hope that the German government will make the appropriate adjustment within the national system.[93] This is the course that Müller-Breuer and Ostermayer pursued after the Constitutional Court rejected their complaints in the 1986 decision.

### *Defeat in the European Commission*

Before the European Commission, the lawyer for Müller-Breuer and Ostermayer argued that the German courts' expanded definition of "force" violated the prohibition of retroactive lawmaking in Article 7(1) of the European Convention. He also argued that the conviction violated the "freedom of peaceful assembly" protected by Article 11 of the Convention. Of course, these arguments closely resembled claims that had already been rejected by the German Constitutional Court under the Basic Law.

The Commission made short shrift of both arguments.[94] On the argument of retroactivity, the Commission acknowledged that, under Article 7, statutes must be drawn with "sufficient precision to enable

[92] 10 BVerfGE, 271, 274 (1960); 34 BVerfGE, 384, 395 (1973); 74 BVerfGE, 102, 128 (1987). See BVerfGG §90.

[93] See generally Nigel G. Foster, *German Legal System and Laws*, 78–79 (London: Blackstone Press, 2nd edn 1996); Klaus Schlaich and Stefan Korioth, *Das Bundesverfassungsgericht: Stellung, Verfahren, Entscheidungen*, 252–55 (Munich: Beck, 5th edn 2001).

[94] European Commission of Human Rights, Decision of 6 March 1989, Application No. 13235/87.

the citizen to regulate his conduct," and "existing offences [may not] be extended to cover facts which previously clearly did not constitute a criminal offence."[95] But the Commission found that "the progressively broader interpretation of the term 'force' [under §240(I) StGB] has adapted the offence . . . to new circumstances and developments in society, which can still reasonably be brought under the original concept of the offence." Moreover, in light of earlier decisions of the BGH, the sit-down protestors could "clearly foresee the risk of punishment."[96]

On the freedom of assembly claim, the Commission concluded that, while the demonstrators' non-violent protest received a measure of protection under Article 11(1) of the European Convention, the convictions could be upheld as "necessary in a democratic society for the prevention of disorder and crime" under Article 11(2) of the Convention.[97] Indeed, the Commission was so certain of its views that it held the protestors' application "manifestly ill-founded" and therefore "inadmissible."[98]

With this conclusive defeat in the European Commission, it would seem that the case of the two Großengstingen demonstrators was finally at an end. Indeed, Müller-Breuer and Ostermayer were so informed by their lawyer in the spring of 1989, after the Commission's judgment. Certainly, counsel for the other Constitutional Complainants in the 1986 *Nötigung* case must have reached the same conclusion.

Yet legal developments sometimes bring considerable surprises, and we will see that—contrary to the universal expectations at the time—Müller-Breuer, Ostermayer, and other protestors would

[95] Ibid., 5.

[96] Ibid., 6.

[97] Ibid., 7. As in the case of Article 8 of the German Basic Law on freedom of assembly, Article 11 of the European Convention is also composed of two sections: the first section sets forth a broad right of "freedom of peaceful assembly," but the second section permits certain limitations on that right if those limitations are "necessary in a democratic society."

[98] Ibid. On the same day, the European Commission of Human Rights dismissed similar petitions of several other German anti-missile protestors, including that of Michael Geywitz, another of the losing complainants in the 1986 decision of the German Constitutional Court. See *Geywitz v. Federal Republic of Germany*, Application No. 13079/87, 60 *European Commission of Human Rights Decisions and Reports*, 256 (1989). See also *C.S. v. Federal Republic of Germany*, Application No. 13858/88 (1989); *Schiefer v. Federal Republic of Germany*, Application No. 13389/89 (1989).

prevail in the end. Yet for these surprising developments to mature, it was necessary for nine years to pass from the date of the 1986 decision in the Constitutional Court—a period in which a number of very important developments occurred. Some of these events reflected a massive revolution on the international scene, while others specifically involved the world of the German Constitutional Court itself.

## Nine years pass

Ordinarily, of course, it is not possible to assess the precise impact of even the most dramatic historical changes on the decision of a particular legal problem. Yet it would be foolish to ignore these changes completely in trying to understand a momentous change of doctrine on an important public issue in a constitutional court.

Of course the first of these changes was the opening of the Berlin Wall and the end of the Soviet Union and the Eastern Bloc, with the accompanying unification of East and West Germany. Indeed, only a few months after the case of Müller-Breuer and Ostermayer was apparently concluded in the European Commission, the Berlin Wall was opened and the Cold War swiftly came to an end. One direct result of these developments was the withdrawal of the opposing armies and the dismantling of much of the nuclear weaponry that had been directed across the European divide. Indeed, the Pershing rockets in Mutlangen were already in the process of removal and destruction in accordance with a treaty signed by Presidents Reagan and Gorbachev in 1987.[99]

Accordingly, the cases involving battles over these missiles had taken on a less urgent quality by the time of the Court's second major *Nötigung* decision in 1995. Moreover, the entire significance of NATO and the Western Alliance began to appear in a rather different light. NATO was still important for its role in maintaining an American military presence in Europe, and it began to undertake military and peace-keeping measures elsewhere in the world. Yet NATO could no longer be viewed as the single force that was absolutely essential in defending the Federal Republic and indeed in preserving its very existence. Accordingly, the past decade's protests against NATO's policies and its missiles no longer seemed to strike at

[99] See Chapter 1.

the very core of West German statehood and its last line of defense against bitterly hostile outside forces. As might well be expected, geopolitical considerations of this kind could play no role in the explicit argumentation of the Court—which was based on somewhat more focused constitutional doctrine—but neither should the influence of such momentous developments be completely ignored.[100]

The second important change that occurred in the nine years between 1986 and 1995 was a considerable turnover in the personnel of the First Senate of the German Constitutional Court.

Unlike their counterparts on the United States Supreme Court, the judges of the German Constitutional Court do not hold their offices for life or "during good behavior." Rather, since 1970, the Constitutional Court judges have been appointed for twelve-year non-renewable terms.[101] The limitation of terms reduces the likelihood that judges will remain on the Court for years after they have lost touch with contemporary circumstances. On the other hand, the advantages of extraordinary judicial careers spanning decades—such as the long tenures of Chief Justice Marshall and Associate Justices Holmes, Brandeis, Black, Douglas, and Frankfurter—are also lost.

As a result of the system of twelve-year terms, only two of the eight judges who participated in the Court's first *Nötigung* decision in

[100] An American analogue might be found in the historical background of *Brown v. Board of Education*, 347 U.S. 483, the great desegregation decision decided by the United States Supreme Court in 1954. The Court did not explicitly argue that racial segregation appeared particularly paradoxical after the United States had fought a bitter war against the racist Nazi regime. Nor did it mention that segregation in the United States greatly weakened the moral and political position of the United States in the Third World. Yet the lessons of World War II, and the perceived imperatives of Cold War foreign policy, may well have contributed to a climate in which the continuation of segregation seemed increasingly anomalous. Mary L. Dudziak, *Cold War Civil Rights: Race and the Image of American Democracy*, 79–114 (Princeton, NJ: Princeton University Press 2002). In this connection, see *Brown v. Board of Education*, Brief for the United States as Amicus Curiae, December 1952, at 6:

> It is in the context of the present world struggle between freedom and tyranny that the problem of racial discrimination must be viewed . . . Racial discrimination furnishes grist for the Communist propaganda mills, and it raises doubts even among friendly nations as to the intensity of our devotion to the democratic faith.

[101] See Chapter 3.

1986 were still present for the second decision in 1995.[102] Accordingly, it has been suggested that the "radical reversal" in the 1995 decision might well be "traced to the changed personal composition" of the Court.[103]

## The 1995 decision: convictions reversed

### *Background and arguments*

The facts of the second *Nötigung* case—decided by the Constitutional Court in 1995—also arose out of protests at the "special weapons depot" for Lance nuclear missiles in Großengstingen. As we saw in Chapter 1, small groups of protestors blocked the entrance to the weapons depot at several points during the day of 9 May 1983. On one of these occasions the four petitioners in the 1995 case—Gunhild Beuter, Wilfried Braig, and Eva and Thomas Moch—sat in the road and blocked the progress of a military vehicle. After the required warnings, these four protestors were carried away by the police. At other times during the day, they stood at the roadside and gave moral support to fellow protestors who were blocking military vehicles, and this supporting activity also played a role in their convictions.[104] In Chapter 2 we traced the complex procedural route of the case of these four protestors—involving seven opinions in five different tribunals—through the German criminal court system.

It is striking to note that the actions of these demonstrators took

[102] The two remaining members were Judges Johann Friedrich Henschel and Otto Seidl. The new members of the First Senate were Judges Dieter Grimm, Evelyn Haas, Renate Jaeger, Jürgen Kühling, Helga Seibert, and Alfred Söllner.

Over the same period of time (from 11 November 1986 to 10 January 1995), only four members of the United States Supreme Court remained in office (Rehnquist, Stevens, O'Connor, Scalia)—also reflecting a significant change of judicial personnel. In contrast, however, over the eleven-year period from 3 August 1994 to the death of Chief Justice Rehnquist in September 2005, the composition of the Supreme Court—quite exceptionally—remained completely unchanged (although in 2005 Justice O'Connor had also announced her retirement, effective upon the confirmation of a successor). Interestingly, as of September 2005, only one of the sitting justices—Justice Breyer—had been in office for less than 12 years, the maximum tenure of the German Constitutional Court judges.

[103] Scholz, "Sitzblockade und Verfassung—Zur neuen Entscheidung des BVerfG," 1995 NStZ 417, 423.

[104] See 92 BVerfGE, 1, 2–3, 5 (1995).

place in Spring 1983—that is, *earlier* than three of the demonstrations that were considered by the Constitutional Court in its first decision in 1986. In part, the great delay between the protest in 1983 and the ultimate decision in 1995 was a result of the complicated path that this case took on its way to the Constitutional Court. Even so, the Court waited for almost six years to decide this case after the Constitutional Complaints were filed in 1989. Indeed, this long delay contrasted dramatically with the requirements of speed which the Constitutional Court has imposed on other courts.[105] There was even "speculation" that the decision had been "intentionally delayed" by the Court.[106]

On this occasion, there was no oral argument in the Constitutional Court, and the case was decided on the written arguments alone. But understandably, these written arguments gave no inkling of the dramatic decision that was actually to follow.

105 See, e.g., Krey, "Das Bundesverfassungsgericht in Karlsruhe—ein Gericht läuft aus dem Ruder (I)," 1995 JR, 221, 228.

106 Schroeder, "Sitzblockade keine Gewalt", 1995 JuS, 875.

In contrast with this long delay in the German tribunal, the United States Supreme Court customarily decides cases before the end of the nine- or ten-month term (October to July) in which oral argument is heard. From time to time, however, a case may be set down for rehearing—with new briefs and new oral argument in the following term. Almost invariably the case is then decided in that term. See, e.g., *Brown v. Board of Education*, 347 U.S. 483 (1954); *Shapiro v. Thompson*, 394 U.S. 618 (1969). Of course, the Supreme Court can delay deciding a *type* of problem by failing to grant *certiorari* in relevant cases over a long period.

It seems reasonably clear that there is a close connection between the institution of oral argument and the rapid decision of cases—as reflected, for example, in the practice of the American Supreme Court. If oral argument is taken seriously, every judge who decides a case should have participated in the oral argument in that case. But if a long period elapses between oral argument and the decision, some judges who heard oral argument may leave the Court before the case is decided. Therefore a swift decision seems imperative. In contrast, if the case is to be decided on written material alone, it might be thought that the material could be as easily read some years after the filing of the Constitutional Complaint as at the outset—a procedure, in any event, that seems to have been followed in the 1995 *Nötigung* case.

It is worth noting, therefore, that in the relatively few cases in which the German Constitutional Court does hear oral argument, a specified date for rapid decision is ordinarily set down in advance. For example, the 1986 *Nötigung* decision of the Constitutional Court was argued in July 1986 and decided in November of the same year, after only four months had elapsed. In contrast, the 1995 *Nötigung* case—in which no oral argument was held—was decided almost six years after the Constitutional Complaints were filed.

Counsel for the four protestors still included Hanns-Michael Langner and Siegfried Nold who, as apprentice lawyers (*Referendare*), had appeared for these defendants in their first trial in 1984.[107] Because counsel felt bound by the Court's 1986 decision, they tried to find a distinction between that decision and the lower court opinions which they were now challenging. Their primary focus of attack was the intervening 1988 decision of the BGH which excluded the protestors' "ultimate goal" (avoiding nuclear war) in determining whether their blockade was "reprehensible" under §240(II).[108] Counsel argued that this flat rule in effect reintroduced the automatic inference of "reprehensible" conduct from a finding of the use of "force"—an inference that the Constitutional Court had been at pains to exclude in its decision in 1986.[109] Federal and State ministries of justice filed quite predictable arguments in their briefs in response.

In the written record, there was only one possible hint or foreshadowing of what was to come. This passage was buried in a brief statement of the Fourth Criminal Senate of the BGH, which had been filed in accordance with the Constitutional Court's practice of seeking advice from the senates of the BGH in cases involving application of the ordinary law.[110] The Fourth Criminal Senate criticized the patterns of prosecution in the *Nötigung* cases, implying that political discrimination affected the enforcement of §240. The Fourth Criminal Senate stated:

> From the standpoint of criminological policy, however, it is regrettable that as a result of the present prosecutorial practice,

107 See Chapter 2. In the Constitutional Court, Hanns-Michael Langner officially represented Eva Moch, while his associate W. Mühlebach represented Thomas Moch. The law firm of Hemeyer, Treimer and Nold represented Gunhild Beuter and Wilfried Braig.

108 35 BGHSt, 270 (1988); see Chapter 2.

109 Constitutional Complaint filed on behalf of Dr. Thomas Moch by W. Mühlebach, 14 June 1989, 7–14; Constitutional Complaint filed on behalf of Gunhild Beuter-Hanke by Siegfried Nold, 8 June 1989, 12–14.

Complainants also argued that imputing criminality to protestors who stood at the side of the road and gave moral support to persons engaged in blockades—as the defendants had done at various points during the day—further attenuated the concept of force in §240(I) in an unprecedented and impermissible manner. As noted in Chapter 2, the defendants' convictions rested, in part, on these grounds. Cf. 92 BVerfGE, 7.

110 For discussion of this practice, see Chapter 3.

> the impression has justifiably arisen that "ultimate goals" (*Fernziele*) would be disregarded only with respect to certain sit-down blockades, whereas the "ultimate goals" result in an omission to prosecute in the case of other blockades—for example, [strikes that] stop businesses or [blockades that] burden long distance traffic. This is detrimental to the acceptance of the *Nötigung* jurisprudence of the Federal Supreme Court (BGH).[111]

In this passage the Fourth Criminal Senate was most likely referring to a famous incident in February 1984 in which long-distance truckers from Germany and elsewhere blocked the Brenner Pass and a related route (Inntal Autobahn) in order to protest delays caused by officials at the Italian border. This economic blockade led to few if any prosecutions in the German courts. Indeed, Franz Josef Strauss, the Minister-President (Governor) of Bavaria, personally visited the blockade and shook the hands of participating truck drivers, assuring them of his "full support".[112] In contrast, the State of Bavaria was energetic in prosecuting anti-nuclear sit-down demonstrators at Neu-Ulm (and elsewhere), and it is difficult to imagine any of these protestors receiving a congratulatory handshake from the powerful Bavarian Minister-President.[113]

### *The Court's opinion*

In a dramatic reversal, the Constitutional Court took a new direction in 1995 and found that the protestors' convictions violated concepts of the rule of law contained in Article 103(2) of the German Constitution.[114] The result of this decision was that even Müller-Breuer, Ostermayer, and Scholl—and many other earlier complainants whose convictions had been upheld by the Court in the 1986 decision—

[111] Letter, dated 18 June 1990, from the President of the Federal Supreme Court (BGH) to the President of the Federal Constitutional Court, VRG 4/90, 4; see also 92 BVerfGE, 11.

[112] Der Spiegel, 9 April 1984, 119.

[113] See, e.g., Hanjörg Reichert-Hammer, *Politische Fernziele und Unrecht*, 64–66 (Berlin: Duncker & Humblot 1991); Hanne and Klaus Vack (eds), *Mutlangen—unser Mut wird langen*! (Sensbachtal: Komitee für Grundrechte und Demokratie e.V., 6th edn 1988), 64–65 (Statement of Fritz Hartnagel). Occasionally, however, officials have claimed that prosecutions for the Alpine truck blockade did actually take place. See, e.g., Schroeder, 1995 JuS, 876.

[114] 92 BVerfGE, 1 (1995).

were entitled to have their cases reopened and their convictions reversed.

This time the Court's vote was five to three in favor of unconstitutionality. As noted, only two of the eight judges remained from the panel that had decided the first *Nötigung* case in 1986; one of these remaining judges was in the majority in 1995 and one joined the dissent.[115] In contrast with the 1986 decision—which contained a complex discussion of the implications of the freedom of assembly guaranteed by Article 8 GG—the decision in 1995 rested principally on the view that the criminal courts' extended interpretation of "force" (*Gewalt*) violated principles of the rule of law contained in Article 103(2)GG.[116]

The Court's opinion concentrated on a rather narrowly focused analysis of statutory language and, for the most part, it avoided the discussion of civil disobedience and political theory that the "defeated" four judges had advanced in 1986. Yet totally apart from any judgment on the correctness of the result, the Court's argument may be criticized for reflecting a rather naive view of the functions of language in the judicial process. Moreover, at the midpoint of its discussion, the Court shifts its focus rather significantly. Although the Court begins by disapproving the extended breadth of the criminal courts' interpretation of "force" in §240(I), it then proceeds to find fault with the vagueness of the term "reprehensible" in §240 (II)—so that its ultimate decision rests at least in part on this second infirmity in the statute as well.

[115] Justice Johann Friedrich Henschel was in the majority, while Justice Otto Seidl voted with the dissent. As this was no longer an equally divided four-to-four decision, the names of the dissenters were disclosed. Indeed, by 1995 the Court's practice in this respect had changed, so that—even if it had been a four-to-four decision—the names of the justices on each side would have been clearly set forth.

[116] For commentary on the 1995 *Nötigung* decision, see, e.g., Amelung, "Sitzblockaden, Gewalt und Kraftentfaltung", 1995 NJW, 2584; Gusy, "Anmerkung," 1995 JZ, 782; Krey, "Das Bundesverfassungsgericht in Karlsruhe—ein Gericht läuft aus dem Ruder", 1995 JR, 221 (Part I), 265 (Part II); Lesch, "Bemerkungen zum Nötigungsbeschluß des BVerfG vom 10.1.1995," 1995 JA, 889; Scholz, "Sitzblockade und Verfassung—Zur neuen Entscheidung des BVerfG", 1995 NStZ, 417; Schroeder, "Sitzblockade keine Gewalt," 1995 JuS, 875; Altvater, "Anmerkung," 1995 NStZ, 278; Offenloch, *Erinnerung*, 183–94.

### *General principles*

The Court began its opinion by reiterating the importance of clarity and "concreteness" in the text of criminal statutes. The point of this requirement is not only to give notice to the individual about what possible conduct may be punishable. The requirement also functions as an aspect of the separation of powers, designed to preserve parliamentary supremacy in lawmaking: the requirement guarantees that the decision on criminality will be made "in advance by the legislature, and not subsequently by the executive or the judiciary."[117] Accordingly, this doctrine imposes limits on the extent of interpretation allowed to the criminal courts.

On the other hand, the Constitutional Court conceded that the legislature must sometimes employ statutory terms that are in particular need of judicial interpretation—in order to take account of the "multifarious nature of life," and because of the generality and abstractness of the criminal law. Yet, even in these situations, a reader of the statute must at least be able to recognize when there is a risk of criminal penalty.[118]

Most important, the constitution prohibits criminalization by analogy or through the invocation of customary law. Accordingly, "every application of law is excluded which goes beyond the content of a statutory norm of prohibition. . . . The possible meaning [*Wortsinn*] of the words of the statute"—as determined from the point of view of the reader of the statute—"marks the farthest boundary of permissible judicial interpretation."[119] The courts may not "correct" a decision of the legislature by interpreting statutory language in a manner that extends "beyond the recognizable meaning [*Wortsinn*] of the rule"—even if the conduct at issue seems to be as worthy of punishment as the conduct prohibited by the statute. It is up to the legislature to decide whether or not to close that "gap."[120]

In these passages, the Court adopts the view that language can establish clear borders for the "meaning of words" and that it is possible to discern with some assurance whether judicial interpretation has observed or exceeded these boundaries. Indeed, in a sense, one could say that "analogy" could be defined negatively as something

117 92 BVerfGE, 12. See, e.g., Gusy, 1995 JZ, 782.
118 92 BVerfGE, 12.
119 Ibid.
120 Ibid., 13.

that goes beyond the bounds of permissible interpretation: where "interpretation" ends, "analogy" begins.[121] Of course, as we have seen, the Court was particularly sensitive about the use of analogy in criminal law because that device was notably employed by the Nazi regime in order to penalize disfavored conduct, without the necessity of defining that conduct in advance.[122]

### *The interpretation of §240(I)*

After these introductory remarks, and after a brief review of the history of §240 StGB, the Court went on to note that the 1986 decision had (unanimously) upheld the constitutionality of §240 StGB on its face. Generally speaking, the Court did not disturb that result.[123] But when the 1995 Court turned to the specific interpretation of the word "force" (*Gewalt*) in §240(1)—as that interpretation was developed in the sit-down decisions of the criminal courts—the Court parted ways with the prevailing judges in the earlier case. In 1986 the Court, in an equally divided four-to-four vote, declined to strike down the criminal courts' interpretation of "force." But, in 1995 the Court, in a five-to-three decision, found that interpretation unconstitutional.[124]

In reaching this conclusion, the Court first reviewed the process of the "spiritualization" (*Vergeistigung*) of the concept of force in the criminal courts. According to the Court, "[t]his development was characterized by the decreasing importance of the application

121 Cf., e.g., Lesch, 1995 JA, 889.

122 Müller, *Hitler's Justice*, 74–75. According to Müller, *Analogie* was only one of the methods of broad statutory interpretation employed by the Nazis in achieving their goals in the criminal law. See generally ibid., 68–81.

123 92 BVerfGE, 13–14. Thus the Court again rejected arguments—heard for decades—that all or part of the *Nötigung* statute is unconstitutional on grounds of undue vagueness or overbreadth. See Amelung, 1995 NJW, 2589; Calliess, "Der strafrechtliche Nötigungstatbestand und das verfassungsrechtliche Gebot der Tatbestandsbestimmtheit," 1985 NJW, 1506, 1507 and n. 13, 1510 and n. 34.

124 In its discussion on this point, the Court followed the *Bastian* case and reiterated its view that the 1986 case had not actually endorsed the criminal courts' interpretation of the word "force" in §240(I). Rather, according to the Court, the equal division of the judges in 1986 meant that the merits of the constitutional issue remained unresolved. 92 BVerfGE, 14, citing 76 BVerfGE, 211, 217 (1987). As we have seen, some scholars vigorously disputed this point, arguing that an equally divided vote of the Court is a holding on the merits in favor of constitutionality. See, e.g., Willms, FAZ, 14 August 1996, 8.

[*Entfaltung*] of physical strength on the part of the offender, and the increasing importance of the coercive effect experienced by the victim." In this development, "the amount of strength that must be applied"—in order for the defendant's act to qualify as force—"was constantly diminished, and the requirement of a bodily coercive effect on the victim of coercion was completely abandoned." Finally in cases such as *Laepple*, the criminal courts sought to protect the freedom of the will against psychological effects "that indeed were more refined (*sublimer*) than applications of bodily strength, but similarly effective."[125]

But, according to the majority of the Court, this extended interpretation violated Article 103(2)GG. The word "force" (*Gewalt*) has various meanings in various contexts, but here it must be examined in light of the structure of §240 StGB. In everyday life we are all subjected to various coercive effects that we would not want to punish under the criminal law. In order to avoid such a result, the statute limits criminality to coercion that is effected through two specified means—"force" and threats of a "substantial evil." Everyone agrees that coercion by other means, such as trickery or suggestion, are not criminalized under §240—even if these means have as severe an effect on the victim as the means set forth in the statute.[126]

Accordingly, Parliament intended that the word "force" should not be considered equivalent to coercion itself. Rather, the phrase "by force" should limit the kinds of "coercion" that would be subject to punishment; and Article 103(2)GG therefore prohibits this limitation of criminality from being abrogated by the judiciary.[127]

The Court indicated that, in contrast with the word "threats," the word "force" accomplished its intended limiting effect through its connection with "bodily application of force on the part of the offender."[128] Accordingly, the Court continued, those "applications of pressure that do not rest on the employment of bodily strength, but rather on a spiritual or psychological influence, could in some

[125] 92 BVerfGE, 14–15. In contrast, a number of German scholars criticized this interpretation of the historical development, arguing that elements of "psychological" coercion were present in the criminal courts' interpretation of the *Nötigung* offense from a very early point—and therefore no significant shift in doctrine had actually taken place. See, e.g., Lesch, 1995 JA, 890–94.

[126] 92 BVerfGE, 16. In these passages, the opinion closely followed the argument of the "defeated" four judges in the 1986 *Nötigung* decision.

[127] Ibid., 16–17.

[128] Ibid., 17.

cases fulfill the statutory element of 'threats', but not however [the requirement of] the application of force (*Gewalt*)."[129] Of course, the criminal courts continued to require some application of bodily strength, but they diluted this requirement so much that nothing more than bodily presence in a place where someone else wished to pass would suffice to constitute "force."

Through this development, the requirement of "force" became so unlimited that it no longer adequately served the function of distinguishing acts of coercion that should be criminalized from those that unavoidably occur in everyday life. To achieve this goal, therefore, the courts were impelled to rely on the requirement of the "reprehensible" nature of the act set forth in StGB §240(II). Accordingly, the BGH began to focus on what it considered to be the "weight"—presumably the seriousness—of the psychological effect on the victim. Yet this concept is even less precise than the concept of force, and consequently it could not dissipate the problems for the rule of law that were raised by the judicial expansion of the concept of force.[130]

The result was that this interpretation of "force" on the part of the BGH had an effect that contravened Article 103(2)GG: one could no longer know with certainty which physical actions that psychologically obstructed the will of another should be legal and which should be illegal. Thus, in cases in which "force consists simply in bodily presence and the pressure exerted on the coerced person is only of a psychological nature," the decision on criminality is not made by the legislature in general abstract form, but rather in each case by the judge "according to his view of whether the act is worthy of punishment."[131]

The result of this development was to introduce a considerable breadth of discretion in prosecutions for *Nötigung*—a breadth of discretion which, the Court indicates, violates Article 103(2) GG. Indeed, these prosecutions have not followed a uniform course—as

129 Ibid.

130 Ibid.

131 Ibid., 18. The Court also denied that the uncertainty evoked by the "expanded concept of force" has been overcome by an understanding that has "stabilized over time." On the contrary, the cases and the literature show that no clear legal view has been established. Moreover, even if the cases would give warning of the risk of criminality, that result cannot be permissibly achieved by judicial interpretation which indeed increases the uncertainty of an already vague norm of the criminal law. Ibid., 18–19.

the Fourth Criminal Senate of the BGH pointed out in its submission to the Constitutional Court. Those engaging in blockades to protest nuclear armaments have been widely prosecuted, while economic protest in the form of blockades against factory closings, increases in fees, decreases in subsidies, and traffic planning regulations have frequently not given rise to criminal prosecutions.[132]

The Court does not explicitly make this point, but the implication seems clear that blockades by groups with political power—such as associations of truck drivers that blocked Alpine passes in order to protest delays at border crossings—are not prosecuted, whereas suspect political minorities which seek to reverse fundamental political choices of the government are, in contrast, subject to systematic prosecution. Indeed, the concerted activity of the anti-nuclear peace movement—growing, as it did, out of the remnants of the 1968 student movement in Germany—was viewed by many as being fundamentally hostile to the West German state. Moreover, the protests were viewed as attacking the basic decision that resulted in the alliance of West Germany with NATO, an undoubted cornerstone of the West German political structure. Indeed, according to some officials, a failure to suppress these demonstrations would lead to chaos.

Viewed in this way, the Court's 1995 decision could be interpreted as ultimately resting on principles of the rule of law under Article 103(2)GG, in combination with weighty considerations of freedom of expression as guaranteed by Article 5 of the Basic Law. According to this view, the criminal courts' broad interpretation of §240 allows too much room for prosecutors to make decisions based on the content of the views put forth by different groups of demonstrators. Moreover, the prosecuting officials, if not the courts, have been exercising that discretion in a constitutionally suspect manner that favors certain political views over others. Under this interpretation, the Court's 1995 *Nötigung* decision may resemble decisions of the United States Supreme Court that have invalidated statutes on the grounds of First Amendment vagueness or overbreadth. In these cases, the Supreme Court has noted that the statutes accord prosecutors and

[132] Ibid., 18. Similar arguments had occasionally been made by the Constitutional Complainants in the *Nötigung* cases. See Constitutional Complaint, dated 27 February 1985, filed on behalf of Karl Wenning by Frank Niepel and Klaus D. Klefke, 41–42.

other officials undue latitude to engage in discrimination on the basis of the content of speech, in their application of the statute.[133]

Perhaps there is another interpretation of this decision that could rest on a form of freedom of expression or assembly. One German commentator has suggested that—although these grounds do not "explicitly" appear in the decision—the Court must have decided that the state's interest in penalizing the sort of attenuated "force" at issue in these sit-down demonstration cases was not strong enough to overcome the important values of freedom of assembly protected by Article 8 GG.[134] According to this view, an important purpose of political assemblies is to "demonstrate power, to impress and in this way to exercise pressure," and this activity "is constitutionally protected" by Article 8 GG. Because in §240 the terms "force" and "reprehensible" serve the purpose of distinguishing constitutionally protected from unprotected examples of assembly, the interpretation of these terms must be influenced by the constitution; and, in these cases, any coercion short of actual physical obstruction should be considered too attenuated to constitute "force" in light of the freedom of assembly protected by Article 8. But in blockades of military bases, "it does not seem plausible" to find a physical barrier "in the mere presence of someone's body. Indeed, a sitting human being is hardly a relevant 'physical' obstacle for [any] military vehicle."[135]

A decision based on a theory of this sort, which was indeed suggested by the four "defeated" judges in the 1986 case, could possibly approach the creation of a constitutionally protected right of civil disobedience—at least when that activity was prosecuted under a statute whose terms were broad or elastic enough to be subject to the "influence" of the constitutional right of free assembly.

[133] *Smith v. Goguen*, 415 U.S. 566, 575 (1974) ("Statutory language of such a standardless sweep allows policemen, prosecutors, and juries to pursue their personal predilections"); Note, "The Void-for-Vagueness Doctrine in the Supreme Court," 109 *University of Pennsylvania Law Review* 67 (1960). See also *Papachristou v. City of Jacksonville*, 405 U.S. 156, 169–70 (1972). For an argument that selective prosecution of the anti-missile protestors violates requirements of equality and non-discrimination in Article 3 of the Basic Law, see Achim Bertuleit, *Sitzdemonstrationen zwischen prozedural geschützter Versammlungsfreiheit und verwaltungsrechtsakzessorischer Nötigung*, 177–80 (Berlin: Duncker and Humblot 1994); see also Hans-Dieter Schwind, Jürgen Baumann *et al.* (eds), I *Ursachen, Prävention und Kontrolle von Gewalt*, 136–37 (Berlin: Duncker and Humblot 1990).

[134] Gusy, 1995 JZ, 783.

[135] Ibid.

### *The dissent*

As might be expected, the three dissenting judges took quite a different view of the problem. The dissent agreed with the majority on the general (and perhaps rather naive) proposition that the courts' interpretation of the term "force" in StGB §240(1) "may not overstep the possible meaning of the words of the norm," judged from the point of view of the actor. Indeed, the dissent went on to note that "even within the possible meaning of the words, the interpretation may not go farther than the purpose and context of the meaning of the norm permit."[136]

Yet the dissent declared that, judged by these criteria, the criminal courts' interpretation of "force" (*Gewalt*) was constitutional. According to the dissent, the term "force" does indeed require a physical operation or effect (*Einwirkung*); yet that can be a physical effect of any kind, and the purpose of the statute does not require any further limitation or narrowing of the term. Accordingly, when coercion is directed toward causing a person to refrain from doing something, the physical operation or effect can consist in the creation of "a bodily obstacle that stands in the way of the intended action—here, the continuation of the [trucks'] passage"—and such an action remains within the "possible meaning of the concept of force." The extent of the applied bodily strength does not matter, no actual touching of the victim's body is necessary, and the defendant's action need not be aggressive.[137]

In this case, the sit-down blockade posed a physical obstacle to the continued passage of the vehicles. Of course, the bodily obstacle did trigger a psychological process that was decisive for the success of the blockade. But even so, the presence of the bodily obstacle was itself sufficient to keep the interpretation within the possible verbal meaning of the concept of "force."[138] The dissent also emphasized that, because of a jurisprudence of consistent interpretation in the criminal courts, the defendants could have been in no doubt about the criminality of their acts.[139]

136 92 BVerfGE, 20.

137 Ibid., 21.

138 Ibid., 22.

139 Ibid., 23–25.

### *The 1995 decision and the question of "overruling"*

The Court's 1995 decision on *Nötigung* came to a result—on the question of the constitutionality of the broad interpretation of "force" by the criminal courts—that was different from and inconsistent with the result that the Court had reached in 1986. In the American system, accordingly, it would be said that the 1995 case had "overruled" the 1986 decision.

But the approach of the German courts and commentators was subtly different from the American approach to these problems. Instead of talking about "overruling" or nullifying the earlier decision, the German commentators tended to talk in a less dramatic manner about the "change" in the jurisprudence. (Indeed, there does not seem to be a verb in German legal language that corresponds to the English "overrule.")[140] In part, this difference in nuance may be related to possible lingering views about the importance of maintaining the "authority" of the courts—not entirely unrelated to the justices' greater reluctance to acknowledge differences within a panel through the use of separate concurring or dissenting opinions.

But a more important factor seems to arise from the prevailing view of the nature of case law in continental legal theory.[141] Because in German theory the cases are not exactly the law—but rather a manifestation of the law—there is no clear concept of *stare decisis* and, therefore, no clear concept of the opposite of *stare decisis*: overruling. Accordingly, there tends to be less focused discussion of the proposition that it may be necessary from time to time to "overrule" or nullify an earlier decision, if a deeper understanding of the law or a significant change in the circumstances require that this be done. Rather, the law is frequently viewed as a continuous stream in which there should be no contradiction or breaks; when there are changes, the theory finds it difficult to accommodate them or to discuss them,

[140] See, e.g., Würtenberger, " 'Unter dem Kreuz' lernen," in Detlef Merten *et al.* (eds), *Der Verwaltungsstaat im Wandel* (*Festschrift für Franz Knöpfle*), 408 (Munich: Beck 1996) (employing the phrase "ein overruling" in a discussion of this issue). In a well-known German work on legal process, another commentator also uses the English word "overruling" although, in addition, he formulates a complex German phrase to express the same idea: "Preisgabe der präjudiziellen Rechtsnorm (abandonment of the precedential legal norm)." Martin Kriele, *Theorie der Rechtsgewinnung*, 247, 286–89 (Berlin: Duncker and Humblot, 2nd edn 1976).

[141] See generally Damaška, "Structures of Authority and Comparative Criminal Procedure," 84 *Yale Law Journal* 480, 497–98 (1975).

except as constituting some sort of imperfection in the system that weakens "legal consciousness." This characteristic of German law may help explain why there was such a vigorous debate about whether the Court's four-to-four decision in the 1986 *Nötigung* case was a holding on the merits or not. If it was a holding on the merits, the 1995 decision would represent the kind of "change" in the doctrine that German legal theory may have difficulty in accommodating. But if the 1986 decision was not a decision on the merits (as the Court maintained) then the stream of constitutional doctrine would flow along more or less undisturbed.

In any case, there does not seem to be in Germany a particularly elaborate or extended literature on the question of when earlier decisions may or should be disregarded or "overruled."[142] When this point was discussed at all in the literature following the *Nötigung* decisions, it seemed to be in tones of regret and alarm for the German "legal culture." This approach is well reflected in the comments of one German authority on the 1995 *Nötigung* decision:

> These sometimes sudden changes of the jurisprudence of the Constitutional Court may be legal, particularly because . . . [the Constitutional Court Act] does not require that the Court be bound by its own decisions. But [these sudden changes] are fundamentally disadvantageous for our legal culture: they impair *the certainty of the law*. They can be the foundation of a severe loss of respect in the sense that in professional circles—especially in the ordinary courts—[the Constitutional Court] will no longer be taken seriously enough as a legal authority.[143]

[142] For a prominent German contribution, see Kriele, *Theorie der Rechtsgewinnung*, 243–309. For well-known American discussions, see Henry M. Hart, Jr. and Albert M. Sacks, *The Legal Process: Basic Problems in the Making and Application of Law*, 545–630 (ed. William N. Eskridge, Jr. and Philip P. Frickey, Westbury: Foundation Press 1994); Israel, "Gideon v. Wainwright: The 'Art' of Overruling," 1963 *Supreme Court Review* 211; Douglas, "Stare Decisis," 49 *Columbia Law Review* 735 (1949); *Burnet v. Coronado Oil and Gas Co.*, 285 U.S. 393, 405–13 (1932) (Brandeis, J., dissenting). See also *Planned Parenthood of Southeastern Pa. v. Casey*, 505 U.S. 833, 854–69 (1992) (opinion of the Court by Justices O'Connor, Kennedy, and Souter).

[143] Krey, 1995 JR, 228 (emphasis in original). See also Altvater, 1995 NStZ, 278.

## The immediate aftermath—acquiescence and patterns of resistance

### *Reopening decisions of the past*

On the surface, the 1995 decision seemed to put an end to almost all prosecutions of sit-down protestors for *Nötigung*.[144] Moreover, lawyers and officials began to debate whether past cases should now be reopened and reversed, as well as fines repaid that were handed down years before.

One state justice minister, Peter Caesar in Rheinland-Pfalz, concluded that the state government itself should review the *Nötigung* convictions of sit-down protestors and, without waiting for individual petitions, reverse the convictions and repay the fines. The governments of Hesse and Baden-Württemberg took a similar position, but the Justice Ministry of Bavaria resisted this trend.[145]

The liberal approach seemed justified by the Constitutional Court Act, which allowed a past criminal judgment to be reopened if it rested on an "interpretation of a norm" which the Constitutional Court has "declared inconsistent with the Basic Law."[146] Nonetheless, this enthusiastic "anticipatory obedience" of the justice ministers was sharply criticized by those who were also critical of the decision itself.[147] The ultimate result, however, was that thousands of previously convicted demonstrators were acquitted in "proceedings for the reopening of judgments" (*Wiederaufnahmeverfahren*) and received repayment of their fines along with legal fees and any court costs that they had been required to bear.

### *Resistance from the BGH*

But, in another strange twist in this complex jurisprudence, the scope of the Constitutional Court's opinion was seriously challenged—only six months after it was handed down—in a controversial decision

[144] Scholz, 1995 NStZ, 423.

[145] See Krey, 1995 JR, 221 and n. 7 (Hesse, Rheinland-Pfalz; Bavaria); Interview with Senior Prosecutor (*Oberstaatsanwalt*) Peter Rörig, Stuttgart, 9 July 2003 (Baden-Württemberg).

[146] BVerfGG §79.

[147] See, e.g., Roellecke, 1995 NJW, 1526; Krey, 1995 JR, 221; see also Schroeder, 1995 JuS, 878; Willms, FAZ, 14 August 1996, 8 (stating that the reopening of these judgments was "a justice-scandal of unprecedented dimensions").

of the Federal Supreme Court (BGH).[148] In this decision the BGH seemed decidedly unsympathetic to what the Constitutional Court had held in its *Nötigung* opinion earlier in the year. In any event, the BGH adopted a very narrow interpretation of that opinion.

The case in the BGH arose when a large group of demonstrators blocked a major German thruway (*Autobahn*), in order to protest the judicial cancellation of a demonstration by the Kurdish community in Augsburg. Although most of the demonstrators conducted themselves peacefully, two protestors (including the defendant) attempted to spray gasoline on police officers while a third sought unsuccessfully to light a match. But despite these serious acts, this case considered only the defendant's conviction for the offense of *Nötigung* by reason of his participation in the blockage of traffic.

Distinguishing this blockade case from the cases of the anti-nuclear protestors, the BGH upheld the convictions for the offense of *Nötigung*. According to the BGH, the Constitutional Court's decision of January 1995 required a reversal of convictions for *Nötigung* only when the "coercion" was "purely psychological." In the case decided by the Constitutional Court in January, the truck driver who stopped at the blockade was facing a small number of protestors directly, and so it would have been physically possible for the driver to have proceeded over them. Thus the "force" that stopped the driver was psychological force only. But in the BGH case, in which a long series of motorists was obliged to come to a stop, only the first in line was psychologically coerced by the demonstrators. According to the BGH, the other drivers were additionally coerced by the *physical* barrier of the stopped vehicle or vehicles in front of them. Thus, according to the BGH, a conviction for coercing these later drivers fell outside of the rationale of the Constitutional Court's decision and would remain constitutional.[149]

There certainly seem to be important distinctions between the *Autobahn* blockade case and the cases of the anti-nuclear protestors. After all, in the *Autobahn* case a mass demonstration blocked a major travel route potentially obstructing hundreds of automobiles—in contrast with the "symbolic" blockade of occasional army vehicles, by a few protestors on a quiet special purpose road, in the 1995 anti-missile protest case. Moreover, the defendant and others apparently tried to set police officers on fire—a far cry from the scrupulous

[148] BGH, Judgment of 20 July 1995; 41 BGHSt, 182.

[149] Ibid., 183–84.

non-violence of the Großengstingen peace protestors Beuter, Braig, and the Mochs.

Yet the specific distinction chosen by the BGH seemed designed to reverse or undo the result of the Constitutional Court's decision in a large number of instances. Indeed, even in many nuclear missile protest cases, more than one successive vehicle was required to come to a stop before the blockade. According to the argument of the BGH, any time a second vehicle came to a stop behind a vehicle that had been "psychologically" coerced to stop at a blockade, the protestors could be convicted of *Nötigung*, notwithstanding the 1995 decision of the Constitutional Court. Writing shortly after the decision of the BGH, one commentator remarked that it was doubtful whether the "argumentation [of the BGH] accords with the spirit of the Constitutional Court's decision, or will be upheld by that Court."[150]

On the face of it, this development in the BGH seems rather peculiar: indeed, one might well wonder how it is possible for the BGH to limit a decision of the Federal Constitutional Court. The Constitutional Court is clearly supreme over all other courts and government agencies in the interpretation of the Basic Law. The BGH is supreme only in the interpretation of federal civil and criminal law; it is *not* supreme on questions of the constitutionality of federal law or on the constitutionality of any particular interpretation of federal law.

Yet, in the course of applying federal law, the BGH must necessarily interpret what the Constitutional Court has said about the constitutional reach of a federal statute. As a practical matter, moreover, if the BGH interprets an opinion of the Constitutional Court, that interpretation may remain undisturbed until it is in turn found

[150] Amelung, 1995 NJW, 2590, n. 67; see also Amelung, "Anmerkung," 1996 NStZ, 230, 231 ("pettifogging" evasion of the Constitutional Court's judgment). For additional criticism of the BGH decision, see, e.g., Hruschka, "Die Blockade einer Autobahn durch Demonstranten—eine Nötigung?", 1996 NJW, 160; Offenloch, *Erinnerung*, 194–96; OLG Koblenz, Decision of 24 June 1996, 1996 NJW, 3351 (the Constitutional Court insisted that *Nötigung* by "force" required the actual application of bodily strength by the defendant, but that element is absent in the sit-down cases whether the blockade stops only one truck or a whole line of trucks). In contrast, however, other commentators approved the decision of the BGH. See Krey and Jaeger, "Anmerkung," 1995 NStZ, 542.

In any event, neither the opinion of the BGH nor the objections of numerous critics seemed to interfere with the reopening of the *Nötigung* judgments and repayments of fines in most cases, pursuant to the Court's 1995 decision.

unconstitutional or incorrect by the Constitutional Court. Accordingly the BGH could (at least theoretically) maintain its position in the *Autobahn* case until reversed by the Constitutional Court.[151]

How do we account for this rather transparent attempt by the BGH to undo a result of the Constitutional Court? Indeed, over the history of the Federal Republic, there have been several notable episodes of tension between the BGH and the Constitutional Court. In these disputes the BGH has often—although not always—taken a more conservative view, seeking to uphold the traditional positions of the "ordinary" law against attempts by the Constitutional Court to extend constitutional rights of individuals into new realms. Indeed, a principal reason for creating a separate Constitutional Court was the apprehension that the ordinary judiciary—trained in the methods of the ordinary law and occupying a quasi-bureaucratic status in the governmental system—would be unable to exercise the sort of independent judgment necessary for the purpose of making constitutional decisions.

Yet one final aspect of the opinion of the BGH is also important to mention. The hostility toward the *Nötigung* decision of the Constitutional Court, evident in that opinion, seemed to be only one aspect of a more widespread bitter hostility to the Court's decision that proceeded principally from the conservative end of the German political spectrum. In the view of some writers, it was as though the

[151] In a similar manner, an American state supreme court or a federal Court of Appeals may interpret the meaning of the Supreme Court's jurisprudence on a particular question, and that interpretation may prevail in the particular jurisdiction until disapproved by the Supreme Court itself. For a prominent recent example, compare *Hopwood v. Texas*, 78 F.3d 932 (5th Cir.), cert. denied 518 U.S. 1033 (1996) (Court of Appeals decision holding that the apparent finding of the Supreme Court's *Bakke* decision, allowing affirmative action in some instances to achieve racially diverse student body, had been undermined by more recent Supreme Court cases) with *Grutter v. Bollinger*, 539 U.S. 306 (2003) (Supreme Court decision reaffirming the diversity rationale of *Bakke*).

Interestingly, in its most recent *Nötigung* decision in 2001, the Constitutional Court explicitly declined to pass on the validity of the 1995 decision of the BGH (see Epilogue). Moreover, in 2002, a screening committee of the Constitutional Court declined to interfere with three (apparently rather unusual) lower court decisions refusing to reopen *Nötigung* convictions, citing the BGH judgment in the *Autobahn* case. Judgment of the 3rd Chamber of the Second Senate, 26 February 2002, 2002 NJW, 2038. Whatever the full Court's future judgment on this question, it is unlikely to have much effect in the anti-missile sit-down cases, because in most of those cases the convictions have long since been reversed and fines and other costs repaid. See supra.

Constitutional Court, in issuing this decision, had allied itself with disruptive, leftist forces that were ranged against NATO, the armed forces, and the traditional structures of the German state. By asserting new, dubious constitutional doctrine—these critics implied—the Court was undertaking questionable experiments that could endanger the foundations of German society.

Interestingly, the *Nötigung* case was not the only decision of its time that evoked bitter complaints of this sort. Indeed, the *Nötigung* case took its place with two other decisions of 1995 which evoked, if anything, even more bitter controversy. Let us proceed, then, to a consideration of the 1995 *Nötigung* decision in this rather dramatic constitutional context.

# Chapter 5

# The great cases of 1995

## Success for the "long march" of 1968?

When the 1995 decision of the Constitutional Court was announced, it immediately became one of the most controversial decisions in the Court's recent history. The debates over the decision reflected deep rifts in the political culture of West Germany. These fissures had become particularly obvious since the 1968 student revolution, but they had existed—in basic principle—since the founding of the Federal Republic itself.

The echoes of the debates of the student movement period were particularly strong.

### Reaction to the 1995 *Nötigung* decision

#### *Voices in politics and the press*

Among the political parties, the SPD and the Greens generally hailed the Court's decision to acquit the sit-down demonstrators. A leading legal theorist of the SPD, for example, welcomed the decision and declared that, in light of the "limitless" extension of the concept of force, thousands of protestors had been unjustly convicted as violent criminals.[1] Certainly most jubilant were members of the Greens—a party whose origins (like those of the peace movement itself) lay in the student uprising of 1968. A representative of the Greens expressed "joy and gratification" over the result.[2]

Yet these favorable reactions encountered deep and sometimes apocalyptic forebodings from the ranks of the CDU and from political conservatives in general—as well as from much of the German

1 FAZ, 17 March 1995, 1 (Herta Däubler-Gmelin).
2 Ibid., 2.

legal establishment. At the outset, for example, political figures from the CDU called the decision "hardly understandable" and "unbearable."[3]

Others, writing from a similar critical perspective, drew explicit parallels with the political struggles of the student movement of 1968. One letter in the *Frankfurter Allgemeine Zeitung* referred to the aspirations of the 1968 movement, and declared that

> [it is] now totally obvious that the [movement's] "march through the institutions" has completely penetrated the Federal Constitutional Court. The politicization of this previously highly respected court has resulted in further concessions to the so-called spirit of the age and thereby promoted the undermining of the [judicial] power.

Referring to Rudi Dutschke—a leader of the student movement who was himself shot and gravely injured in 1968[4]—this writer concluded that the *Nötigung* decision of 1995 was "Dutschke's revenge."[5]

A law professor from Marburg, also writing to the *Frankfurter Allgemeine Zeitung*, declared that the *Nötigung* decision of the Constitutional Court "is a political decision"—that is,

> a decision that proceeds from the result and . . . seeks to change the existing law on the basis of its own political convictions. The Court's judgment is based upon the following political thesis: Whoever pursues the noble goal of peace, whoever wants to preserve humanity from the dangers of nuclear fission, cannot possibly be a "felon", or—stated more simply—the end justifies the means. This point of view evokes vivid memories of the time of the "student revolution."

This writer concluded that, as a result of the Court's reinterpretation of the concept of force, "the authority of the law and therefore of the state is endangered."[6] Along similar lines, the respected legal correspondent of the *Frankfurter Allgemeine Zeitung* argued that the decision of the Constitutional Court "is obviously animated

3 Ibid., 1.

4 See Chapter 1.

5 FAZ, 22 March 1995, 13 (Ernst-Ulrich Hantel).

6 FAZ, 28 April 1995, 15 (Prof. Dr. Ekkehard Kaufmann).

[*getragen*] by a silent sympathy for the peace demonstrators, who enjoy opposing the German army."[7]

Other publicists expressed their disapproval in apocalyptic terms. One eminent law professor and university president proclaimed that the decision created a deplorable "legal vacuum" and showed that "with arguments from the Constitution, the Constitution itself can be altered and even endangered."[8] Another correspondent declared:

> Once again a high [German] court has issued an opinion that not only leaves one at a loss, but also brings a flush of anger (*die Zornesröte*) to the face . . . This bad decision, when clearly examined, is a further milestone on the path of the Federal Republic into political decline.[9]

Other correspondents stated that "the decision of the Federal Constitutional Court was—to put it mildly—incomprehensible,"[10] and that such a trend of political decisions could impair confidence in the judiciary and "call into question the existence of our democratic order."[11]

Other correspondents, similarly emphasizing a note of "cultural despair,"[12] seemed to view the decision as an attack by the Constitutional Court on the substance of the West German state itself—as that state was represented by its (ordinary) judges and civil servants. Predicting that the decision would give rise to 10,000 acquittals of previously convicted defendants and arguing that the decision had overturned long-standing precedents, one eminent professor of criminal law inquired whether the Constitutional Court understood "what it means that the Court [now] certifies that tens of thousands of servants of this state—judges, prosecutors, police officers and university teachers—have acted unconstitutionally for eight decades." This law teacher continued:

7 FAZ, 17 March 1995, 1 (Friedrich Karl Fromme).

8 FAZ, 9 June 1995, 10 (Prof. Dr. Bernd Rüthers).

9 FAZ, 27 March 1995, 13 (Ulrich Lampert).

10 FAZ, 11 April 1995, 9 (Claus Groth).

11 FAZ, 5 April 1995, 9. See also FAZ, 20 June 1995, 10 (Dr. Bernhard Müllenbach) (Such decisions would decrease "legal consciousness in our society").

12 Cf. Fritz Stern, *The Politics of Cultural Despair* (Berkeley: University of California Press 1974).

> The decision produced incomprehension—but for many [it was] also a shock. How should a university teacher explain to his students the difference between right and wrong, when he must expect that even an established doctrine can be declared retroactively unconstitutional after decades if the majority in the Constitutional Court has changed? What will law students think when [acts] that they learned [were] wrong can retroactively be declared to be right? Particularly for young jurists, this decision will lead to a serious shock to their view of law. Psychologically, this decision can be handled only by a radical change in one's attitude toward law. [Law's] meaning no longer [lies] in the differentiation between right and wrong. [Rather,] it is an instrument for carrying out one's own interest, and it must be stretched [*strapaziert*] until it justifies that interest. Those who do not wish to participate in this transformation of legal consciousness will turn away from the Federal Constitutional Court, deny the persuasive force of its decisions and seek the cause of this loss of legitimacy. Both are disastrous for the polity.[13]

Along similar lines, an eminent commentator on criminal law—and one of the two "expert" authorities in the 1986 oral argument—complained that a thin majority of the Court "had disavowed an entire generation of judges which had held to the prevailing doctrines of the law" and that the taxpayers would have to bear the "immense" costs of a multitude of new proceedings.[14] In these remarks we see, again, the interesting view that by holding unconstitutional a judicial interpretation of the criminal courts, the Constitutional Court was in effect issuing a moral condemnation of those tribunals.

Finally, another correspondent complained that appointment to the highest judicial positions depends most on party affiliation and least on competence. "With judgments of this kind," the writer continued, even those who support the judiciary "will soon lose their childish belief (*Kinderglauben*) in our legal order."[15]

[13] Prof. Dr. Friedrich-Christian Schroeder, "Wenn aus Unrecht Recht wird," FAZ, 5 May 1995, 16.

[14] FAZ, 11 April 1995, 5 (Prof. Dr. Herbert Tröndle).

[15] FAZ, 22 March 1995, 13 (Dr. Erich Müller).

### *The legal commentary*

The more extended legal commentary in the professional journals—although somewhat more temperate in expression—was also highly critical of the Court's 1995 *Nötigung* decision.[16] One eminent constitutionalist (and CDU politician and legal advisor) stated that the Constitutional Court must ask itself "whether it is really correct and appropriate to discard [*verwerfen*] a completed and well-established legal structure [*Rechtsentwicklung*] from one day to the next—with only a single changed judicial vote."[17] In a later passage this author—in somewhat dramatic tones—argued that the institution of civil disobedience, at issue in this case, could endanger the state:

> [T]he state's monopoly of force is challenged in a very graphic manner. The state's monopoly of force means nothing other than the state's monopoly of law—as well as the state's monopoly in protecting justice, peace and equality . . . But this [monopoly] is called into question if, under the protective covering of "civil disobedience" or something similar, individuals or certain groups assume the authority to decide on their own competence what is legal and what is not legal—with the further consequence that they believe they are allowed to impose their will on the organs of state and on their fellow citizens. One must take steps against this, for a *Rechtsstaat* which renounces the enforcement of law—that is, equality in the enforcement of law—in the end abandons itself.[18]

This writer concluded that the legislature must adopt a revised definition of "*Nötigung*," under which the sit-down protests could be constitutionally punished.

[16] See, e.g., Scholz, "Sitzblockade und Verfassung—Zur neuen Entscheidung des BVerfG," 1995 NStZ, 417; Roellecke, "Bio-Recht oder die Sanftmut von Gesäß-Protestierern," 1995 NJW, 1525; Schroeder, "Sitzblockade keine Gewalt," 1995 JuS, 875. For a more favorable view, see Gusy, "Anmerkung," 1995 JZ, 782; see also Hruschka, "Die Blockade einer Autobahn durch Demonstranten—eine Nötigung?," 1996 NJW, 160, 161 n. 10.

[17] Scholz, 1995 NStZ, 417.

[18] Ibid., 423–24.

### *Proposals for legislative reform*

Indeed, almost from the date of the announcement of the decision, voices from the CDU and CSU proposed that the definition of *Nötigung* be amended in the criminal code so that "psychological" force would be expressly included in the text and the extensive judicial interpretation—disapproved by the Constitutional Court—would no longer be necessary. But this proposal—and a related proposal to include an expanded definition of "force" that would apply throughout the criminal code[19]—have not been successful. One professor of criminal law has noted that to include an expanded definition of "force" in the code would raise incalculable problems and dangers, and that any change in response to the Court's opinion must focus on changes in the laws relating to demonstrations or in the traffic laws—rather than on an attempt to revise concepts relating to *Nötigung*.[20] Because of the very complicated technical problems involved in amending a legal code in which the same word is used in a number of different contexts—and also probably due to the unwillingness of the SPD and the Greens to take any steps that would extend the constitutional coverage of the *Nötigung* statute—it has been impossible for the opponents of the 1995 decision to effect any of these proposed statutory amendments.

But the *Nötigung* case was not the only controversial decision handed down by the Constitutional Court in 1995. Indeed, it was only one of a trio of opinions of that year which drew massive criticism from the conservative spectrum of German politics and precipitated a crisis over perceived trends in the Constitutional Court. Reviewing these and other decisions, one prominent jurist declared:

> In a short time the confidence [in the Court] that was built up over decades has suddenly collapsed; agreement has turned into disapproval; respect into contempt; admiration into complaint . . . Opponents and supporters of the new jurisprudence agree, the Constitutional Court is caught in a crisis of legitimacy.[21]

19 See, e.g., FAZ, 13 May 1995, 1.

20 Samson, "Wenn die Drohung schwerer wiegt als die Tat," FAZ, 19 May 1995, 12; cf. also Scholz, 1995 NStZ, 424.

21 Isensee, "Bundesverfassungsgericht—quo vadis?," 1996 JZ, 1085, 1086; see also Isensee, "Karlsruhe ist nicht mehr unangreifbar," FAZ, 26 September 1996, 13.

Similarly, Professor Jutta Limbach, who was President of the Court during this period, declared that these decisions of 1995 aroused a "barrage of criticism" that was a sort of lesson "for a republic that more than others must confront the question of how stable democracy remains in its land."[22] Other authors, whether writing in approval or disapproval, noted that with these decisions criticism of the Court had "reached a new dimension"—indeed, a "general reproach" of the entire institution.[23]

An examination of the background, decisions, and reactions in these two other great cases of 1995 will help establish a constitutional context for our final reflections on the 1995 *Nötigung* case.

## The *Soldiers* case

In the prolific attacks on the Court's 1995 *Nötigung* decision, the critics frequently drew explicit parallels with another important opinion of the Court, also handed down in 1995. In the critics' view, both decisions could impair the functioning of the German army (*Bundeswehr*)—a pillar of the German government—and therefore, in an important sense, could threaten the stability of the German state. In both decisions, moreover, the Court ruled in favor of the

[22] Jutta Limbach, "*Im Namen des Volkes*": *Macht und Verantwortung der Richter*, 165, 200 (Stuttgart: Deutsche Verlags-Anstalt 1999). See also Jutta Limbach, *Das Bundesverfassungsgericht*, 68 (Munich: Beck 2001); Jutta Limbach, *Die Akzeptanz verfassungsrechtlicher Entscheidungen* (Münster: Regensberg 1997); Interview with Jutta Limbach, *Der Spiegel*, 35/1995, 34–38.

[23] Wahl, "Quo Vadis—Bundesverfassungsgericht? Zur Lage von Verfassungsgerichtsbarkeit, Verfassung und Staatsdenken," in Bernd Guggenberger and Thomas Würtenberger (eds), *Hüter der Verfassung oder Lenker der Politik*?, 83–84 (Baden-Baden: Nomos 1998). See also Redeker, "Der moderne Fluch der Versuchung zur Totalität," 1995 NJW, 3369. To the "register of judicial sins"—that is, the list of controversial opinions—Wahl adds decisions of the Court's Second Senate suggesting constitutional limits on the criminalization of some uses of marijuana and providing immunity for certain former East German spies. Wahl, in *Hüter der Verfassung*, 82 n.8; see 90 BVerfGE, 145 (1994); 92 BVerfGE, 277 (1995).

For more general criticism of the expanding reach of the Court's jurisprudence in this period, see Großfeld, "Götterdämmerung? Zur Stellung des Bundesverfassungsgerichts," 1995 NJW, 1719; for a response, see Benda, "Wirklich Götterdämmerung in Karlsruhe?," 1995 NJW, 2470.

For a comprehensive—albeit somewhat tendentious—discussion of the controversial cases of 1995, and the attack on the Court that these decisions evoked, see Rolf Lamprecht, *Zur Demontage des Bundesverfassungsgerichts* (Baden-Baden: Nomos 1996).

suspect German peace movement in the context of its resistance to the NATO double-track decision and the stationing of the Pershing missiles. Finally, the critics claimed that the rulings would cast the judiciary into disrepute and weaken public confidence in the German legal system.

This controversial decision considered whether a speaker could be criminally punished for publicly declaring that soldiers are "murderers"—or "potential murderers."

### *Background of the* Soldiers *case*

As is frequently the case in German constitutional controversies, the *Soldiers* case has its roots deep in the Weimar period.[24] Writing in a special "peace" issue of the well-known journal *Die Weltbühne* in 1931, the pacifist author Kurt Tucholsky discussed the battlefields of World War I. In this article Tucholsky remarked: "For four years, there were whole square miles of land on which murder was obligatory—while a half an hour away it was forbidden with equal rigor. Did I say: murder? Naturally murder. Soldiers are murderers."[25]

At the instigation of the War Ministry, the Weimar authorities responded by prosecuting Carl von Ossietzky, the editor of the journal (and later a Nobel Peace Prize winner) for defamation of the Wehrmacht, the German army of the time.[26] But in an unusual legal victory for the Left in Weimar Germany, Ossietzky was acquitted of these charges—on the grounds that Tucholsky's remarks were too general to incur liability. The Court suggested that such

[24] This was the era of the first democratic constitution in Germany, which extended from 1919 until Hitler's assumption of power in 1933.

[25] *Die Weltbühne*, 4 August 1931, reprinted in Michael Hepp and Viktor Otto (eds), *"Soldaten sind Mörder": Dokumentation einer Debatte 1931–1996* (Berlin: Links 1996), 25–26. See generally Sudhof, " 'Soldatenurteil': Aus einem Land vor unserer Zeit," 1990 *Rechtshistorisches Journal* [RJ], 145.

[26] Tucholsky—the author of the lines—was already in self-imposed exile in France, in reaction to the growing Nazi threat. Nonetheless, he considered (and rejected) advice that he should return to Germany for the trial. Kurt Tucholsky, *Unser ungelebtes Leben: Briefe an Mary*, 536–41 (ed. Fritz J. Raddatz; Reinbek bei Hamburg: Rowohlt 1982); Hepp and Otto, 16–18. At the time of trial, Ossietzky was already in prison for "treasonable" publication, as a result of disclosures in *Die Weltbühne* that the German army was violating the Versailles Treaty by purchasing military airplanes. Sudhof, 1990 RJ, 147–48; Ronald F. Bunn, *German Politics and the Spiegel Affair: A Case Study of the Bonn System*, xix–xx n.3 (Baton Rouge: Louisiana State University Press 1968).

remarks could only be punished if they were directed to a determinate group of individuals, such as the soldiers of the German army who had taken part in World War I.[27] This judgment evoked a major uproar, but then these issues were swallowed up by the Nazis' seizure of power and World War II, and there the matter rested for five decades.

It was mainly in the disputes arising from NATO's double-track decision and the stationing of the Pershing II rockets in West Germany that members of the peace movement revived Tucholsky's slogan from the Weimar period. The dispute was memorably sharpened in a panel discussion about war, peace, and the stationing of Pershing II rockets, at a school in Frankfurt in 1984. In the course of the discussion Dr. Peter Augst, a physician representing a peace organization, turned to a *Bundeswehr* captain, who was also on the panel, and declared: "All soldiers are potential murderers, and that includes you."

As a result of this provocative remark, Dr. Augst was prosecuted for the criminal offense of libel or "insult" (*Beleidigung*) under §185 of the German Criminal Code.[28] He was convicted in the first instance but was acquitted on appeal (*Berufung*) in the Frankfurt State Court (*Landgericht*). The appeals court noted that questions of "military defense" and "weapons of mass destruction" were "naturally subjects of special interest" and controversial discussion in society.[29]

The acquittal in this case—which came against the background of a jurisprudence that seemed to favor convictions in similar circumstances—sent a shock wave through the ranks of defenders of the *Bundeswehr*.[30] Moreover, a long train of subsequent proceedings in the Augst case kept the matter in the public eye.[31] Indeed,

[27] Hepp and Otto, 63–70. An appeal (*Revision*) by the prosecution was also rejected. Ibid., 83–92.

[28] Dr. Augst was also prosecuted for a hate speech crime (*Volksverhetzung*) under StGB §130.

[29] Judgment of LG Frankfurt, 8 December 1987, 1988 NJW, 2683, 2685.

[30] See, e.g., Dau, "Der strafrechtliche Ehrenschutz der Bundeswehr", 1988 NJW, 2650; Giehring, "Die sog. 'Soldatenurteile'—eine kritische Zwischenbilanz," 1992 StV, 194.

[31] The acquittal of Dr. Augst was in turn reversed by the State Appellate Court in a *Revision* proceeding (see 1989 NJW, 1367), but in a new trial the State Court acquitted Augst for a second time. In handing down the second acquittal, the State Court noted that issues such as those raised by the NATO double-track decision were of "existential" importance for the German population and that, in the tense atmosphere of the period, the army captain knew he could expect "tough debate" on the

Tucholsky's slogan was increasingly adopted by the peace movement, and pacifists inscribed it on banners and bumper stickers and employed it in public debates on the Pershing II missiles and related topics.

In contrast with the acquittals of Dr. Augst, a significant number of these activists were convicted of criminal libel in other courts in West Germany.[32] In 1994 one of these convictions—involving an automobile bumper sticker with the slogan "Soldiers are murderers" —was reversed by a preliminary screening panel of the Constitutional Court and returned to the criminal courts for further action.[33] The reversal of this conviction evoked particular outrage among politicians from many sides of the political spectrum—as one commentator put it, a "grand coalition of indignation."[34]

subject. 1990 NStZ, 233, 234; see also Frankfurter Rundschau (FR), 28 October 1989, 10–11 (setting forth oral opinion of the Court).

This second acquittal evoked renewed expressions of official outrage. Chancellor Kohl announced that he was "appalled" (*entsetzt*) by the decision, and a CDU/ CSU official spoke about prosecuting the trial judges for "perversion of justice" (*Rechtsbeugung*). FR, 26 October 1989, 4; FR, 27 October 1989, 2–3. See also Brammsen, "Anmerkung," 1990 NStZ, 235 (disapproving the result on legal grounds). After the second acquittal, the government again prevailed in a *Revision* proceeding, but the prosecution was ultimately dropped after the defendant agreed to pay a small fine in settlement. Hepp and Otto, 138. See Judgment of OLG Frankfurt, 11 March 1991, 1991 NJW, 2032.

32 See, e.g., Hepp and Otto, 95–124.

33 1994 NJW, 2943 (3rd Chamber of First Senate, 25 August 1994); see also 1992 NJW, 2750 (3rd Chamber of Second Senate, 10 July 1992). The defendant was subsequently acquitted in the criminal court system. Hepp and Otto, 209–12.

34 Hill, "Tucholskys Schuh—Anmerkungen zum 'Soldaten-Urteil'," 1994 DRiZ, reprinted in Hepp and Otto, 193; see generally ibid., 125–212.

Politicians of the ruling conservative coalition called the decision a "scandal" and a "disgrace for the German judiciary." FAZ, 21 September 1994, reprinted in ibid., 146–47. Moreover, for the "first time in the history of the German Parliament, the major parties convened a parliamentary debate for the purpose of distancing themselves in a public manner from a decision of the Constitutional Court." Limbach, "*Im Namen des Volkes*," 166; see also Lamprecht, *Zur Demontage*, 27–28.

For academic and newspaper commentary disapproving the screening panel's decision, see Herdegen, " 'Soldaten sind Mörder'," 1994 NJW, 2933; cf. FAZ, 19 January 1995, 12 (Friedrich Karl Fromme). One report in a prominent national newspaper noted that all three judges on the screening panel had been supported by the SPD and suggested that "now the '68ers'—those who were influenced by the student unrest of 1968—were sitting in the highest German court." *Welt am Sonntag*, 25 September 1994, in Hepp and Otto, 177 (Jochen Kummer).

Apparently taken aback by the vehemence of the reaction, the Constitutional Court issued a special clarifying press release, explaining that the screening panel had *not* held that it was "generally permissible to characterize Bundeswehr soldiers as murderers."[35] Moreover, Justice Dieter Grimm, who was the Court's Reporter (*Berichterstatter*) for free speech matters, sought to explain and defend the Court's jurisprudence on the freedom of expression in a comprehensive law journal essay.[36] Grimm's contribution to the debate, in turn, evoked some further controversy.[37]

### *The Soldiers case: the Court's decision*

Finally, in 1995, four similar cases came before the full Constitutional Court. In a decision that enraged many conservatives in Germany, the Court reversed all four convictions on the grounds that they did not adequately respect the freedom of expression guaranteed by Article 5 of the Basic Law. The cases were sent back to the lower courts for reconsideration.[38]

These four cases presented further variations on the same basic theme. In one case, a conscientious objector protested NATO army

[35] Announcement of the Press Office of the Constitutional Court, No. 38/94, reprinted in Hepp and Otto, 171–72.

[36] Grimm, "Die Meinungsfreiheit in der Rechtsprechung des Bundesverfassungsgerichts," 1995 NJW, 1697; see also "Interview: 'Wir machen das Meinungsklima nicht'," 1994 ZRP, 276.

In these publications, Grimm focused on controversial free speech decisions that preceded the *Soldiers* cases. For example, in the early 1990s the Court had been vigorously criticized for overturning judgments against speakers or publications that had suggested that the former Minister-President (Governor) of Bavaria was a "democrat by necessity" only (*Zwangsdemokrat*), 82 BVerfGE, 272 (1990); charged that federal officials had employed "Gestapo methods" in carrying out night-time deportations, 1992 NJW, 2815; and referred to a paraplegic soldier, who sought to take part in military maneuvers, as a "born murderer," 86 BVerfGE, 1 (1992); see Sendler, "Kann man Liberalität übertreiben?," 1994 ZRP, 343, 345–46.

In another controversial free speech decision of the period, the Constitutional Court reversed a conviction for the distribution of a photo-collage that purported to show a person urinating on the German flag. 81 BVerfGE, 278 (1990). For commentary on this case, compare Sendler, 1994 ZRP, 350, with Quint, "The Comparative Law of Flag Desecration: The United States and the Federal Republic of Germany," 15 *Hastings International and Comparative Law Review* 613 (1992).

[37] See, e.g., Zuck, "Gerechtigkeit für Richter Grimm," 1996 NJW, 361.

[38] 93 BVerfGE, 266 (1995). The vote in three of the cases was five to three; in one case the Court was unanimous.

maneuvers by hanging a bed-sheet at a street crossing, displaying the slogan "A SOLDIER IS A MURDER (*sic*)."[39] In another case, a teacher responded to a German army display at a vocational school by circulating a protest leaflet with the following text:

> Are soldiers potential murderers? One thing is certain: Soldiers are trained to become murderers. "You shall not kill" becomes "you must kill". Worldwide. And in the Bundeswehr, too . . .[40]

In a third case, a newspaper published a letter supporting Dr. Augst, the physician who had recently been acquitted in the trial in Frankfurt. In a provocative closing passage the writer stated: "I declare my complete solidarity with [Dr. Augst] and herewith publicly declare: 'All soldiers are potential murderers.' "[41] In the fourth case, demonstrators appeared at an army information stand and displayed a large banner that proclaimed: "Soldiers are potential MURDERERS."[42]

In approaching these cases, the Constitutional Court first noted that the various statements of the petitioners were expressions of opinion which are generally protected by Article 5 GG—the fundamental guarantee of freedom of expression in the Basic Law.[43] Yet, the Court noted, Article 5 does not protect expressions of opinion absolutely. In a structure that is parallel to that of Article 8 GG (right of assembly), which we examined in Chapter 4, Article 5 GG sets forth a broadly stated right of freedom of expression in its first section but then goes on to provide for significant limitations on that right in section 2. Accordingly, under section 2, the expression of opinions can be limited by "the rules of the general laws" and "the right of personal honor." Moreover, §185 of the Criminal Code, which provides penalties for "insult"—or libel—falls into the category of laws that limit expression mentioned in Article 5(2).[44]

Indeed, §185 serves to protect human dignity and the "general right of personality" of the defamed person, which are also constitutionally protected interests. Yet, on the other hand, the limiting

39 Ibid., 268–75.

40 Ibid., 275.

41 Ibid., 280–84.

42 Ibid., 284–88. For interesting background on these cases, see Hepp and Otto, 223–32.

43 For the full text of Article 5 GG, see Appendix. For general discussion of freedom of expression in German constitutional law, see, e.g., David P. Currie, *The Constitution of the Federal Republic of Germany*, 174–243 (Chicago, IL: University of Chicago Press 1994).

44 93 BVerfGE, 289–90.

legal rules referred to in Article 5(2)—"general laws" and a law of "personal honor", such as §185 StGB—cannot completely remove the protection of expression of opinion. Rather, an accommodation of the competing interests—expression of opinion and the rights of the defamed person—is necessary. Indeed, the criminal code itself seeks to accommodate these countervailing interests.[45]

With these background principles in mind, the Constitutional Court came to the specific problems of the cases before it. In a very interesting opinion, the Court avoided the adoption of broad or absolutist free speech principles—principles that might have clearly prevented any future prosecutions for statements of this type. Indeed, the Court reversed the convictions in a very nuanced, narrow, and one might even say cautious opinion.

The Court's careful method of interpretation was particularly striking because broad grounds of decision were at least theoretically available. It could be argued, for example, that the right of personal honor is implicated only when specific, named individuals are defamed, and that the values of personal honor are not affected by criticism of huge groups of people—such as all soldiers of the *Bundeswehr*. Indeed—by way of comparison—Anglo-American law generally does not recognize an offense or tort of group libel when such large groups are attacked.[46]

Yet in a case handed down shortly before the Court's *Soldiers* decision, the Federal Supreme Court (BGH) had explicitly confirmed that the offense of "insult" under §185 StGB could include the defamation of large groups under some circumstances. Derogatory statements about a group could violate §185, if the group could be clearly defined, if the insulting statement referred to a characteristic

[45] Ibid., 290–92. See §193 StGB.

[46] See, e.g., *Knupffer v. London Express Newspaper Ltd.* (1944) A. C., 116; American Law Institute, Restatement of the Law Second (Torts 2nd) §564A (1976); 93 BVerfGE, 299–300. On this argument, see generally Gounalakis, " 'Soldaten sind Mörder'," 1996 NJW, 481, 483–84; see also Sendler, "Blüten richterlicher Unabhängigkeit und Verfassungsgerichtsschelte", 1996 NJW, 825, 826.

To the extent that broader ideas of group libel may possibly survive in Anglo-American law, they seem limited to the possible protection of racial, ethnic, or religious groups against discriminatory hate speech. See *Beauharnais v. Illinois*, 343 U.S. 250 (1952); Arkes, "Civility and the Restriction of Speech: Rediscovering the Defamation of Groups," 1974 *Supreme Court Review* 281. But see *Collin v. Smith*, 578 F.2d 1197 (7th Cir.), *cert. denied*, 439 U.S. 916 (1978). This sort of speech was not at issue in the *Soldiers* cases although German law does also provide broad prohibitions in this area.

that was present in every member of the group, and if the group was not unmanageably large, such as "all Catholics" or "all women." In its decision the BGH found that the members of the German army met these criteria, and therefore defamatory statements about all members of the *Bundeswehr* could give rise to civil or criminal actions by individual soldiers against the speaker.[47] In its *Soldiers* decision, the Constitutional Court expressly endorsed this position put forth by the BGH. So long as the insulting statements referred to all members of the *Bundeswehr* (but not to a larger group, such as all soldiers anywhere), the speaker might be constitutionally punished for insult to individual *Bundeswehr* members.[48]

Another broad theory of decision might have been suggested by American constitutional doctrine. The Constitutional Court could have decided that—although the words might be considered to be directed against a large group of individual soldiers—the speaker was actually directing his attack against the *Bundeswehr*, one of the most prominent of German governmental institutions. In this view, any law that restricted criticism of such an institution would actually represent a form of "seditious libel" law—that is, a law that penalized speech because it was critical of the government. But—the argument could further continue—central concepts of democracy require that the people remain free to level even the harshest criticism against governmental institutions. In the United States Supreme Court, this position is most clearly set forth in the famous case of *New York Times v. Sullivan*,[49] and it is further developed in the work of the influential free speech theorist Harry Kalven, Jr.[50]

[47] 36 BGHSt, 83 (1989). See 93 BVerfGE, 300–2.

[48] Ibid., 302–3.

[49] 376 U.S. 254 (1964).

[50] Kalven, "The New York Times Case: A Note on 'The Central Meaning of the First Amendment'," 1964 Supreme Court Review 191; Harry Kalven, Jr., *A Worthy Tradition: Freedom of Speech in America*, 62–68 (ed. Jamie Kalven; New York: Harper & Row 1988) ("[According to the doctrine of seditious libel,] criticism of government is viewed as defamation and punished as a crime. [But after the *New York Times* case] seditious libel, like heresy, is now firmly outside the American tradition."). Moreover, the general principles of the American case of *Cohen v. California*, 403 U.S. 15 (1971), could also be invoked for the argument that any verbal formulation employed in criticizing the government must remain largely within the choice of the speaker—even if the speaker chooses an epithet that is scurrilous or shocking. Cf. 1990 NStZ, 235.

For a general comparison of the American and German constitutional law of defamation—emphasizing the more extensive protection extended to defamatory

Yet the Constitutional Court also ignored any possible arguments of this kind. Indeed, the Court appeared to imply that even express criticism of the *Bundeswehr* as an institution might be constitutionally punishable under certain circumstances.[51]

Instead of asserting a new free speech principle, therefore, the Court pursued its traditional approach in these cases. According to the Court's technique, each dispute must be resolved through a careful weighing of the countervailing interests—free expression and personal honor—in the individual circumstances of the case.[52] The required balancing is to be undertaken primarily by the "ordinary" criminal courts. But the ordinary courts must undertake this balancing within the proper constitutional framework, and if they do not do so, the Constitutional Court may intervene.

The Constitutional Court reversed these four decisions, therefore, by finding that the "ordinary" criminal courts had misapplied the constitutional free speech balancing principles in each of these cases. In reaching this conclusion, the Court focused on three rather specific aspects of the problem.

First, the Court noted that, in these cases, the ordinary courts had not closely examined the speakers' language to determine whether the statements really insulted the soldiers—or whether the statements were susceptible of a less drastic interpretation. For example, in the vocational school leaflet case ("Soldiers are trained to become murderers"), the author may not have meant that soldiers had killed as a result of a "base character," as required in the statutory offense of murder.[53] Rather, the author may have been criticizing the soldiers' training and education in the waging of war—an interpretation that would presumably be less insulting to the individual soldiers.[54] The Court emphasized that each statement must be carefully examined in its specific context, and all possible interpretations considered.

speech in American law—see Grimm, 1995 NJW, 1701–2. But for a vigorous exposition of the view that American free speech jurisprudence is irrelevant for Germany, see Tettinger, "Das Recht der persönlichen Ehre in der Wertordnung des Grundgesetzes," 1997 JuS, 769, 775.

51 See 93 BVerfGE, 291, 293. Cf. StGB §§ 90, 90a, 90b; Giehring, 1992 StV, 195–96.

52 93 BVerfGE, 292–93. For fuller discussions of the Court's balancing technique in free speech cases, see Currie, 178–207; Quint, "Free Speech and Private Law in German Constitutional Theory," 48 *Maryland Law Review* 247 (1989).

53 See StGB §211 ("aus niedrigen Beweggründen").

54 93 BVerfGE, 307.

Otherwise—if a less insulting statement was actually conveyed—there could be the danger that permissible statements might be unconstitutionally suppressed.[55]

The Court's second point also focused on the criminal courts' failure to examine the precise wording and context of the statements with adequate care. In discussing group defamation, the Court had found that an action for "insult" could arise from statements about the members of the *Bundeswehr*—but not from broader statements referring to soldiers in general.[56] Accordingly, the criminal courts were required to examine the precise formulation of the protestors' statement in order to determine whether the broader or narrower meaning was being conveyed.

According to the Constitutional Court, however, the lower tribunals had fallen short in this respect. For example, in the case of the bed-sheet displayed near a NATO maneuver, the criminal courts did not explain why the inscribed motto ("A SOLDIER IS A MURDER (*sic*)") referred specifically to the soldiers of the *Bundeswehr* and not to those of other armies.[57] In addition, in the case of the banner at the *Bundeswehr* information stand, the protestors' statement was general in form ("Soldiers are potential MURDERERS"), and the ordinary

[55] Ibid., 295–99. The Court had employed a similar technique in earlier cases. See 82 BVerfGE, 272, 282–83 (1990) (Democrat by necessity); 1994 NJW, 2943 (*Soldaten* bumper sticker; 3rd Chamber of First Senate).

This technique of close examination of the speaker's language has evoked sharp criticism. See, e.g., Gounalakis, " 'Soldaten sind Mörder'," 1996 NJW, 481, 483. For a particularly pointed commentary by an eminent former chief judge of the highest administrative court, see Sendler, 1994 ZRP, 349:

> [If the speaker] leaves open only a small, almost hidden tiny back door, which allows an interpretation of the insult as being harmless, one can be certain that the Constitutional Court will find this hidden back door and will slip through it with single-minded determination . . . and with admirable richness of imagination [the Court] will take into its progressive consideration even the most remote possibilities of interpretation.

In contrast, Dieter Grimm, the Court's Reporter (*Berichterstatter*) for cases relating to freedom of expression, acknowledged that this technique is a "source of discomfort and criticism." But without such a technique, he maintained, "an adequate protection of the freedom of expression would no longer be possible." Grimm, 1995 NJW, 1701. For a similar view, see Mahrenholz, " 'Kritik an der Justiz gehört zur Sache,' " 1995 DRiZ, 35 (interview).

[56] 93 BVerfGE, 302–3. Interestingly, it was on these general grounds that Ossietzky was acquitted in the criminal courts in 1932. See above, pp. 210–11.

[57] Ibid., 305–6.

courts did not explain how they concluded that the statement referred specifically to members of the *Bundeswehr*.[58]

Finally, the Court addressed the finding of the ordinary courts that these statements constituted such an outrageous defamation (*Schmähkritik*) that a balancing of the values of free speech and personal honor was no longer required. The Court reaffirmed its view that there was indeed a narrow category of defamation that was so outrageous, and so predominantly directed toward personal abuse, that a defendant could be convicted of "insult" without the necessity of any judicial balancing. But, the Court continued, this category of defamation ordinarily involves personal feuds in which no important public question is being discussed. In contrast, the present cases involved the issue of the maintenance of the armed forces and their "readiness to kill in war"[59]—presumably a public question of considerable significance. The criminal courts were therefore obliged to undertake an individual balancing of the competing interests in the specific context of each case. Their failure to do so also required that the cases be reversed and remanded for further proceedings.[60]

Even though the Court reversed all four cases, we can see from the form of the argument that its cautious opinion rested on rather narrow grounds. Most important, the Court left open the possibility that defamation of the German military might be punishable in the future under certain circumstances. Indeed, in a noteworthy concluding statement, the Court emphasized that it was remanding the cases because the criminal courts might have reached different conclusions if they had applied the proper constitutional standards. But, the Court continued, its decision had not acquitted the defendants, nor had the Court found that it was permissible to defame "individual soldiers or the members of specific armed forces by statements such as 'soldiers are murderers.' Rather, each of the respective statements must be evaluated anew [by the criminal courts] under the [constitutional] requirements that have been set forth" in the opinion.[61]

[58] Ibid., 311–12.

[59] Ibid., 310.

[60] For an earlier decision also narrowing the concept of *Schmähkritik*, see 82 BVerfGE, 283–85 (*Zwangsdemokrat*).

[61] 93 BVerfGE, 312.

### *The* Soldiers *case: the dissent*

Although there were three dissenting judges in the *Soldiers* case, only Judge Evelyn Haas published a separate opinion. Her main contention was that the criminal courts had the authority to interpret the criminal law and to balance the contending interests. The Constitutional Court is authorized to intervene only when the criminal courts clearly disregard constitutional principles. Moreover, in Haas's view, the conviction of the defendants was proper, because their statements represented gross defamation (*Schmähkritik*). This part of the opinion was little more than another installment in a running dispute among the justices, and in academic commentary, over the scope of the Constitutional Court's authority to set aside decisions of the ordinary courts.[62] Indeed, we have already seen examples of this debate in aspects of the 1986 and 1995 *Nötigung* decisions.

But the concluding passages of Haas's dissenting opinion were considerably more interesting, and they seemed to reveal certain underlying structures of political thought in a more candid manner. In these passages, Judge Haas employed conceptions that seemed to have a pre-democratic, almost feudal tone—ideas, indeed, that also characterize the traditional German law regulating the civil service. Judge Haas invoked the "reciprocal relationship between protection and obedience" in the armed forces and found that this relationship, in particular, supported the protestors' convictions. Haas declared:

> A legal order that imposes the obligation of armed service upon young men, and requires obedience of them, must guarantee protection to those who meet this obligation if they are grossly defamed [*geschmäht*] because of their service as soldiers and publicly characterized as murderers. This is not a question of creating a special "soldiers' honor". Rather it is a question of the quite self-evident proposition that the Constitution—if it does not want to lose its credibility—must not leave persons defenseless who follow its commands and are attacked precisely (and exclusively) for that reason. The reciprocal relationship between protection and obedience belongs to the elementary principles of a legal order. That cannot and must not remain unconsidered.[63]

[62] See, e.g., Mager, "Meinungsfreiheit und Ehrenschutz von Soldaten," 1996 Jura, 405, 408.

[63] 93 BVerfGE, 318–19.

Overall, this remarkable argument seemed rather to invoke the pre-modern ethos of the old Prussian army than the spirit of contemporary "citizens in uniform."[64]

But the Court's majority explicitly rejected this argument, denying that there was a constitutional principle according to which "certain duties of obedience are to be compensated by increased protection of honor." Rather, the Court remarked, the legal protection of honor flows from the constitutional protection of personality, "which accrues to all persons in an equal manner."[65]

## *Reaction to the* Soldiers *case*

Notwithstanding the careful and nuanced nature of the majority opinion, the Court's decision in the *Soldiers* case was met with a torrent of hostility perhaps even more violent than that evoked by the decision in the 1995 *Nötigung* case. This reaction echoed the criticism of the previous year after the Court's three-judge screening panel reversed a similar conviction.[66]

### *Voices in politics and the press*

Among the politicians of the conservative coalition the reaction was particularly sharp. One CDU official referred to the Court's 1995 judgment as "incomprehensible in the highest degree",[67] and another called it "disappointing and unrealistic."[68]

Much of the reaction in newspaper columns and correspondence followed along similar lines. Indeed—as was also the case after the *Nötigung* decision—the Court's judgment in the *Soldiers* cases evoked grim forebodings about tendencies in German politics and society. Some writers claimed, for example, that decisions of this kind

[64] See, e.g., F.L. Carsten, *The Reichswehr and Politics: 1918 to 1933*, 3 (Oxford: Clarendon Press 1966):

> When Prussia, in the nineteenth century, became an industrial country its officer corps retained the characteristics of a pre-industrial world. The bond which linked the officer to the person of the "Supreme War Lord" was a modern variant of the nexus between the vassal and his liege lord.

[65] 93 BVerfGE, 304–5.

[66] See note 34 above.

[67] FAZ, 8 November 1995, in Hepp and Otto, 237 (CDU General Secretary).

[68] Mitteldeutsche Zeitung, 8 November 1995, in ibid., 241 (official of CDU/CSU parliamentary caucus).

undermined basic certainties and contributed to a damaging permissiveness. In this context, one writer complained darkly about the "increasingly aggressive libertine-like formlessness of life" and deplored "the loss of values as well as tastelessness and instability." According to this writer, the Constitutional Court—departing from its past contributions to the polity—"recently has taken the incomprehensible course . . . of opening the gates wide to the permissive and uncivil [*zivilschädlich*] spirit of the age."[69]

Others argued that the *Soldiers* decisions could have ominous political consequences. According to one eminent professor of law, the 1994 *Soldiers* decision "destroys any consciousness of community—[a quality] that no state can do without if it wants to preserve itself." Expression of the view "soldiers are murderers" "poisons the international atmosphere," contradicts basic principles of international law, and "casts into question" the loyalty of Germany with respect to its allies. In sum, the Court's decisions arose from a system of values "that destroys itself because, in the last analysis, it only recognizes the unlimited sphere of freedom [*Freiheitsraum*] of the individual."[70] Another correspondent declared that the "bad effects" of the 1994 *Soldiers* decision "will reach far into the future."[71]

Moreover, the parliamentary commissioner for defense matters, who viewed the 1994 decision with "incomprehension and indignation," claimed that the *Soldiers* decision was having a negative effect on the *Bundeswehr*.[72] Indeed, another important CDU official argued that—because of the decision—persons subject to conscription will find it difficult to have a "positive inner attitude to the Bundeswehr."[73] The General Inspector of the *Bundeswehr* also concluded that "a society that allows soldiers of the Bundeswehr to be called murderers should not be surprised if qualified young people no longer make themselves available for service as soldiers and . . . if

69 FAZ, 16 December 1995, 11 (Josef W. Jech).

70 FAZ, 20 January 1995, 12 (Prof. Dr. Karl Doehring).

71 FAZ, 3 April 1995, 11 (Dieter Lueg). As indicated in the text, some of the arguments presented here are reactions to the 1994 *Soldiers* decision of the Constitutional Court's third screening panel (see above), while others are reactions to the full opinion of the Court in October 1995. These arguments and reactions are discussed together here, in order to present a unified portrait of responses.

72 FAZ, 8 March 1995, 4.

73 *Landesweiter Basisdienst*, 21 September 1994, in Hepp and Otto, 145–46 (remarks of Heiner Geißler).

compulsory military service [*Wehrpflicht*] eventually collapses as a result."[74]

Others anticipated or followed Judge Haas in claiming that soldiers deserved particularly strong protection against defamation because of their pledge of obedience to the state. For example, one retired general declared: "The equation of soldiers with murderers is unbearable and [it is] an insult to those who have pledged themselves to loyal—that is, selfless and responsible—service to their fatherland."[75] In a parliamentary debate on the subject, an official of the CDU/CSU declared that if military recruits are to fulfill their duty they must be protected from being defamed as murderers when they do that duty; moreover, the federal Defense Minister wondered whether he should send German troops to Bosnia if he could not protect them from defamation.[76] In a contrasting view, however, an SPD official seemed to allude to well-known problems of the past when he warned against creating "an elevated [*herausgehobene*] officers' caste that will be cut off from society through a privileged legal position."[77]

Other writers seemed to reach the curious conclusion that the Court, in upholding the speech rights of these defendants, was somehow endorsing the truth of what the defendants had said—i.e., "soldiers are murderers."[78] These writers seemed to miss the quite basic point that rights of expression have their own value in a democratic system and that, in upholding those rights, the courts are not taking a position on the truth or falsity of opinions that may be put forth in vigorous political debate.[79]

74 *Berliner Morgenpost*, 16 November 1995, in ibid., 242.

75 FAZ, 24 January 1995, 9 (Joachim v. Schwerin). See also, e.g., FAZ, 11 November 1996, 6 (Rupert Scholz).

76 FAZ, 9 March 1996, 1–2. See also *Süddeutsche Zeitung*, 9 March 1996, in Hepp and Otto, 313.

77 FAZ, 9 March 1996, 2 (quoting FAZ summary of statement).

78 See, e.g., FAZ, 27 January 1995, 10 (Jan-Wolfgang Berlit).

79 Others claimed that the Court was showing insufficient judicial self-restraint in giving greater protection to the freedom of expression. In this connection, one writer invoked the *Flag Desecration* case and the 1994 *Soldiers* case in arguing that the state based on the rule of law was declining into a state ruled by courts. FAZ, 10 March 1995, 10 (Prof. Dr. Peter Schade). Another correspondent cited the 1995 *Soldiers* case as evidence of a "regrettable development" away from judicial restraint. FAZ, 16 November 1995, 11 (Matthias Schollen). Moreover, the respected journalist Friedrich Karl Fromme argued that if the Court continued to protect the interests of minorities in a way that deviated from the views of the majority of citizens,

On the other hand, representatives of the Greens congratulated the Court for being willing to "stand firm in favor of freedom" and emphasized that the decision underscored the importance of freedom of expression.[80] Moreover, several publicists and correspondents supported this view. Some were bemused, for example, that these general statements of pacifist principles had drawn such a vehement public reaction. One writer remarked:

> All this excitement seems to me to be intelligible only against the background that, even in the democratic state of the Federal Republic of Germany, the military power [*bewaffnete Macht*] is viewed as the heart and core of the state. The expression "soldiers are murderers" is very likely viewed as an attack on the heart of the state.[81]

Another writer noted that the 1994 decision by the Constitutional Court:

> simply repeats the acquittal [of von Ossietzky] by the Reichsgericht in 1932. But while at that earlier time it was only the Nazis and their close allies who foamed with anger and indignation, today an almost united political class, including members of the military and commentators, take issue with the liberal constitutional judges . . . The German political class has totally . . . forgotten all of the lessons of the [twentieth] century.[82]

the Court would lose the "high reputation" it has enjoyed. FAZ, 8 November 1995, reprinted in Hepp and Otto, 243–45.

A much-noted judicial reaction came from a lower court judge in Mainz who had received one of the four *Soldiers* cases on remand from the Constitutional Court. The judge declared that he was obliged by the Constitutional Court's reasoning to acquit the defendant. Yet, in a blistering attack, the judge bitterly criticized the Court's decision, finding that it was "arrogant, judicially questionable, and false as a matter of social policy." Sendler, 1996 NJW, 826; Lamprecht, *Zur Demontage*, 100–4.

80 FAZ, 8 November 1995, in Hepp and Otto, 238; *Süddeutsche Zeitung*, 8 November 1995, in ibid., 240. Indeed, the SPD (and the PDS) also approved the Court's 1995 decision. Ibid., 295.

81 *Süddeutsche Zeitung*, 25 November 1995, in Hepp and Otto, 268 (Sigurd Asper).

82 junge Welt, 22 September 1994, in Hepp and Otto, 165 (Gerhard Zwerenz). See also Karlsruher Kultur-Magazin, November 1994, in ibid., 185–86:

> Standing shoulder to shoulder with our brave troops was always proof of a blameless character. So it was under the Wilhelmine Empire, so it was in the Weimar Republic, also in the Third Reich, in the East German state and—as

Another writer pointed out that "even shrill stupidity and injurious exaggerations are covered by the right of free expression,"[83] and another author noted that, in issuing the 1994 decision, the Constitutional Court had "understood its most important task: it has kept the door open for contentious debate."[84]

### *Reactions in the legal periodicals*

Finally, the predominant commentary on these decisions in the legal journals was heavily negative, perpetuating and drawing upon academic criticism of preceding years which held that the Court was according undue favor to the freedom of expression.[85] One critic

> it now turns out—also in unified Germany . . . The excitement about [this] decision is the threadbare attempt to pack [our soldiers] in cotton wool, and to extract them from the conflict of opinions of a pluralistic society.

For a similar view, see *die tageszeitung*, 8 November 1995, in ibid., 252 (Dieter Rulff):

> The honor of soldiers still receives more votes in Germany than the freedom of expression. Accordingly, the reaction to the opinion of the Constitutional Court throws a more revealing light on the political culture in this country than on the judgment itself.

And cf. Fritz Stern, *The Failure of Illiberalism: Essays on the Political Culture of Modern Germany*, xl (New York: Columbia University Press 1992): "It is necessary to remember that [in earlier periods the German] army was not only a military machine but the embodiment of certain conscious and unconscious values."

83 *die tageszeitung*, 22 September 1994, in Hepp and Otto, 170 (Matthias Geis).

84 *Hannoversche Allgemeine*, 20 September 1994, in Hepp and Otto, 141–42 (Joachim Jahn). See also *junge Welt*, 8 November 1995, in ibid., 246–247 (Angelika Beer): "[W]e must have the right to criticize the Bundeswehr, and the Bundeswehr must be in a position to accept criticism."

85 See, e.g., Schmitt Glaeser, "Meinungsfreiheit, Ehrenschutz und Toleranzgebot," 1996 NJW, 873, 874 and n. 11; Zuck, 1996 NJW, 361; Zuck, "Anmerkung," 1996 JZ, 364; Scholz, "Meinungsfreiheit und Persönlichkeitsschutz: Gesetzgeberische oder verfassungsgerichtliche Verantwortung?," 1996 AfP, 323; Tettinger, "Das Recht der persönlichen Ehre in der Wertordnung des Grundgesetzes," 1997 JuS, 769.

For more general debate about the Court's apparent preference for freedom of expression over the protection of "honor," compare Kriele, "Ehrenschutz und Meinungsfreiheit," 1994 NJW, 1897, with Soehring, "Ehrenschutz und Meinungsfreiheit," 1994 NJW, 2925.

For discussion of the *Soldiers* cases in the American literature, see Edward J. Eberle, *Dignity and Liberty: Constitutional Visions in Germany and the United States*, 214–20 (Westport: Praeger 2002); see also Kommers, *Constitutional Jurisprudence*, 388–95. For a more general analysis of "insult" and "honor" in German law, see Whitman, "Enforcing Civility and Respect: Three Societies," 109 *Yale Law Journal* 1279 (2000).

charged, for example, that the Court's apparent preference for freedom of expression over the protection of honor was "a dangerous change of course" in the interpretation of basic constitutional principles.[86] Moreover, in failing to defer to the balancing undertaken by the ordinary criminal courts, the justices were guilty of a "dangerous invasion" of the authority of those tribunals.[87] In sum, according to this critic, the decision further solidified a "false development" [*Fehlentwicklung*] in the Court's jurisprudence.[88] Another author claimed that the general tendency of the Court's free speech jurisprudence is leading to a "brutalization of political behavior, in which state symbols that are directed toward [societal] integration end up in the dust bin."[89]

In contrast, however, a few authors in legal journals—sometimes invoking the considerably more libertarian English or American jurisprudence—applauded the result of the *Soldiers* decisions and even criticized the opinions as ultimately not giving enough protection to the freedom of expression.[90] But even among those who approved the result, there was some criticism of the Court's technique. According to one writer, for example, the Court's arguments were "inconsistent and half-hearted": instead of achieving clarity, the Court issued "a Janus-headed decision, perhaps in the illusory hope that it could appease both opposing groups . . . But what the Court supplied were stones instead of bread." In any case these questions "belong in the realm of public discussion . . . and not in the court-room."[91]

### *Proposed legislation*

In light of the great public outcry, the governing coalition introduced a measure in Parliament for the purpose of seeking to undo the Court's *Soldiers* ruling—a step that echoed the government's reaction after the Court's *Nötigung* decision. Interestingly, the proposal also paralleled a decree issued by President Hindenburg—as an

[86] Zuck, 1996 JZ, 365; see also Scholz, 1996 AfP, 325.

[87] Zuck, 1996 JZ, 365. For further criticism on this point, see also Schmitt Glaeser, 1996 NJW, 874; Scholz, 1996 AfP, 324; see generally Sendler, 1994 ZRP, 346–47.

[88] Zuck, 1996 JZ, 365.

[89] Tettinger, 1997 JuS, 775.

[90] Gounalakis, 1996 NJW, 481; Mager, 1996 Jura, 405. See also Wrase, "Meinungsfreiheit und Ehrenschutz," 1996 JuS, 88; Mahrenholz, 1995 DRiZ, 35 (interview).

[91] Gounalakis, 1996 NJW, 486–87.

"emergency measure"—following the acquittal of Carl von Ossietzky in the original *Soldiers* case in 1932.[92]

The coalition's proposal would impose up to three years' imprisonment or a fine on anyone who "publicly, in an assembly or through the distribution of written material, defames [*verunglimpft*] soldiers, in connection with their service, in a manner calculated [*geeignet*] to degrade the esteem of the Bundeswehr or its soldiers in public opinion."[93] According to its proponents, the purpose of this provision was to protect the "viability of the Bundeswehr and its readiness to protect the country, the combat readiness [*Einsatzwille*] of the individual soldiers, and the readiness of citizens" to enter the Bundeswehr.[94] This proposal, however, made little progress in Parliament.[95] Certainly, it is difficult to see what the proponents of this measure might accomplish by its passage, because it seems likely that the measure would be subject to the same limitations—in favor of freedom of expression—that the Constitutional Court has imposed on prosecutions for "insult" under §185.[96] Moreover, the proposed statute could well violate the free speech provisions of the European Convention on Human Rights, by which Germany is also bound.[97]

## The *Crucifix* case

Unlike the *Nötigung* and *Soldiers* cases, the final decision that we will consider in the trio of controversial constitutional opinions of 1995 did not grow out of contentious political battles that were widely reported in the press before they came to the courts. Rather, this case arose from a quiet but tense dispute between parents and school officials in Bavaria over the placement of a crucifix or cross in public school classrooms. Yet, when the case was ultimately decided by the First Senate of the Constitutional Court in May 1995, it seemed

[92] Hepp and Otto, 293, 298.

[93] BT-Drucks. 13/3971, reprinted in Hohmann and Grote, "Funktionalismus und Funktionsfähigkeit der Bundeswehr," 1997 JR, 364, 365.

[94] Quoted in Scholz, 1996 AfP, 327. For discussion of this proposal, see ibid., 327–30.

[95] See Stamm, "Das Bundesverfassungsgericht und die Meinungsfreiheit," APuZ 2001 (B 37–38), 16, 23.

[96] See Nolte, " 'Soldaten sind Mörder'—Europäisch betrachtet," 1996 AfP, 313, 322; see also v. Arnauld, "Überlegungen zu dem Entwurf eines neuen §109b StGB," 1997 ZRP, 110, 112–13 (arguing that a special "protection of honor" for soldiers might violate concepts of equality in the Basic Law).

[97] Nolte, 1996 AfP, 317.

to strike a particularly sensitive nerve among traditionalists in Germany.[98]

As in the *Soldiers* case, the Court's *Crucifix* opinion was by no means absolutist in nature. Indeed, in a nuanced way, the majority attempted to strike a balance between contending values. Nonetheless, the three cases—the *Nötigung*, *Soldiers*, and *Crucifix* cases—were often bracketed together as perceived examples of a new extremist left-wing trend in the jurisprudence of the Constitutional Court, and particularly in its First Senate.

## *Background of the* Crucifix *case*

In 1968 the Bavarian Constitution was amended to provide that pupils in the public schools "will be instructed and educated according to the principles of the Christian confessions."[99] In an important decision in 1975, the Federal Constitutional Court examined this provision and found that it was constitutional under the Basic Law.[100] For the purpose of implementing the values of this provision, the Bavarian government issued a rule requiring that a cross be placed in every public school classroom.[101]

The complainants in the *Crucifix* case were two parents who followed the tenets of the "anthroposophical world-view" as set forth in

[98] See Peter Pappert (ed.), *Den Nerv getroffen. Engagierte Stimmen zum Kruzifix-Urteil von Karlsruhe* (Aachen: Bergmoser & Höller undated) [*Den Nerv*].

[99] Bayr. Verf. Art. 135. The Bavarian Constitution also declares that the goals of public education include instilling "fear of God [and] respect for religious convictions" and that, in the schools, "the religious feelings of all are to be respected." Ibid., Arts 131, 136. For the history of provisions of this kind, growing out of a "culture-compromise" in the Weimar Constitution, see Link, "Stat Crux?: Die 'Kruzifix'-Entscheidung des Bundesverfassungsgerichts," 1995 NJW, 3353, 3354.

[100] 41 BVerfGE, 65 (1975); see also 41 BVerfGE, 29 (1975); 41 BVerfGE, 88 (1975); for commentary, see Eberle, "Religion in the Classroom in Germany and the United States," 81 *Tulane Law Review* 67, 92–99 (2006). The Court found that the Basic Law gave the states considerable leeway in balancing the rights of parents who preferred religion in public schools against the rights of those who did not. See Art. 7(1)GG. If the schools did not insist on the truth of Christian doctrine and did not act as missionaries, the Court found, the rights of the protesting minority would not be infringed. In another important case, decided four years later, the Court held that it was permissible for a "non-confessional" prayer to be said in the public schools, so long as objecting students were not required to participate. 52 BVerfGE, 223 (1979).

[101] 93 BVerfGE, 1, 2 (1995).

the teachings of Rudolf Steiner. These parents objected to the placement of a cross or crucifix—i.e., a cross with the representation of a "dying masculine body"—in their children's classrooms.[102] When efforts to arrange a compromise failed, the parents sought relief in the Bavarian administrative courts. These courts ruled against them, and they filed a Constitutional Complaint in the Federal Constitutional Court.

The parents based their Complaint on Article 4(1) of the Basic Law, which states that "the freedom of belief and of conscience, and the freedom of religious and philosophical [*weltanschaulichen*] creed, are inviolable." The parents also based their claim on "the natural right of the parents" over the "care and upbringing of children" as protected by Article 6(2) of the Basic Law. The parents argued that the placement of a crucifix in the classroom would exert an "intensive" religious influence on children, whose ability "to form an independent judgment is considerably less than that of adults."[103] The Bavarian court had rejected these arguments, however, concluding that the complainants' rights must give way to the rights of other children and parents who wanted a crucifix in the classroom. According to the Bavarian court, the cross was actually not the expression of a particular confessional belief, but rather a cultural object of the "general western-Christian tradition." Indeed, by merely displaying a crucifix, the school was not engaging in active missionary endeavor. Those who objected must accept the cross under the requirement of tolerance for the "world-view" of others.[104]

### *The Crucifix case: the Court's decision*

In a decision of profound significance for Germany as a multicultural country, the Constitutional Court held that a state regulation requiring a crucifix or cross in a public school classroom was unconstitutional.[105] Yet, as in the *Soldiers* case, the Court developed its view

[102] Ibid., 2. The parents took this position although it was not entirely clear that Steiner's "world-view" actually required it. See, e.g., Redeker, " 'Der moderne Fluch der Versuchung zur Totalität,' " 1995 NJW, 3369; Maier, "Geschichtsblind und schulfremd," in Alexander Hollerbach *et al.* (eds), *Das Kreuz im Widerspruch: der Kruzifix-Beschluss des Bundesverfassungsgerichts in der Kontroverse*, 55 and n.8 (Freiburg/B: Herder 1996).

[103] 93 BVerfGE, 7, 6.

[104] Ibid., 4–6.

[105] 93 BVerfGE, 1 (1995).

in a careful and nuanced opinion that seemed designed to give some comfort to both sides in the dispute. As in both the *Nötigung* and *Soldiers* decisions, questions of the interpretation of language and symbols or symbolic action were prominent.

The Court began by making clear that Article 4(1) GG not only protects the freedom to hold a belief and to act in accordance with that belief, but also guarantees the right to remain free from the religious activities of others—to a certain extent at least.[106] Of course, one may often be confronted with unwanted religious symbols in everyday life—and one must accept that—but a situation created by the state in which one is forced to confront those symbols is something different.[107] Indeed, there is a general requirement of state neutrality in questions of belief, arising from Article 4(1) and other constitutional provisions.[108] Yet the Court also made clear that this requirement of neutrality was not absolute and that opportunities for accommodation with religion were not inconsiderable.

In applying these general principles, the Court first rejected the view—adopted by the Bavarian court—that the cross was a cultural and not a religious symbol. Indeed, the Court emphasized, the cross is Christianity's main symbol. "It makes manifest [*versinnbildlicht*] the salvation of humanity from original sin, accomplished through the sacrificial death of Christ." The placement of a cross on a building, therefore, shows the owner's profession of Christian faith and may be viewed by non-Christians as a symbol of Christianity's missionary expansion. Moreover, the Court continued, the cross may well have a particular effect on students, whose beliefs may not be firm or certain and who may be particularly susceptible to influence.[109]

[106] Ibid., 15.

[107] Ibid., 16.

[108] Ibid., 16–17. On this point, the Court invoked the equality provisions of the Basic Law (Arts 3 and 33(1)GG), as well as three provisions of the Weimar Constitution that had been incorporated into the Basic Law by reference: Article 136(1)WRV (religious freedom); Article 136(4)WRV (no compelled participation in religious observance); and Article 137(1)WRV ("There is no state church"). See Art. 140 GG. For the relationship between the Basic Law and incorporated religious provisions of the Weimar Constitution, see Eberle, 81 *Tulane Law Review*, 72–78.

[109] 93 BVerfGE, 19–21.

For extensive debate on the symbolic meaning of the cross—in light of the Court's decision in the *Crucifix* case—compare Czermak, "Zur Unzulässigkeit des Kreuzes in der Schule aus verfassungsrechtlicher Sicht," in Winfried Brugger and Stefan Huster (eds), *Der Streit um das Kreuz in der Schule*, 22–29 (Baden-Baden:

Yet even with this background, the Court sought to accommodate other contending interests. Accordingly, the Court noted that the Complainants' constitutional right of belief could be limited by countervailing constitutional values, such as the right of belief of other parents—who might seek a Christian education and a crucifix in the classroom—as well as the constitutional authority and obligation of the state to supervise the public schools.[110] This conflict of contending rights and interests must be resolved through the principle of "practical concordance," which states that no interest will be granted an automatic preference and requires that a settlement be reached which is most considerate to all.[111]

In this light, the Court indicated, the state may strike the necessary compromise by allowing religious influences in the schools, but by also seeking as far as possible to exclude pressure or coercion of students. In particular, the school must not act as a missionary and must not claim that Christian belief is obligatory. This approach also requires acceptance of the doctrine of tolerance which also excludes any disparagement of non-Christian beliefs. Only under such an interpretation was the Court able to uphold the Christian influence in schools in Bavaria and Baden in earlier cases.[112]

In this view, the Court concluded, the display of the cross in the classroom goes too far. As noted, the cross "symbolizes the essential core of Christian belief."[113] Moreover, the choice between countervailing interests cannot simply be resolved according to the principle of majority rule, because the specific purpose of freedom of belief is to protect minorities.

Accordingly, with respect to religion in the schools, the basic principle must be one of voluntariness: school prayers and other religious ceremonies may be permissible if dissenting children have the opportunity to avoid them. But that cannot be the case with respect to the cross. Because it is always on the classroom wall,

Nomos 1998), with Geis, "Zur Zulässigkeit des Kreuzes in der Schule aus verfassungsrechtlicher Sicht," in ibid., 47–51. See also Brenner,"Der Kruzifix-Beschluß des Bundesverfassungsgerichts," 1996 ThürVB1, 145, 149–50.

110 See Article 7(1)GG. Indeed, the Basic Law allows the state to create public schools with certain religious goals (*Bekenntnisschulen*) and expressly provides that religious instruction will constitute a normal part of the curriculum in most public schools. Art. 7(3),(5)GG.

111 93 BVerfGE, 21.

112 Ibid., 21–23. See 41 BVerfGE, 65 (1975); 41 BVerfGE, 29 (1975).

113 93 BVerfGE, 23–24.

its presence and putative spiritual demands cannot be avoided by dissenting students. In conclusion, according to the Court,

> [it] would not be consistent with the requirement of practical concordance fully to ignore [*zurückdrängen*] the feelings of the dissenters, with the result that students of the Christian faith—in addition to religious instruction and voluntary prayer—would also be entitled, even in secular courses, to study under the symbol of their belief.[114]

## *The* Crucifix *case: the dissent*

Three of the eight Constitutional Court judges dissented. They emphasized that the Basic Law accorded the states broad discretion over education and the structure of the school system.[115] Displaying the cross is nothing more than the communication of general "Christian-western values and ethical norms"—a goal that the Court has upheld as permissible.[116] Under Article 4(1) GG, Christian parents have a "positive" right to observe their religion, and dissenting parents have a "negative" right not to be confronted with other religious beliefs—and the state must weigh these two values. But, in the end, the requirement of tolerance indicates that the dissenting parents must "accept the presence of the cross."[117] Any resulting psychic injury is of "relatively slight weight," as the children are not forced to participate in religious ceremonies or to engage in particular religious conduct. Finally—in Bavaria at least—people are frequently confronted by crosses in everyday life; therefore, "the cross in the classroom remains in the realm of the usual; it does not have a missionary character."[118]

[114] Ibid., 24.

[115] Ibid., 25–28 (opinion of Judges Haas, Seidl, and Söllner). Judge Haas also issued a separate dissent on procedural matters.

[116] Ibid., 28. Indeed, it could be argued that the decision of the *Crucifix* majority was inconsistent with earlier cases allowing Bavarian schools to instruct and educate "according to the principles" of Christianity. 41 BVerfGE, 65 (1975); see Würtenberger, " 'Unter dem Kreuz' lernen," in Detlef Merten *et al.* (eds), *Der Verwaltungsstaat im Wandel* (*Festschrift für Franz Knöpfle*), 408–9 (Munich: Beck 1996).

[117] 93 BVerfGE, 32–33.

[118] Ibid., 33.

### *Religion in the schools: an American comparison*

Although the result in the *Crucifix* case is consistent with the result that would be reached in the United States, the doctrinal background is considerably different in the two systems. Under the Establishment Clause of the American First Amendment, the placement of a cross or crucifix in a public school classroom would clearly be unconstitutional. But the American doctrine goes considerably further. Under the American cases, any sort of official religious practice in public schools—including the least sectarian of religious prayers—is also unconstitutional, even if those who object are excused from participation.[119] In contrast, under the "practical concordance" or balancing technique of the German Constitutional Court, certain prayers are allowed in the German schools—so long as no dissenting student is required to take part.[120] In addition, Article 7 of the Basic Law makes specific provision for a special class period of religious teaching in most public schools—although, again, any objecting student must be excused from attendance.

As a matter of doctrine, the Establishment Clause—which yields individual rights indirectly, by prohibiting an undue relationship between church and state—has assumed a position of great prominence in the American cases. In Germany, the Basic Law incorporates Article 137 of the Weimar Constitution, which declares that there shall be no "state church."[121] Nonetheless, most cases that would be decided under the Establishment Clause in the United States are thought to raise issues of the "negative" freedom of conscience and belief under Article 4(1) of the German Basic Law—an individual right to be free of certain religious influences and pressures—and, as we have seen, this "negative" religious freedom may have to be weighed against the "positive" religious freedom of others. Indeed, in general, the idea of "non-establishment"—the clear separation of church and state—is not recognized in German constitutional law. Rather, the German courts have adopted a concept of state "neutrality" which, as indicated above, permits the accommodation of significant religious influences.[122]

[119] *Engel v. Vitale*, 370 U.S. 421 (1962); see also *Abington School District v. Schempp*, 374 U.S. 203 (1963).

[120] 52 BVerfGE, 223 (1979).

[121] See Art. 140 GG.

[122] For a comprehensive discussion of the German law concerning church and state and religious freedom, see Currie, *Constitution of the Federal Republic of Germany*,

## *Reaction to the* Crucifix *decision*

### *Voices in politics and the press*

The reaction to the *Crucifix* decision was sharp and immediate, and even more widespread than the reactions to the *Nötigung* and *Soldiers* cases. Chancellor Kohl referred to the decision as "incomprehensible" (*unverständlich*).[123] Moreover, some other political leaders —at least in their "first rage" against the Court's opinion—called for actual resistance to the decision, a rare, perhaps unprecedented official reaction to a decision of the Constitutional Court.[124] As one commentator wryly remarked: "For the first time, people who consider themselves conservative are resorting to the rhetoric of resistance which has been cultivated for decades by their political opponents. Now they too want to have their Mutlangen."[125]

The critics were animated by a number of common themes, and many of the writers extended their complaints about the *Crucifix* decision to cover the *Nötigung* and 1994 *Soldiers* cases as well.[126] As with the *Nötigung* and *Soldiers* decisions, several critics viewed the *Crucifix* opinion as revealing the Court's acceptance of the principles of the revolutionary movement of 1968. One writer suggested, for example, that "the old ideological fetishes of the left" were being finally brought into reality.[127] Another declared more forthrightly that the *Crucifix* decision "proves again how successful the 'march through the institutions', which commenced in 1968, has become."[128]

244–69; see also, e.g., Robbers, "State and Church in Germany," in Gerhard Robbers (ed.), *State and Church in the European Union*, 57–73 (Baden-Baden: Nomos 1996).

123 FAZ, 12 August 1995, 1.

124 See Sendler, "Blüten richterlicher Unabhängigkeit und Verfassungsgerichtsschelte," 1996 NJW, 825; see also Lamprecht, "Verführung zum Rechts-Ungehorsam," 1996 NJW, 971; FAZ, 24 August 1995, 2 (quoting Coburger Tageblatt).

125 Jan Ross, "Hüter der Verfassung," FAZ, 23 August 1995, 35. In Bavaria, moreover, tens of thousands of people marched in protest of the Court's decision, bearing the slogan "The cross remains—yesterday—today—tomorrow." Brenner, 1996 ThürVBl, 145; Lamprecht, *Zur Demontage*, 77–80.

126 See, e.g., FAZ, 23 August 1995, 10 (Michael Müller); FAZ, 14 August 1995, 1 (FAZ commentary); FAZ, 14 August 1995, 1 (CSU politician); FAZ, 18 August 1995, 8 (Prof. Dr. Werner Kinnebrock).

127 FAZ, 29 August 1995, 6 (Judge Hans Lothar Graf).

128 FAZ, 16 August 1995, 9 (Dieter Löhmann).

Sounding another common theme, several writers maintained that the decision was "anti-federal," impairing the authority of the states in the constitutional order.[129] Similarly, an important Bavarian politician advocated limitations on the Constitutional Court in order to prevent "such fundamental interferences with the rights of the *Länder*."[130] Some academic critics also argued that the Court's failure to give adequate weight to the constitutional recognition of the states' authority over education in Article 7 GG was one of the greatest failings of the majority opinion.[131]

Other commentators—quite extraordinarily—drew an analogy between the decision and the anti-religious policies of the Nazis. One writer, for example, declared that the "miserable" decision of the "Karlsruhe Five" (the Court's majority) had parallels with the Nazis' policy of removing crosses from the public schools.[132] Another complained that what "the Nazis were not able to do everywhere—that is, to banish the cross from the schools—the Constitutional Court has achieved."[133] Yet another writer declared that in 1941, "the National Socialists demanded the removal of the cross; today [it is] the Federal Constitutional Court. I do not understand our world anymore."[134]

This provocative argument, however, did not go unchallenged. One writer, for example, found the analogy "shameful," noting that the motivation of the Constitutional Court judges is "indeed quite different from that of the [Nazis] . . . Whoever draws such comparisons

129 See FAZ, 17 August 1995, 6 (Erich Einwachter); see also FAZ, 11 August 1995, 1.

130 FAZ, 18 August 1995, 3 (remarks of CSU leader Theo Waigel). Another writer claimed that the decision is a "massive invasion . . . of the religious and cultural identity of Bavaria." *Augsburger Allgemeine*, reprinted in *Den Nerv*, 121 (Dr. Hubert Gindert). See also FAZ, 1 September 1995, 10 (Supreme Administrative Court Judge Heinz Honnacker) (Decision seems to have been "quite intentionally anti-Bavarian.")

131 Geis, in Brugger and Huster, 53–55. See also Hollerbach, " 'Der Staat ist kein Neutrum,' " in *Das Kreuz im Widerspruch*, 28.

132 FAZ, 20 September 1995, 14 (Prof. Dr. Konrad Repgen).

133 FAZ, 15 August 1995, 6 (Hans Beckmann).

134 FAZ, 18 August 1995, 8 (Gertrud Spode). Compare FAZ (Eberhard Jüngel), reprinted in *Den Nerv*, 218.

Rather more moderately, another critic of the *Crucifix* decision noted that the return of crosses to the classrooms after 1945 expressed the break with the National Socialist regime "and therefore the new basis of political ethics." Würtenberger, in Merten *et al.* (eds), *Verwaltungsstaat im Wandel*, 409 n. 62. See also FAZ (Hans Maier), in *Den Nerv*, 223–24.

should rather re-examine his understanding of democracy. We are now living in a state under the rule of law."[135]

A significant number of correspondents objected to the Court's insistence that the constitution is intended to protect minorities, considering that view to be "dangerous."[136] One writer asked whether "a small minority may rob the majority of an important symbol," and, referring in a disparaging manner to the "dictatorial intolerance of a small minority," predicted "a 'class struggle' if the decision were put into effect."[137] Another claimed that the decision, by imposing "the interests of a minority on the majority," reaches a result that "attacks the absolutely necessary basic consensus [of society] at its core"—as also happened in the 1994 *Soldiers* case. In sum—this writer argued—"small radical minorities try everything in order to discredit or repress the institutions, values and symbols of our state."[138] A conservative politician even suggested that "the majority of the German population" needs protection against "blackmail by minorities."[139]

In some ways, these correspondents advanced the most fundamental criticism of the Constitutional Court's approach by refusing to accept the view—important in the Court's majority opinion and, if anything, even more important in the United States—that constitutional review exists in large part to protect the rights and interests of minorities against governmental oppression and majoritarian power. These correspondents seemed to revert to an earlier view in which the constitution is seen as a necessary integrating factor in society—without which conservative fears of societal disintegration might well become justified.

Along similar lines, numerous writers also insisted that the principle of tolerance required that the minority—who might be offended

[135] *Kölnische Rundschau* (Eduard Bopp), in ibid., 47. See also Straubinger Tagblatt (Martin Lakermeier), in ibid., 65: "But certainly it is significantly different if a measure is set down by dictators who scorn humanity or if a judgment is spoken by the highest German court in a proceeding under the rule of law."

[136] FAZ, 18 September 1995, 8 (Dr. Horst Leutheußer).

[137] FAZ, 18 August 1995, 8 (Ursula Liesner).

[138] FAZ, 26 August 1995, 8 (Wolfgang Tücks). For similar views, see also FAZ, 23 August 1995, 10 ("Constitutional Court again . . . supports extreme minority views"); FAZ, 15 August 1995, 6 (Hans Beckmann) ("Unbelievable that . . . minorities determine what we are allowed to do and not to do"); *Kölnische Rundschau* (Joachim Uebing), in *Den Nerv*, 128 ("[A] small minority is given the right to injure the Christian world-view of the great majority of the population").

[139] FAZ, 14 August 1995, 1 (remarks of the chair of the CDU/CSU parliamentary caucus).

by the presence of the cross in the classroom—should accede to the religious sensibilities of the majority.[140] From an American perspective, at least, this appears to be a peculiar argument because the principle of toleration is generally perceived as an obligation of the majority not to oppress the minority on account of its religious or political views. To interpret this principle as requiring the minority to agree to what it sees as its own oppression by the majority has, in contrast, a somewhat Orwellian tone.[141] Indeed, the fact that such an argument is so often heard in this debate reveals the strength of a general view that is particularly tenacious in German constitutional law—the view that the constitution is an integrating factor, in which the positions of the majority, rather than those of the minority, may deserve a special measure of constitutional protection.

Other writers attacked the *Crucifix* decision as reflecting the decay or loss of substantive spiritual or social values—an argument also heard in connection with the *Nötigung* and *Soldiers* cases. One writer declared that, with the *Crucifix* decision, "the Rubicon has now been crossed, and the way has been shown into the totally liberal, neutral, confession-less and value free state."[142] Along the same lines, a preacher from Bockau wrote: "Perhaps in future one should hang an empty picture frame in our class-rooms as a symbol of spiritual solidarity, or a picture of Mickey Mouse as a symbol of the lowest common spiritual denominator."[143] Certainly this argument had important political implications as well. An official of the CDU expressed the views of many when he declared that religion was an essential pillar of government; if religion were banished from

140 See, e.g., *Passauer Neue Presse* (Msgr. Josef Aidenbach), in *Den Nerv*, 81; *Aachener Volkszeitung* (Pfarrer Hans Tings), in ibid., 73–74. This position was also asserted by the three dissenting judges in the *Crucifix* case. 93 BVerfGE, 33. For illuminating discussion of this argument in light of more general political philosophy, see Forst, "A Tolerant Republic?," in Jan-Werner Müller (ed.), *German Ideologies since 1945: Studies in the Political Thought and Culture of the Bonn Republic* (New York: Palgrave Macmillan 2003), 209–20.

141 For recognition of this point in the German literature, see Rozek, "Anmerkung," 1996 BayVBl, 22, 23–25; Lamprecht, *Zur Demontage*, 77–78; Czermak, 1995 NJW, 3351–52: What kind of "outrageous liberality" is it that allows "the minority to be so tolerant that they dance to the pipe" of the majority?

142 FAZ, 23 August 1995, 10 (Dr. Jens Eugen Baganz).

143 FAZ, 23 August 1995, 10 (Jochen Härtwig).

activities of the state, he argued, "the constitutional order itself will be threatened with danger of collapse."[144]

### *Reactions in the legal periodicals*

Reaction to the *Crucifix* decision in the law journals was also, by and large, sharply critical.[145] A former President of the Constitutional Court went so far as to call the decision "almost incomprehensible."[146] One professor complained that, among other things, the decision ignored German federalism because the Basic Law accorded special competence over public schools to the states.[147] But in his conclusion, this writer saw even greater problems for the institutions of the state in tones that again seemed to evoke the historical theme of cultural despair:

144 FAZ, 28 August 1995, 10 (Christoph Böhr). See also General-Anzeiger (Dieter Felbick), in *Den Nerv*, 112 ("If we go further along this course, we will undermine the foundation of this commonwealth"); *Schwäbische Zeitung* (Richard Baumann), in ibid., 72–73:

> If we continue to proceed with the de-Christianization of our society . . . then in a few years this Republic will no long be governable . . . [P]eople and country will end in anarchy and chaos if the last inalienable values and traditions of the Christian West are abandoned.

These remarks seem to reflect the views of many observers—from the founding of the Federal Republic onwards—that, in light of Nazi atrocities, only an alliance with the Christian religion can preserve the stability of a liberal state. See Forst, in *German Ideologies*, 216–17.

Finally, as in the *Nötigung* and *Soldiers* cases, correspondents argued that the *Crucifix* decision impaired the reputation of the Court and "the acceptance of its decisions." According to one writer, the result is that "the state based on the rule of law is damaged, as are we all." FAZ, 1 September 1995, 10 (Judge Heinz Honnacker). For similar complaints about the Court's lost reputation, see also FAZ, 18 August 1995, 8 (Prof. Dr.-Ing. Wilhelm Schwier); 30 August 1995, 8 (Dr. jur Klaus-Dieter Uelhoff). As in the *Soldiers* and *Nötigung* cases, several writers also questioned the juristic competence of the judges. FAZ, 26 August 1995, 8 (Prof. Dr. Egon Wetzels); see also FAZ, 19 August 1995, 8 (Dr. Hans-Jürgen Rösgen).

145 See, e.g., Brenner, 1996 ThürVBl, 145; Redeker, 1995 NJW, 3369; Link, 1995 NJW, 3353.

146 Benda, 1995 NJW, 2470.

147 Müller-Volbehr, "Positive und Negative Religionsfreiheit", 1995 JZ 996. For additional criticism on this point, see Brenner, 1996 ThürVBl, 151–52: "The increasing unitarization of the German Federal State has obviously now reached the schools, and federalistic diversity has been sacrificed, through this decision, to the leveling of a central-state uniformity." But for a different view on this question, see Czermak, in Brugger and Huster (eds), *Streit um das Kreuz*, 35–38.

> The Constitutional Court continues its long-observed trend of evaluating the individual rights of minorities as substantially higher than the countervailing Basic Rights of third persons, and other constitutional values. This exaggerated protection of minorities is regrettable because, as a result of the further development of the so-called pluralistic society, there is a growth in the number of minorities which, invoking the criteria developed by the Constitutional Court, can successfully bring an action against all traditional, historically developed forms of expression of the life of the state . . . Under the cloak of tolerance and protection of minorities, any minority at all will feel itself encouraged toward further campaigns against institutions, values and symbols of the state . . .
>
> Of course, the [*Crucifix*] decision must be judged as a signal of the advanced de-Christianization of society . . . The banishment of religion from public life results in a loss of traditions and [the loss of] a way of life for a significant part of society. A state that is cut off from the root of its order of values falls into the emptiness of a value-vacuum. A complete freedom to choose values [*unverbindliche Wertbeliebigkeit*] could lead the state based on the rule of law, with its concept of human rights, into a crisis. The frequently-invoked openness of society and its multi-cultural setting [*Kulisse*] will hardly be able to replace the loss of the Christian heritage as the leading factor in the value order of the state.[148]

Along similar lines, another author noted that the *Crucifix* decision of the Constitutional Court was just one part of the Court's "recent tendency increasingly to dissolve the fundamental values of the Basic Law, in favor of individual constitutional rights"—a development which prepares the way for a "society of egotistic and egocentric individuals that no longer feels any obligation to any values whatsoever."[149]

[148] Müller-Volbehr, 1995 JZ, 1000 (footnote omitted). See also Redeker, 1995 NJW, 3370: In the *Crucifix* decision, the "social community . . . has almost faded away [and] the other values which . . . can fill this social community with inner life are scarcely considered."

[149] Brenner, 1996 ThürVBl, 152. See also, e.g., Eberl, "Anmerkung," 1996 BayVBl, 107 (denying that a constitutional right of "negative" religious freedom can be

### *The judges respond*

The immediate flood of criticism led to two interesting reactions from judges of the Constitutional Court. First, the Chairman of the Court's First Senate, Johann Friedrich Henschel, issued public statements that seemed to interpret or qualify the decision by declaring that only government-mandated crosses were affected by the Court's opinion: if parents agreed with school officials on the matter, a cross might indeed remain in the classroom as a voluntary matter. These statements, along with a corresponding press release of the Court amending an official headnote of the case, drew renewed criticism.[150] Many spoke of the sloppiness (*Schlamperei*) of the justices in not expressing this qualification more clearly in the original decision.[151] Moreover, it was certainly open to question whether an opinion of the Court could be subsequently altered or interpreted by the senate's chairman in this informal manner.[152] Eventually, indeed, the State of Bavaria took up the view suggested by Henschel and enacted a statute which generally provided for

derived from Article 4 GG, and indicating that the *Crucifix* decision was an "extraordinarily serious discrimination against the Christian majority").

Notwithstanding the overwhelming criticism in the law journals, a few writers did endorse the Court's *Crucifix* decision. One commentator, for example, declared that the decision remained within the general scope of the Court's earlier religion cases, and welcomed the "new accent" that the Court had placed on the relationship between "negative" and "positive" freedom of religion. Goerlich, "Krieg dem Kreuz in der Schule?," 1995 NVwZ, 1184. Another writer, agreeing that the decision followed from earlier jurisprudence, noted that the administrative courts had routinely found that teachers wearing non-Christian religious symbols injured the "negative" religious rights of students and parents. "The obvious question," this author continued, "is why should something else suddenly apply in the case of a state-ordered cross in the school." Rozek, "Anmerkung," 1996 BayVBl, 22, 24. Yet another author—a Bavarian Administrative Court judge—found the decision "convincing and difficult to contradict," and predicted that the decision would mark a proud moment in the history of the Federal Republic. Czermak, 1995 NJW, 3350, 3353.

150 Announcement of the Press Office of the Constitutional Court, 22 August 1995, reprinted in *Den Nerv*, 250.

151 See, e.g., *Saarbrücker Zeitung*, 23 August 1995, in ibid., 192; *Köln Express*, reprinted in FAZ, 23 August 1995, 2.

152 FAZ, 24 August 1995, 3. See also FAZ, 31 August 1995, 8 (Dr. Kurt Hackenbracht) ("A final judgment is subsequently altered by the chairman of the panel. I know of no comparable case in the literature. Please, which *Crucifix* judgment is now in effect—the original one, or the one that was fundamentally altered . . . by a single judge?").

crosses in schoolrooms but, in cases in which parents complained, allowed the local school authorities to balance all of the competing interests and thereafter to remove the cross, if the authorities thought best.[153]

A second response to public criticism of the *Crucifix* case came from Judge Dieter Grimm, who had been among the prevailing justices in the 1995 *Nötigung* and *Soldiers* decisions, as well as in the *Crucifix* decision. Judge Grimm contributed a brief comment to the *Frankfurter Allgemeine Zeitung* in which he pointed out that if politicians encourage noncompliance with the Court's decisions—as seems to have happened after the *Crucifix* decision—those politicians are actually undermining the constitutional structure that supports their own work.[154]

Grimm's comment drew an emotional response from another well-known lawyer and teacher who argued that Grimm had understated the political nature of the Court's basic task.[155] Indeed, this writer expanded his remarks to attack all three of the decisions we have been examining—the *Nötigung* and *Soldiers* cases, as well as the *Crucifix* case—on the ground that these cases were unduly absolutist and lacked a "Solomonic" bridge of compromise that would allow the Court to determine unconstitutionality in the specific case while providing a method for resolving the problem that would be considerate to all. "Three times now," declared this writer,

> has the First Senate ignored this wisdom of constitutional judicial decision-making. Three times it has disdained . . . the honorable and overwhelming feelings of the part of the population that upholds the state, in order to protect marginal groups of society. Whether it is the aggressive peace-advocates, who portray their peace in such a manner that they defame soldiers; or whether it is those who obstruct the passage of other people because they want to impose their world-view on third persons; or finally [whether it is] those who want to oppose what is self-evident to the people of Bavaria . . . When, as has occurred, a senate three times acts like a willful schoolmaster and disregards

[153] See, e.g., Biletzki, "Das Kreuz im Klassenzimmer," 1996 NJW, 2633. See also Epilogue.

[154] Grimm, "Vor dem Gesetz," FAZ, 18 August 1995, 29. Grimm's article is translated in full in Kommers, *Constitutional Jurisprudence*, 483–84.

[155] FAZ, 28 August 1995, 8 (Prof. Dr. Dieter Feddersen).

the traditional legal concepts of a legally-aware populace, there is cause for anxiety.[156]

## The three cases reconsidered

This critic, among many others, saw that the *Nötigung* decision resembled the *Soldiers* and *Crucifix* cases in a number of important ways, even though the precise subject matter and argumentation of each appeared, at first glance, to be significantly different from that of the others. In order to understand the broader constitutional context of the *Nötigung* case, therefore, it will be useful to pursue this point and seek to identify the factors that united these three important cases of 1995 in the eyes of their critics as well as their supporters.

First, from the standpoint of constitutional doctrine, all three cases are concerned with important rights of belief and expression. In the *Nötigung* cases, a deep concern over the dangers of nuclear war led the protestors to express their views through forms of passive resistance, according to the teachings of Gandhi and Martin Luther King. Accordingly, the Constitutional Court recognizes that even this form of protest falls within the general area of coverage of the right of assembly set forth in Article 8 of the Basic Law. Although in the end such blockades are not protected by Article 8 GG and therefore may be punishable under some conceivable legislation, they *cannot* be constitutionally punished under the present *Nötigung* section of the criminal code because of the unduly extended judicial interpretation required to achieve that result. At the core of the decision seems to be the fear that the undefined extension of the statute has allowed officials to choose among political views in deciding which cases to prosecute—a course that violates central ideas of the freedom of expression, which ordinarily prohibits penalization on the basis of political views and should be applied with particular stringency to protect the expression of minorities.

The *Soldiers* case of course also protects the (particularly vivid) expression of deeply held beliefs, in this case "pacifist" beliefs. Indeed, like the expression at issue in the *Nötigung* cases, these views arose from protests against the stationing of nuclear rockets in Germany and also represented the opinion of a minority that was received with hostility by more mainstream political forces.

[156] Ibid.

Rights of belief and expression are also at issue in the *Crucifix* case, albeit in a somewhat different form. Here, the Court upheld the "negative" religious rights of parents and children with minority religious views—indeed distinctly minority views in the cultural setting of conservative Bavaria. The Court found that these children had a constitutional right not to be required by law to confront the constant symbolic expression of the majority's differing religious beliefs in the form of a cross or crucifix on the classroom walls.

But beyond this important point of doctrinal similarity, there is a more fundamental political point that binds these cases together in the eyes of the critics, and in the eyes of the decisions' supporters as well. In each of these decisions, the Constitutional Court upholds the rights of rather small minorities that might be viewed as being on the margins of German society: certain perhaps extreme members of the anti-nuclear movement in the *Nötigung* cases, and of the peace movement in the *Soldiers* cases—in each case, with antecedents in the student uprisings of 1968—as well as religious minorities in the State of Bavaria in the *Crucifix* case. Moreover, in each case the rights of these marginal minorities are upheld against important traditional institutions of German society.

When we emphasize the Court's protection of the rights of minorities against traditional institutions, we come to the focal point of the critics' disapproval—the common factor that seems to have evoked bitter protest against all of these decisions. For in some way each of these decisions has been viewed by critics as not only an attack on certain traditional practices or institutions, but also as an attack against the structure of the state that these institutions support and protect—whether the challenged institutions be NATO and the *Bundeswehr* in the *Nötigung* and *Soldiers* cases, or Christianity and the church in the *Crucifix* case.

Indeed, the critics' bitter reactions suggest that they see the carefully constructed society of post-war Germany as being threatened in this manner. In the *Nötigung* and *Soldiers* decisions, the institution perceived to be under attack is, directly or indirectly, the *Bundeswehr* or army, which is still an important pillar of the German state in a tradition extending—with long baneful passages—back to the eighteenth century. Also under attack in these cases is NATO which formed the guarantor of West German sovereignty in the post-war period. In the *Crucifix* case, the attack seemed to be directed against Christianity and the institution of the church whose doctrine and tradition, still in the eyes of many, provide the basic values of the state. Many traditionalists, therefore, saw these cases as an attack on these central institutions of German life and, moreover, as an attack on the state itself which was supported by these institutions.

Of course, in the history of the Federal Republic, there have been many disputes which might be seen as pitting minority interests or views against traditional governmental institutions, and therefore—it might be said—against the stability of the state. In a number of important instances, moreover, the constitutionality of these measures has come before the Constitutional Court. But in the most important of these instances—before 1995 at least—the Court has generally protected the interests of the state and has strongly and reliably ruled against the minorities. In these earlier cases, therefore, the Court could be viewed as an integrating factor, protecting the interest of the general community and giving short shrift to what might be viewed as the disruptive efforts of minorities.

Certainly, in the earlier years of the Federal Republic, the Constitutional Court could generally be relied upon to protect and vindicate traditional interests of the security and stability of the state. Thus, in early decisions, the Constitutional Court imposed bans against radical political parties, including the neo-Nazi Socialist Reich Party (SRP) and the KPD, the Communist Party of West Germany.[157]

At approximately the same time—and specifically in the context of the West German peace movement—the Court struck down the plans of two German states to hold advisory plebiscites on whether the *Bundeswehr* should be equipped with atomic weapons and whether atomic missiles should be deployed in Germany. These forms of nuclear armaments were strongly supported by the Federal Government of Konrad Adenauer, and the plebiscites, which were sponsored by SPD state and local governments, were viewed as attempts to mobilize political opposition to the government's nuclear plans.[158] Although the plebiscites were to have been completely advisory and would not have had any legal effect in any event, the Court endorsed the government's view that merely holding the plebiscites would be

[157] 2 BVerfGE, 1 (1952)(*SRP Case*); 5 BVerfGE, 85 (1956)(*KPD Case*).

[158] 8 BVerfGE, 104 (1958); see 1 Dennis L. Bark and David R. Gress, *A History of West Germany*, 406–7 (Oxford: Blackwell 1989); Heinz Laufer, *Verfassungsgerichtsbarkeit und politischer Prozeß*, 433–47 (Tübingen: Mohr Siebeck 1968).

an unconstitutional incursion of the states into a subject (defense) that lay within exclusive federal competence. In a companion case, moreover, the Court found that the unwritten constitutional principle of "friendly behavior toward the federation" required the states to prevent their localities from holding such plebiscites.[159] In these cases, therefore, the Court seemed to go out of its way to protect the interests and plans of the central government and of the armed forces.

A few years later, in the famous *Spiegel* case, the Court was called upon to consider a massive police raid on a journal's editorial offices, in response to an article which was unfavorable to the *Bundeswehr* and which might have disclosed "secret" information. This police action raised considerable anxiety in Germany as it was eerily reminiscent of similar incursions at the beginning of the Nazi regime. Yet in this matter—in which the interests of the *Bundeswehr* were also under challenge—the Constitutional Court (by an equally divided four-to-four vote) declined to intervene.[160]

Along similar lines, in an opinion of almost intemperate language asserting the security interest of the state, the Court in 1975 upheld legislative and administrative measures that were designed to exclude "radicals" from the civil service (*Beamtentum*).[161] In all of these cases, therefore, the Court could be seen as willing to allow limitations on political speech of various forms in order to protect what the government thought to be necessary in order to maintain state security interests.[162]

In other notable decisions of the 1970s the Court similarly seemed to accede to conservative fears of social and institutional disintegration in striking down what traditionalists considered to be radical and disruptive legislation enacted by Social Democratic governments. For example, the Court invalidated state legislation seeking to "democratize" the universities by weakening the traditional

[159] 8 BVerfGE, 122 (1958).

[160] 20 BVerfGE, 162 (1966).

[161] 39 BVerfGE, 334 (1975).

[162] In another case that raised issues of privacy and rights of association (including political association), the Court upheld constitutional and statutory provisions allowing secret electronic surveillance in national security cases when necessary to protect the "free democratic basic order." 30 BVerfGE, 1 (1970) (*Klass Case*). See generally Uwe Wesel, *Der Gang nach Karlsruhe: Das Bundesverfassungsgericht in der Geschichte der Bundesrepublik*, 327–31 (Munich: Blessing 2004).

hierarchical power of the full professors.[163] The Court also struck down a measure that was intended to make it easier for draftees of the *Bundeswehr* to claim exemption from military service by abolishing the requirement of a hearing and allowing the draftee simply to file a notice of conscientious objection by mail.[164] Finally, in probably the best-known decision of the period, the Court struck down a measure enacted by the *Bundestag* that would have made abortions freely available in the first three months of pregnancy.[165]

Of course, even in these earlier periods, the Court did not always find in favor of the interests of traditional institutions or security interests asserted by the state. In some of these cases—generally of lesser importance—the Court did protect minority rights.[166] Yet, in light of the Court's rulings in the most important of these cases, a justified impression could arise that the Constitutional Court would favor the government and other official institutions in the most important instances when traditional values of the German state and society were at issue.

But in the 1995 cases—at least in the eyes of the critics—the

[163] 35 BVerfGE, 79 (1973). For historical background, see Fritz K. Ringer, *The Decline of the German Mandarins: The German Academic Community, 1890–1933* (Hanover: University Press of New England 1990).

[164] 48 BVerfGE, 127 (1978). In a later case the Court upheld a statute that subjected conscientious objectors working in hospitals, clinics, etc., to a longer period of service than that required in the *Bundeswehr*—even though the text of the constitution appeared to prohibit the longer term. 69 BVerfGE, 1 (1985); cf. Art. 12a GG.

[165] 39 BVerfGE, 1 (1975).

On the tensions between the Constitutional Court and the Social Democratic governments of the 1970s, see generally Richard Häußler, *Der Konflikt zwischen Bundesverfassungsgericht und politischer Führung*, 52–74 (Berlin: Duncker & Humblot 1994); Christine Landfried, *Bundesverfassungsgericht und Gesetzgeber* (Baden-Baden: Nomos 1984); Rolf Lamprecht and Wolfgang Malanowski, *Richter machen Politik: Auftrag und Anspruch des Bundesverfassungsgerichts* (Frankfurt/M: Fischer Taschenbuch Verlag 1979).

[166] For two interesting examples, see 47 BVerfGE, 198 (1978) (Marxist and Communist parties are entitled to broadcast campaign advertisements, even directed against present political structures, so long as the parties have not been banned by the Constitutional Court); and 63 BVerfGE, 266 (1983) (Lawyers are not bound by the same stringent requirements of political loyalty that are applicable to civil servants). In another interesting decision—a forerunner of the *Crucifix* case—the Court found that a cross must be removed from a courtroom, in response to the objection of a lawyer or litigant of the Jewish faith. 35 BVerfGE, 366 (1973).

Court seemed to have taken a firm position on the other side, supporting the arguments of the marginal minority against traditional institutions supporting the state. Accordingly, in the minds of many—and particularly in the minds of older conservative jurists who represented the "prevailing" doctrinal view on such subjects—the three cases of 1995 (along with a few others of the same period) very severely weakened their previous assurance that in the most important cases the Constitutional Court would support traditional institutions against the incursions of marginal outsiders.

Of course, there had been a few slightly earlier decisions that seemed to point in the same direction—particularly in the Constitutional Court's First Senate. In 1985, for example, we have seen that the *Brokdorf* case seemed to expand the rights accorded to political protestors.[167] Moreover, in a much criticized decision in 1990, the First Senate upheld the expressive rights of a political journal whose scurrilous collage was designed to cast the German flag into disrepute.[168] The Second Senate also handed down a controversial decision suggesting limitations on possible punishment for personal use of marijuana.[169]

But the three cases of 1995—which specifically concerned the armed forces and the church, two of the traditional pillars of German society—seemed to elevate this development to a new level. In these cases, the Court appeared to betray a deep skepticism about the claims of the state and of the church. Moreover, in the *Nötigung* and *Soldiers* cases, the Court favored the traditional opponents of the army and (many thought) of the state itself—peace protestors who frankly sought to reduce the role of the *Bundeswehr* in German life.

The critics' response to the Court's perceived shift of allegiance appears to have been a mixture of bewilderment and rage: the Court's services to governmental stability in the past are readily acknowledged; but why has the Court shifted its position now? Some appear to blame what they consider to be an unduly political method of choice of justices—sometimes referred to as appointment by the "party book." Yet a political process of this nature seems inevitable in choices for constitutional courts in any system—and the German Constitutional Court has boasted many eminent and distinguished members over the years.

[167] 69 BVerfGE, 315 (1985); see Chapter 3.
[168] 81 BVerfGE, 278 (1990).
[169] 90 BVerfGE, 145 (1994).

But many of the critics of the 1995 decisions seem to have drawn a different conclusion. Indeed, some critics note that the radical students of 1968 vowed to undertake a "long march through the institutions" of West Germany; and for these critics—with the passage of years—that radical "long march" had succeeded in the First Senate of the Constitutional Court. In this view the 1995 decisions, which attack certain central institutions of the state, indicate that the radical views of 1968 have finally prevailed within a central branch of the state itself. According to these critics, this reversal of a worldview threatens the German state because it threatens the worldview that supports the state.

This is a rather apocalyptic position and may tell us something about the persistence of certain strands of conservative pessimism in German intellectual life. But certainly there are a number of other ways in which to view the controversial cases of 1995. For example, one could argue that these cases represent increased emphasis on the rights of expression and rights of minorities in what is becoming a more open and multicultural German society. One could also argue that these cases represent a diminution of the strong role of certain traditions that have not always served Germany well in its history.

But it may also be that these cases could be viewed in a slightly different light. From the point of view of comparative constitutional law set in the context of post-war German history, it may make sense to view these cases as one more episode—a judicial episode—in the Americanization of German political and cultural life that, according to some historians, has been in progress to a greater or lesser extent from the end of World War II (and indeed, according to some, from the beginning of the twentieth century).[170]

At any rate, each of the three 1995 cases contains elements of similarity with important aspects of First Amendment doctrine in American constitutional law. Certainly, the *Soldiers* case moves in the general direction of American doctrine—although only part of the way—in protecting political speech that would clearly be

[170] See generally Anselm Doering-Manteuffel, *Wie westlich sind die Deutschen? Amerikanisierung und Westernisierung im 20. Jahrhundert* (Göttingen: Vandenhoeck and Ruprecht 1999); see also, e.g., Ralph Willett, *The Americanization of Germany, 1945–1949* (London: Routledge 1989); Schildt, "Vom politischen Programm zu Populärkultur: Amerikanisierung in Westdeutschland," in Detlef Junker (ed.), *Die USA und Deutschland im Zeitalter des Kalten Krieges 1945–1990. Ein Handbuch*, 955–65 (Stuttgart: Deutsche Verlags-Anstalt 2001); Lammersdorf, "Verwestlichung als Wandel der politischen Kultur," in ibid., 966–77.

constitutionally protected in the United States; indeed, the remarks at issue in those cases would almost certainly not even give rise to damages in the United States or England under applicable common law doctrines of group libel.[171] Similarly, the *Crucifix* decision is consistent with American doctrine which also goes considerably further and prohibits not only crosses or crucifixes but also the least sectarian of religious prayers in the public schools. Finally, the *Nötigung* decision of 1995 seems to parallel American doctrines of First Amendment vagueness and the concomitant fear that undefined provisions may evoke censorship by virtue of discriminatory enforcement on the basis of disfavored political views—something that actually seems to have occurred in the German cases.

Yet behind this Americanization—if that is indeed what is occurring in these cases—may lie a more general development. In German theory the concept of the state has always played a much more important role than it has in England or the United States. But after German unification and the end of the Cold War, many of the intense pressures, anxieties, and fears that led to what might be seen as excessive protection of the state in the Federal Republic have now at least to a significant extent disappeared. At the same time, the generation of legal scholars with experience in the more repressive periods of the Wilhelmine Empire and the Nazi period—scholars who in many cases seemed more favorably disposed toward doctrines of societal integration than to claims of minority rights—have almost vanished from the scene, and even their immediate students are nearing retirement age.[172] Furthermore, the German state seems to be inexorably facing a slow process of gradual (partial) dissolution into the more capacious, and by definition less nationalistic, structures of the European Union—in which the existence of a great patchwork quilt of minorities will, if anything, accustom the German legal culture to focus even more on minority rights. With all of the

[171] On parallels with American doctrine, see Eberle, *Dignity and Liberty*, 217–20. In connection with the possible influence of American views on the opinion in the *Soldiers* case, see Whitman, 109 *Yale Law Journal*, 1313 n.89 (noting the prominent role played by Judge Dieter Grimm, a "scholar oriented toward America," in the *Soldiers* cases). Indeed, at least one other member of the majority in the 1995 *Soldiers* case—Helga Seibert—also held an American LL.M. degree. See, e.g., Muth, "Helga Seibert," in Bernhard Großfeld and Herbert Roth (eds), *Verfassungsrichter: Rechtsfindung am U.S. Supreme Court und am Bundesverfassungsgericht*, 426 (Münster: LIT 1995).

[172] Cf. Wesel, *Gang nach Karlsruhe*, 367–68.

inevitable wandering and uncertain paths that characterize a case law system of constitutional doctrine, the great cases of 1995 seem to mark an important milestone in this gradual development away from a principal concentration on the traditional claims of the state toward a less anxious and fearful society more welcoming to claims of minority rights.

# Epilogue

With the Constitutional Court's *Nötigung* decision of 1995 and the repayment of the fines to most of the protestors who had been convicted in the Großengstingen, Mutlangen, and other sit-down demonstrations, the history of the anti-missile sit-down protests as an important political movement came to an end. By 1988, the Pershing and other missiles were being dismantled and destroyed, pursuant to the INF agreement for arms reduction entered into by Presidents Reagan and Gorbachev. Moreover, as we have seen, the dissolution of the Soviet Bloc, and the end of the Cold War, led to further disarmament in Germany and a shift of international tensions toward other problems.

In subsequent years, very small groups—including the international group Plowshares—have attempted various forms of civil disobedience, including incursions on the property of the headquarters of American forces in Europe (EUCOM), located in Stuttgart. Moreover, occasional tense blockades have been directed against trains and other transport vehicles carrying radioactive waste to the storage center at Gorleben.[1] But—unlike the anti-missile protests of the 1980s—these isolated "actions" have had little popular or political support.

Moreover, on the level of constitutional doctrine, there seemed to be a broad consensus that the constitutional status of the application of the coercion (*Nötigung*) statute to sit-down demonstrations had been generally resolved. Yet, in a legal system that relies on doctrines developed in individual cases, very few legal issues are ever completely decided. The general principles set forth in a case—applied to

1 FAZ, 11 November 2003, 4; FAZ, 13 November 2003, 5. See Chapter 1.

the particular facts of that case—can yield a form of clarity that is ultimately deceptive. The principles, as stated, are often developed in the context of the facts of the specific case, and do not (and really cannot) fully take into account the application of the principles to a range of other—similar but distinct—factual circumstances.

And so it was that in two cases in 2001 the Constitutional Court—perhaps rather surprisingly—reached back to events that had taken place in 1986 and 1990 to issue an opinion that adjusted and refined the result of the 1995 *Nötigung* decision—most likely without disturbing it in a major way—and provided some answers to questions that had been left open in that opinion. In contrast with the 1995 decision, however, the Court upheld the convictions in both cases.[2]

In the first of these decisions, ten protestors participated in a chain blockade—very much like the 1981 chain blockade in Großengstingen—at the main gate of the construction site of the planned nuclear waste-processing plant in Wackersdorf.[3] The blockade lasted for approximately three hours before the police cut the chain and carried the demonstrators away. Approximately twenty vehicles were obliged to halt at the blockade; and only some of these were able to enter the construction site from another fairly distant gate. Among other things, an important goal of the demonstrators was to call attention to the dangers of atomic energy. The two defendants in this case were convicted of *Nötigung* in the criminal courts.

In the second case, 600 members of the Sinti and Roma (gypsy) communities in Germany parked their automobiles, mobile homes, and buses in the middle of a main auto route near the Swiss border. Having been denied entry to Switzerland, this group hoped that a blockade could elicit a meeting with the United Nations High Commissioner for Refugees in Geneva—so that the demonstrators could argue for their right to remain in Germany or Switzerland. The defendant (the leader of the group) told police that any attempt to clear the thruway "would lead to a catastrophe."[4] The blockade continued for more than twenty-four hours and required a major rerouting of traffic. The defendant in this case was convicted of *Nötigung* in the criminal courts.

As noted, the Constitutional Court upheld the convictions in both cases. In the *Wackersdorf* case, the use of the chain to bind the

2 104 BVerfGE, 92 (2001).

3 See Chapter 1. The Wackersdorf blockade in this case took place in 1986.

4 104 BVerfGE, 98.

protestors together and to lock them to the metal posts of the gate was sufficient in the view of the Court to distinguish this case from the reversals of the convictions of Beuter, Braig, and the Mochs in the Court's 1995 decision. In the 1995 case it was simply a question of "bodily presence" in the road and the coercive effect was "of a psychological nature only." In the *Wackersdorf* case, the Court found that the use of the chain added an element of "force"—making it more difficult for the police to clear the entrance to the construction site. Moreover, this additional element provided a sufficiently clear distinction from mere bodily presence to satisfy the requirements of clarity contained in Article 103 (2) GG.[5]

The Court also found that the blocking of the thruway by numerous automobiles of the Sinti and Roma community could be constitutionally interpreted as the use of "force" under §240(I). The accumulation of the *protestors'* vehicles on the thruway constituted a physical—rather than a merely "psychological"—barrier and raised the risk that those who tried to resist the blockade might be injured. The Court explicitly noted that it did not have to consider the argument of the Federal Supreme Court (BGH) that any automobiles of *non-protestors* that might be obliged to stop at the blockade constituted another physical barrier which could also lead to a finding that the protestors were using "force."[6]

The finding that the defendants' actions could constitutionally be

[5] Ibid., 102. Two judges dissented on this point, arguing that the use of the chain—a "minor, non-aggressive" means of assistance, imposed by the protestors on themselves—could not constitutionally be interpreted as the use of "force" just because the chain might make it more difficult for the police to remove them. To call this the use of "force," the two judges argued, departs "too far from the text of the statute" and therefore violates Article 103(2)GG. In the view of these two judges, the *Wackersdorf* blockade still relied upon "spiritual"—rather than physical—pressure and therefore the principles of the 1995 *Nötigung* case required reversal of the convictions. 104 BVerfGE, 124–25 (opinion of Judges Jaeger and Bryde).

For additional criticism of the majority opinion along these lines, see Sinn, "Gewaltbegriff—quo vadis?," 2002 NJW, 1024. For commentary on the decision, see also Werner Offenloch, *Erinnerung an das Recht. Der Streit um die Nachrüstung auf den Straßen und vor den Gerichten*, 197–206 (Tübingen: Mohr Siebeck 2005). Judge Offenloch points out that during the period between the 1995 *Nötigung* opinion and this decision in 2001, the composition of the Constitutional Court had again changed so that only two judges—including Judge Jaeger, one of the dissenters—remained from the earlier period. Thus again, a "new generation" of justices was on the bench. Ibid., 202.

[6] 104 BVerfGE, 102–3. See 41 BGHSt, 182 (1995), discussed in Chapter 4.

held to represent the use of "force" under §240(I) required that the Court proceed to consider the lower courts' finding in both cases that the actions were "reprehensible." Because in 1995 the Court had struck down the application of the term "force" to the demonstrators' actions, it did not have to confront problems relating to the application of the term "reprehensible" in §240 (II). The Court's discussion on this point, therefore, seemed to answer some questions that may have been left open in the 1995 decision.

The Court first set forth its general view (previously expressed by the four "defeated" judges in the 1986 *Nötigung* decision) that the determination of whether a blockade is "reprehensible" under StGB §240(II) must take into account constitutional values, including those of the right to assembly in Article 8 (1) GG.[7] But the Court also emphasized that, in order to fall within the scope of Article 8 GG, the demonstration must be directed primarily toward influencing or participating in the creation of public opinion—that is, communicating a general point of view by virtue of the demonstration.

In this light, the Wackersdorf chain demonstration did fall within the scope of Article 8 because that blockade was primarily intended to "call attention to the dangers of atomic energy."[8] On the other hand, the thruway blockade of the Roma and Sinti demonstrators did not fall within the protection of Article 8, because that blockade was primarily intended to force a discussion with the High Commissioner for Refugees in Geneva and was not directed primarily toward the general formation of public opinion.[9]

In this interesting passage, therefore, the Court draws a line between what Ronald Dworkin has called "persuasive" and "non-persuasive" forms of civil disobedience.[10] Only the "persuasive" form—directed toward the general formation of public opinion—will receive coverage under Article 8. In contrast, if the primary purpose of the blockade is to force governmental acquiescence through the imposition of some sort of administrative burden, that form of civil disobedience will fall outside the scope of Article 8.

[7] In addition, the courts must take into account the constitutional principle that a penalty must be proportionate to guilt, a value protected by Article 2(1)GG. 104 BVerfGE, 108.

[8] Ibid., 104.

[9] Ibid., 105. Interestingly, a requirement of this kind was also suggested by the four "defeated" judges in the 1986 *Nötigung* case. 73 BVerfGE, 206, 259.

[10] Ronald Dworkin, "Civil Disobedience and Nuclear Protest," in *A Matter of Principle* (Cambridge, MA: Harvard University Press 1985), 109; see Chapter 1.

In this discussion, therefore, the Court makes clear that Article 8 GG, protecting freedom of assembly, is closely aligned with the values of Article 5 GG (freedom of expression) and does not necessarily protect assemblies that fail to reflect those values. With this finding, the conviction resulting from the Sinti/Roma blockade was essentially upheld, and further discussion in the opinion focused principally on the convictions of the Wackersdorf demonstrators.

In its discussion of the *Wackersdorf* case, the Court noted that coverage under Article 8 GG also requires that the assembly or demonstration in question be "peaceful." Drawing on a unanimous section of the 1986 opinion, the Court found that the Wackersdorf chain protest was not "unpeaceful" under Article 8 (1) GG, because "unpeacefulness" requires "aggressive rioting [*Ausschreitungen*] against persons or property" or similarly violent or dangerous actions. The "passive protest" of the chain demonstrators did not raise that level of danger and was therefore "peaceful"—notwithstanding that it was appropriately classified as involving the use of "force" under §240 StGB.[11]

The Court also clarified the constitutional status of the long-term goals of the demonstrators' communication. In the balancing required under StGB §240(II), the courts must give significant weight to the fact that the protestors were expressing their opinion on a "controversial question of significance to the public"—here, the peaceful use of atomic energy. On the other hand, the courts are *not* allowed to evaluate the protestors' substantive position on that question—i.e., whether the use of atomic energy should or should not be pursued—and accord increased weight if they believe that the protestors' position is useful or valuable. On these matters, the state (including, presumably, the courts) must remain neutral.[12]

In this way, the Court resolved the question of the weight to be accorded the protestors' "ultimate goals" in a manner that paralleled a resolution long advanced in cases involving the freedom of expression more generally. In the constitutional balancing, the Court will accord high value to speech on public issues—in contrast with speech that furthers private interests only. But the nature of the substantive position taken on a public question—whether for or against a particular measure—will not be taken into account.

[11] 104 BVerfGE, 105–6; see 73 BVerfGE, 248–49, discussed in Chapter 4.

[12] 104 BVerfGE, 110.

Also following the 1986 decision, the Court found that the requisite balancing of the countervailing interests should take into account the duration and intensity of the demonstration and other elements bearing upon the seriousness of the burden imposed by the protestors. Moreover, the balancing should also take into account the relationship between the subject of the protest and the persons adversely affected by the demonstration. If there is a relationship between the particular theme of the demonstration and the persons adversely affected, there is an increased likelihood that the demonstration could be "socially tolerable" and therefore not "reprehensible."[13]

In this respect, the Court found, the criminal courts ignored proper constitutional principles by not taking the values of Article 8 GG into account in determining the "reprehensible" nature of the Wackersdorf action—and by "falsely" finding that the blockade violated the human dignity of the persons whose travel was interrupted.[14] Even so, the Court declined to reverse the convictions because, in its view, the criminal courts would have concluded that the blockade was "reprehensible," even if the proper factors had been taken into account. Rather mysteriously, however, the Court does not further explain this finding. Perhaps the justices ultimately concluded that atomic power plants and their ancillary facilities posed smaller risks—and were thus less likely to justify civil disobedience—than was true in the case of the stationing of the Pershing II nuclear missiles.

The Court's conclusion on this point was challenged by two dissenting judges who argued that the balancing of the relevant factors must be undertaken by the criminal courts in the first instance—and therefore the case should have been returned to the criminal courts for a decision in accordance with the proper constitutional principles. The dissenters also objected to the Court's view that because the appropriate factors had been considered by the criminal courts in issuing a very mild penalty, that process somehow cured the criminal courts' error in finding guilt according to an improper constitutional standard.[15]

[13] Ibid., 112.

[14] Ibid., 113.

[15] Ibid., 125–26 (opinion of Judges Jaeger and Bryde).

It is worth noting that, in several places in its opinion in this case, the Constitutional Court responds rather sharply to arguments made in the separate concurring opinion of a particular named justice (Evelyn Haas). See ibid., 104, 107, 108,

The result of this decision, therefore, was to clarify the 1995 *Nötigung* opinion in some respects and to amplify the Court's jurisprudence on this subject in general. First, the Court made clear that the constitutional limitation on the interpretation of "force" in §240(I)—set forth in the 1995 decision—does not extend to large demonstrations using massive physical objects such as automobiles. These demonstrations clearly involve the use of "force" because they constitute "physical" as opposed to merely "psychological" blockades. Furthermore, little protection will be extended to demonstrations whose purpose is the immediate constraint of governmental officials to accede to certain demands. Rather, the purpose of the demonstration must be "symbolic" and "persuasive"—that is, its main purpose must be to change governmental policy through its effect on the judgments of public opinion in general.

The other lesson of this decision is that the constitutional protection extended in the 1995 decision stands right on the borderline. It seems that the employment of any physical obstacle in addition to the mere presence of the demonstrators exercising civil disobedience allows the criminal courts to qualify the demonstration as the use of "force" under StGB §240(I). This decision is perhaps an indication that the Constitutional Court viewed the anti-missile sit-down protests as so clearly directed toward a general campaign of public opinion, and so clearly based upon principles of "non-violence," that it would be perverse to interpret these "symbolic" communications as the exercise of "force." (Moreover, as suggested in the 1995 opinion, there was a clear record of unequal enforcement of the *Nötigung* statute according to political views, in the context of the anti-missile sit-down demonstrations.) But if the demonstrators go any further—using automobiles as actual physical hindrances, or even physical hindrances so mild as the chain in the *Wackersdorf* case—the analogy with intellectual political communication becomes sufficiently attenuated that an extended interpretation of the term "force" in §240(I) may prevail.

In this way, the Court seems to be drawing a line between what it sees as true political communication, on the one hand, and a phenomenon that it might view as more ominous, on the other.

109; see also ibid., 125 (opinion of Judges Jaeger and Bryde). This combative technique—which is common in the Supreme Court of the United States—remains unusual in the German opinions, and its appearance here might herald a break from what has ordinarily been a rather lapidary and impersonal style. See Chapter 3.

Ironically, however, the 2001 decision would seem to withdraw the coverage of constitutional protection for the initial chain demonstration at Großengstingen—whose participants fell squarely within the Gandhian tradition of non-violence. But, in any case, Wolfgang Müller-Breuer and Hansjörg Ostermayer had long since received their judgments of acquittal and the repayment of their fines and costs, in the collateral proceedings (*Wiederaufnahmeverfahren*) after the Court's 1995 decision. As far as they were concerned, therefore, their proceedings had indeed successfully drawn to a close.

Thus although the 2001 *Nötigung* decision cut back somewhat on possible expansive interpretations of the 1995 decision, it generally endorsed the basic principles of that case, which resulted in a form of constitutional protection for non-violent civil disobedience by a protesting minority. In this respect the decision was far from unique. In other areas, also, the contemporary Court seems to be continuing a general trend toward the development of significant protection for minorities.

In later cases involving the freedom of religion, for example, the Court has also generally tended to continue to protect the rights of minorities—although these more recent cases have not raised quite the same level of controversy that followed the issuance of the *Crucifix* decision in 1995. In one recent case, for example, the Constitutional Court found that the freedom of religion (and the free development of personality) required that a statute be interpreted to allow Muslim butchers to continue to sell meat that had been slaughtered in accordance with their religious views—even though this method of slaughter would otherwise have been illegal.[16] According to one commentator, the *Muslim Butchers* case is "a landmark case on religious liberty" that is particularly sensitive to minority rights.[17] Another writer similarly finds that the Court's decision "is of utmost importance for the status of Muslims in Germany" but adds—on a rather more ominous note—that the case "has provoked harsh reactions [from] those who perceive the Court's decision as a further . . . step toward multiculturalism," instead of assimilation.[18]

[16] 104 BVerfGE, 337 (2002).

[17] Eberle, "Free Exercise of Religion in Germany and the United States," 78 *Tulane Law Review* 1023, 1056–63 (2004).

[18] Langenfeld, "Developments—Germany," 1 I. CON, *International Journal of Constitutional Law* 141, 146 (2003). The decision was also opposed by animal

In another case protecting the rights of religious minorities, the Constitutional Court reversed a decision of the Federal Administrative Court, which had denied the Jehovah's Witnesses church access to the advantageous status of a "corporation under public law" on the grounds that the church, viewing the state as part of the "World of Satan," had prohibited members from voting in national or local elections.[19] In remanding this case, the Court noted that the citizen's support of the state cannot be "compelled through a duty of obedience, and certainly not through penalties."[20] In a more recent decision, the Court found that public school officials could not constitutionally reject a Muslim teacher's employment application on the ground that she intended to wear a headscarf during class for religious reasons; the Court did indicate, however, that this result rested on the lack of clear legislative authority for such a prohibition.[21]

Specifically in the aftermath of the *Crucifix* decision, however, the administrative courts and the Constitutional Court of Bavaria have approved a statute—drawing on a narrow interpretation of that decision by Judge Henschel in press statements and an "amended" headnote—that allows crosses and crucifixes to remain in the classrooms unless specifically challenged by a student, parent, or teacher.[22] Although the statute favors compromise in such circumstances, the Federal Administrative Court has been ready to order the exclusion of the crucifix from a classroom when such a challenge is based on "serious and evident grounds of belief or world view."[23]

Finally, in 2002, the Constitutional Court decided one additional case protecting minority groups that raised bitter objections which were similar to those evoked by the cases of 1995. In this decision, the Court upheld a federal statute that provided official recognition

protection groups, and apparently it was a factor in the adoption of a constitutional amendment adding explicit animal protection language to the Basic Law's environmental provision. Ibid.; see Art. 20a GG.

19 102 BVerfGE, 370 (2000).

20 Ibid., 398.

21 108 BVerfGE, 282 (2003). Therefore, the Court did not decide the underlying question of whether the wearing of such a headscarf by a teacher should receive full constitutional protection as an exercise of "positive" religious freedom. As several states have enacted or are likely to enact prohibitory legislation, this issue will almost certainly return to the Court. See generally Battis and Bultmann, "Was folgt für die Gesetzgeber aus dem Kopftuchurteil des BVerfG?," 2004 JZ, 581.

22 1995 BayGVBl, 850. On Judge Henschel's amended headnote, see Chapter 5.

23 See 109 BVerwGE, 40 (1999).

of long-lasting "life partnerships" between persons of the same sex. The Court rejected the argument that the "special protection" of marriage contained in Article 6 GG excluded the possibility of other forms of official "life partnerships" that could compete with marriage.[24] There were vigorous objections to this decision,[25] yet it differed in an important respect from the decisions of 1995. In the "Life Partnership" case, the Court upheld a *majoritarian* parliamentary decision to recognize certain minority rights. It was not a decision of the Court itself to confer constitutional status on minority claims that ran contrary to statutes or to patterns of decision in the civil or criminal courts—as was true of the great cases of 1995.

And what about the participants in the long legal odyssey of the *Nötigung* cases? A number of the lawyers—such as Hanns-Michael Langner and Siegfried Nold, who first appeared as apprentice counsel for Beuter, Braig, and the Mochs, as well as Karl Joachim Hemeyer, who represented Müller-Breuer and Ostermayer—are still relatively young, and continue to engage in legal practice in Tübingen and the surrounding area. Nold and Hemeyer, in particular, are still active in the kind of peace movement cases that extend as far back as the litigation over the anti-missile sit-down protests.

Judge Werner Offenloch who was among the most active and prominent of the judges handing down convictions in the Amtsgericht in Schwäbisch Gmünd has recently retired, joining in that status his former colleague Wolfgang Krumhard—the judge who changed his mind and handed down acquittals for a substantial period. As we have seen, Judge Offenloch has recently published a book on the *Nötigung* cases.

Judge Thomas Rainer, the judge who excluded the apprentice lawyers Langner and Nold, is still active, and is still the sole criminal court judge in Münsingen on the high Swabian plateau. Although he has always had some sympathy with the political engagement of the demonstrators (and declares that he was himself influenced by the 1968 movement of his student years), he still strongly believes that his decisions in the hundreds of *Nötigung* cases over which he presided were correct—indeed, he has no doubts.[26]

24 105 BVerfGE, 313 (2002).

25 See, e.g., Tettinger, "Kein Ruhmesblatt für 'Hüter der Verfassung,' " 2002 JZ, 1146.

26 Interview with Thomas Rainer, Münsingen, 8 July 2004.

As for the demonstrators, a number of them have continued to follow an "alternative" style of life, perhaps marked indelibly by their early experiences in the peace movement. Hansjörg Ostermayer is a professional storyteller for children and adults, traveling around Germany to shows, birthday parties, wedding anniversaries, and church festivals with his collection of Celtic tales, Arthurian legends, and stories from the Brothers Grimm. One of Ostermayer's particular specialties is folk legends from areas of the world that are threatened by atomic testing—such as Shoshone myths from the area of the Nevada atomic testing grounds.[27] Wolfgang Müller-Breuer is working in a small town outside of Cologne as an advisor and counselor for children and youthful immigrants to Germany. He is employed by a social agency operated by the Catholic church and funded by the Federal Ministry of Youth.

As noted in Chapter 4, Karl Wenning—the only defendant whose conviction was reversed in the 1986 decision—has been a clown and cabaret performer, sometimes using the experiences from his own sit-down blockade, and the resulting case, as material for his performances. Luise Scholl has been active as an artist in a small town not far from Stuttgart—although, according to Scholl, difficult economic circumstances in Germany have made this sort of work precarious from time to time.

For more than fifteen years Eva Moch has conducted an active practice as a midwife, giving advice and assisting at home births. But she has refused to work in hospitals because the highly charged atmosphere—and what she views as the excessive use of caesarean sections for normal births—do not accord with her views of the requirements of non-violence. According to Eva Moch, her form of work is not particularly well paid. But it may be that she is now leading the sort of non-violent life that she envisaged at the peace camp of the Tent Villages in 1982.

Having studied medicine in order to use his skills in the Third World, Eva's brother Thomas Moch spent three years in the Amazon in Brazil, building a hospital and then helping to operate it. Thereafter, he was an anesthetist in emergency medicine in Hamburg, Germany; but he also continued his work in the Third World, traveling abroad for short periods to treat patients in emergency

[27] Interview with Hanjörg Ostermayer, Tübingen, 27 July 2004; see also Uwe Painke and Andreas Quartier, *Gewaltfrei für Atomteststopp*, 171–73 (Tübingen: Books On Demand 2002).

situations—for example, in East Timor and in Bam, Iran, following the catastrophic earthquake there in 2003. Currently, Thomas Moch has joined the German Red Cross, working on the management of medical emergencies. Gunhild Beuter carries on an active practice as a family therapist, counseling families and other small groups—particularly groups of young people—on how to overcome personal problems and deal successfully with difficult situations. Perhaps her work could be viewed as an attempt to create a sort of peace within these groups of people. Wilfried Braig is one of the few demonstrators of this group who has followed a more mainline business career—being the co-founder of a successful management relations consulting firm.

In Mutlangen itself, veterans of the 1980s peace movement have organized a peace center in the one-time "press cabin" (*Pressehütte*), near the former Pershing missile depot, and they have continued to provide "trainings" in non-violent techniques for interested participants. The Affinity Group Gustav Heinemann has also remained in existence (with some departures and some new additions over the years), and it has engaged, among other things, in working to help political asylum seekers in the Tübingen area. But in one of the sudden reversals of fortune that are not uncommon in recent German history, the group's most prominent member, Tübingen professor Walter Jens (now in his eighties)—the rhetorician who engaged in a well-known debate with Judge Offenloch—has been confronted with scholars' reports that his name is included in the card index of World War II Nazi Party members preserved in the German Federal Archive; Jens responds that he knows nothing about any such membership.[28] In Germany, as has often been remarked, the past is not dead; it is not even past.

And as for the protestors whose cases we have followed through so many twists and turns of the German legal system—how do they look back on their protests and civil disobedience of more than twenty years ago? In general they harbor little doubt about the correctness of their paths in the 1980s, and of the dangers posed by the Pershing and other nuclear missiles which they protested so vigorously. Many also continue to reflect a skepticism and distrust of the arguments and positions of the government in general.

[28] See FAZ, 25 November 2003, 35; *Die Zeit*, 15 January 2004, http://www.zeit.de/2004/04/W_Jens.

Yet on the other hand, many of their opponents in these long legal struggles—the prosecutors and judges—also remain convinced of the rightness of their actions. This particular political dispute has now dissipated—and the legal issues that it evoked have been resolved, to a significant extent at least—but in many ways the positions that animated this dispute have not significantly changed. Only, perhaps, the gradual change of generations—and the new problems evoked by history—will eventually elicit new occasions for civil disobedience and provide a new focus for the ancient antinomy between the citizens' asserted right to withhold obedience and the opposing claims of society and the state.

# Appendix

## Selected constitutional and statutory provisions

### Selected provisions of the Basic Law

#### *Article 1 (1)* [Human Dignity]

Human dignity is inviolable. It is the obligation of all state power to observe and protect human dignity.

#### *Article 2 (2)* [Life and Bodily Integrity]

Everyone has the right to life and bodily integrity. The freedom of the person is inviolable. These rights may be curtailed only pursuant to statute.

#### *Article 3* [Equality]

(1) All people are equal before the law.

(2) Men and women have equal rights. The state will further the actual accomplishment of equal rights for women and men and will work toward the elimination of existing disadvantages.

(3) No one may be disadvantaged or preferred on the basis of gender, ethnic origin, race, language, native place or place of origin, belief, or religious or political views. No one may be disadvantaged on the grounds of handicap.

#### *Article 4* [Freedom of Belief]

(1) The freedom of belief and of conscience, and the freedom of religious and philosophical creed, are inviolable.

(2) The undisturbed exercise of religion is guaranteed. . . .

### *Article 5* [Freedom of Expression]

(1) Everyone has the right freely to express and to disseminate his opinion in words, writing and pictures and to inform himself without hindrance from generally accessible sources. Freedom of the press and freedom of reporting through broadcasting and film are guaranteed. There will be no censorship.

(2) These rights find their limits in the rules of the general laws, the statutory provisions for the protection of youth, and in the right of personal honor.

(3) Art and learning, research and teaching are free. The freedom of teaching gives no dispensation from loyalty to the constitution.

### *Article 6* [Marriage and Family]

(1) Marriage and family stand under the special protection of the order of the state.

(2) The care and upbringing of children are the natural right of the parents and their most important duty. The community of the state watches over this activity. . . .

### *Article 7* [Schools]

(1) The entire school establishment stands under the supervision of the state.

(2) Parents or guardians have the right to decide whether the child will participate in religious instruction.

(3) Religious instruction shall be an ordinary subject of study in the public schools, with the exception of non-denominational schools . . . No teacher may be required to give religious instruction against his will. . . .

### *Article 8* [Right of Assembly]

(1) All Germans have the right of peaceful and unarmed assembly, without a requirement of registration or a requirement that permission be received.

(2) For assemblies in the open air, this right may be limited by statute or on the basis of a statute.

### *Article 20* [Basic Principles]

(1) The Federal Republic of Germany is a democratic and social federal state.

(2) All state authority proceeds from the people. State authority is exercised by the people in elections and voting and through the separate organs of legislation, the executive power, and the judiciary.

(3) Legislation is bound by the constitutional order, and the executive power and the judiciary are bound by law and justice.

(4) All Germans have the right of resistance against anyone who undertakes to overthrow this constitutional order, if no other redress is possible.

### *Article 24 (1)* [Transfer of Sovereign Rights]

The federation may, through a statute, transfer sovereign rights to international institutions.

### *Article 26 (1)* [Aggressive War]

Activities that are directed toward, and undertaken with the intention of, disturbing the peaceful coexistence of nations, and particularly making preparations for the waging of aggressive war, are contrary to the constitution. These activities are to be subjected to criminal punishment.

### *Article 59 (2)* [Treaties]

Treaties which regulate the political relations of the federation, or relate to subjects of federal legislation, require the approval or the participation of the governmental bodies that have authority in the relevant area, in the form of a federal statute. . . .

### *Article 93 (1)* [Constitutional Court: Jurisdiction]

The Constitutional Court issues decisions:

(1) concerning the interpretation of this Basic Law, as a result of disputes about the scope of the rights and duties of a principal governmental organ or of other participants that are provided with their own rights under this Basic Law . . .;

(2) concerning differences of opinion or doubts about the formal or substantive conformity of federal or state law with this Basic Law . . . upon the motion of the federal government, a government of a state, or one third of the members of the Bundestag; . . .

(4a) concerning Constitutional Complaints, which may be filed by any person who claims that he has been injured by public authority in one of his Basic Rights or in [certain other constitutional] rights . . .

### *Article 94* [Constitutional Court: Judges]

(1) The Federal Constitutional Court shall be composed of judges from the federal courts, as well as other members. Half of the members of the Federal Constitutional Court shall be chosen by the Bundestag and half by the Bundesrat. They may not be members of the Bundestag, the Bundesrat, the federal government, or the corresponding organs of a state.

(2) A federal statute shall regulate the Court's constitution and procedures . . .

### *Article 100 (1)* [Referral to Constitutional Court]

If a court finds a statute unconstitutional, and if the validity of the statute is relevant to the decision, the proceeding must be suspended and . . . if a violation of this Basic Law is at issue, the decision of the Federal Constitutional Court must be obtained. . . .

### *Article 103* [Procedural Protections] . . .

(2) An act may be punished only if its criminality was determined by statute before the act was committed.

(3) No one may be punished more than once for the same act on the basis of the general criminal laws.

## Selected statutory provisions

### *BVerfGG [Law Concerning the Federal Constitutional Court]*

#### *§79 (1) [Reopening of Criminal Judgments]*

A proceeding may be reopened . . . for the purpose of reconsidering a final criminal judgment that rests on a norm that has been declared inconsistent with the Basic Law . . . or for the purpose of reconsidering a final criminal judgment that rests on an interpretation of a norm if that interpretation has been declared inconsistent with the Basic Law by the Federal Constitutional Court.

### *StGB [Criminal Code]*

#### *§240 [Coercion]**

(1) Whoever illegally coerces another person, through force or by the threat of a substantial evil, to undertake an action, to allow something to happen, or to omit to do something, will be punished by up to 3 years imprisonment or by a fine, or, in particularly serious cases, by imprisonment from 6 months to 5 years.

(2) An act is illegal if the application of force or the threat of the evil, for the purpose of achieving the intended end, is to be viewed as reprehensible.

(3) An attempt [to commit the above offense] is also punishable.

#### *§32 [Necessary Defense]*

(1) Whoever commits an act that is required by necessary defense does not act illegally.

(2) Necessary defense is the defense that is required in order to avert a present illegal attack upon oneself or upon another person.

* Version considered by the Federal Constitutional Court in 1986 and 1995; see 73 BVerfGE, 206, 209 (1986).

*§34 [Justified Action in Emergencies]*

Whoever—in the case of a present and otherwise unavoidable danger to life, body, freedom, honor, property or other legal interest—commits an act in order to avoid the danger to himself or to another person does not act illegally if, through a balancing of the contending interests (particularly the affected legal interests and the degree of the dangers that threaten those interests), the interest that is being protected substantially outweighs the interest that is infringed upon. This is only the case, however, to the extent that the act is an appropriate means for avoiding the danger.

# Select bibliography

## Books


Arendt, Hannah, *Crises of the Republic* (San Diego: Harcourt Brace 1972)

Badura, Peter and Dreier, Horst (eds), *Festschrift 50 Jahre Bundesverfassungsgericht* (Tübingen: Mohr Siebeck 2001)

Bark, Dennis L. and Gress, David R., *A History of West Germany*, Vol. 1: *From Shadow to Substance 1945–1963*; Vol. 2: *Democracy and its Discontents 1963–1988* (Oxford: Blackwell 1989)

Bedau, Hugo Adam (ed.), *Civil Disobedience in Focus* (London: Routledge 1991)

Bedau, Hugo Adam (ed.), *Civil Disobedience: Theory and Practice* (New York: Pegasus 1969)

Bedford, Sybille, *The Faces of Justice: A Traveller's Report* (New York: Simon & Schuster 1961)

Bell, John, *French Constitutional Law* (Oxford: Clarendon Press 1992)

Benedict, Hans-Jürgen, *Ziviler Ungehorsam als christliche Tugend* (Frankfurt/M: Athenäum 1989)

Bertuleit, Achim, *Sitzdemonstrationen zwischen prozedural geschützter Versammlungsfreiheit und verwaltungsrechtsakzessorischer Nötigung* (Berlin: Duncker & Humblot 1994)

Bickel, Alexander M., *The Morality of Consent* (New Haven, CT: Yale University Press 1975)

Bissinger, Manfred (ed.), *Günther Anders: Gewalt—ja oder nein* (Munich: Knaur 1987)

Blackwood, Caroline, *On the Perimeter* (London: Heinemann 1984)

Bloch, Susan Low and Krattenmaker, Thomas G., *Supreme Court Politics: The Institution and Its Procedures* (St. Paul: West 1994)

Böll, Heinrich, *Ende einer Dienstfahrt* (Köln: Kiepenheuer & Witsch 1966)

Brandt, Willy *et al.* (eds), *Ein Richter, ein Bürger, ein Christ: Festschrift für Helmut Simon* (Baden-Baden: Nomos 1987)

Brugger, Winfried and Huster, Stefan (eds), *Der Streit um das Kreuz in der Schule* (Baden-Baden: Nomos 1998)

Brzezinski, Zbigniew, *Power and Principle: Memoirs of the National Security Advisor 1977–1981* (New York: Farrar Straus Giroux, rev. edn 1985)

Bunn, Ronald F., *German Politics and the Spiegel Affair: A Case Study of the Bonn System* (Baton Rouge: Louisiana State University Press 1968)

Burns, Rob and van der Will, Wilfried, *Protest and Democracy in West Germany: Extra-Parliamentary Opposition and the Democratic Agenda* (New York: St. Martin's Press 1988)

Busche, Jürgen, *Die 68er: Biographie einer Generation* (Berlin: Berlin Verlag 2003)

Carsten, F.L., *The Reichswehr and Politics: 1918 to 1933* (Oxford: Clarendon Press 1966)

Carter, Jimmy, *Keeping Faith: Memoirs of a President* (New York: Bantam 1983)

Cooney, Robert and Michalowski, Helen (eds), *The Power of the People: Active Nonviolence in the United States* (Philadelphia, PA: New Society Publishers 1987)

Cooper, Alice Holmes, *Paradoxes of Peace: German Peace Movements since 1945* (Ann Arbor: University of Michigan Press 1996)

Currie, David P., *The Constitution of the Federal Republic of Germany* (Chicago, IL: University of Chicago Press 1994)

Dahrendorf, Ralph, *Über Grenzen: Lebenserinnerungen* (Frankfurt/M: Fischer Taschenbuch 2004)

Doering-Manteuffel, Anselm, *Wie westlich sind die Deutschen? Amerikanisierung und Westernisierung im 20. Jahrhundert* (Göttingen: Vandenhoeck and Ruprecht 1999)

Dörr, Dieter, *Die Verfassungsbeschwerde in der Prozeßpraxis* (Köln: Schmidt, 2d edn 1997)

Dubber, Markus D., *Criminal Law: Model Penal Code* (New York: Foundation 2002)

Dudziak, Mary L., *Cold War Civil Rights: Race and the Image of American Democracy* (Princeton, NJ: Princeton University Press 2002)

Dutschke, Rudi, *Jeder hat sein Leben ganz zu leben: Die Tagebücher 1963–1979* (ed. Gretchen Dutschke; Cologne: Kiepenheuer & Witsch 2003)

Dutschke, Rudi, *Mein langer Marsch: Reden, Schriften und Tagebücher aus zwanzig Jahren* (Reinbek bei Hamburg: Rowohlt 1980)

Dworkin, Ronald, *A Matter of Principle* (Cambridge, MA: Harvard University Press 1985)

Eberle, Edward J., *Dignity and Liberty: Constitutional Visions in Germany and the United States* (Westport, CT: Praeger 2002)

Ebke, Werner F. and Finkin, Matthew W., *Introduction to German Law* (The Hague: Kluwer 1996)

Eppler, Erhard, *Die tödliche Utopie der Sicherheit* (Reinbek bei Hamburg: Rowohlt 1983)

Fikentscher, Wolfgang, *et al.*, *Wertewandel, Rechtswandel* (Gräfeling: Resch 1997)

Fink, Carole *et al.* (eds), *1968: The World Transformed* (Cambridge: Cambridge University Press 1998)

Finkh, Ute and Jens, Inge (eds), *Verwerflich? Friedensfreunde vor Gericht* (Munich: Knaur 1985)

Fionda, Julia, *Public Prosecutors and Discretion: A Comparative Study* (Oxford: Clarendon Press 1995)

Foster, Nigel G., *German Legal System and Laws* (London: Blackstone, 2nd edn 1996)

Fraser, Ronald (ed.), *1968: A Student Generation in Revolt* (New York: Pantheon 1988)

Gandhi, M.K., Hind Swaraj *and Other Writings* (ed. Anthony J. Parel; Cambridge: Cambridge University Press 1997)

Glotz, Peter (ed.), *Ziviler Ungehorsam im Rechtsstaat* (Frankfurt/M: Suhrkamp 1983)

Gorbachev, Mikhail, *Memoirs* (New York: Doubleday 1996)

Grimm, Dieter, *Die Verfassung und die Politik* (Munich: Beck 2001)

Großfeld, Bernhard and Roth, Herbert (eds), *Verfassungsrichter: Rechtsfindung am U.S. Supreme Court und am Bundesverfassungsgericht* (Münster: LIT 1995)

Grüninger, Sibylle and Frommann, Anne (eds), *"Wo diese schweigen, so werden die Steine schreien": Seniorinnen und Senioren für den Frieden* (Mössingen-Talheim: Talheimer 1989)

Gugel, Günther, *Wir werden nicht weichen: Erfahrungen mit Gewaltfreiheit* (Tübingen: Verein für Friedenspädagogik e.V. 1996)

Gugel, Günther and Furtner, Horst, *Gewaltfreie Aktion* (Tübingen: Verein für Friedenspädagogik e.V. 1983)

Guggenberger, Bernd and Würtenberger, Thomas (eds), *Hüter der Verfassung oder Lenker der Politik?* (Baden-Baden: Nomos 1998)

Haksar, Vinit, *Civil Disobedience, Threats and Offers: Gandhi and Rawls* (Delhi: Oxford University Press 1986)

Hannover, Heinrich, *Die Republik vor Gericht, 1975–1995* (Berlin: Aufbau 1999)

Hart, H.L.A., *Law, Liberty and Morality* (Stanford, CA: Stanford University Press 1963)

Häußler, Richard, *Der Konflikt zwischen Bundesverfassungsgericht und politischer Führung* (Berlin: Duncker & Humblot 1994)

Hepp, Michael and Otto, Viktor (eds.), *"Soldaten sind Mörder": Dokumentation einer Debatte 1931–1996* (Berlin: Links 1996)

Herf, Jeffrey, *War by Other Means: Soviet Power, West German Resistance, and the Battle of the Euromissiles* (New York: Free Press 1991)

Herzog, Roman, *Strukturmängel der Verfassung? Erfahrungen mit dem Grundgesetz* (Stuttgart: Deutsche Verlags-Anstalt 2000)

Hinton, James, *Protest and Visions: Peace Politics in Twentieth-Century Britain* (London: Hutchinson 1989)

Hollerbach, Alexander *et al.* (eds), *Das Kreuz im Widerspruch: der Kruzifix-Beschluss des Bundesverfassungsgerichts in der Kontroverse* (Freiburg/B: Herder 1996)

Ingman, Terence, *The English Legal Process* (London: Blackstone, 6th edn 1996)

Iyer, Raghavan (ed.), *The Essential Writings of Mahatma Gandhi* (Delhi: Oxford University Press 1991)

Jens, Walter (ed.), *In letzter Stunde: Aufruf zum Frieden* (Munich: Kindler 1982)

Jens, Walter, *Republikanische Reden* (Munich: Kindler 1976)

Jensen, Lloyd, *Bargaining for National Security: The Postwar Disarmament Negotiations* (Columbia: University of South Carolina Press 1988)

Jescheck, Hans-Heinrich and Vogler, Theo (eds), *Festschrift für Herbert Tröndle zum 70. Geburtstag* (Berlin: de Gruyter 1989)

Junker, Detlef (ed.), *Die USA und Deutschland im Zeitalter des Kalten Krieges 1945–1990. Ein Handbuch* (Stuttgart: Deutsche Verlags-Anstalt 2001)

Kalven, Harry Jr., *A Worthy Tradition: Freedom of Speech in America* (ed. Jamie Kalven; New York: Harper & Row 1988)

Kempton, Murray, *Part of Our Time: Some Ruins and Monuments of the Thirties* (New York: Modern Library 1998)

Kennedy, Ellen, *Constitutional Failure: Carl Schmitt in Weimar* (Durham, NC: Duke University Press 2004)

King, Martin Luther, Jr., *Stride Toward Freedom: The Montgomery Story* (New York: Harper 1958)

Knef, Hildegard, *The Gift Horse: Report on a Life* (trans. D. Palastanga; New York: McGraw-Hill 1971)

Komitee für Grundrechte und Demokratie, e.V., *Ziviler Ungehorsam: Traditionen, Konzepte, Erfahrungen, Perspektiven* (Sensbachtal 1992)

Kommers, Donald P., *The Constitutional Jurisprudence of the Federal Republic of Germany* (Durham, NC: Duke University Press, 2nd edn 1997)

Kommers, Donald P., *Judicial Politics in West Germany: A Study of the Federal Constitutional Court* (Beverly Hills, CA: Sage 1976)

Kraus, Henry, *The Many and the Few* (Los Angeles, CA: Plantin Press 1947)

Kraushaar, Wolfgang, *1968 als Mythos, Chiffre and Zäsur* (Hamburg: HIS 2000)

Kriele, Martin, *Theorie der Rechtsgewinnung* (Berlin: Duncker & Humblot, 2nd edn 1976)

Laduch, Manfred *et al.*, *Mutlanger Heide. Ein Ort macht Geschichte* (Schwäbisch Gmünd: Remsdruckerei 1990)

Laker, Thomas, *Ziviler Ungehorsam: Geschichte—Begriff—Rechtfertigung* (Baden-Baden: Nomos 1986)

Lamprecht, Rolf, *Zur Demontage des Bundesverfassungsgerichts* (Baden-Baden: Nomos 1996)

Langbein, John H., *Comparative Criminal Procedure: Germany* (St. Paul: West 1977)

Langguth, Gerd, *The Green Factor in German Politics: From Protest Movement to Political Party* (trans. Richard Straus; Boulder, CO: Westview Press 1986)

Laqueur, Walter and Hunter, Robert (eds), *European Peace Movements and the Future of the Western Alliance* (New Brunswick: Transaction 1985)

Laufer, Heinz, *Verfassungsgerichtsbarkeit und politischer Prozeß* (Tübingen: Mohr Siebeck 1968)

Lechner, Hans and Zuck, Rüdiger, *Bundesverfassungsgerichtsgesetz* (Munich: Beck, 4th edn 1996)

Lewis, Anthony, *Make No Law: The Sullivan Case and the First Amendment* (New York: Random House 1991)

Limbach, Jutta, *Das Bundesverfassungsgericht* (Munich: Beck 2001)

Limbach, Jutta, *"Im Namen des Volkes": Macht und Verantwortung der Richter* (Stuttgart: Deutsche Verlags-Anstalt 1999)

Mandel, Michael, *The Charter of Rights and the Legalization of Politics in Canada* (Toronto: Thompson, rev. edn 1994)

Markovits, Andrei S. and Gorski, Philip S., *The German Left: Red, Green and Beyond* (New York: Oxford University Press 1993)

Mechtersheimer, Alfred (ed.), *Nachrüsten? Dokumente und Positionen zum NATO-Doppelbeschluß* (Reinbek bei Hamburg: Rowohlt Taschenbuch 1981)

Menzel, Jörg (ed.), *Verfassungsrechtsprechung* (Tübingen: Mohr Siebeck 2000)

Merryman, John Henry, *The Civil Law Tradition* (Stanford, CA: Stanford University Press, 2nd edn 1985)

Morrison, Fred L., *Courts and the Political Process in England* (Beverly Hills, CA: Sage 1973)

Müller, Ingo, *Hitler's Justice: The Courts of the Third Reich* (trans: Deborah Lucas Schneider; Cambridge, MA: Harvard University Press 1991)

Müller, Jan-Werner, *A Dangerous Mind: Carl Schmitt in Post-War European Thought* (New Haven, CT: Yale University Press 2003)

Müller, Jan-Werner (ed.), *German Ideologies since 1945: Studies in the Political Thought and Culture of the Bonn Republic* (New York: Palgrave Macmillan 2003)

*Mutlanger Erfahrungen: Erinnerungen und Perspektiven* (Mutlangen: Friedens- und Begegnungsstätte Mutlangen e.V. 1994)

Negt, Oskar, *Achtundsechzig: Politische Intellektuelle und die Macht* (Göttingen: Steidl 1995, 2001)

Nick, Volker *et al.* (eds), *Mutlangen 1983–1987: Die Stationierung der Pershing II und die Kampagne Ziviler Ungehorsam bis zur Abrüstung* (Mutlangen 1993)

Offenloch, Werner, *Erinnerung an das Recht. Der Streit um die Nachrüstung auf den Straßen und vor den Gerichten* (Tübingen: Mohr Siebeck 2005)

Packer, Herbert L., *The Limits of the Criminal Sanction* (Stanford, CA: Stanford University Press 1968)

Painke, Uwe and Quartier, Andreas, *Gewaltfrei für Atomteststopp* (Tübingen: Books On Demand 2002)

Pappert, Peter (ed.), *Den Nerv getroffen. Engagierte Stimmen zum Kruzifix-Urteil von Karlsruhe* (Aachen: Bergmoser & Höller undated)

Rehnquist, William H., *All the Laws but One: Civil Liberties in Wartime* (New York: Knopf 1998)

Rehnquist, William H., *The Supreme Court: How It Was, How It Is* (New York: Quill 1987)

Reichert-Hammer, Hansjörg, *Politische Fernziele und Unrecht* (Berlin: Duncker & Humblot 1991)

*Reporting Civil Rights Part I: American Journalism 1941–1963* (New York: Library of America 2003)

Robbers, Gerhard (ed.), *State and Church in the European Union* (Baden-Baden: Nomos 1996)

Rochon, Thomas R., *Mobilizing for Peace: The Antinuclear Movements in Western Europe* (Princeton, NJ: Princeton University Press 1988)

Rogowski, Ralf and Gawron, Thomas (eds), *Constitutional Courts in Comparison: The U.S. Supreme Court and the German Federal Constitutional Court* (New York: Berghahn 2002)

Russell, Peter H. and O'Brien, David M. (eds), *Judicial Independence in the Age of Democracy: Critical Perspectives from around the World* (Charlottesville: University Press of Virginia 2001)

Schlaich, Klaus and Korioth, Stefan, *Das Bundesverfassungsgericht: Stellung, Verfahren, Entscheidungen* (Munich: Beck, 5th edn 2001)

Schmidt, Helmut, *Menschen und Mächte* (Berlin: Siedler 1999)

Schmitt Glaeser, Walter, *Private Gewalt im politischen Meinungskampf* (Berlin: Duncker & Humblot, 2nd edn 1992)

Schoenbaum, David, *The Spiegel Affair* (Garden City, NY: Doubleday 1968)

Schwind, Hans-Dieter, Baumann, Jürgen *et al.* (eds), *Ursachen, Prävention und Kontrolle von Gewalt* (Berlin: Duncker & Humblot 1990)

Seidman, Joel, "*Sit-Down*" (New York: League for Industrial Democracy 1937)

Sinn, Arndt, *Die Nötigung im System des heutigen Strafrechts* (Baden-Baden: Nomos 2000)

Stern, Fritz, *The Failure of Illiberalism: Essays on the Political Culture of Modern Germany* (New York: Columbia University Press 1992)

Stern, Fritz, *The Politics of Cultural Despair* (Berkeley: University of California Press 1974)

Stern, Robert L., Gressman, Eugene *et al.*, *Supreme Court Practice* (Washington D.C.: Bureau of National Affairs, 8th edn 2002)

Thoreau, Henry David, *Walden and Civil Disobedience* (New York: Penguin 1983)

Tröndle, Herbert, *Antworten auf Grundfragen* (Munich: Beck 1999)

Tucholsky, Kurt, *Unser ungelebtes Leben: Briefe an Mary* (ed. Fritz J. Raddatz; Reinbek bei Hamburg: Rowohlt 1982)

Vack, Hanne and Klaus (eds), *Mutlangen—unser Mut wird langen!* (Sensbachtal: Komitee für Grundrechte und Demokratie e.V., 6th edn 1988)

Watley, William D., *Roots of Resistance: The Nonviolent Ethic of Martin Luther King, Jr.* (Valley Forge: Judson 1985)

Wesel, Uwe, *Der Gang nach Karlsruhe. Das Bundesverfassungsgericht in der Geschichte der Bundesrepublik* (Munich: Blessing 2004)

Wesel, Uwe, *Die verspielte Revolution: 1968 und die Folgen* (Munich: Blessing 2002)

Wolpert, Stanley, *Gandhi's Passion: The Life and Legacy of Mahatma Gandhi* (New York: Oxford University Press 2001)

*Zerreißprobe Frieden: Baden-Württemberg und der NATO-Doppelbeschluss. Katalog zur Sonderausstellung im Haus der Geschichte Baden-Württemberg* (2004)

Zuck, Rüdiger, *Das Recht der Verfassungsbeschwerde* (Munich: Beck, 2nd edn 1988)

## Articles

Albers and Eckertz-Höfer, "Helmut Simon zum 80. Geburtstag," 2002 NJW, 41

Altvater, "Anmerkung," 1995 NStZ, 278

Amelung, "Anmerkung," 1996 NStZ, 230

Amelung, "Sitzblockaden, Gewalt und Kraftentfaltung," 1995 NJW, 2584

Arkes, "Civility and the Restriction of Speech: Rediscovering the Defamation of Groups," 1974 *Supreme Court Review* 281

v. Arnauld, "Überlegungen zu dem Entwurf eines neuen §109b StGB," 1997 ZRP, 110

Arzt, "Anmerkung," 1988 JZ, 775

Battis and Bultmann, "Was folgt für die Gesetzgeber aus dem Kopftuchurteil des BVerfG?," 2004 JZ, 581

Biletzki, "Das Kreuz im Klassenzimmer," 1996 NJW, 2633

Brennan, William J., Jr., "In Defense of Dissents," 37 *Hastings Law Journal* 427 (1986)

Brenner, "Der Kruzifix-Beschluß des Bundesverfassungsgerichts," 1996 ThürVBl, 145

Brohm, "Demonstrationsfreiheit und Sitzblockaden," 1985 JZ, 501

Brunnée, "The Reform of Legal Education in Germany: The Never-Ending Story and European Integration," 42 *Journal of Legal Education* 399 (1992)

Burbank, "Alternative Career Resolution II: Changing the Tenure of Supreme Court Justices," 154 *University of Pennsylvania Law Review* 1511 (2006)

Calliess, "Der strafrechtliche Nötigungstatbestand und das verfassungsrechtliche Gebot der Tatbestandsbestimmtheit," 1985 NJW, 1506

Calliess, "Sitzdemonstrationen und strafbare Nötigung in verfassungsrechtlicher Sicht," 1987 NStZ, 209

Casper and Zeisel, "Lay Judges in the German Criminal Courts," 1 *Journal of Legal Studies* 135 (1972)

Clark, "The Selection and Accountability of Judges in West Germany: Implementation of a *Rechtsstaat*," 61 *Southern California Law Review* 1795 (1988)

Czermak, "Der Kruzifix-Beschluβ des Bundesverfassungsgerichts, seine Ursachen und seine Bedeutung," 1995 NJW, 3348

Dam, "The American Fiscal Constitution," 44 *University of Chicago Law Review* 271 (1977)

Damaška, "Structures of Authority and Comparative Criminal Procedure," 84 *Yale Law Journal* 480 (1975)

Davis, "Power on the Court: Chief Justice Rehnquist's Opinion Assignments," 74 *Judicature* 66 (1990)

Douglas, "Stare Decisis," 49 *Columbia Law Review* 735 (1949)

Dubber, "American Plea Bargains, German Lay Judges, and the Crisis of Criminal Procedure," 49 *Stanford Law Review* 547 (1997)

Eberl, "Anmerkung," 1996 BayVBl, 107

Eberle, "Free Exercise of Religion in Germany and the United States," 78 *Tulane Law Review* 1023 (2004)

Eberle, "Religion in the Classroom in Germany and the United States," 81 *Tulane Law Review* 67 (2006)

Eilsberger, "Die Kölner Strassenbahnblockade," 1970 JuS, 164

Eser, "Justification and Excuse," 24 *American Journal of Comparative Law* 621 (1976)

Felstiner, "Plea Contracts in West Germany," 13 *Law & Society Review* 309 (winter 1979)

Fletcher, "A Trial in Germany," 18 *Criminal Justice Ethics* 3 (winter/spring 1999)

Frase, "Comparative Criminal Justice as a Guide to American Law Reform," 78 *California Law Review* 542 (1990)

Frase and Weigend, "German Criminal Justice as a Guide to American Law Reform: Similar Problems, Better Solutions?," 18 *Boston College International and Comparative Law Review* 317 (1995)

Frowein, "Die Versammlungsfreiheit vor dem Bundesverfassungsgericht," 1985 NJW, 2376

Galtung, "Violence, Peace, and Peace Research," 6 *Journal of Peace Research* 167 (1969)

Ginsburg, Ruth Bader, "Speaking in a Judicial Voice," 67 *New York University Law Review* 1185 (1992)

Gounalakis, " 'Soldaten sind Mörder'," 1996 NJW, 481

Gray and Payne, "Victory is Possible," *Foreign Policy*, No. 39, 14 (summer 1980)

Grimm, "Die Meinungsfreiheit in der Rechtsprechung des Bundesverfassungsgerichts," 1995 NJW, 1697

Grimm, "Interview: 'Wir machen das Meinungsklima nicht'," 1994 ZRP, 276

Gusy, "Anmerkung," 1995 JZ, 782

Herf, "War, Peace, and the Intellectuals: The West German Peace Movement," 10 *International Security*, No. 4, 172 (spring 1986)

Herrmann, "Bargaining Justice—A Bargain for German Criminal Justice?," 53 *University of Pittsburgh Law Review* 755 (1992)

Herrmann, "The Rule of Compulsory Prosecution and the Scope of Prosecutorial Discretion in Germany," 41 *University of Chicago Law Review* 468 (1974)

Holmes, "The Path of the Law," 10 *Harvard Law Review* 457 (1897)

Hruschka, "Die Blockade einer Autobahn durch Demonstranten—eine Nötigung?," 1996 NJW, 160

Hughes, "Civil Disobedience and the Political Question Doctrine," 43 *New York University Law Review* 1 (1968)

Isensee, "Bundesverfassungsgericht—quo vadis?," 1996 JZ, 1085

Israel, "Gideon v. Wainwright: The 'Art' of Overruling," 1963 *Supreme Court Review* 211

Jeffries, "Legality, Vagueness, and the Construction of Penal Statutes," 71 *Virginia Law Review* 189 (1985)

Kalven, "The New York Times Case: A Note on 'The Central Meaning of the First Amendment'," 1964 *Supreme Court Review* 191

Karpen, " 'Ziviler Ungehorsam' im demokratishen Rechtsstaat," 1984 JZ, 249

Kaufmann, "Der BGH und die Sitzblockade," 1988 NJW, 2581

Kelsh, "The Opinion Delivery Practices of the United States Supreme Court 1790–1945," 77 *Washington University Law Quarterly* 137 (1999)

Krey, "Das Bundesverfassungsgericht in Karlsruhe—ein Gericht läuft aus dem Ruder," 1995 JR 221 (Part I), 265 (Part II)

Krey and Jaeger, "Anmerkung," 1995 NStZ, 542

Kriele, "Ehrenschutz und Meinungsfreiheit," 1994 NJW, 1897

Kühl, "Sitzblockaden vor dem Bundesverfassungsgericht," 1987 StV, 122

Lacovara, "Un-Courtly Manners: Quarrelsome justices are no longer a model of civility for lawyers," *American Bar Association Journal* 50 (December 1994)

Lamprecht, "Verführung zum Rechts-Ungehorsam", 1996 NJW, 971

Langbein, "Land Without Plea Bargaining: How the Germans Do It," 78 *Michigan Law Review* 204 (1979)

Langbein, "Mixed Court and Jury Court: Could the Continental Alternative Fill the American Need?," 1981 *American Bar Foundation Research Journal* 195

Langenfeld, "Developments—Germany," 1 I.CON, *International Journal of Constitutional Law* 141 (2003)

Larsen, "States Federal, Financial, Sovereign and Social. A Critical Inquiry into an Alternative to American Financial Federalism," 47 *American Journal of Comparative Law* 429 (1999)

Lerner, "The Intersection of Two Systems: An American on Trial for an American Murder in the French *Cour d'Assises*," 2001 *University of Illinois Law Review* 791

Lesch, "Bemerkungen zum Nötigungsbeschluß des BVerfG vom 10.1.1995," 1995 JA, 889

Levitin, "Putting the Government on Trial: The Necessity Defense and Social Change," 33 *Wayne Law Review* 1221 (1987)

Link, "Stat Crux?: Die 'Kruzifix'-Entscheidung des Bundesverfassungsgerichts," 1995 NJW, 3353

Lippman, "Reflections on Non-Violent Resistance and the Necessity Defense," 11 *Houston Journal of International Law* 277 (1989)

Lutz, "Sind erstschlagsfähige Nuklearwaffen verfassungswidrig?," 38 *Frankfurter Hefte*, No. 9, 17 (1983)

McKillop, "Anatomy of a French Murder Case," 45 *American Journal of Comparative Law* 527 (1997)

Mager, "Meinungsfreiheit und Ehrenschutz von Soldaten," 1996 Jura, 405

Mahrenholz, " 'Kritik an der Justiz gehört zur Sache,' " 1995 DRiZ, 35

Meador, "German Appellate Judges: Career Patterns and American-English Comparisons," 67 *Judicature* 16 (1983)

Meurer and Bergmann, "Gewaltbegriff und Verwerflichkeitsklausel," 1988 JR, 49

Müller-Volbehr, "Positive und negative Religionsfreiheit," 1995 JZ, 996

Munday, " 'All for One and One for All'," 61 *Cambridge Law Journal* 321 (2002)

Mushaben, "Grassroots and *Gewaltfreie Aktionen*: A Study of Mass Mobilization Strategies in the West German Peace Movement," 23 *Journal of Peace Research*, No. 2, 141 (1986)

Nadelmann, "The Judicial Dissent: Publication v. Secrecy," 8 *American Journal of Comparative Law* 415 (1959)

Nolte, " 'Soldaten sind Mörder'—Europäisch betrachtet," 1996 AfP, 313

Note, "Recent Emergency Legislation in West Germany," 82 *Harvard Law Review* 1704 (1969)

Note, "The Void-For-Vagueness Doctrine in the Supreme Court," 109 *University of Pennsylvania Law Review* 67 (1960)

Offenloch, "Der Streit um die Blockaden in rechts- und verfassungstheoretischer Sicht," 1992 JZ, 438

Offenloch, "Geforderter Rechtsstaat," 1986 JZ, 11

Oswald, "Verfassungsbeschwerde-Verfahren ohne mündliche Verhandlung?," 1972 ZRP, 114

Ott, "Anmerkung," 1969 NJW, 2023

Otto, "Sitzdemonstrationen und strafbare Nötigung in strafrechtlicher Sicht," 1987 NStZ, 212

Otto, "Strafbare Nötigung durch Sitzblockaden in der höchstrichterlichen Rechtsprechung und die Thesen der Gewaltkommission zu §240 StGB," 1992 NStZ, 568

Prittwitz, "Sitzblockaden—ziviler Ungehorsam und strafbare Nötigung?," 1987 JA, 17

Quint, "The Border Guard Trials and the East German Past—Seven Arguments," 48 *American Journal of Comparative Law* 541 (2000)

Quint, "The Comparative Law of Flag Desecration: The United States and the Federal Republic of Germany," 15 *Hastings International and Comparative Law Review* 613 (1992)

Quint, "Free Speech and Private Law in German Constitutional Theory," 48 *Maryland Law Review* 247 (1989)

Quint, "Leading a Constitutional Court: Perspectives from the Federal Republic of Germany," 154 *University of Pennsylvania Law Review* 1853 (2006)

Redeker, " 'Der moderne Fluch der Versuchung zur Totalität,' " 1995 NJW, 3369

Reimann, "Legal Education in the United States and in Germany: Lessons for Korea?," 41 *Seoul Law Journal* 293 (2000)

Reynolds and Young, "Equal Divisions in the Supreme Court: History, Problems, and Proposals," 62 *North Carolina Law Review* 29 (1983)

Roellecke, "Bio-Recht oder die Sanftmut von Gesäß-Protestierern," 1995 NJW, 1525

Roggemann, "Der Friede—ein Strafrechtsgut wie jedes andere?," 1988 JZ, 1108

Rozek, "Anmerkung," 1996 BayVBl, 22

Rudolph, "Blockierende Richter—eine Herausforderung für den Rechtsstaat?," 1988 DRiZ, 131

Schenke, "Anmerkung," 1986 JZ, 35

Schmitt Glaeser, "Meinungsfreiheit, Ehrenschutz und Toleranzgebot," 1996 NJW, 873

Schmitt Glaeser, "Politisch motivierte Gewalt und ihre 'Fernziele'," 1988 BayVBl, 454

Scholz, "Meinungsfreiheit und Personlichkeitsschutz: Gesetzgeberische oder verfassungsgerichtliche Verantwortung?," 1996 AfP, 323

Scholz, "Sitzblockade und Verfassung—Zur neuen Entscheidung des BVerfG," 1995 NStZ, 417

Schroeder, "Die Bestimmtheit von Strafgesetzen am Beispiel des groben Unfugs," 1969 JZ, 775
Schroeder, "Sitzblockade keine Gewalt," 1995 JuS, 875
Sendler, "Blüten richterlicher Unabhängigkeit und Verfassungsgerichtsschelte," 1996 NJW, 825
Sendler, "Kann man Liberalität übertreiben?," 1994 ZRP, 343
Sendler, "Was dürfen Richter in der Öffentlichkeit sagen?," 1984 NJW, 689
Sinn, "Gewaltbegriff—quo vadis?," 2002 NJW, 1024
Soehring, "Ehrenschutz und Meinungsfreiheit," 1994 NJW, 2925
Stamm, "Das Bundesverfassungsgericht und die Meinungsfreiheit," APuZ 2001 (B 37–38), 16
Starck, "Anmerkung," 1987 JZ, 145
Sternstein, "Die 68er und die Gewaltfrage," 2001 Wissenschaft und Frieden (W&F), No. 2, 47
Sudhof, " 'Soldatenurteil': Aus einem Land vor unserer Zeit," 1990 *Rechtshistorisches Journal*, 145
Tettinger, "Kein Ruhmesblatt für 'Hüter der Verfassung,' " 2002 JZ, 1146
Tettinger, "Das Recht der persönlichen Ehre in der Wertordnung des Grundgesetzes," 1997 JuS, 769
Wald, "The Rhetoric of Results and the Results of Rhetoric: Judicial Writings," 62 *University of Chicago Law Review* 1371 (1995)
Whitman, "Enforcing Civility and Respect: Three Societies," 109 *Yale Law Journal* 1279 (2000)
Wolter, "Gewaltanwendung und Gewalttätigkeit," 1985 NStZ, 193
Wrase, "Meinungsfreiheit und Ehrenschutz," 1996 JuS, 88
ZoBell, "Division of Opinion in the Supreme Court: A History of Judicial Disintegration," 44 *Cornell Law Quarterly* 186 (1959)
Zuck, "Gerechtigkeit für Richter Grimm," 1996 NJW, 361

# Index

www.ingramcontent.com/pod-product-compliance
Lightning Source LLC
LaVergne TN
LVHW011116300926
849160LV00008B/404
* 9 7 8 0 4 1 5 4 4 3 5 3 1 *